W9-CTI-434

CIO Wisdom

HARRIS KERN'S ENTERPRISE COMPUTING INSTITUTE

ENTERPRISE COMPUTING SERIES

CIO Wisdom

Best Practices from Silicon Valley's Leading IT Experts

**Dean Lane,
Change Technology Solutions, Inc.,
and Members of the Silicon Valley
Community of Practice**

www.ciowisdom.org

Prentice Hall PTR, Upper Saddle River, NJ 07458
http://www.phptr.com

Library of Congress Cataloging-in-Publication Data

Editorial/Production Supervision: *Mary Sudul*
Acquisitions Editor: *Gregory G. Doench*
Editorial Assistant: *Brandt Kenna*
Marketing Manager: *Debby vanDijk*
Manufacturing Manager: *Alexis R. Heydt*
Cover Design Direction: *Jerry Votta*
Cover Design: *Talar Boorujy*
Series Design: *Gail Cocker-Bogusz*

© 2004 Prentice Hall PTR
Prentice-Hall, Inc.
A Simon & Schuster Company
Upper Saddle River, NJ 07458

Prentice Hall books are widely used by corporations and government agencies for training, marketing, and resale.

The publisher offers discounts on this book when ordered in bulk quantities.
For more information, contact Corporate Sales Department, Phone: 800-382-3419; fax: 201-236-7114; email: corpsales@prenhall.com or write Corporate Sales Department, Prentice Hall PTR, One Lake Street, Upper Saddle River, NJ 07458.

Printed in the United States of America

2nd Printing

ISBN 0-13-141115-2

Pearson Education LTD.
Pearson Education Australia PTY, Limited
Pearson Education Singapore, Pte. Ltd
Pearson Education North Asia Ltd
Pearson Education Canada, Ltd.
Pearson Educación de Mexico, S.A. de C.V.
Pearson Education — Japan
Pearson Education Malaysia, Pte. Ltd
Pearson Education, Upper Saddle River, New Jersey
Editora Prentice-Hall do Brasil, Ltda., *Rio de Janeiro*

Contents

Chapter 1

Within and Beyond: Understanding the Role of the CIO 1
By Stuart Robbins and Al Pappas

Chapter 4

The Tao Perspective   51
by George Lin

Chapter 5

Communications: Communication Excellence in IT Management 71
by Brenda J. Fox

Contents

Chapter 6

IT Organization   95
by Guy de Meester

Chapter 7

Governance   **123**

by Danny Maco

Chapter 8

Architecture   151

by John Dick, Holly Simmons, Maureen Vavra, and Steve Zoppi

Chapter 12

IT Infrastructure Management and Execution   253
by Joe Feliu

Chapter 13

Budgeting   299
by Bob Denis, Maureen Vavra, John Dick

Chapter 14

Marketing the Value of Information Technology 335
by Judy Armstrong and Steven Zoppi

Chapter 15

The Metrics of IT: Management by Measurement 355
by Shel Waggener and Steve Zoppi

Foreword by Regis McKenna

I've had the good fortune to work with many information professionals during my forty years in technology and business marketing. Contrary to the popular notion that the IT professionals are technical nerd or incapable of addressing the needs of customers, I have found that they have much to offer beyond their functional expertise.

More often than not, I am stimulated by their imaginations and their innovative visions of what is possible. They are men and women who love to exchange ideas, to explore the impact they and their decisions have on their companies and customers, and to discuss the nature of work as well as business processes, leadership, and financial management. Often our conversations revolve around qualitative ideas such as process management, customer empowerment, branding, and the governance of information technologies. IT is taking them to places they had not anticipated, and teaching them to explore well beyond the silos of traditional, hierarchical organizations.

Consider for a moment that IT spending, as a percentage of total corporate capital expenditures, has grown steadily over the past 40 years from roughly 15 percent to an expected 50 percent in the near future. It is no surprise that in this age of information, IT has become a powerful strategic asset, vital to the enterprise. Worldwide expenditures by IT professionals are expected to exceed $1.5 trillion by 2005. This means that the talents, expertise, and investment decisions of the CIO and other information professionals will have profound effects on every business process within the modern enterprise.

xix

The term "information age" is not simply a cliché. Indeed, the evidence of its significance is everywhere; it is clear that the modern enterprise has developed an insatiable appetite for easily-accessed, real-time, user-defined information. IT transforms everything—employees, processes, costs, operational interdependencies, cultures, competition, productivity, R&D, marketing, and customers. As a result, every industry and business today faces market demands and unforeseen challenges far more complex than ever before. For one thing, IT infrastructures are much more powerful, distributed, complex, universally accessible, and costly than in the past, and these trends will continue. Even as they address the needs of the persent, however, executives cannot fail to keep looking beyond the observable horizon.

The most important business trend we have seen in the past few decades, emerging from the dramatic reduction in IT and communication costs, is the growth of network and software-based service economies. Indeed, almost half the employees in the advanced economies of the world market—the United States, Britain, Germany, Japan, and France—are employed in the service sectors. As services evolve, IT becomes a more crucial resource in maintaining customer relationships, managing distribution, discovering value-added revenue growth opportunities, and sustaining competitive productivity.

In the industrial era of the past, many leading corporations saw their manufacturing-based positions fade due to lack of competitive factories and increasing labor costs, which resulted in declines in productivity and competitiveness. When labor began to consume a large percentage of production costs, automation changed the economics of manufacturing and new leaders emerged. This same phenomenon dramatically altered the structure and leadership of the retail and banking industries. _

Today, all business are facing a similar challenge—only this time, it stems from rising service costs. With approximately 80 percent of American jobs currently related to the service sector, the pressure to expand services while improving productivity will hasten the development of IT supply chain and self-service solutions.

Already, we can see the trend toward IT-based services with such advances as CRM, real time service networks, dynamic content management, supply chain management, personalization tools, identity management, and the synchronization of diverse data centers with transaction access points. Marketing, for example, is rapidly becoming an architecture of mass-customized services. More than half of all marketing infrastructure functions will soon be fulfilled by software and intelligent networks.

Foreword by Regis McKenna

The extent to which the modern enterprise has become, in effect, an information resource broker points to the emergence of the information professional and a new kind of leadership. This new leadership has both the general business and relationship skills and the specialized expertise needed to make informed choices and judgments concerning the management of the enterprise's core asset—information.

The new IT-smart leadership understands that the creative application of information technology is essential for coordinating all the various elements of the business: operations, investment, and innovation, as well as sustaining competitive market positions and customer loyalty. The fact is that most successful enterprises today are energized by high-speed information networks and applications tailored to every function and business process. Functional silos are giving way to networked organizational models, and those who have grasped this concept are well ahead of the game. For it is the IT network that provides the glue that holds the enterprise's knowledge assets together, and most IT professionals understand very well that it is incumbent on them to understand both the user's needs and the technology in order to deliver dependable, quality solutions.

Our real time, complex, interconnected world demands a rethinking of how best to manage the enterprises of the 21st century. We need more and better knowledge of the information infrastructure and process in order to express imagination and creativity in the necessary context—that is, within a competitive, purposeful, value-added, and sustained business process.

Great business leaders are made, not born. Unique, personal experience is what equips individuals to lead. Not all information professionals will bring together the right mix of experience, knowledge, and insight to become successful CEOs, but the CIO is well-positioned to grasp the golden ring because he or she is already on the fast-track learning curve, dynamically engaged with every core function and asset of today's enterprise. Every element of a successful information age business will find that innovation lies in the knowledge and understanding of the IT-smart executive.

This book was written by a group of IT executives. It is a brief but rewarding glimpse into their thoughts and ideas, not only about their future as IT professionals but about the emerging IT-smart enterprise of the 21st century.

Foreword by Maynard Webb (COO of eBay)

I didn't start my career expecting to be in IT. I found myself thrown into it along the way. I've always gravitated toward the big, visible challenges no one else wanted to tackle and have found the greatest personal reward in turning tough problems into routine, repeatable processes. During successful stints as the head IT guy for four major public companies, I chalked up some of the most humbling and rewarding experiences of my life. Many folks aspire to the top IT job, but it looks better from a distance! The job is tough, and you're the one everyone is counting on for the answers. A guidebook like this would have been an invaluable resource for many of the challenges I've faced. This book is packed with practical advise from a group of highly accomplished IT veterans. Whether you're a seasoned CIO or aspiring to be one, I think you'll find this collection of ideas to be useful and thought provoking.

There is no single recipe for IT. The book begins with Understanding the Role of the CIO, where the authors discuss the multi-faceted, evolving role of the IT leader, and offer three perspectives on the role of the CIO. Every situation is unique and each of us brings unique perspectives and talents to bear. When I was at Quantum, the challenge was to make it easier to do business, while reducing costs. At Bay Networks, it was about implementing major ERP capability and exploiting the Internet to accelerate the supply chain. At eBay it's been about fulfilling the destiny of the company and leveraging technology to enable it. Regardless of the particular situation, we all face the common challenge of needing to lead while appearing to serve. As the book describes, it's all about bringing credibility and strategic insight to the table - while your colleague can't get their PC to work or their business is suffering because of network problems! It's a constant battle to achieve the right IT vision while doing the day job really, really well.

For me, success has meant applying conventional methods and tools in unconventional ways. With that, the chapter, The First 90 Days, resonated deeply with me. When I joined eBay in 1999 as President of eBay Technology, I knew I was walking into problems. The business was taking off like a rocket ship yet there were severe system issues. On my first day on the job, I was chagrined to find CNN in the lobby interviewing Meg Whitman, my new boss, about problems with the site. Not an auspicious beginning! Now conventional wisdom would have said to freeze all product changes and focus on stability and scale. But because of eBay's unusual potential and unique position in the marketplace, we chose to take significant risks and fix the stability and scale problems, while at the same time we accelerated the rate of product development and site changes by 4x. Applying conventional methods in out of the box ways, we were able to fuel the aggressive business growth while rearchitecting the site for infinite scalability. Had we not done so, eBay may not have become the market leader it is today. As these authors will teach you, "Decide and act with a sense of urgency". "Make aggressive commitments and meet them." "Strive for excellence through continuous improvements." Words to live by.

I've always felt that one of the hallmarks of a successful CIO is the ability to lead and manage alignment across the business. In The Tao of IT Leaders, the author writes about the business-focused IT organization, and the power and leverage this brings. The most successful IT executives I have known are those who not only have the vision to determine where the business needs to go, but have the credibility and service orientation to have the company enjoy the journey!

Sharing the secrets of their success, this group of seasoned CIOs gives you real world advise on developing and communicating IT strategy, developing true partnerships with the business, considerations for organizational design and tools for managing projects. Their collective wisdom has come together to be no less than a career's worth of mentoring in a paperback.

Listen to these folks. Then figure out the unique circumstances you're trying lead your company through and create your game plan. I look forward to reading your chapter in the next edition.

Maynard Webb
Chief Operating Officer
eBay, Inc.
December 2002

Foreword by Dean Lane

The research for this book began more than 30 years ago and is based on the experience, learning and real-world practices of more than 18 people who currently are, or have been, in the role of the Chief Information Officer (CIO). The combined knowledge, expertise and skills have been leveraged on individual chapters as well as groups of chapters to ensure practical information that can be easily understood.

The concept or idea behind this written work began about a year ago, when I had cause to reflect on all of my experiences as a CIO (both good and bad). What were my successes, failures, frustrations and accomplishments? One of my revelations was that we (the IT industry) had not communicated clearly enough what it is that we do. Quite to the contrary, many lower level IT professionals cause greater frustration by promoting the thought that they are magicians who work on black boxes.

To help bridge the chasm, I decided that a book, of CIOs, by CIOs and for CIOs was indicated. I first floated the concept past War Department 470 - the supreme authority in all the land ...my wife. She normally tells me to keep my day job and get back to work, but this time she thought it was a capital idea.

I first presented my idea to several long time friends who also happen to be CIOs. I was cautiously optimistic that they would like what was then the young concept of a "CIO book", but I did not expect the enthusiastic response that I received from my colleagues. The reception to the idea was overwhelming. In a matter of days, I had 15 stakeholders in this book. The collective brain always being better than a single unit, caused us to add and delete more topics/chapters. We also modified the definitions of some chapters and added, deleted and combined topics. Everyone signed up to write a chapter, and teams formed around certain topics that required greater attention.

It had only been a matter of weeks and this quite knowledgeable group of people had taken over the book. I was relegated to the role of providing leadership and, of course, writing my own chapter. I knew this to be an honorary position …you try to lead a group of 15+ CIOs and push them in a direction. First there was the discovery phase that each author went through to thoroughly understand their topic and outline what would be included, and what would not.

The true leadership came from the sub-groups, like the Technical Architecture team who spent numerous hours together and with others to ensure a pure message. The collaborative effort was also demonstrated by those who wrote individual chapters like "Types of CIOs", combining and ripping them apart before producing their final product. Importantly, where there was strengthening required, the smaller groups would combine chapters, as in Planning and Setting Priorities.

Everyone completed their assignments to their committed dates. We only had one chapter actually fall off the map, due to a physical illness. The topic being too important to ignore, saw one author writing a solid six pages and working with other authors to incorporate it into the book.

The story surrounding the book gets much more interesting. None of the authors were on a quest have their name(s) attached to the actual chapter that they wrote. This is because of the collaborative efforts associated with this book. Three people have served as "lead authors" reviewing and providing feedback on individual chapters. Many jumped in to help another author who got busy at work and might have missed a deadline. Still others have rewritten sections and incorporated them into other chapters.

To give you the essence of these authors, is to tell the story of how we decided what to do with the proceeds from the book. I was sitting next to one of the authors at our regularly scheduled monthly meetings. He suggested that we create a scholarship fund for disadvantaged students who wanted to pursue a career in Information Technology. This was, perhaps, the most satisfying part of my experience with this book since every author, without exception, was quick to endorse this idea… without question. 100% of the proceeds that any author receives will be donated to the scholarship fund that we have established.

This book has been a collaborative effort right from the beginning, when I sat down with a CIO to review a list of the top 20 topics/chapters, up to and including this forward… that I asked a different CIO to rewrite. Have no doubt that all members of the team, beginning with modifying the list of chapters, have had input the entire way, up to and including the Book Title and how the author's name would appear. CIOs more than any other executive cannot perform his/her job without being collaborative. This book was the epitome of a collaborative effort. The strength of this book is due to the ego-less collaboration of these CIOs, my colleagues, …most importantly, my friends.

Within and Beyond: Understanding the Role of the CIO

By Stuart Robbins and Al Pappas

Bringing a variety of special skills and experiences, Stuart Robbins and Al Pappas provide two perspectives on the role of the Chief Information Officer (CIO) in business today. Each expresses a unique view of what it means to be a CIO.

The CIO is a relatively new executive management position in many organizations. Introduced in the early 1980s to address the special needs of enterprises in maintaining the critical IT infrastructures that support their business processes, the CIO's role has grown in importance as it has evolved through the 1990s and into the new millennium.

In the previous decade, a major CIO role shift was needed to address the impact of the Internet on the business environment. This is being now superseded by another transformation: in the 2000s, the role and responsibilities of the CIO are extending beyond normal IT boundaries to encompass key partnerships with customers, businesses, and suppliers.

Comparing and contrasting the views of Robbins and Pappas, you will notice that some common threads and key messages emerge.

- *CIOs play many different roles in a variety of organizations today.*
- *The role of the CIO continues to evolve as the business environment changes.*
- *CIOs have become key members of the senior management team.*
- *CIOs continue to move from traditional technical roles to more strategic roles.*
- *CIOs are assuming a special responsibility to ensure that investments in IT really provide value to their organizations .*
- *CIOs will be key change agents, mentors, leaders, protectors of business assets, and technologists, among their others roles.*

This chapter provides an excellent foundation for the chapters that follow. As you read on, you will see that each author provides new and more detailed perspectives on these key messages.

In 1981 a new executive title was introduced into business: Chief Information Officer.[1] Designed as a response to the ever-increasing need to maintain the internal technology infrastructures upon which corporations relied, the role was transformed in the late 1990s as the Internet introduced dramatic changes into our business environment.

Like the railroads and telephone systems of earlier decades, the Internet altered business processes, management methodologies, and product strategies—and with them, the role of the CIO. By 2000, the CIO's responsibilities extended beyond the corporate boundaries to include e-business partnerships, mirroring institutional changes. With an emphasis on business relationships and cross-institutional data exchange, the CIO's role evolved into a primary relationship with customers, suppliers, and partners.

The economic downturn of late 2001 and the abrupt reversal of fortune for many technology giants brought another shift in the role of the CIO. Those executives who had become business partners in a net-based system of interrelated services were now at risk, as the emphasis

---

1. Carol Brown, Graduate School of Business, Indiana University, "The Successful CIO: Integrating Organizational and Individual Perspectives," 1993, p. 400.

on that extended network diminished. Those executives who had focused on the technology were now at risk, as they represented (to their executive teams and directors) an irrational investment that had not yet produced the promised dividend. And those executives who remained "hands-on" managers of their institutions' infrastructure operations found themselves without budgets, losing employees, and now directly supporting their internal customers, who had come to expect a high level of service. As the recession impacted revenue streams, numerous companies removed the position of CIO entirely.

In each business and historical phase, the position of CIO can be seen as a mirror of the broader environment within which it operates. To better understand this phenomenon, we present two CIO perspectives, each of which examines the role from a very particular point of view, reflecting a profession that has transformed and been transformed by the rapid development of new technologies and economies.

An adage that is well-known within the IT community is worthy of note as we introduce these essays: Ask 10 CIOs what they think, and you will get ten very different answers. It is one of the quintessential challenges of "selling to the CIO," because we are a community of unique personalities. Any strategy for accomplishing this task must be constructed with that individualized approach.

As you listen to our various and sometimes conflicting points of view, however, some consistent themes emerge. It is often valuable to combine these contrasting perspectives to allow those underlying truths to emerge.

We therefore offer our two perspectives on the role of the CIO, with great respect for the unique ideas represented by each. Together, they provide a glimpse of what it means to be a CIO, an outline for success amid turbulent times.

▶ Perspective 1: The Extended Enterprise CIO

by Stuart Robbins

One of the many transformations in our business institutions during the past decade has been the growing importance of the extended enterprise.[2] As our businesses have changed, so have the information systems that support them; indeed, the information systems are mirrors of that change. As the networks of our businesses have changed, so have the mandates of those responsible for managing them.

Therefore, the changing roles of those systems and of the executives responsible for them become a map for the broader transformations—in our commerce, in our culture, and in our socioeconomic relationships. By better understanding the changing role of the CIOs in these institutions, we can better understand the institutions themselves. Indeed, the changing landscape of the CIO's charter becomes an excellent metaphor for commercial society, including the business leaders, citizens, and participants in the broader communities these institutions serve.

Examples can be found in every segment of our economy. Financial institutions now rely upon 24/7 derivative calculations and zero-latency reporting, federal institutions are tasked to become interoperable with state and local efforts because of eGovernment requirements and "homeland security" imperatives, technology vendors are constructing virtual (electronic) marketplace networks, and manufacturing companies are refining their supply chains and service provider networks. In every business and every social organization, we are witnessing a dramatic shift in the universe of our jobs. Parents send urgent messages to kindergarten teachers via alphanumeric pagers. Salespersons find a special color or size in their franchise locations around town. Craftspeople in Africa can sell their wares directly into New York homes. Midwives in China can obtain immediate triage assistance from the emergency pediatrics specialist at the University of Maryland.

The "extended enterprise CIO" is a partner in a networked community designed to deliver systems and services with and between customers, vendors, and partners, a matrixed role in a network of associations for which some executives are suited and others are not.

CIOs at every level of business and trade have become responsible for managing and maintaining this interconnectedness of daily life. These

---

2. For the purposes of this essay, let us define the extended enterprise as the metropolitan view of the institution: all external systems, processes, alliances, and customer/user interactions in combination with the (internal) operations of the institution taken together as the amalgam of all internal and external functions, the full geography of the institution's reach, both by design and by necessity.

new responsibilities influence every aspect of our daily activities and have become central to the definition of "success" in our profession.

- The "eTransformation" that has occurred in our business is reflected in our charter and daily responsibilities: CIOs for corporations large and small are now directly involved with customers, becoming advisors to venture capital firms, constantly interviewed by analysts and the press.

- A major percentage of our time—in some cases 60 to 70 percent of our time—is now dedicated to issues "beyond the firewall," with internal issues assigned to subordinates in our IT organizations. The top issues within this "extended" responsibility include supply chain integration and data flow, network distribution and globalization, corporate intellectual asset management, and strategic alliances.

- As our institutions have been influenced by the shift from a commodity-based economy to a knowledge-based economy, the impact on our professional development, and our organizations' professional growth, changes have been required in our management approach and philosophy. We have become business partners with our suppliers, our service providers, our customers, and our executive team. The essential values of that partnership at the CIO level are based upon this central attribute: We tell the truth.

- As "our" systems become more dependent on "their" systems (and as our processes become more dependent upon theirs), the impact can be seen in the renewed emphasis on technology standards such as XML and SOAP, in which the exchange of information not only between legacy systems but between institutions must be automated in real time and accessible 24/7, the data integrity must be unquestioned and completely auditable, and yet the systems supporting that analysis are transparent.

- As mentors to junior IT professionals who aspire to become CIOs, our advice and teaching has changed in response to the extended responsibilities of our office. Additional skills and attributes are encouraged for our teams and managers to become successful in the extended enterprise. We now teach our managers to listen—to their internal customers, to their employees, to each other—and to better understand the essential business problem.

Some of these changes, indeed, are temporary (driven by budgets and the economy), and others have introduced a fundamental shift back to operational fundamentals, such as cost containment and support. However, the core responsibilities of the IT executive now extend beyond the corporate boundaries, and those responsibilities—for supply chain management, vendor control, data center operations, customer information (accumulation, analysis, distribution) and network security—are not going away. Rather, they are the fundamental building blocks of an integrated information technology environment.

Who are some of the successful eTransformation or e-business CIOs, and why? As Bud Mathaisel, VP and CIO for Solectron, reminded me during a recent lunch and discussion of this topic, responsibility for the extended enterprise is not a new phenomenon. Indeed, companies such as Solectron have long established successful business networks in order to maximize supply chain, manufacturing, and procurement issues. Our profession is populated with individuals who have incorporated this approach during the past decade.

Two individuals, however, come to mind as key examples of success in the extended enterprise—Mohamed Muhsin, VP and CIO for the World Bank Group, and Phil Thompson, VP of eTransformation and CIO for IBM.

I first met Mohamed Muhsin several years ago at an IT conference sponsored by *The Economist*. There, he presented the World Bank's mission of ending world poverty and emphasized the fundamental role that information and communications technologies must play in the realization of that lofty goal. The objectives of the Bank, according to Mohamed, are not met simply by loans and grants, but rather by leveraging knowledge among the bank's many customers through a clearly articulated coordination of expert support systems and a fully globalized network of technology resources, from servers in Washington to teletraining facilities in Africa or portals in Palestine, Zambia, and India.

For Mohamed's exceptionally dedicated IT staff, the role of IT cannot be separated from the role of the financial institution that it enables, nor can it be separated from the broad network of intellectual assets in dozens of languages that are now provided via the Web, allowing villagers in one hemisphere to directly benefit from the cumulative knowledge of subject matter experts around the world. ICT (Information and Communications Technology) is a fundamental aspect of the World

Bank's charter, extending well beyond the traditional roles of processing vendor payments (which they also do quite efficiently).

Phil Thompson of IBM is responsible for a broad range of internal and external functions that extend far beyond the direction of IT investment for the company. He sets the company's business transformation strategy, leads overall business process reengineering and e-business initiatives, and aligns e-business investments and collaborative processes with all of IBM's customers, partners, suppliers, and employees. At IBM, moreover, the CIO is a partner to the company's strategy team, increasingly involved in an ongoing effort to share transformation insights with customers.

The emphasis on knowledge sharing among IBM and its customers and partners is epitomized by Phil and his team and should be seen as a critical aspect of success in the extended enterprise. According to Phil, who emphasized this point to the Federal CIO Council last year when they met with CIOs from around the country to discuss business transformation, information is becoming the primary source of competitive advantage. A knowledge-based economy empowers people inside and outside the company, multiplying their contributions in ways that would not be possible in a commodity-based economy. Indeed, this may be the central difference between those CIOs who focus exclusively on internal operations and those, such as Mohamed and Phil, who are responsible for the entire end-to-end business process and the technologies that enable it.

More and more, CIOs are the executives who are forging alliances and ensuring alignment with critical owners of business relationships, both within and outside the corporate boundary. For many years, successful CIOs have been business strategists, capable of translating the value of technology in terms that can be understood by the business leaders of the institution. Now that skill set is being externalized.

Subsequently, standard IT "best practices" and management principles, once the key to success for internally focused CIOs, are being supplemented by an additional set of values and requisite skills. The new CIO must be an entrepreneur, a matrix manager of teams that do not report into IT and may not even belong to the company, an architect and e-business visionary, an evangelist, a relentless recruiter, a mentor, and an expert in the psychology as well as the implementation of (constant) change management.

The capacity of the successful extended enterprise CIO to serve as both visionary and customer advocate, someone who is both a consumer and a supplier of services, is directly proportional to his or her ability to migrate to an externalized system of services and foundational infrastructure. This CIO must be able to comprehend, and then teach, the essential importance of intellectual property that resides on a corporate intranet, even if that intranet exists on another company's servers and is maintained by another company's employees.

Successful CIOs must be able to transform the old "federal versus state" funding analogy—the politics of centralized versus decentralized control that erupt annually in budget cycles often requiring months to resolve—into a new variation: the "global versus personal" requirements of net-based messaging and information delivery. They must deliver core internationalized architectures that can be translated into dozens of languages, yet offer individual views of information that are unique to each business role.

Struggling CIOs will continue to be distressed about who is paying for what, and why 80 percent of what is being asked is simply impossible. Forward-thinking CIOs will initiate conversations within their companies about how they must architect products and services to serve a multicultural, multilingual Internet community on desktops that are unique for each user.

Struggling CIOs, if they can retain their jobs in difficult economic times, will be challenged to explain why they need ten people instead of five, or five instead of two, to support their systems. Forward-thinking CIOs will be educating their executives and their customers about customized Web services and how new standards such as XML and SOAP can help them deliver additional revenue or additional value to their partners, customers, and employees.

Struggling CIOs will be asked to once again explain why so much money has been spent on technology in the past year. Forward-thinking CIOs will be reminding their executive teams of the substantial accomplishments that were enabled by information technology, and they will be building upon that framework to continually refine business processes within and beyond the corporation.

▶ Perspective 2: Back to the Basics—What is a CIO?

by Al Pappas

Overview of the CIO Role

Originally, the position of CIO was derived from the data processing leaders of the past. The title is less than 20 years old, but represents the culmination of the significant impact that technology has had in most of the modern world's business communities. The evolution of the CIO role has mirrored the dependencies of business upon information technology and its associated operational functions.

Recent surveys have found that the average IT executive has many years of experience in fields other than IT and many have substantial international experience. And contrary to the "techie" stereotype, more appear to be extroverts, not introverts. Technology still takes up more than half of their time, but not much more; IT executives devote a substantial portion of their working lives to business issues. CIOs were once the consummate corporate insiders, focused on internal systems, internal customers, and internal IT staff, but today's CIOs are out in the wider world, doing work that has more in common with a secretary of state than a systems developer.

Leadership and communication are two of the most critical capabilities that modern CIOs must master, not least because most need to deal with more people across the entire organization than other executives. Today's CIOs recognize the importance of these skills, and many are still developing and honing them.

The following paragraphs portray the variety of styles and behaviors that many CIOs have developed to become successful in a variety of unique business situations. Because each enterprise's business leadership—CEO, COO, board of directors, and so on—is unique, and because this business leadership establishes both the corporate culture and eventually the expectations imposed upon the CIO, there is no one-size-fits-all approach for ultimate CIO success. CIOs need to fully comprehend the requirements of their positions, their incentives, and the expectations of their direct reports to ensure that they remain as closely aligned as possible.

Background of the CIO—Technology Versus Business

The role of the CIO has become as varied as the business models in place today. Many of us have evolved into these roles from a variety of early disciplines, such as technology, finance, manufacturing, service, and so on. The particular expertise that a CIO has developed over his or her career becomes a determining factor in the roles he or she fulfills, but is equally a key determinant of the type of business that might employ him or her. I believe that the corporate leadership determines the type of CIO required based upon their own expectations of the CIO role, which often include the following:

The Technology Leader: Traditionally, leaders of IT were drawn from information systems departments with which they were applications, operations, or business analysis leaders. This avenue of growth continues to provide the largest number of CIOs. There are alternatives, however. As an example, I received my initial CIO assignment when the leaders of a large software organization asked me to consider assuming the role of the CIO (as well as vice president of information systems). I was then a director of engineering, with numerous responsibilities, including engineering infrastructure services. This new role incorporated the various engineering and information technology functions within a common functional area. The business of software technology clearly mapped my technology background, which enabled improved business and technology relationships. I believe that this experience has been replicated in many high-tech environments in which leaders from engineering, software development, and the like have successfully transitioned their careers into the IT arena.

The Business Leader (with a technology bent): Business leaders from services, manufacturing, or marketing have also transitioned into CIO roles, a phenomenon that has become more commonplace over the last 10 years. The need to comprehend the specific business needs of the corporation has led to the emergence of the business-driven CIOs. At the same time, leaders in the areas noted have taken ownership of some IT-based tools and systems to satisfy their business requirements, which required that they become more knowledgeable about the these tools and systems. These CIOs have assumed their positions not only to leverage the technology skills they developed as business leaders, but also because it has provided a vehicle for promotion to a CXX position.

The Strategist and Mentor: The strategist and mentor type of CIO operates in a fashion similar to that of a Chief Technology Officer (CTO) in a high-tech environment. These individuals can be characterized both by their focus upon strategic directions for the corporation and by the roles that they perform as mentors and advisors to the corporate staff members (that is, other CXOs).

These CIOs are typically grounded in strategic thinking and play an active role in the product or service development side as well as the marketing and sales side. By focusing on issues such as business and IT alignment, they attempt to uncover IT-enabled business opportunities and apply IT initiatives to streamline business processes. These CIOs are the best candidates to become the CEOs or COOs of their organizations. They have developed an all-encompassing view of the enterprise and therefore become key mentors to both the CEO and COO in particular. An excellent example of such an individual is the president of eBay Systems, Maynard Webb; he came from the CIO ranks and was recently promoted to COO of eBay.

The Corporate Influencer: The role of the CIO is directly shaped by the type of business environment he must support, and his influence is driven by the characteristics of the business, including their relative maturity levels. The two areas of focus are likely to be strategy and execution, and most CIOs are expected to play an equally important role in both arenas. The strategic side of the CIO requires a focus on business and IT alignment and IT-enabled opportunities, while the execution side requires active participation in the execution of major projects in areas like ERP, CRM, and so on. (The role of the CTO has evolved over the last few years to further delineate between an execution-based CIO role and a strategic-based one rather than combining these aspects. The CTO has been more focused on operations, technology, and product development. This role has not evolved significantly and remains doubtful in this author's opinion.)

Business Environments and the CIO's Role

The following paragraphs elaborate upon the way various business environments affect the CIOs role.

The Startup IT Environment: The startup business model requires a CIO who can literally roll up her sleeves and build an IT organization while the business evolves. This requires understanding of the key business demands associated with strategies and plans and the ability to delineate the IT-specific functions required to enable them. In addition, a fundamental understanding of basic IT infrastructure usually becomes the early focus area, quickly followed by business-specific applications or initiatives that enable the growth of various business units (such as sales automation, customer service call tracking, and so on).

The High-Tech Environment: High-tech businesses require a CIO who is well grounded in the technology products or services provided by that type of enterprise. The CIO needs to be aware of the technical challenges faced by the development organizations as well as the associated marketing, sales, and services required to promote and sustain the customer communities. The IT support expected by the technology teams emphasizes a secure and highly integrated infrastructure and the ability to relate to these needs and to sustain a highly productive and communicative work environment is key. Therefore email, networking, video conferencing, development labs, and like elements are a given.

The Brick-and-Mortar Environment: The brick-and-mortar businesses are characterized by a more traditional business approach and associated IT infrastructure. I would place financial, health care, and government institutions in this category. The CIO focus in these businesses can be quite varied and diverse based upon the business models, the existing IT infrastructures, and the focus upon IT to enable business changes.

The Internet Environment: The Internet phenomenon changed the methods and practices that most CIOs follow. The term "Internet speed" became the byword that most companies in this arena were expected to emulate—get the products to market before competitors at all costs, and eliminate the processes followed by most traditional businesses. This placed substantial burdens upon CIOs who wanted to apply the best practices of good business processes before embarking upon technological solutions; the technology was expected to be deployed and functional while the business models were evolving, and in many instances before any real business existed. My role at an Internet business encompassed more than the traditional IT requirements but actually included product development for the site's operations as well the enablement of all Internet-based business functions. This is the typical model for Internet companies today; the CIO is more engaged in business enablement than is ever expected at the more traditional companies, including even the high-tech variety.

The Established Business Environment (over 10 years): CIOs at more established corporations (such as AT&T, Lucent, HP, and so on) have a more traditional business focus for IT than those mentioned previously, characterized by more established business models that require minimal investments in innovative technologies. They deal with established infrastructures and applications, and focus most of their attention on cost reduction and improvement of existing business processes. The CIOs in these environments are well-grounded in the basic business practices of the corporation and typically spend a great deal of time with the executive staff, while their direct reports focus on the specific entities that support divisional or business unit needs. HP and Lucent are good examples, since their dedicated IT personnel support a variety of divergent business needs from both a business analysis and operations perspective. The major challenges facing these CIOs are the significant focuses on streamlining operations and reducing overall costs.

Reporting Relationships, Hierarchy, and the CIO's Role

The role of the CIO is significantly affected by the reporting relationships involved. The following paragraphs delineate some of the possibilities.

The Chief Financial Officer (CFO): The CIO who reports to a CFO is typically part of the administrative side of the business and is always expected to focus on cost reduction as a key strategy for the IT organization. The utility role of the CIO is a key expectation of the CFO as it is for his direct reports in finance, human resources, facilities, and related administrative business functions. In some instances, the CFO has eclipsed or eliminated the CIO role and has subsumed the responsibilities entailed. This is done partly to reduce costs and partly because the CFO wishes to drive the IT agenda directly.

The Super-CIO (a la Lucent and HP): A business unit or divisional business model typically drives the CIO that resides in this environment within which either a centralized and decentralized IT model can exist. Two of my closest CIO associates are CIOs within the Lucent family, and I became a CIO within the HP family as a result of an acquisition. Our experiences differed somewhat due to our varying business climates.

For HP, decisions about business independence directly affected the degree of incorporation within the HP corporate infrastructure (that is, the adoption of all HP systems, the use of HP networks, HP email, and so on). As an independent business unit, these adoptions were deemed unnecessary, but as an integrated division of HP, they became absolutes; the strategies adopted by the parent directly affected the IT practices needed. We began as an independent company and then migrated into a divisional operation; then that same division was spun off for sale. At Lucent, my peers faced a more difficult reduction and downsizing scenario, and their focus was clearly consolidation and cost reduction.

Higher authorities and the current business climates clearly drove the role of the CIO at both HP and Lucent. The need to collaborate with the various centralized IT organizations as well as the various business units supported by them was paramount to success. The super CIOs in these environments were absolutely expected to be business aligned and focused exclusively on strategy as opposed to execution.

The Chief Executive Officer (CEO) and Chief Operating Officer (COO): The CIO who reports to either the CEO or COO possesses a higher degree of freedom and responsibility than a comparable CIO who reports to the CFO. The CEO/COO usually has a broader base of responsibilities for the overall business, and the CIO is expected to play an equally critical role in applying IT strategies to assist the CEO/COO's directions to the fullest. In this reporting relationship, the CIO's role is focused upon managing a project portfolio for business results instead of upon whether those projects are within a given time line or within budget. These CIOs are expected to work very closely with other business units, including the CFO, to ensure that projects are selected to bring the highest value to the corporation.

In particular, CIOs who report to the CEO differ from other IT executives in two significant ways: Their corporate role is more centered on business issues, yet they are far less likely to find themselves focusing on correcting misalignment between the IT environment and the business. It may be that the reporting relationship has helped to create, or is a sign of, a better-aligned IT function.

Others: Board of Directors, Engineering, Services, Business Units: CIO reporting relationships to other entities are a rarity in most corporations today. The exception that stands out most significantly is that of the reporting relationships at Cisco, where the CIO reported to the executive responsible for services. This was clearly intended to build a customer service environment that utilized all the latest technologies available for the Internet and led to a breakthrough application that enabled Cisco to provide the optimum interaction with its customers while reducing the need for direct contact.

The CIO for 3Com reported to the chairman of the board and possessed the highest degree of business focus that I have encountered. His strategies and associated activities resembled those of a CEO. This brand of CIO must develop and have the ability to create and manage the highest level of external and internal relationships.

Understanding the Dynamic Role of the CIO

The current economic downturn has created a crisis for IT professionals as business leaders begin to question the value of the investments they have made in technology. The downsizing of IT organizations, initiatives, and salaries, as well as the role of IT executives in the overall business, has placed the CIO at a critical juncture in the brief history of the position. Three distinct developments have been noted in the press:[3]

1. The CIO has been able to navigate the economic crisis and has become a central member of the executive team in businesses that are dependent upon IT partnerships and value.

2. The CIO has returned to an operational focus, in many cases assuming a hands-on role in the tactical aspects of the infrastructures she supports.

3. The role of the CIO has been eliminated, replaced by corporate operational executives, finance systems experts, or sales opera-

---

3. Excerpted from *CIO Insight,* April 2002. Reprinted with permission of Ziff Davis Media. All rights reserved.

tions professionals. In such cases, actual IT organizations are decentralized and become part of the functional units that they support.

The CIO is a mirror of the institution; each of these trends in the CIO's role reflects the changed direction of the broader institutions that employ him or her and of our technology and economy.

The CIO is a mirror of a global economy. As such, the technology executives who are responsible for information flow in an information-based economy will continue to be central to an institution's success.

The CIO is at the center of our cultural crossroads. As business people, we are responsible for zero-latency information that drives executive decision making and critical alliances. As technologists, we are responsible for business continuity and availability. As individuals, we are responsible for telling the truth and doing what is right. The CIO is therefore an architect and a plumber, a strategist and a tactician, a communicator and a craftsperson, an employer and a service provider.

The CIO is a change agent for business processes and cultural norms. The limitations of our institutions are often the reasons for our lack of success, and in order to prevail, we must address them.

The CIO is a mentor and a leader. We must lead and teach by example and by the accumulation of best practices as we have learned them over the years.

The CIO is the gatekeeper of the company's intellectual assets and operational resources, taken for granted when things go well and blamed when things go badly. It is a career that no one should ever seek—yet so many of us cherish it, seated at the center of our institutions' failures and successes.

Women CIOs

by Judy Armstrong

Judy Armstrong provides a personal perspective on women CIOs from a woman's point-of-view. She highlights an important concern—within an overall workforce comprising over 50 percent women, only 20 percent of the IT workforce are women, and far fewer are CIOs. Something definitely appears to be wrong with this picture.

It has been clearly demonstrated that many women bring valuable skills to IT organizations. Moving into the new millennium, companies that can learn to recruit, develop, and retain women CIOs and managers will be far ahead of the others. How can we better tap this vast resource? Ms. Armstrong explores this issue in detail, based on her real-life experiences as a CIO as well as the experiences of others. She provides an interesting discussion of issues such as:

- *Why IT is unfriendly to women.*
- *What IT is really losing by limiting women in the workforce.*
- *How IT can change to attract and retain more women.*
- *Why some women have been successful despite the constraints and limitations.*
- *How can we learn from the experiences of other women CIOs.*

While women appear to face some unique issues, many of these issues arise from common problems that all CIOs face—man or women, young or old. This chapter highlights the importance of looking at common issues from different perspectives. Successful CIOs do this every day.

▶ Why Single Out a Particular Group of CIOs?

This could have been a chapter on diversity in general, and there is no doubt that adverse conditions and challenges exist for other minority groups as well as for men; however, in order for women to recognize and step up to leadership roles in technology jobs, they must cultivate special skills that are not required by most men.

It is important to note that women make up over 50 percent of the workforce and approximately 20 percent of the IT workforce, and yet hold few of the top jobs. What is worse, there continues to be a decrease in young women entering the technical and scientific fields. A few statistics may help you understand why it is important to devote a chapter to women in leadership positions, specifically in technology management.

According to a study by the Department of Labor Women's Bureau, women receive only 9 percent of engineering-related bachelor's degrees and fewer than 28 percent of computer science bachelor's degrees. This represents a decline of 37 percent over the past 20 years. Several other recent surveys indicate that few women become CIOs because the life-style and the work environment are unfriendly to women.

Women CIOs have success stories, but the truth is that most people— including those in our own profession—don't hear about them or seem to care.

My belief is that it is important to take a closer look at why IT is unfriendly to women, what IT is losing by remaining unfriendly, what we can do about it, and most importantly, to highlight the attributes of those women who, in spite of all this, have been successful.

▶ Why Is IT Unfriendly to Women?

A short answer might be the "glass ceiling." But I believe it is more than that. Is there a glass ceiling? Yes, depending on your definition. Some 60 percent of women say the glass ceiling is a reality in IT; they define it as gender bias, stereotypes, and the perception that women are less knowledgeable than their male counterparts. Interestingly enough, the same survey showed that 62 percent of men believe there are no barriers to women.

In many ways, IT is unfriendly because of the nature of the job. IT is a 24/7 job. Achieving any significant position in IT often means putting your career before many other aspects of your life. You will find yourself putting in 70- or 80-hour weeks, becoming deeply committed to both the short-term and long-term needs of your career, and this will result in the loss of time spent with family or in personal activities.

When asked in a recent survey if their IT jobs were meeting expectations, 52 percent of women said they worked more hours than expected. The same survey stated that 40 percent of the men felt the same way. It is hard work, and most people, especially those who want to participate in a significant family life, are not willing to make the sacrifice. In *The Feminine Mystique,* Betty Friedan asked the question that caused millions of women to examine the role of housewife, mother, and caretaker: Is this all? Many women trying to balance a full-time career and a family are asking the same question today. There is no good answer.

Before the Civil Rights Act was passed in 1964, women consistently received less money than men for the same jobs. On my first job, I earned 50 cents an hour less than a man who started the same day. At that time, this was legal and clearly stated in the salary matrix. While equal opportunity has helped, the thinking that allowed that inequality still exists—that assumption that women are best suited for administrative, teaching, and nursing jobs; that we aren't tough enough; that we can't make quick decisions or think like a man; that we can't command respect. When pressed to allow women in, the fraternity will do so, but it is reluctant to open up its inner workings to us.

You might be interested to know that Title VII of the Civil Rights Act of 1964, which prohibits employment discrimination based on race, color, religion, sex, or national origin, did not originally include sex. A senator trying to create a filibuster thought that if he included sex, no right-thinking senator would vote to pass the act. He was wrong, and by accident women were included.

These traditional glass ceiling and work-versus-family issues are very real, but there are other factors that contribute as well. I believe the unfriendliness is as much one of expectations as it is of gender. The glass ceiling can be and is being shattered, but not without extraordinary time and effort.

We need to understand what a true loss this is to the IT profession and look at ways to attract more women and keep them in our ranks. It is also interesting to understand how some women have been successful despite the unfriendliness.

What Is IT Losing When Women Leave the IT Workforce?

Many studies show that women excel at collaboration, juggling multiple tasks, and prioritization. Women have a very different way of looking at problems. Research suggests that women see more nuances and have a more holistic approach than men, who are more linear thinkers. Without both kinds of thinking, you lose the breadth of perspective that can approach a problem from multiple directions, resulting in creative solutions otherwise unavailable.

Women managers who possess the inherent skills required of a good manager often add compassion, nurturance, and sensitivity to the role. While this is not vital to success, it does help to build teams that work well together.

Women look to maximize, not necessarily to win, in competitive situations. Often, it is not as important to win as it is to achieve the maximum gain.

Another loss is that of sheer talent. The more people you have in the talent pool, the better your chances of success. Getting and keeping good talent is expensive; replacing a valued worker can cost a company two to three times her annual salary.

Diversity also adds to the overall health of a profession. Individuals and organizations need to work on creative ways to attract this diversity, not only in gender but in all other ways as well. We would be no healthier if current balances were reversed.

▶ What Do We Need to Change to Attract More Women into the IT Profession?

A critical area of focus is on adolescent girls.

- A recent report, which completes a two-year study analyzing previous research, teacher survey responses, and focus groups of middle school and high school students, suggests girls must be attracted to technology at an early age.

- Educators should focus on what is wrong with the computing culture and how to change it rather than on why girls don't like technology. Educators must also focus on teaching girls complex technology skills beyond the traditional word processing and presentation tools.

- Girls are influenced against technology at an early age by computer games that are designed and marketed toward boys. These games are violent and often boring. They are not attractive to girls, who want games that are more interactive, engaging, and creative.

Once we do engage women and attract them to the profession, we need to keep them. The hiring organizations have a responsibility, as do the women themselves.

- As women, we need to take personal responsibility for making change. We need to take the best practices that men have developed and learn to make them work for us in our own way. Take networking as an example. Men spend more time networking to further their careers. Women network too, but we tend to network with people whom we like and who share our value systems. We need to retain those aspects of our networking but incorporate this style into the business world. We need to also realize that liking someone and being able to work with that person are two separate issues. The end game is success, and you need every possible resource to achieve it.

- Women must mentor other women. We must help them learn early what it took us years to learn, and we must find as many ways as possible to share what we know.

- Organizations can contribute by putting reasonable work and family programs in place. Practices such as telecommuting and flextime help everyone achieve balance. (Remember, however, that visibility is a key factor in success, and if you use telecommuting, for example, you must make an extra effort to be in the office at the right times to support your efforts.)

- Women often do carry extra family burdens, and managers can help by supporting creative scheduling. Several years ago, when I was programming and raising children, my manager let me leave early to care for my children and then return to work after the children were in bed and finish my hours. This was very innovative at the time. It was a win for everyone because I was onsite when many of the programs had problems and was able to fix these and keep someone else at home and asleep.

Work/life balance will always be a challenge, and it is up to us to keep working on better ways to achieve it.

▶ Why Do Some Women Prevail and Others Do Not?

It is interesting to note that even with the challenges presented to women, some women have been very successful. Do they do something differently that helps them to succeed?

When I speak with other women CIOs and technology leaders, the most prominent common trait is that they "never knew they couldn't be a leader or a CIO."

I love this quote from one of my colleagues in the Community of Practice, Maureen Vavra: "The intrigue of this field is that, in 30 years, I have never had a boring day. You have to relish that part and the stress that comes with it to love this work. The most important things a woman can bring into this profession are willingness to ask tough—and sometimes obvious—questions, belief in her own abilities, and a tendency to find great humor in painful circumstances."

This does not mean that Maureen and I, and many other women, did not feel the pressure of the ceiling and the unrelenting demands on our time. We all have many stories to tell about gender bias, family trials and tribulations, and so on. The difference with us is that we never saw the problems as barriers, only as obstacles to overcome. Without this belief, most of us would not have been successful. If you believe that it is not possible, it probably won't be.

Women who aspire to be CIOs, more often then men, must find unique ways to balance family and job or in many cases forgo having a family. Okay, I hear a lot of mumbling from some of you women saying, "But men don't have to give up having a family." That is only partially true. Many successful men have been divorced several times or are estranged from their families, and many have remained bachelors until they have reached a certain level of success. True, others have wives who stay home and raise the children, but remember that those women chose to be stay-at-home moms. There is nothing to stop you from finding and marrying a stay-at-home dad or a man who wants to share your success by taking on extra work at home. Often, it is your own views on how you should act as a wife and mother that limit your opportunities.

Finally, the successful women are willing to take on projects and tasks that no one else wants or is willing to do. Tackling projects that your boss does not want to do will challenge your skills and stretch your abilities, leading to growth and exposure. Visibility is absolutely essential to your growth and can be enhanced by taking on those unpopular tasks. This may be the very key to your success.

The women who have become successful CIOs have all had to use strategies as well as tactics to achieve their successes. Other chapters in this book focus on these skills. Successful men and women alike use those skills. But do women do anything differently?

▶ What Is Different for Women CIOs in Their First 90 Days?

Women executives face a few unique challenges when starting in a new position. One of the biggest challenges is that they can't use the men's room. You think that's funny, and it is, but it's also true! Any man reading this chapter will know there are many issues discussed and potentially resolved in the men's room. How do I know? Because a few places I have worked have had the walls of the ladies room back-to-back with the men's room and enough air ducts to allow conversation to flow freely between facilities. I have no easy answer for this one. The best I personally have been able to do is to ask the men whom I have influence with and with whom I have built relationships to tell me when a critical conversation or decision has been made when I am not present. Making it funny by mentioning the proverbial "men's room" always helps.

On a more serious note, we will not automatically be accepted into the club. We need to spend time building the relationships, trust, and support that may come automatically to a man in the same position. However, men can't keep those inherited gifts without doing the same work. The difference is that we have to earn it up front. So, focus on finding key influencers and building those relationships first. And remember that these influencers are not necessarily your fellow executive staff members.

Your staff will most definitely test your mettle. We may not like it, but some of the staff will view you as "a woman" and test you to see if you have backbone. It is not necessary to overcompensate; you need to be yourself and rely on all the terrific skills that got you where you are. But be careful to recognize when you are being tested, consider the source of the test, and respond to achieve the result you want. Show respect for the existing staff, give everyone a chance, and don't take anyone else's word for another's behavior—learn for yourself.

Your first 90 days are your time to assess. You should be gathering and understanding the most critical business needs, validating them, assessing how your staff is prepared (or not) to handle them and whether you are staffed and organized correctly to achieve the expected results. This establishes the expectations against which you want to be assessed and reviewed; in the end, they will appreciate your strategy and reward your execution.

This is no different than any other CIO would do. The key is in the handling of both soft and technical skills, which must be kept in balance.

While all of this takes skills that require time to learn as well as the will to overcome some special challenges, you can do it if you have the desire. If you are willing to make some sacrifices, there is a special reward in leading a technical team to success and building and maintaining a sound IT infrastructure to support the success of your company.

There are not enough pages to recount the stories of all the successful women CIOs. In order to support the idea that women make great technology leaders, however, I would like to present for you a few who are worth emulating.

Who Are Some of the Successful Women CIOs, and Why?

I have known many successful women in the IT profession and it was hard to chose three from this terrific group of friends and business associates. I have chosen the individuals who represent three different industries: biomedical, high tech, and aerospace. All of these women have had successful careers and have been active in supporting diversity in their respective companies. All three—Pat Anderson, CIO of Lockheed Martin's *Space Systems Company*; Polly Moore, former CIO of Genentech and currently attending a seminary; and Tama Olver, formerly CIO at Amdahl, Informix, and Quantum, and currently CIO of Applera—have been recognized as being among the top 100 women in the IT profession, and all continue to represent the best that women bring to the business.

I asked each of these esteemed ladies to answer six questions regarding their experiences as CIOs.

Pat Anderson, CIO of Lockheed Martin's Space Systems

How long have you been a CIO?

I have been a CIO for about a year, but was also one for three years several years ago.

What was your educational background and career path?

I have a bachelor's degree in psychology. I began my career as a human factors engineer working on the Trident I missile system. For the next 20 years I worked on that program in supervision and management in a variety of disciplines—product assurance, reliability engineering, field operations and support, factory operations, and program management. I then spent the next three years as a CIO/executive vice president to the CIO (of a 4,000-person organization), then three years as the program manager of a large corporate project, and now CIO again.

What are the three most important factors contributing to your success?

A real desire to learn, the willingness to take risks, and the ability to work very, very hard. I also think having an easy personality with strong interpersonal skills in a culture that is hard on people helped a lot.

What were your biggest success and your most memorable failure? What was the impact of each?

My biggest success was the large, complex corporate project I managed. The complexities and diversity of the corporation, the magnitude of the change, the complexities of the organizations that matrix personnel to work the project, and the mix of functions working the project all led to an enormous amount of risk. Yet, the project has been phenomenally successful—nearly flawless in its implementations and enthusiastically received by the companies in the corporation, which has enabled the seeding of a corporate culture for the first time and a software product that has reduced cost and improved service.

My biggest failure was a CIO position that was deputy to the corporate CIO. The organization was virtual and just coming into place, I worked remote from the CIO and rarely saw him, and I did not have distinct responsibility and authority. All these ingredients, coupled with a trauma in my personal life, left me somewhat less than effective. The impact was a truncation of my career.

What advice do you have for young women considering entering the IT field and women aspiring to become CIOs?

The IT field is extremely interesting and challenging and hospitable to women (unlike some of the more engineering-centric disciplines.) That means it is possible to have a career of constant growth and opportunity, and one where the emerging technologies mean you will never need to be bored.

Being an effective CIO means adopting a strong sense of the business. Therefore, to be a CIO, I think incumbents should also have direct experience in the business itself. The job is exceptionally challenging and requires extraordinary interpersonal skills, with a heavy dose of diplomacy, as well as strong management and leadership skills. It is a wonderful career objective for someone with those interests and attributes.

What were the most serious glass-ceiling barriers you encountered in making your way up the corporate ladder?

In the early and middle parts of the corporate ladder climb, I didn't have a perception of a glass ceiling. I was rising quickly, there were other women at my level, and everyone was working so hard there wasn't much time to complain. But then I reached the level where there were no women ahead of me, and things all of a sudden looked different. When I was promoted to VP, and especially when I was made a member of the Operations Committee (the company's senior management team), it began to feel as if my gender had been part of the reason I had made it that far. While I was happy to be at the table (and boy, did they need a fresh voice, even if they didn't listen very often!), in retrospect I had been promoted beyond what they were comfortable with, and it turned out to be the beginning of the end of my CIO career. The good news is that once the company had made the leap and promoted a woman to VP, the next such promotion was much easier. Within a few years, the senior management team was well balanced and has remained so.

Polly Moore, Former CIO of Genentech

How long have you been a CIO?

I spent 18 years at Genentech, building its computing organization. Four of those years I was a VP, which is as close as they had at the time to a CIO. I retired two and a half years ago.

What was your educational background and career path?

I have a Ph.D. in math and always intended to teach. Teaching jobs were scarce when I graduated, so I went into industrial applied mathematics and worked for several years as an applied mathematician (which I loved). The opportunity came to get into biotech when it was still a young field, and it seemed like too much fun to be on the sidelines. So I took a job managing scientific computing and doing statistical consulting at Genentech. I didn't really have the background to be managing a computing group, but I learned fast! In retrospect, one of the reasons our computing activity was successful over the years is that we evolved it to fit the company's needs rather than knowing how it was "supposed" to be done. When the company finally got big enough that it really needed the more formal MIS-style approach, it was time for me to move on anyway.

What are the three most important factors contributing to your success?

Above average intelligence, a willingness to respond to opportunity, and having a mentor. It's always useful to be smart, especially when intelligent people surround you. And while it's wonderful to be able to plan a career, sometimes you just have to jump at an unplanned oppor-tunity. (I gave a career-planning talk on this once and titled it "Plan When You Can, But Dance If There's a Chance.") Much has been writ-ten about the value of having a mentor, and it's all true. If someone in the organization looks out for you and wants you to succeed, it vastly increases your chances. When that support evaporates, watch out.

What were your biggest success and your most memorable failure? What was the impact of each?

The biggest success was melding a freewheeling scientific computing group and a strait-laced MIS group into a single department. It took a while, but each group learned from the other, and the company bene-fited.

The biggest failure came from taking over the leadership of a manufac-turing systems project that had not been well thought out. It was too late to save it, and in the end it had to be killed. Fortunately, there was a clause in the contract that allowed us to recoup some of our invest-ment in hardware, so the biggest impact was lost time. The company went on to do a much larger (and successful) manufacturing systems project years later when it was really ready for it.

What advice do you have for young women considering entering the IT field and women aspiring to become CIOs?

IT is a great field for women. The glass ceiling is still there, but it has a lot more holes in it than in some other fields. Find a way to stay cur-rent with technology (which is a lifelong challenge) and find a mentor. As you rise in management, the job becomes less and less about tech-nology (at least, about your being able to do it yourself) and more and more about people.

At the CIO level, it's really a business position, not a technical one. Keep a focus on the people aspects—I'm convinced that the key to suc-cessful computing in an organization is to understand how people use technology in their jobs, which is a much more people-centric view than most computer executives have. Keep your eye on the politics (there is always politics) because even if you don't play hardball your-self, you can lose out if you don't understand what's happening around you.

What were the most serious glass-ceiling barriers you encountered in making your way up the corporate ladder?

For the first 20 years of my career, I had as much, if not more, opportunity as my peer group, since all of my promotions occurred with far less tenure than normal for my peer group, which fundamentally was white male. I broke through the glass ceiling several times, being the first female to achieve three of the top four levels of senior management in my company. In this regard, I also believe I was the first female in the corporation to achieve these levels. I was the first female vice president of a functional organization. The first female vice president managed a staff function. So, I can't say that I personally encountered any glass ceilings in this regard. However, I believe the people here before me did. I was just the one who got to break them!

Tama Olver-CIO of Applera

How long have you been a CIO?

I have over 30 years in technology and have been a CIO since 1994.

What was your educational background and career path?

I knew I wanted to be a computer programmer when I entered college. I took a degree in mathematics at Michigan State University and included computer science courses as electives. My other education has taken the form of university short courses and training programs in management and technology.

What are the three most important factors contributing to your success?

Commitment to lifelong learning. I am especially careful to recognize when I start to think I have "the answers" in an organizational setting; I try to refocus on asking the right questions. As I moved to more responsible positions, my commitment to learning helped with the transition from mastering technology to mastering leadership skills.

Commitment to add value to everything I do. When I focus on adding value, I am able to eliminate work and reapply the resources to higher value tasks. Focus on this commitment requires that I be present and listening consistently.

Commitment to the success of everyone and every effort in which I am involved. For me, this final commitment is an aspiration. It is not easy to stay committed to the success of people who have, from my point of view, let me down or are competing with me for scarce resources. To the extent I can stay totally accountable for everything, including everyone's success, I am able to make far more extraordinary contributions to an organization.

What were your biggest success and your most memorable failure? What was the impact of each?

The biggest successes have related to implementing change where everyone said, "It will never happen here." An example that comes to mind is a work request process in an IT organization that truly believed it could not be done "here." The consequence was not only a positive result for the organization, but also the opportunity to tackle other tough changes with support from the team as a whole, rather than skepticism.

The biggest failures have related to inability to get the right team in place to meet business needs. The consequence has generally been that I lost the opportunity to do the job.

What advice do you have for young women considering entering the IT field and women aspiring to become CIOs?

For young women: IT is at an inflection point where basic infrastructure will be in place and the challenge is in integration and exploitation of the tools to innovate in business. If you are a systems thinker with interest in technology and business innovation, IT is a good field to explore. Although the pendulum swings back and forth, I believe that pure IT roles over time will be in centralized infrastructure companies where there will be careers in systems management and technology adoption for operational effectiveness. Most roles outside the infrastructure arena will be in business units where knowledge of both technology and business disciplines will be needed.

For women aspiring to be a CIO: Focus on relationship and influencing skills, as well as work habits that keep you current with technology. Develop understanding of processes, how to introduce them, and how to keep them healthy in the organization. Understand the importance of vision and organizational culture, and develop related skills. Finally, build a plan and skills for balancing your life across work, personal, and health issues. Any executive role is a huge commitment and will be fun only if it fits into a life you have designed to meet your needs overall.

What were the most serious-glass ceiling barriers you encountered in making your way up the corporate ladder?

The very first one was my interview with a large computer manufacturer when I graduated from college. I met with a recruiter new to the firm. When I told him my interest in being a computer programmer, he said "I don't think we hire women for those jobs. The job requires lifting boxes of line printer paper." I told him that I believed he was mistaken. Our university had equipment made by his firm, and I had met women among the team who installed the equipment. I asked him to check with the company, and he said he would. In a few days I got a registered letter asking me to come to their headquarters for job interviews. The interviews led to an offer and over seven years of great technical and leadership work to launch my career. This may not sound like a "glass ceiling" problem on the surface; however, it was motivated by the recruiter's view that women in his industry held manufacturing, finance, and administrative jobs—not technical ones. I knew better and was assertive enough to say so. Other women may not have fared as well.

A more serious problem occurred later in my career when my advancement in management stalled. I was being passed over for promotions to director, and neither my manager nor I could figure out why. He wanted to promote my career greatly and tried hard to understand what I needed to do to be seriously considered for a more senior role. Over time, I received coaching about personal behavior, all of which I was able to address. For example, I was told I was not "tough" enough to be given more responsibility. I took on some visible assignments that demonstrated the ability to drive for results and overcome resistance, especially where I needed to influence senior management. At the end of a year my manager asked decision makers their current opinion of my "toughness." He was told that I was now viewed as "plenty tough enough." One senior vice president said, "Tough? She's downright persistent!" Still, openings for positions at the director level came and went, and I was not considered. I thought about leaving the company, [but] decided to stay. I was being compensated at the director level without the responsibility. My view was that the problem was more likely than not to follow me into another company rather than being solved by moving.

Finally, an organizational crisis occurred that led to heart-to-heart conversations with senior management who viewed me as not promotable. For all the "right" reasons, I had been doing many counterproductive things with respect to earning a promotion. I was oblivious to the formal power structure in the organization, preferring the informal network I had developed over a decade. I had been stepping up to responsibilities outside my formal role for altruistic reasons in my own mind, out of dedication to overall business success. My actions were perceived as political, motivated by ambition to show my boss and peers to be weaker than I, and outside acceptable norms of behavior for the executive team. I was abashed by the negative interpretation of my actions, especially since, in my heart, I knew my motives really were pure. At the same time, my ability to see my actions through another perspective gave me the freedom to learn a lot of political sophistication quickly. I did not, in fact, need to change my actions much. I did need to learn how to position what I was doing properly with the right influencers and to clear the air quickly of any perception that I was intent on using the bodies of failed colleagues as stepping stones to my success. Within three years I was promoted twice and became part of the executive team.

I learned from the experience that having the right mentors and sources of candid information about how you are viewed as an executive, or as executive material, is key. I had been trapped in a version of the myth about heads-down hard work and results being the key to advancement. To be invited into the executive team, they must trust you. Marketing your performance in an authentic context that builds trust and alignment with other executives is as important as the performance itself. Once again, this may not seem like a glass-ceiling problem on the surface. I believe there was a component of gender, however, in the lack of early schooling I got about "the ropes" in an organization. During the years when the young men were building relationships and getting advice about how to climb the ladder, I was in a much more transactional relationship with my employer. Executives liked my work; however, they did not view me as one of them. At first, this was because "women work for three years, then get married and leave the work force." I was hired out of college a grade level lower than the men based on that reasoning. (The fact that I got an extra promotion in the first three years and more than caught up with peers in salary was unexpected, since it was not planned that I would be there in the fourth year.) Later, I had missed early political development steps and did not know how to ask for mentoring and support from the right people. I do now.

▶ The Value of Women in IT

With women in top IT spots, we can continue to help build diversity into the IT profession. Women bring many invaluable skills to IT organizations, skills that are equally useful to men. Relationship management, flexibility, and diplomacy are just some of the skills CIOs need to bring to and foster in today's business climate. Many IT organizations are learning, to their benefit, that women executives do extremely well in these areas.

The First 90 Days

by Mark Egan

Mark Egan describes the most important period in a CIO's career—the first 90 days. This is a honeymoon period during which executive management and the board of directors may be most receptive to the new CIO's needs and concerns, including requests for special resources like staff and funds to help the new CIO get a good start. It is also the only period in which the new CIO has the advantage of a "third-party" view of the IT organization; soon enough, the new CIO must begin demonstrating real value and return on investment while effectively handling day-to-day operational problems.

In this chapter, Egan explores:

- *The importance of identifying issues and concerns within the IT organization that were not discussed during the hiring process.*

- *The three major areas on which the new CIO should focus.*

- *The importance of developing a tactical plan to address time-critical issues and decisions.*

- *How to conduct an IT organizational analysis leading to recommendations.*

- *The importance to developing a two-year strategic plan for IT.*

- *Why the first 90 days is a great opportunity to make sweeping changes within the company and IT organization.*
- *Why it is important to establish a rapport with management during this early phase.*
- *The importance of building management support to implement your recommendations.*
- *The importance of communication during this timeframe, especially in clarifying what you plan to accomplish and when.*

This chapter highlights the importance of establishing an overall plan that balances strategic and tactical issues. Many of the issues touched on here, such as strategic planning, IT infrastructure, management, and leadership, are explored in more detail in later chapters.

I had just started my new CIO job and settled into my large corner office with a great view of the water. The job search had been a long one, almost six months, as the market was more competitive due to the demise of the Internet boom. I'd been able to negotiate a good package and was confident this was the right company for me, one in which I could make a difference and have a real impact on the business.

The phone rang; it was my boss, who wanted to discuss a few issues we hadn't had the chance to discuss during the interview process. On the way to his office, my operations manager stopped by to let me know that our ERP system had just crashed, and although they were not sure what happened, they were working hard to bring the system back online. My boss started out by welcoming me to the company and saying how happy he was to have me on board. He then mentioned that we'd had a security breach the previous week and that the board of directors wanted me to present my recommendation at their next meeting the following week. He also mentioned that we were spending way too much on IT and that he would like my recommendations on how we could cut the budget by 20 percent. On the way back to my office I ran into my applications manager, who gave me his resignation because he was upset about not being considered for my job and had found another position.

The question at this point was, What am I going to do? The honeymoon had just ended, and the perfect job was now looking somewhat different from what I had expected. The bottom line, however, was that the company had hired me because it had some problems, and it was up to me to turn the situation around.

▶ Key Takeaways

- The first 90 days is the most important period in your CIO career at a new company.
- Expect to find many issues and concerns within the IT organization that were not discussed during the interview process.
- Focus on three major projects: a tactical plan to address time-critical issues and decisions, an IT organizational analysis with recommendations, and an IT strategic plan for the next two years.
- The first 90 days is a great opportunity for you to make sweeping changes within the company and the IT organization.
- Establish a strong rapport with management during this time-frame, as you will need management support to implement your recommendations.
- Communication is essential during this period, as you need to be extremely clear on what you plan to accomplish and when.

▶ Overview

The first 90 days is the most important period in your career at a new company. You need to quickly assess the current situation and develop a corrective plan. You can also develop a strategic plan, as management does not expect a large number of improvements to be accomplished during this period. It is a great opportunity to establish a strong rapport with the management of the new company and create a positive first impression.

The remaining portions of this chapter explore the key components of the first 90 days:

- 90-day tactical plan

- IT organizational analysis and recommendations
- IT strategic plan

These are the essential areas that you need to focus on during this time-frame. Each topic is reviewed in detail, and examples are provided to assist in the process.

▶ Ninety-Day Tactical Plan

It would be helpful to be left alone for the first 90 days. The reality, however, is that your boss hired you because your organization has real-world problems that must be quickly addressed. You need to be responsive to the fact that your ERP system is going down and no one seems to know why. You have to be prepared to present to the board of directors on your recent security incident and explain what you are going to do about it. And you have a significant staff opening that you need to address before you have had a chance to fully evaluate the organization. At this point, I would caution you to resist the natural urge to go completely into tactical mode. You will be able to address some of the burning issues, but you need to balance this against the long-range strategic goals of the IT department.

I recommend that you develop a 90-day tactical plan that includes the following:

- High visibility issues that must be addressed immediately.
- Critical decisions that cannot be postponed.
- Quick wins that can be accomplished and gain management support.
- Major architectural decisions and large expenditures that can be deferred until the overall IT strategy has been developed.

This tactical plan sends a message to management that you are aware of the key issues and have plans to address them now. It also gives you an opportunity to establish a rapport with management who may not be pleased with the IT organization and to show that you can make a difference.

In my initial discussions with management, I make a point of understanding their future business strategy along with existing pain points. I look for "quick wins" that can be accomplished during the first 90 days that can gain some management support for longer term strategic initiatives. Be sure to identify business champions of new IT initiatives, as they will need to drive the funding process. This is a delicate balance between devoting time to immediate tactical issues and developing the overall IT architecture.

Communication is extremely important during the first 90 days; I try to "overcommunicate" whenever possible, including both good and bad news. Further, I spend a great deal of time with both management and IT staff in order to fully understand current circumstances before drawing any conclusions. One technique that I have found effective is to develop a consistent status report to communicate the progress during the first 90 days. This fosters communication using a common methodology and minimizes misunderstandings. An example of a project report template that can be tailored for your organization is provided in Figure 3–1.

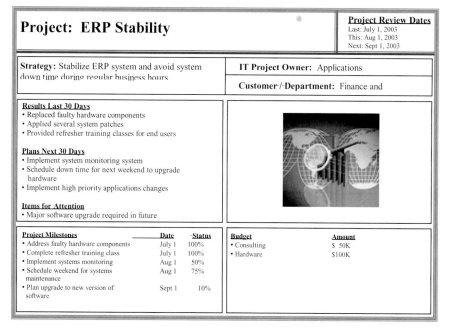

Figure 3–1 Project report template.

This template includes key information such as objectives, recent results, and upcoming milestones. Project reports of this kind can be used to monitor progress on key issues as identified by management.

You can consider yourself successful in your first 90 days if you have accomplished the following:

- Addressed some of the current pain points within the organization.
- Established a rapport with key members of management.
- Set up a consistent mechanism for tracking status of projects.
- Avoided the urge to make major architectural decisions until you have conducted adequate research.

The last point to keep in mind is that because no two companies are the same, you will have to customize your tactical activities. The key objective is to immediately make a positive impact on the organization while you are developing your strategic plan. Executive management will probably not remember exactly what you did in the first 90 days, but rather that you addressed some key issues and put together a long-term strategy.

▶ IT Organization Review

Having a strong IT organization is the foundation for accomplishing your objectives. In order to get anything done, you need a strong team that is well aligned with the business. It is extremely important that you critically evaluate the overall structure and staff of the organization during the first 90 days and make the necessary adjustments.

Common problems within IT organizations include the following:

- Dysfunctional structure with unclear roles and responsibilities.
- "Rogue" IT organizations established by departments who are unhappy with services provided by IT and decide to form their own organization.
- Ineffective team members.

- Poor teamwork within the IT team and/or the business overall.
- Lack of IT alignment with business.

In initial discussions with management, I make a point of discussing their opinions of existing IT staff and the service currently provided. I also discuss their preferences for service in the future. Companies vary considerably, and you must align the IT organization with business preferences.

IT organizational structure can have many forms. The model in Figure 3–2 can serve as a starting point for designing the future organizational structures:

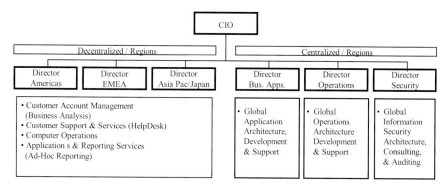

Figure 3–2 IT Organizational model.

Key organizational concepts that I follow when designing the organization I want include the following:

- Establish a customer-focused IT organization.
- Align IT organization with internal customers.
- Provide customers with a single point of contact for IT services.
- Make it *very* easy to do business with IT.
- Provide customers with the highest level of service possible.
- Ensure each department within the IT organization has a customer.
- Achieve a healthy balance of centralized/global and decentralized/regional functions within the organization.

Companies normally follow a centralized or decentralized organization model, and the IT organization needs to align with this structure. The actual details of IT structure are secondary to ensuring the organization provides the best service possible to its internal customers. Within IT, be sure to establish clear roles and responsibilities; this allows you to focus on delivering services to your customers rather than on deciding who is responsible for addressing a particular issue.

The following provides some guidelines on assigning functions to the different organizational models:

Centralized/Global: Functions that need to be consistent on a global basis, including the following:
- Information security, due to the high risks of systems being compromised.
- Enterprise business applications development, as you should avoid multiple systems such as ERP.
- Network design and management, so you can deliver seamless systems access on worldwide basis.
- Email administration, to enable communication across the company.
- Other shared infrastructure components, such as the network, as appropriate.

Decentralized/Regional: Functions that require close coordination with internal customers, including the following:
- Business analysis, as business practices and regulations vary around the world, and the IT solutions must address these needs.
- Help desk and end-user support, so that you can be responsive to internal customers.
- *Please note* that decentralized functions should still follow global standards whenever possible, to reduce costs and improve service.

Hybrid Model: Balances both centralized and decentralized functions and provides both global consistency and regional responsiveness.

I generally design the new organization first and then evaluate the existing staff to determine how well they can fill the new roles. This approach helps you avoid being constrained by your existing staff and gives you an opportunity to review the model with internal customers and existing staff without regard to staff who may be moved into these roles.

The final step is to match up the existing staff with the various roles in the new organization. I recommend that you carefully evaluate your existing staff, as it is likely that they will not be able to fill all the new roles effectively. Do not expect to have all the staff in place within 90 days, but rather to define the organization's structure and identify any missing talent. I also recommend that you address as many issues as you can during the organization design as opposed to reorganizing the IT group multiple times over the course of the year. Reorganizations are time consuming and distract the staff from their primary responsibility of delivering services to their internal customers.

Make sure you communicate about the process of reviewing the IT organization and announce its new structure. This process can be time consuming, and team members will be apprehensive about their new roles within the organization. Further, this is an excellent time to instill some core values in the IT organization, both by example and directly. I have outlined some recommendations in the following:

- IT must be passionate about providing the best service possible to its internal customers.
- Support for internal and external customers is the sole reason for IT's existence.
- Decide and act with a sense of urgency.
- Strive for excellence through continuous improvements.
- Commit to learning and the application of intellect.
- Believe in the collective strength of teamwork.
- Make aggressive commitments and meet them.
- Communication is a two-way process; do it openly, constantly, and effectively.
- Encourage the team to develop a healthy balance between work and home life.
- Act always in the highest standards of honesty, integrity, and professionalism.

The first 90 days constitute an excellent opportunity to making sweeping changes in the IT organization, and your ability to obtain management support is high. The IT organization must be aligned with the business, and the appropriate organizational model will vary dramatically from company to company. IT is a services organization, and you need to provide service in the manner that your internal customers prefer and expect.

▶ IT Strategic Plan

Developing and maintaining an IT strategy is essential to the success of the organization. The IT strategic plan is the roadmap for transforming the systems within a company, and you must communicate the plan in simple terms that can be understood by a nontechnical audience. You should also communicate the process that you plan to follow in developing the strategic plan.

The process for developing a strategic plan should include both an assessment of the IT environment as is and a vision of the IT environment to be. The five-step process shown in Figure 3–3 can be used in creating the IT strategic plan.

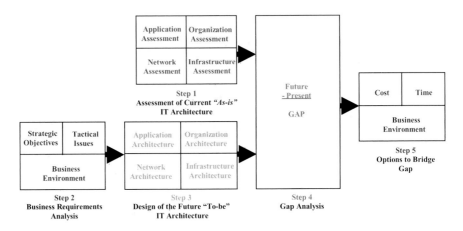

Figure 3–3   IT architecture approach and methodology.

Step 1

Assess the current IT architecture to determine its present state. The objective of this step is to become familiar enough with the existing environment to understand the current issues and architecture. This should not be an exhaustive documentation of the existing environment, as that level of detail is not required and frankly wastes a lot of time. Questions that you need to answer during this step include the following:

- What business applications are being used to support the major requirements for the company (for example, ERP)?
- How well do these applications meet business needs?
- What is the network topology for the company, and what business needs are not being met?
- How well does the current IT organization support internal customers?
- How reliable is the current computing infrastructure?

Step 2

Determine current and future business requirements for the IT organization. The majority of this analysis consists of interviews with key management within the company. This includes evaluating the following three areas:

Business Environment
- What is the company's line of business?
- What changes are expected in this industry over the next couple years?
- What unique systems challenges or opportunities exist?

Strategic Objectives
- What are the company's long-range strategic goals?
- What major initiatives are expected over the next 12 to 18 months?
- What are the systems and services requirements for meeting these objectives?

Tactical Issues
- What are the shorter term tactical issues for the company?
- What are the automation alternatives?

Step 3

Evaluate the possibilities for the environment to be, based on the company's business objectives and needs. The initial analysis should be broad and unconstrained, as the goal is to define a long-range plan that will later be constrained by what the company is willing to invest. Examples of elements within your description of the future environment might include the following:

- Changes and/or upgrades to enterprise applications, such as the introduction of an integrated CRM system.
- Outsourcing of key components of the IT infrastructure for cost or competitive reasons.
- Reorganization of the IT group.
- Improvements to the network to improve customer satisfaction and reduce costs.

Step 4

Conduct an analysis of the gap between the current state and future state to determine the optimal future environment. This is the most important step in the process, as you need to develop a good list of alternatives for management. I rely heavily on my peer group for suggestions in this area, as they have often faced similar challenges and I place a lot of trust in their opinions. I also consult with independent research analysts such as META Group to validate these peer recommendations and gain additional insight into possible solutions. Finally, I work with suppliers to understand their current product offerings and future strategies. The goal of this step is to compile a list of alternatives for step 5.

Step 5

Present management with alternative approaches for transforming the IT environment. These alternatives must be stated in business terms and specify the ways in which they will enable the company to accomplish its goals, which may include the following:

- Increase revenue.

- Improve staff productivity.
- Improve customer satisfaction.

Each alternative must also be explicitly clear about what is being proposed, how much it will cost, and how long it will take to deliver. I usually float these alternatives to the management to test their acceptance during the course of the first 90 days rather than wait until the end, as some of the changes being proposed may not be acceptable to them or the costs may be beyond what they are willing to invest in IT.

▶ IT Architecture Blueprint

The final IT architecture must be easily understood by management and address critical business objectives. In developing the architecture, be sure to establish overall guiding principles that will be followed when migrating to systems built upon it. Some recommendations for these guiding principles are outlined below:

- Speed and flexibility are absolutely essential.
- Adopt proven leading-edge technologies.
- Balance packaged solutions with internal development to meet legitimate customer needs.
- Prefer integrated solutions from a single supplier over multisupplier best-of-breed solutions.
- Use comprehensive architectural planning to ensure that all elements of the total IT solution are defined and planned.
- Design solutions for global operations from the outset rather than local solutions that are later to be "enhanced" for "international idiosyncrasies."
- Organize IT to ensure local responsiveness and global consistency.
- Focus on internal IT core competencies to address essential value-added activities and outsource other IT activities.
- Manage all of the company's data as a corporate asset, beginning with customer information.

Architecture Overview

The overall IT architecture for most companies can be described using the diagram in Figure 3–4. The back-end or ERP systems, front-end or CRM systems, and management reporting or data warehousing systems are key components of any overall architecture. These major applications are also supported by a collaborative applications environment, or workflow package such as Lotus Notes, and everything runs on the IT infrastructure.

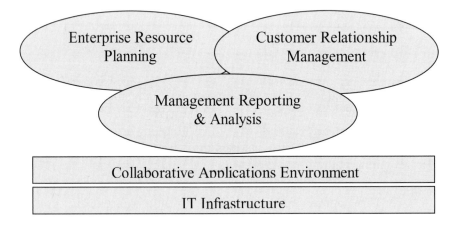

Figure 3–4   Overall IT architecture.

Be sure to start with simple, high-level, diagrams that convey your ideas, followed by additional levels of detail. Normally, at least one of these major areas, and possibly more than one, has serious issues that must be addressed. If you start with a diagram of the overall computing environment, it is easier to drill down and explain the issues to the management of the company.

▶ Management Recommendations

The first 90 days is your best opportunity during your career at a company to recommend bold, sweeping changes to existing systems. You have been hired because things are not working well; management is looking for you to tell them what needs to be done. You need to seize this opportunity now and make significant recommendations, as you will never get as good a chance again.

Management must be provided with a list of alternatives for migrating to the future systems environment along with the costs, benefits, and timeframes of each. As previously noted, the recommendations must be presented in business terms and address three major areas: revenue, staff productivity, and customer satisfaction.

Two final points on IT architecture: Set realistic expectations and don't overcommit. The costs associated with your recommendations are going to be significant and will normally require board approval. You must deliver on these commitments.

▶ Pulling It All Together

The results of your efforts during the first 90 days should be summarized in a strategic plan for the IT organization. This plan serves as the roadmap for the next one to two years. You need to maintain a high level of communication during this timeframe and test your recommendations to determine management acceptance.

The actual document should contain the following information and features:

- A management summary that is 25 pages or less.
- A summary of the process used to develop the architecture.
- Alternative solutions based on bold recommendations.
- Roadmaps for implementation.
- Highly graphical presentation.

My recommendation is to use the first 90 days to turn the IT organization around and set the company on course for the development of its future system architecture. Ninety days is enough time to get things on track and start making visible progress. Remember always: You would not have been hired if things were going well. Your situation at your new company is an opportunity to excel rather than a problem that needs to be fixed.

The Tao Perspective

by George Lin

In this chapter George Lin notes that nothing affects the success of a CIO and the strategic value of the IT organization more profoundly than the CIO's ability to lead and manage. For a fortunate few, this is a gift. Others develop this ability through careful observations of successful leaders while making leadership and management their highest priorities.

Tao means "the enlightened way." Tao IT leadership is the enlightened way in which CIOs can enable business success through wisdom rather than brute force. Mr. Lin developed the concept of the Tao of IT Leaders to deal with challenging leadership, management, and alignment issues surrounding IT.

The Tao of IT Leaders is comprised of five fundamentals of leading by example, five strategies for uniting the forces, and two practices for sustaining success.

The five fundamentals lead to both alignment within IT and alignment between IT and the business, creating an environment in which IT can be an effective service provider and a valuable business enabler. The five strategies enable alignment within the business, leveraging IT's role as a business partner. The two practices enable a sustainable upward success spiral for the CIO.

In this chapter Mr. Lin discusses:

- *Why IT leaders should "think deep" and "plan well."*
- *Why IT organizations should be business-focused, not technology-focused.*
- *The importance of leading by example.*
- *How to become a trusted advisor to your business counterpart.*
- *Why the CIO's top priorities should be leadership, management, and high-level IT strategies.*

The Tao of IT Leaders is heavily influenced by the philosophy of Lao-Tzu, who lived some 2,500 years ago in ancient China. As Lao-Tzu wrote in *Tao-Te Ching*, "When the best leader's work is done and the goal accomplished, the people say, 'We did it ourselves.'" Indeed, this form of "doing without doing" is the ultimate expression of leadership.

Lao-Tzu's *Tao-Te Ching* conveys a sense of harmony and the natural order of the world. The power of physical nature and human nature is limitless. Power belongs to the leader who can understand nature and use it to his own advantage. Once nature is on his side, he can then lead the world with little or no effort, achieving his goals as if by magic.

I developed the Tao of IT Leaders to encourage a similar approach of understanding and leveraging, but focused on business nature and human nature in relation to IT. Use wisdom instead of brute force. CIOs can apply the Tao of IT Leaders as a tool to effortlessly create extraordinary value for the business and to ensure the success of IT.

The Tao of IT Leaders is by no means a complete leadership and management toolbox, and it is not a substitute for leadership and management experience. It is, however, a set of leadership and management concepts and suggestions that, if properly applied by practicing CIOs, can effectively break the 18-month "career is over" syndrome, turning ordinary CIOs into extraordinary IT leaders and managers for the long haul.

▶ An Indirect but Fundamental Approach

As CIOs, we often try to attack conflicts and problems head on and to maintain tight control, thinking that by doing so we can better achieve our goals. More often than not we achieve exactly the opposite result while expending a huge amount of effort. Even if we are successful in some situations, our position and credibility may become weakened over time.

Newton's third law tells us that whenever a force is exerted, it will generate an equal and opposite force in return. I think Sir Isaac Newton is right on. His third law applies not only to physical nature, but often to human nature as well.

So why not take an indirect approach? If we don't employ force head on, we won't experience an opposing force in return. Let us change the paradigm: Instead of using brute force to directly attack conflicts and problems—which are often only the symptoms in any case—the Tao of IT Leaders encourages CIOs to focus on observing and understanding the most fundamental things and use the wisdom gained to create subtle yet powerful influences. In the hands of a skilled practitioner, this approach can enable us to resolve conflicts and problems almost effortlessly. Further, this method often cures the root cause because it encourages us to think deep and plan well.

▶ CIO Challenges

To appreciate the power and simplicity of the Tao of IT Leaders, we must first understand the challenges faced by CIOs today.

The CIO role is inherently challenging because it is constantly beset by conflicts and problems. A CIO has to wear many hats: service provider, business enabler, business partner, strategic visionary, and company executive.

Unlike his other executive peers, a CIO not only has to resolve issues internal to his own functional unit, but as a service provider and a business enabler, he has to resolve issues between IT and other functional and business units. As a business partner, he has to facilitate and resolve issues among various functional and business units. Throwing in the uncertain and fast-changing pace of technology and the relationships that he has to build and maintain with his vendors, suppliers, and service providers, it is no wonder the acronym CIO is said to stand for Career Is Over.

But this multiplicity of roles is only the beginning. The CIO is also supposed to add value to the enterprise as a strategic visionary and a company executive.

Only after a CIO has accomplished the seemingly impossible—creating alignment among constituents with different and often conflicting agendas and requirements—will he be a success wearing his first three hats as service provider, business enabler, and business partner. The Tao of IT Leaders shows CIOs the enlightened way to this success so that they can have a chance to properly fulfill the other two roles: strategic visionary and company executive.

▶ Creating a Business-Focused IT Organization[1]

The root cause of most of the challenges confronting IT organizations today is the CIO's inability to lead and manage alignment, starting with IT/business alignment. Not only must the CIO's vision be strategic and well aligned to the business, his entire IT organization, from top to bottom, needs to be well aligned both internally and to the business.

Misalignment causes a multitude of symptoms, such as IT project delays and cost overruns, poor and unresponsive IT service, runaway IT spending, frequent infrastructure outages, a general business perception of low IT value, and a sense of definite problems with IT, the solutions to which are not clear.

It is not surprising that IT and the business it supports can easily become misaligned. IT staff are often attracted to the IT profession by their love of technology. IT managers tend to employ the most technically oriented and experienced IT specialists to cope with the increasing complexity of information technology and the accelerating pace of change. Combining these two phenomena, we frequently find IT organizations staffed with "propeller heads" at all levels. Such IT organizations can be described as technology-centric.

IT is not about technology, however, but rather about applying information technology to create a competitive advantage for a business. A

---

1. For simplicity and readability, the rest of this chapter is focused on for-profit public companies. The concepts discussed can easily be applied to public sectors such as non-profit organizations and government agencies.

technology-centric IT organization is likely to be inundated with technical details and thus distracted from its ultimate goal, which is to improve shareholder value. IT organizations that lose focus in this way may find themselves doing IT for the sake of IT.

A technology-centric IT organization becomes absurd in this analogy: a packaged software vendor staffed only with software developers, without marketing, sales, professional services, and customer support people. As CIOs, would we buy packaged software from this vendor? Of course not; this vendor is not equipped to make us or the business we support successful. Why then would a CEO buy IT solutions and services from a CIO leading this sort of IT organization?

In a business-focused IT organization, on the other hand, IT staff are more interested in understanding the business—and the people, processes, and organization that make up the business—than they are in the technology for its own sake. These staff members possess a balanced set of soft skills, business acumen as well as analytical and technical skills. They think about business process first and technology second. The solutions they propose tend to be more complete, often involving people, process, and organization as well as technology, which is seen as simply a tool. Interacting with such an organization yields an experience similar to that expected from Big Four consulting firms, but with the added intimacy and insights only an internal organization can provide.

More importantly, IT/business alignment becomes a nonissue because it is natural to a business-focused IT organization, the very DNA of its staff. There is no need to expend effort specifically on IT/business alignment because the business-focused IT organization thinks and acts like the business that it serves and is an integral part of that business.

The Tao of IT Leaders calls on us to build a business-focused IT organization because by doing so we confront the root causes and not merely the symptoms of IT/business alignment issues. Once we have a business-focused IT organization, IT/business alignment issues are effortlessly resolved—doing without doing.

Few of us have the luxury of building an entire IT organization from scratch. In most cases we need to transform a traditional technology-centric IT organization into a business-focused one. One practice that I have used successfully is actively filling key IT positions and openings with appropriate employees from other functional or business units within the company. This is not stealing employees from my executive peers; in fact, my company encourages internal transfers because this practice is beneficial to the business at large. It is especially beneficial to IT because these transferees bring a wealth of knowledge about the business and are naturally aligned to it.

For example, since I work for an enterprise software business, I recruited as my director of IT services the former director of product development. Also, my IT business analyst team is made up of internal transferees.

While some IT positions can be filled with appropriate internal transfers or by hiring technology-inclined business people from outside the company, most IT staff have to undergo a transformation to become business-savvy technologists. Although the term business-savvy technologist may seem like an oxymoron, the next section explains how this transformation can be effortlessly accomplished.

▶ Leading by Example: Five Fundamentals for Better IT/Business Alignment

If a CIO can convince his IT staff to internalize his beliefs and priorities—in essence, sharing the CIO's DNA—the CIO can lead his IT organization with little or no effort, doing without doing as depicted by Lao-Tzu. In such an IT organization, everyone believes in the same vision and acts accordingly.

How does a CIO create such an internally aligned IT organization? Through his or her own actions. Lead by example. But note that leading by example is not acting; acting backfires. Successful leaders are simply being themselves, and in so doing, they become magnets. Leading by example is an especially useful change-management tool for a CIO leading change in an IT organization.

In leading by example, a CIO may focus on different aspects of his organization. I believe, however, that there are five especially important fundamentals that a CIO needs to be cognizant of, regardless of the current focus. If internalized by IT staff, these fundamentals can dramatically transform a technology-centric IT organization into a business-focused one, almost without effort:

- Passion
- Humility
- Openness
- Clarity
- Agility

Each of these fundamentals reinforces the effect of the others. Again, leading by example is not acting. If we look at ourselves in the mirror and can't convince ourselves that we truly believe in these five fundamentals, my best advice is that we leave the responsibility of leading and managing in IT to somebody who does.

Passion

There is no substitute for a CIO's passion for the industry and the business that he is in. In general, executives are hired not only for their professional qualifications but also for their experience in a particular industry, which enriches the collective wisdom of the senior management team. But CIOs are often hired for their professional qualifications alone, regardless of their experience in the industry. This is not a desirable practice.

I remember attending an executive panel discussion in which CEOs frankly shared what they thought about IT and CIOs in general. One CEO said something that struck me: "I feel CIOs work for the IT industry and not for my business." So CIOs are merely internal sales reps for IT vendors? What a revelation! I think CEOs, CFOs, and COOs have some responsibilities too. To begin with, they need to hire the right CIOs.

If a CIO is interested only in IT, I would question his potential value to the business. Without developing a passion for the industry and the business that he or she is in, it will be difficult for the CIO to develop the insights, acumen, and big-picture mindset needed to help the business to achieve its goals. If a CIO's only value is running IT like a utility, there is little reason to keep that IT organization inhouse. Many IT outsourcing vendors can probably do better in this regard, at the least through economies of scale.

IT is about creating a competitive advantage for the business. This starts with a CIO who has passion well beyond IT.

Humility

In the not-too-distant past, there was a huge technology gap between the haves and the have-nots—that is, between management information systems (MIS) professionals and business users. MIS professionals were seen as all-knowing people who wielded the power of mysterious machines in the basement. Then came the revolution of the personal computer and VisiCalc. For the first time, business managers could perform rudimentary forecasts without the help of MIS.

Some might argue that it was all downhill for IT from there. On the contrary, I think that these events actually set the stage for IT professionals to leave the basement for good. IT is not about control, as in the old mainframe days. IT is about empowering IT customers to unleash their potential to succeed in whatever they set out to do. The more technically inclined IT customers are, the easier it is to empower them. The less time IT spends on technology, the greater the effort IT can devote to the business, and the more business value IT can generate.

As CIOs, therefore, not only should we not feel challenged by technically inclined customers, we should try to learn from them. Seeking first to understand is the key to creating alignment. We should learn from all of our constituents: IT staff, executive peers, internal IT customers, our business's customers and partners, vendors, industry peers, analysts, everyone. We should strive to understand their goals, visions, concerns, fears, likes, dislikes, and even their own technical solutions, everything that we can possibly learn. We learn from people's successes, and at other times we learn from their mistakes…and that is extremely valuable too.

CIOs should stop talking, and start listening with humility. Only by understanding our constituents can we possibly become a trusted partner and help IT become more closely aligned with the business.

Openness

Most of us would agree that the only constant in IT is change. Some of us may also believe that being a change agent is an important part of a CIO's role. But there are times at which the actions taken by IT lead our constituents to believe that we are the most conservative functional unit in a company. We do three- or six-month-long Phase Zero analyses. We do endless discoveries, looking for that perfect technology path. We test applications to death. At the end of the day (or after a couple of year's worth of development efforts), what we deliver may turn out not to be what our constituents are looking for after all.

No doubt, most CIOs are successful and smart people. Over the years, we build up certain beliefs and rituals. Things have got to be done in a particular way or they will fail; after all, we've tried all the alternatives. We have our battle scars to prove our point. But my challenge to CIOs is this: If we keep doing what we were doing yesterday, how can we possibly create a competitive advantage for our business when our competitors are moving forward? Is it perhaps time to leave our baggage behind?

I start every day as a new day, like starting with a blank sheet of paper. Clearing my mind of any prejudice that I may have helps me to make the right decisions. My job is not to come up with solutions. My job is to make the right decision at the right time. The only way to ensure that I can consistently do my job well is to have an open mind in making decisions. Having an open mind allows me to embrace outside-the-box thinking, to take calculated risks, which are often critical to the success of all my constituents.

If a CIO encourages a sense of openness throughout his IT organization, IT staff will be more inclined to be creative, think outside the box, take risks, and perform often-needed "miracles."

Clarity

Clarity is the ability to see the fundamentals, to be able to turn complex, muddy issues into simple, clear concepts and solutions. Clarity is a necessary skill for leaders; successful leaders use clarity in order to direct.

An IT organization, armed with its knowledge and tools, can add great value to a business by providing relevant and timely information so that business leaders can have clarity. Providing both clarity and the information that others need to have clarity is in fact at IT's root.

As CIOs, we should stay true to our roots. We should provide clarity in every interaction with our constituents, and we should inspire all our constituents, especially IT staff, to do the same.

IT is sometimes perceived by our customers as providing the opposite of clarity. In fact, IT often seems to make everything more complex than necessary. In conveying a sense that it is doing IT for the sake of IT, IT becomes a runaway freight train. This problem is especially prevalent among technology-centric IT organizations. It is a dangerous problem to have. Whether the CIO is at fault or not, he may quickly loose his credibility.

As both IT and the business it supports become more complex, CIOs should seize the opportunity to be true leaders. Instead of getting tangled up in complexities, CIOs should practice simplicity, the best antidote. Ask simple, insightful questions to seek practical solutions. Consider everything in terms of its most basic fundamentals. Soon, you can become a leader of clarity, revered for your uncommon wisdom.

Agility

Agility—the ability to move quickly and effectively—can be thought of as the result of applying passion, humility, openness, and clarity. Passion gives us insight into the business that we support. Humility encourages us to listen to and understand all of our constituents. Openness enables us to embrace new ideas and to make the right decisions. Clarity allows us be wise and able to direct proper actions. These four fundamentals, if combined and implemented, should almost always produce a competitive advantage in the form of increased speed for the business, such as quicker time to market, increased inventory turns, and so on.

This should not come as a surprise; one of the functions of IT is to make a business more agile. But I want to make one clarification. While some say that technology can make a business more agile, I think this is misleading. Technology by itself can never make a business more agile, but the right IT people applying the right technology at the right time can.

Agility can also be considered separately, and can support the other four fundamentals. Think agile! Be proactive! Get something done! Treating agility as a separate fundamental is especially important to IT. While IT is helping the business to become more agile, IT needs to become more agile itself. I am sure that many of us have had the experience of having the business perceive IT as an obstacle to agility.

To achieve better agility within IT, the CIO needs to put passion, humility, openness, and clarity into action, and encourage IT staff to think and act agile.

In today's hyper-competitive but cost-conscious environment, agility is not only a much-sought-after virtue, but one that can mean the difference between success and failure for the business that we support.

▶ Uniting the Forces: Five Strategies to Align the Business

In practicing the Tao of IT Leaders concepts and techniques—using an indirect but fundamental approach, aligning IT to the business, and leading by example—we find that the CIO job suddenly requires less effort than before. We find ourselves spending significantly less time in dealing with symptoms and achieving more success in stomping out root causes.

At this stage, the IT organization is both better aligned internally and better aligned to the business. The business's perception of this well-aligned IT organization is that IT has become a more valuable service provider and can be counted on to deliver additional tactical value to enable business success. But this is only the beginning. By leveraging and building on these achievements, we can elevate IT to the next level: becoming a true business partner.

While IT may now be better aligned to the business, we need to ponder whether the business is well aligned with itself in the pursuit of its goals. All of us have experienced the common "islands of information" phenomenon in one way or another. This phenomenon may be mistaken as a systems problem, and the blame conveniently placed on IT. But if a business system is merely a representation of the business itself, the "islands of information" problem reflects how an enterprise really operates: business and functional units working in silos rather than in a crossfunctional, collaborative way.

This is when the CIO role becomes strategic and why CIOs should step up to deliver strategic value as a business partner. A CIO, regardless of whom he reports to or whether it is an enterprise or a divisional role, is often a central touchpoint behind the scenes. This role is strategic because it can profoundly shape the business in a cross-functional way. The flip side, though, is that playing the role well is critically important.

Most business projects require some form of IT support and inevitably have IT components, whether they are application, infrastructure, or service-related. Sadly, we know that business/functional units don't always collaborate well with one another; they are the silos of an enterprise. But even silos would need something from IT in order to execute their projects, so they all must work with IT. If IT is well aligned to the business and is viewed as an effective service provider and a valuable business enabler, it can then become a central touch point that everyone works with. As CIOs, we can passively support these projects or we can take on an active role. By leveraging IT's crossfunctional role, a CIO can create a subtle yet powerful influence to help the forces in various business and functional units to unite and focus on common goals.

Earlier, I discussed how effective an IT organization can become if it is well aligned internally. This holds true at a larger, enterprise level. If all business and functional units within an enterprise are well aligned and work collaboratively and in support of one another, the enterprise can achieve far greater success than it otherwise could.

There are five important strategies a CIO can use to help align his business:

- Start with business processes.
- Be a diplomat: Empower all constituents to seek win-win.
- Cultivate business partnerships.
- Mandate customer participation in IT projects.
- Provide thought leadership.

For the rest of this section, I discuss how a CIO can use these strategies in his role as a business partner to entice forces in various business and functional units to unite. Not only can the CIO thus add strategic value to the business in a crossfunctional way, he will also find that the problems and challenges commonly associated with large IT projects disappear as if by magic.

Start with Business Processes

IT organizations are traditionally responsible for implementing business systems and rolling out major applications. IT staff are usually experts at the technology aspect of these projects, such as programming. Today, however, technology is more about packaged software solutions. So we find IT doing configurations, customizations, tuning, upgrades, and system management.

Setting the technology aside, all these systems and applications are really tools to help automate business processes. No system or application can help a business process if the process is broken to begin with. As a matter of fact, automating a bad business process can quickly worsen the business; in such cases it is better not to automate it at all. This brings to mind the dotcom economy. Every widget sold made a certain e-tailer lose a few dollars; the more widgets the e-tailer sold, the quicker it went bankrupt.

As CIOs, we need to help both IT and the business focus first on business processes. Figure out the current process. Understand the goals and how we want the right process to look. Do a gap analysis so that we can devise a realistic strategy to migrate the business from its current state to its goals.

Focusing everyone on the business process gives IT the obvious benefit of business insights so that IT can deliver the right systems and applications. Going through the business process exercise yields two other significant results that are beneficial to the business as a whole:

1. The business may discover that incremental improvements do not necessarily require an additional investment in technology. Sometimes, even improving certain manual processes can yield immediate and significant gains without a huge capital investment in technology;

2. Understanding the business process helps the business to understand handoff points and interdependencies. This is the key to fostering meaningful crossfunctional collaborative work.

Be a Diplomat: Empower All Constituents to Seek Win-Win

Some of us may wonder why IT should be facilitating business process work rather than hiring outside consultants. There are a lot of good reasons to hire consultants. Consultants are not in the forest, so presumably they can see well. But if IT can fulfill the objective role of a consultant, I believe it can help the business to know what is best for itself.

The business has to come up with its own solutions to solve its own problems; for me, there is no way around this. What the business needs in business process work are facilitation, methodology, objectivity, encouragement, and common sense. IT can certainly act like a consultant and provide the business with these value-adds. And unlike an outside consultant, IT possesses insights available only to an internal organization, such as an intimate knowledge of the people, organization, culture, and history involved.

Obviously, IT has an ulterior motive in facilitating business process work; a clear and efficient business process is the prerequisite for IT to deliver a successful business system implementation. Adding up these reasons, it does make sense for IT to engage.

There is little doubt that when IT delves deeper into business processes, disconnects within organizations and between organizations will surface. Even in the best-run companies, opportunities for improvement abound.

My experience is that if we put motivated people in a room and tell them where the disconnects are, nine times out of ten they will figure out a workable solution, often a good one. The problem has frequently been that people assume others know what they themselves know, and others sometimes don't! I am oversimplifying, but that is the essence.

The CIO role is inherently a crossfunctional role. We already possess the crossfunctional know-how; it requires only minor effort to extend ourselves into a more strategic role as a business partner. To that end, CIOs should learn to become effective diplomats to help various parts of the business become better aligned with one another. An aligned business is always a more profitable business. I have a mentor who once said, "We may not be right, but we are not confused." That is alignment in the business.

How do we learn to become effective diplomats? Learn from our favorite statesmen. A quicker alternative is to use the Tao of IT Leaders.

Religiously practice the five fundamentals discussed earlier: passion, humility, openness, clarity, and agility. They give us a better read of our constituents. Once we have the insight into everyone involved, becoming a great diplomat is not difficult. All we need to do is to guide our constituents toward common goals. Common goals create alignment. Alignment sparks win-win opportunities.

Cultivate Business Partnership

If IT is to become a business partner, CIOs need to actively cultivate business partnerships internally. As CIOs, we already know how to cultivate strong partnerships with vendors and suppliers. Why does it always seem difficult for us to have the same kinds of relationships internally?

A partnership is a symbiotic relationship; a successful and sustainable business partnership requires all partners to benefit. If one partner loses, the partnership will not last long. With our vendors and suppliers, we typically put effort into building and maintaining the relationship, including clearly understood benefits to all partners, and they do the same in return. Each partner has incentive to maintain the partnership, and partners typically know what incentives are needed to keep the partnership strong.

Cultivating similar business partnerships internally encourages us to strive to ensure the success of our partners, because we benefit in turn from the continuation of the partnership. Applying this mentality to day-to-day crossfunctional collaborative work is quite powerful, encouraging everyone to ask, What's in it for me? and What's in it for him? Understanding everyone's concerns solidifies relationships and generates the oomph behind whatever the partnership has set out to accomplish—for example, a major IT enhancement project involving IT and a few other business and functional units. Interactions within a partnership build stronger relationships among partners, paving the way for future partnerships and successes.

Mandate Customer Participation in IT Projects

Generally, IT projects have an unusually low success rate when compared to non-IT projects within an enterprise. IT projects fail for many reasons, but seldom for purely technical ones. Most often, failure is ultimately a result of people, process, and organizational issues. In post-mortem analysis, we hear reasons such as that the business had unreasonable requirements, the project scope crept, the timeline was too compressed, IT wasn't given enough money or resources, and so on.

How can a CIO improve the odds? It is actually deceptively simple: Hold the business accountable for IT projects.

One root cause for the high failure rate of IT projects is that there are too many unnecessary IT projects—those with dubious benefits, unclear business ownership, and questionable business commitment. A large percentage of all IT projects are unnecessary and are doomed to fail.

A CIO can significantly reduce the number of unnecessary IT projects by encouraging the business to work on business processes, playing diplomat to align conflicting business and functional units and their requirements, and being a trusted business partner—the three strategies for uniting the forces discussed so far.

The remaining IT projects, by definition, are necessary, must-do projects that the business can agree on and see a compelling value in executing. The CIO still has to ensure proper prioritization and implementation of these projects.

One strategy that I have employed successfully in weeding out unnecessary IT projects is to mandate customer participation. Participation is not simply that the business sponsor receives weekly updates from IT, but rather that the business and IT are working together on the project, at all levels and across all functions, from the business sponsor to users, from project financials to project management.

If an IT project is truly necessary—must-do—obtaining that level of business commitment is easy. The business wants IT to succeed because the business has a vested interest; IT and the business are in the same boat. In such a situation, everyone is motivated to make the project successful in order to reap benefits from it.

At my company, if I didn't have that high level of business commitment, I would simply veto the project as a waste of IT's time and the business's money, although this hasn't happened yet, since IT and the business are well aligned at my shop. Issues are resolved well before I need to use that stick.

Another mechanism that we have employed rather effectively to ensure that all IT investments are properly linked to business goals and attainable ROIs is our funding and approval process for capital expenditure.

We use a "business-funded" model to encourage responsible IT investments (and for that matter, all capital investments). The burden of justifying capital spending falls on the beneficiary business/functional VP. All capital funding requests, both IT and non-IT related, go to a capital approval board, which consists of three members: the CFO, the corporate controller, and the CIO. Funding approval requires the consensus of all three members.

Provide Thought Leadership

Providing the right thought leadership is important because it can compel people to think. Thought leadership also has the potential to change people's behavior and organizational structure in a fundamental way. Such thoughts should be simple so that a large population can easily identify with them.

Providing thought leadership can be the hardest thing for a CIO to do—or it can be the easiest. Unfortunately, I don't have a theory on how CIOs can better provide thought leadership other than to keep practicing the Tao of IT Leaders and look for appropriate opportunities, but I can provide a couple of examples for illustrative purposes.

Maintaining a high customer-satisfaction level and keeping our product quality high are top priorities at my company. IT therefore champions the internal use of our products as a means to improve customer success and product quality goals. Our internal slogan reads, "Documentum IT is Documentum's first and best customer." Indeed we are. IT has tremendous crossfunctional support in this effort. Our experience with our products and our experience as a customer are being leveraged daily by the rest of the company in continually enhancing our products and service offerings for our customers.

Since we are one of the leading enterprise software companies and since IT is about enterprise software, the challenge that I put forward to my own organization is this: Can we afford to not be an IT leader when the company is a leader in enterprise software? Now IT has a mission. IT staff members are compelled to think outside the box, often a step ahead of what is considered industry best practice. Major IT projects are completed in unheard-of record time. The business has benefited immensely from this highly motivated and effective IT organization.

▶ Sustaining Success: Two Practices

So far, I have discussed how a CIO can apply the Tao of IT Leaders concepts and techniques to enable IT to become an effective service provider, a valuable business enabler, and a trusted business partner. In this section, I discuss two practices that CIOs can use to sustain and further their success.

Hire Complementary IT Leaders

A CIO, like other executives, is probably a specialist in a limited number of areas and a generalist in most others. Unlike other functional units, IT is broad and deep, plus it deals with the added dimension of change. For a CIO to manage a highly successful IT organization, he must have a staff of topnotch IT leaders who can complement his strengths and make up for his weaknesses. These senior staff members should also be able to complement each other's skills and personalities well.

I want to share with you a personal "if I can do it, anybody can do it" story as both an inspiration and a concrete illustration of what I have discussed in this chapter.

My IT career path is atypical. I don't have some twenty-plus years of IT experience. I graduated from UC Berkeley with a liberal arts degree. I am probably the least technical person among senior management staff at my company. I am 32 years old. Yet I run a successful IT organization at one of the leading enterprise software companies, a job that is probably an order of magnitude more difficult than a regular CIO's, since all my internal customers are IT pros andI have to stay always ahead of the game.

I took on IT not because it is easy but because it is hard. I was on a mission to prove that with the proper focus on leadership and management, perhaps even the most unwieldy organization can be tamed. Before leading IT, I used the same focus to successfully manage two other unrelated functions with which I also had zero previous experience.

In IT, I provide the vision and high-level strategies. I devote myself full time to leading and managing, using the Tao of IT Leaders that I've developed. Since I need to focus only on this limited number of tasks, I do them very well. For the same reason, I need to hire and retain the most talented IT staff that I can find to implement my vision and strategies.

I learned the golden rule of hiring quite early in my career. I always hire people who not only can do what they are hired to do, but who also have the potential to do my job someday. My ulterior motive is that I don't want to get stuck in a position—I want to move on and move up. Hiring capable employees ensures that I can reach my own personal career goals. Over time, the organizations that I build tend to have extremely capable employees from top to bottom. This brings a tremendous value to the business.

Improve People, Processes, and Organization Continually

Improving people, processes, and organization continually is a simple concept, but it is often difficult to implement. A typical IT organization is probably already inundated with issues. How can a CIO afford to devote precious time, effort, and resource on these "soft" issues? My question is, how can he afford not to?

Continually invest in people, fine tune processes, and align the IT organization internally. These are investments that can offer high returns. If an IT organization is in bad shape, make such investments to stop the downward death spiral. If an IT organization is in good shape, make such investments to create an upward success spiral.

I think the most effective way is not to make a limited number of big-bang course changes but to make frequent incremental course corrections over time. Big-bang course changes have the potential to create more harm than good, especially if a wrong turn is made. The benefits of frequent incremental course corrections made over time can add up substantially.

Making these frequent incremental corrections requires the CIO to have a keen sense of his IT organization and its relationship with other organizations. The CIO has to be a good coach. He must have a good read on IT staff, understanding their goals, assisting them in growing effectively, and ultimately matching them to the right roles at the right times. If the matching is done well, work can be accomplished twice as fast with half the effort.

As CIOs, we need to understand that work ultimately has to be done by the people whom we lead and manage. Our success depends on them. The only thing that we can effectively control to improve our own success is to make leadership and management our highest priorities, day in and day out.

▶ In Closing

In this chapter, I have discussed the Tao, or the Enlightened Way, of IT Leaders. This approach is about observing and understanding the most fundamental of things and using the wisdom gained to create subtle yet powerful influences. When solving problems, CIOs should not perform frontal assaults on symptoms. Instead, go for the root cause. Use wisdom instead of brute force. The problem can often be resolved effortlessly if it is approached from an indirect yet fundamental perspective.

To solve IT/business alignment issues, transform a technology-centric IT organization into a business-focused one. Leading by example is the best change management tool for such a transformation in IT. Practice the five fundamentals in leading by example. A business-focused IT organization is naturally aligned to the business, and is usually an effective service provider and a valuable business enabler.

Having IT aligned to the business is of limited value if other parts of the business are not well aligned with one another. CIOs should provide strategic value as a trusted business partner fostering overall business alignment, practicing the five strategies in uniting the forces. A better-aligned business is a more profitable business and also makes a CIO's job exponentially easier.

To ensure the effectiveness of the IT organization and its continued success, CIOs need to hire and retain complementary staff members. A CIO should focus primarily on leadership and management, and on providing vision and high-level strategies for IT. Those are his top priorities. CIOs should strive to continually adjust people, processes, and organization to realize incremental improvements, which add up over time.

I want to share one parting thought: When there is change, there is opportunity. Be proactive. Do something different today to begin leading IT's transformation into an extraordinary organization.

Communications: Communication Excellence in IT Management

by Brenda J. Fox

In this chapter Brenda Fox covers an essential skill of all successful CIOs—the special ability to communicate.

Covering many areas, communication means going out and working with users, customers, other business units, executive management, partners, suppliers, and other organizations. It is the only way the CIO can understand everyone's needs and all the requirements to effectively run the business. It means taking a proactive role in the business—not simply reacting to problems—as well as marketing and selling the IT organization. For the CIO to be successful, the CIO must help users, customers, and others succeed too. Brenda Fox discusses:

- *How to break down stereotypes that threaten good communication.*

- *The essential management practices that produce good communication.*

71

- *What to keep in mind when implementing communication tools and practices.*
- *How to be a better communicator.*
- *How to know when communication is effective.*

Communication is an essential skill that is highlighted throughout the book, particularly in the chapters on leadership, governance and budgeting. Remember, to be a successful CIO, you must communicate, communicate, and communicate.

"I don't want to see any more f***ing slides with any more f***ing arrows!"

This isn't the kind of thing you want to hear during your first big presentation to the executive staff. But that is how the VP of operations responded three slides into my 30-slide presentation on the current crisis facing our IT department.

As the recently hired CIO, I had spent hours analyzing the company's systemic IT problems and untold additional hours putting together this presentation. In the hiring process, the executive team had been extremely excited about my ability to finally solve their problems, and this was my first chance to take them through it step by step. As a computer science person, that's how I'd always attacked a problem. Diagram it, get it in front of the group, and discuss the best solution.

Three slides into my presentation, I discovered that the rest of the world doesn't think the same way. I was bewildered and speechless, and that was the end of my presentation.

I didn't realize it right away, but that moment brought me face to face with the fundamental communication gap between IT people and non-IT people in any business. At the time I couldn't fathom why anyone on the executive staff wouldn't want to understand the problem. The truth is, non-IT people only want to know how IT problems will affect what they do. Everything else is too confusing, too complex, or too time consuming.

As CIO, I learned to be aware of who I was communicating with and what essential information they needed. In the case of the executive staff, they wanted to know only the gist of the problem, what I was doing about it, the cost and the timeframe, the impact on the business, and what was required of them.

That meeting was a turning point for me because I realized that succeeding as a CIO meant getting good at communicating both on a personal level and as an organization. I was like a medical student who, on his first day as a real doctor, realizes that nothing in school taught him how to have a good bedside manner.

Since then, I have learned a few things that make good communication possible. In this chapter, you'll learn ways to attack this problem, including:

- How to break down stereotypes that threaten good communication.
- Essential management practices that produce good communication.
- What to keep in mind when implementing communication tools and practices.
- How to make yourself a better communicator.
- How you know when communications are good.

▶ The Problem: Us Versus Them

The fundamental communication gap between IT people and non-IT people begins with a few deeply entrenched stereotypes. Non-techies often feel like the dog named Ginger in that famous *Far Side* comic strip (Figure 5–1): The dog listens to the owner's explicit commands, but all the dog understands is "BLAH, BLAH, BLAH, GINGER…BLAH, BLAH, BLAH, GINGER!"

When the Gingers of the world see IT people, they see a bunch of nerds. Why?

Let's create a profile of a stereotypical IT professional to help illustrate. Like engineers, IT people excel in logistical, binary, and abstract thinking. IT people also tend not to be people persons, often leave the impression of sarcasm or superiority, and in general do not value communication skills—or those who have them. IT people may appear unconcerned with the larger process and success of the business. IT people may also appear to have no standard process or priority when handling incoming requests.

Figure 5–1 *Far Side* comic sketch.

That is what the Gingers see. They don't realize (or appreciate) the underlying causes of these appearances. They don't realize that solving IT problems requires an intense focus on the details (not the bigger business picture) and that the speed of technological change sometimes does not allow IT people to step back and see that bigger picture. They don't realize that compared to other business processes like finance and engineering, IT is in its infancy, and standard practices from customer support to software rollouts have not been established since mainframe-era practices were abandoned.

If nothing is done to dispel these stereotypes and appearances, miscommunication and mistrust will continue from both sides. Non-IT people will continue to see IT people as:

- Unwilling to speak except in confusing technical jargon.
- Living in a separate world and unconcerned about the business.
- Self-centered, arrogant, and passive-aggressive.
- A roadblock to the organization's success.
- A group that should be managed by another executive.

Figure 5–2   Targeted as IT stereotypes.

IT people will continue to see themselves as

- Misunderstood geniuses.
- Wrongly treated like second-class citizens.
- Victims of circumstance.
- Overworked, underpaid, and unappreciated.
- Not to blame for third-party software and hardware failures.
- Totally justified in indulging in this kind of behavior.

Figure 5–3   Misunderstood techie.

As CIO, your success depends on breaking down these appearances on both sides of the IT fence. You must set the example from the top down and ensure that your department delivers from the bottom up.

Consider how former New York Mayor Rudy Guiliani reduced crime and improved the quality of life in the city. He began by ticketing jay-walkers, loiterers, and double-parked cars. By raising the standards on what criminal behavior the city was willing to tolerate, he changed the willingness of would-be criminals to commit all crimes. I am not suggesting that you start putting bad communicators in handcuffs. The lesson here is that improving the little things—by creating a systemic improvement in what is expected—can improve the big things in the process.

Many of you may feel that you lack the skills to tackle what is considered a "touchy-feely" problem. I am here to tell you that you already have all the skills, but are lacking one key distinction:

Good communication practices should be viewed as deliverables, identical to any other business objective in your department. Give them the same priority you would give any mission-critical enterprise system rollout.

As CIO, you already have the skills and experience to roll out a major system implementation. Good communication is not that different, except that in this case the deliverables are the tools and processes necessary for creating good communication. Let's begin by discussing:

▶ How to Break Down Stereotypes That Threaten Good Communication

Changing entrenched stereotypes and misperceptions begins with you. Whatever initiatives you undertake, you as an individual have to buy into the idea that there is real benefit in making these changes. You will be the evangelist, the one dragging everyone else to new places, so here are a few essentials for success.

Lead by Example

The best way to get people to follow is to lead by example. Don't expect anyone else to buy into anything that you don't believe in yourself. Make communication a priority and be passionate about the way IT is perceived, and the way IT performs and communicates. Because IT touches every department, your changes can have a big impact on your own department and on communication throughout the company.

Know Your Audiences

As I learned from my shocking first executive staff meeting, you must be aware of who you are communicating with and what essential information they need. Let's examine the four principle groups that you regularly communicate with (as shown in Figure 5–4) and what to be aware of for each.

Executive Level (board of directors, executive staff, your direct manager, and possibly executive committees). Communication should:

- Be high level.
- Address their concerns in their language.
- Focus on impact on business and ROI.
- Be immediate.
- Take hierarchy into consideration (depending on the culture).

IT Staff Level (direct reports, entire local and remote staff, consultants and outsource vendors, and possibly special projects teams for which you are the executive sponsor). Communication should:

- Be detailed.
- Explain the technical background and architecture.
- Outline and explain requests, and justify outcomes.
- Contain clear instructions and clear conditions for satisfaction of requests.

Internal Customers Level (peers, other functional groups, desktop and network users, major application users, remote site users, and all mobile users). Communication should:

- Be clear, concise, and simple.
- Quick and precise.
- Explain the when, where, why, and why not.

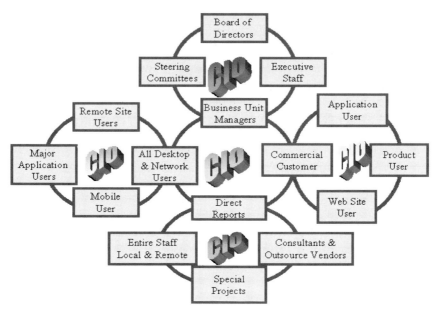

Figure 5–4 Total communication loops.

- Exhibit extreme patience.
- Be repeated over and over again.
- Make it easy for recipients to access facts on their own.

External Customers Level (commercial customers using the company's products, external users of the company's Web site or major applications, and both formal and informal organizations). Communication should:

- Be politically correct.
- Be aware of revenue impact.
- Be conscious of security and breach of contract issues.
- Take the lead from the marketing and sales departments as to the approved methods of communicating with outside customers.

Create Awareness of the Lines of Communication

It is important that not just you, the CIO, be aware of these different audiences and how to deal with them. All members of the IT staff should be familiar with all lines of communication and with what behavior is expected of them in each scenario. Push communication awareness down through your organization.

Start Thinking Like a Service Organization

You are managing a service organization, and as such, all that matters is how your "customers" perceive you. Spend time with them, learn their processes, and constantly ask for feedback. Pay extra attention to your help desk and customer service because this is where many of the perceptions of IT communication are derived. They are the main windows into IT for most of your users.

There is no secret to success regarding good customer service. Service management by nature is a day in, day out, ongoing, never-ending, unremitting, persevering, and compassionate enterprise.

Ask Your Staff for Help

The people in the trenches know what is really going to work and what is going to end up in the dumb idea file. Use your staff of experts to build your communication tools and processes. By asking for help, you can build team spirit and tackle the problem of stereotypes and misperceptions together.

Stop the Blame Game

It has puzzled me that IT shops often tend to be their own worst enemies. The applications group and the operations group fight with each other, the network group fights with everyone, and the desktop group always tells users it is not their fault. Not exactly a formula for success, or for creating a positive perception of your IT department. The lines of communication are quite complex within IT.

There are many diverse skill sets and levels of technical knowledge, as shown in Figure 5–5. These subgroups should be communicating and planning together or they will continue to fight and blame each other for problems.

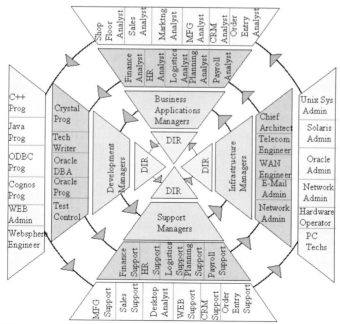

Figure 5–5   Internal IT lines of communication.

The fastest way to work on a cure to this problem is mandatory inter-group planning and review sessions, in which responsible individuals are required to review their plans and status publicly and facilitate open discussions to resolve interdependencies. The first few can be rather ugly but don't give up on them. There is no simple solution to stopping the blame game, but here are a few more pointers.

Provide Accurate Information

Make sure everyone in IT gets the same timely information. Require individuals to communicate their plans consistently and to be accountable for their actions. No hiding out, no whining! Institute *communication protocols* between your major groups.

> **Production Control.** Policies and procedures to manage the handoff between the Applications group and the Operations group.

Figure 5–6 No whining.

> **Problem Management and Corrective Action.** Policies and procedures to manage performance issues and ensure that the same problem is not happening repeatedly. This will also give the customer service group a voice and provide them with the tools and status to report back to the customers.
>
> **Product Release Updates.** Maintain current update information on all changes to products in production. This will assist all groups in understanding the impact of the changes or updates, and ensure that all dependencies are compatible before these updates or changes go into production. This process can be adapted from those used by commercial product development groups releasing product updates for sale. In particular, it is imperative that the networking group treats the network as a product, and applies the same disciplines. How many times have we heard, "It should not have affected any-

thing" from an engineer who made what she considered a minor change to the network, with the result that no one could log into a mission-critical application for hours. This type of thing builds bad blood among your own IT groups, shutting down many layers of communication and trust—not to mention aggravating your users.

Foster Teamwork

Integrating the groups within IT requires you to build and provide an atmosphere that fosters teamwork. Studies indicate that the major considerations involved in the integration of people from many disciplines into an effective team are:

- Effective communication from the leader and within the team.
- Sincere interest by the leader and the team in the professional growth of team members.
- Commitment to the group's success.

Let's examine the barriers to creating such an atmosphere (see Table 5–1).

To foster teamwork in your department, you must learn what encourages active participation and minimizes conflict. This requires skills in leadership, administration, organization, and technical expertise on the project. Having human resource professionals tightly linked to the entire IT planning process can be key in this effort; if your HR department cannot provide this assistance, you may have to seek outside advice. The CIO *must* ensure that someone qualified and skilled is making certain that education, career concerns, reward systems, job design, teambuilding, leadership skills and the like are factored into IT, because they are major building blocks of effective teamwork.

Changing entrenched stereotypes and misperceptions can seem like an enormous task. However, you don't have to enact all the above-mentioned changes. Most importantly, breaking down these stereotypes and making good communication a priority begins with you.

Barrier	How to Minimize or Eliminate Barriers
Differing outlooks, priorities, and interests: IT organization team members are often aligned to a particular hardware or software component, find it very difficult to accept a change, and will refuse to support (or even sabotage) the success of projects. Alternatively, if team members have their hearts set on getting into the "new fun stuff", morale issue can arise if the projects are not approved or the team members are not assigned to them.	Identify these conflicts and "sell" the team concept to the team members involved. Try to blend individual interests to support overall department objectives. Clearly discuss the importance of making this cultural shift in IT, and the benefits and rewards that will result from it. Lay out your general expectations for team collaboration, and what behavior is not acceptable. Finally, if a staff member remains uncooperative in supporting change and continues to spread negativity, replacement should be considered.
Role conflicts. Team development efforts can be quickly thwarted when ambiguity exists over who does what and who is responsible—and more importantly, accountable—for what. Good examples include the role differentiation between desktop support and LAN support, or that between applications development and database administration.	Starting by asking each staff member where they see themselves fitting in, and what they are responsible and accountable for. Examine gaps and overlaps and resolve them with the team to ensure that all bases are covered in an efficient and unambiguous manner. Uncovered responsibilities are as much of a problem as duplicated ones, and both can cause fighting within a team. Here is where regular production control and open ticket analysis meetings can rally the whole team around a common cause.
Unclear objectives. Unclear goals, deliverables or definitions of success can lead to conflict, ambiguities, and power struggles. Not to mention hours of wasted labor on non-mission-critical tasks.	Assure that the entire IT organization understands overall and interdisciplinary objectives. Clear and frequent communications from the CIO and senior management become critically important. Regular status meetings can be used for feedback. Invite the CEO, president, and other executive staff to attend your status meetings so your staff can begin to see the importance of IT within the company.

Table 5–1 Barriers vs. minimized or eliminated barriers.

Dynamic environments. Many companies and IT organizations operate in a continuous state of change. I have been at organizations in which the common joke was that you could duck this change because another one was just around the corner.	If you are operating in such an environment, your attempts at making a cultural change n your group may be met with great skepticism. Here is where you must "sell" this direction to the whole team. You must make a personal long-term commitment to make this happen; it won't happen over night. Staff members will be watching you to see if you are committed and serious before they make a their own commitments to change their behavior. Set a strong example to follow.
Communication Problems. Not surprisingly, poor communication is a major enemy of effective team development. This can exist on multiple levels: among IT staff members, between staff members ad IT management, between IT and top management, and between IT and internal customers	The CIO and IT management should devote considerable time to communicating with individual team members. Also, a strong cautionary note: make sure your direct reports have bought into your initiatives first, or you will have difficulty with their entire groups. Watch out for personality conflicts between your senior managers and functional department managers, or communication with that whole customer group will be bad. In addition, you should provide vehicles for encouraging communication among individual staff members. Tools for enhancing communication include production control meetings, regular brief status review meetings, all hands updates at which group managers are required to give updates and individual staff members give technical updates, and establishing regular and thorough communication with internal customers and top management.
Lack of senior management support.	Roll up your sleeves and actively participate in making this cultural shift happen. You'll need the support of the senior IT managers, but this responsibility cannot be delegated downward— you must stay involved to give the effort the priority and visibility it must have to be successful.

Table 5–1   Barriers vs. minimized or eliminated barriers (continued).

▶ Essential Management Practices That Produce Good Communication

Without accurate and understandable information, there is not much hope that good communication will improve your department's performance. Communication tools and processes break down in most companies because the information moving through those channels is inaccurate, out of date, or incomprehensible to the person who needs it. Good communication begins with having the ability to collect and deliver reliable information on a consistent basis.

As CIO, you need to consistently collect accurate information about all IT initiatives. You need to aggregate and interpret that information in order to make beneficial adjustments. Then you need to deliver this information to each group in a way that enables that group to make use of it. Figure 5–7 shows the relationship of business processes to the generation of information.

Whether you are dealing with servo systems, financial results, or even your own abilities, good communication is dependant upon feedback information generated by ongoing initiatives within the organization. Thus the first step in implementing good communication practices is implementing some key management practices.

The following is a set of IT management practices that must be in place to support good communication. These topics are discussed in detail in other chapters of this book; here we show how each practice supports good communication.

Plan

If your company does not plan well, you may be inclined not to plan at all. Unfortunately, that makes communicating especially difficult. Without planning, including monitoring and review processes, it is hard to accurately evaluate status, to keep everyone on the same page, and to communicate what you need to complete a given project.

Set IT Policy and Standards

Without the ability to set policy and ensure that it is followed, your IT organization will constantly be at war with the rest of the organization.

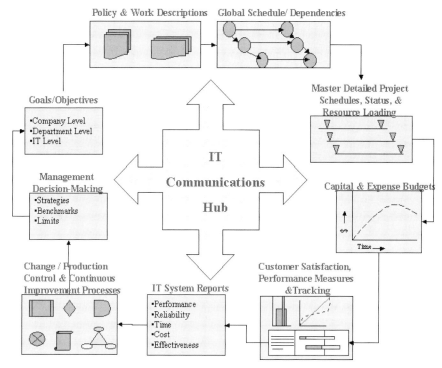

Figure 5–7   IT communications hub.

Having standards in place allows others to have accurate expectations of IT, which improves communication.

Understand the Company's Commitments, Schedules, and Dependencies

As CIO, you must know what is happening throughout the entire organization. Otherwise, your IT department will be frequently blindsided and perceived as a roadblock. Take time to sit in on department staff meetings, or implement your own planning meetings with key executives on a regular basis to ensure you are up to speed with their plans. This allows you to communicate to your staff and plan accordingly.

Integrate Project Planning

Often, each business unit or each unit within IT develops its own planning documentation. Since most projects involve more than one unit, this lack of integration can put you behind the eight ball before a project even begins.

Budget as a Team

Budgeting must be done with the executive team. Awareness of approved, and more importantly non-approved, initiatives must be communicated across the organization. Also, the budget must never be used as an excuse. Users hate to hear "It's not in the budget." This feeds the stereotyped perception of IT people.

Control Production Changes

Without formal production control practices, your applications, operations, network, and desktop staff will continually fight and blame each other when changes create problems across your systems. If you do one thing as a result of reading this chapter, put a production control function in place.

Continuously Improve Quality

Customers may forgive you the first time something goes wrong, maybe even the second or third. After that, don't expect any repeat business. Root-cause analysis procedures and corrective action plans must be part of your process. Include your whole team in the corrective action plan. This puts the focus on improving as a team and learning lessons without placing blame.

Be Explicit in Your Decision-Making Process

Base your decisions on visible and logical factors. When the decision-making process is transparent and explicit, the objectives, standards, costs, policies, and schedules become visible guidelines to your team and to the entire organization.

Good communication can be a lifesaver in times of crisis; it cannot cover up for consistently poor performance. With these solid IT management practices in place, communication within your department and across the organization will improve by default. With the accurate measurements and clear expectations established by these changes, you will be well on your way to good communication.

What to Keep in Mind When Implementing Communication Tools and Practices

Deliver Information That Each Group Requires

Creating helpful communication tools and practices will depend in large part on making sure these tools and practices deliver the information you are generating in a form and manner that is understandable and accessible to its intended users. Figure 5–8 shows typical communication tools and practices in IT organizations.

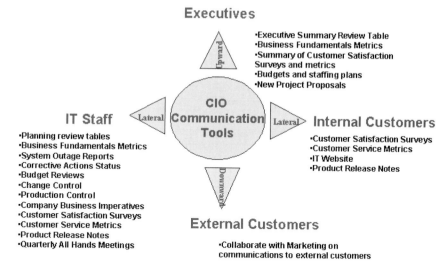

Figure 5–8   Communication patterns in the organization.

Communication Tools Depend on Accurate Process-Level Information

Now that we have defined the management practices that generate good information, we need to learn how to make it understandable for each intended group. Especially for large organizations, the challenge is not only to provide good information, but also to provide a coherent procedural framework that allows IT staff and non-IT staff to work and communicate with each other. The complexity of these relationships is illustrated in Figure 5–9.

Figure 5–9   Interrelationship of IT management activities and resulting communication materials with various functional and organizational levels.

IT Is a Team Sport

Figure 5–10 shows an example of how to implement a set of planning and control systems, with corresponding communication tools across the entire organization. These changes ensure that everyone is getting the same information on a timely basis and that all members of IT are actively involved in the creation of good information.

Communication Tool		Creation and Review			Communication Delivery Matrix		
		CIO	IT Managers	IT Staff	Executives & Board	Internal Customers	External Customers
P L A N N I N G	Objectives	✗	✗●		⊖		
	Planning & Project Review Tables	✗	✗●	✗●	⊖		
	Strategies	⊖	✗●	✗●			
	Implementation Plans	⊖	✗●	✗●		⊖	
	Budgets & Staffing	✗	✗●	✗●	⊖		
M E T R I C S	IT Business Fundamentals & Metrics	⊖	✗●	✗●	⊖		
	Customer Satisfaction Survey & Metrics	⊖	✗●	✗●	⊖	✗●	✗●
	System Outage report	⊖	✗●	✗●			
C O N T R O L	Corrective Action & Problem Management Reports	⊖	✗●	✗●			
	Production & Change Control	⊖	✗●	✗●			
	Product Releases	⊖	✗				⊖
	Operations and Management Control & Status Reports	⊖	✗				
Quarterly All Hands meeting		✗	✗	⊖			

Legend : ✗ Create ⊖ Review (Present to) ● Create & Review

Figure 5–10   Communication tools by creator and audience.

Tools Must Measure Project Status at All Levels

If you don't measure the specific tasks related to an objective, you have no way to accurately communicate status. Use a systematic approach that creates a direct link from your broad objectives down to specific implementation tasks. That way you can deliver both detailed and broad status information. And when you get your team using the same reporting system, you can quickly coordinate and plan for interdepartmental dependencies and quickly roll plans up for an executive review. See Figure 5–11.

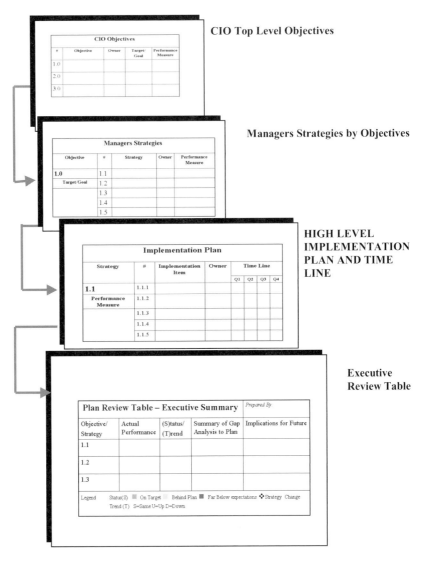

Figure 5–11 Systematic reporting.

▶ How to Make Yourself a Better Communicator

While we all have experience as communicators in various situations, the nature of these experiences and our comfort levels vary. For a CIO, being a good communicator means having the ability to successfully deal with the world, having good managerial and leadership abilities, and having responsibility and care for others. Are you able to express your intentions and take responsibility for the commitments and perceptions they generate? Here are a few guiding principals to assist you.

Assess Yourself

To be a great communicator, you do not have to be Winston Churchill. You must however convey the perception that you are sincere and can be trusted.

Know Your Audience

Communicate in terms that your audience will understand. In all communication, keep in mind whom it is for and what they need out of it.

Set and Manage Expectations

If there is a gap between what others expect of you and your IT department and what you actually deliver, you will be dealing with a frustrated and disappointed organization. Think of your communications as a set of requests and promises. Make sure that when you promise something you can follow through. If not, make sure you renegotiate your commitment.

Insist on Accountability

Accountability means being totally answerable for the satisfactory completion of a specific assignment. Take extra care to ensure that the lines of accountability are clear, both for yourself and for your team members. Eliminate from your own and your team's conversations statements such as "It's not my fault," "They made me do it," "It's not my job," "No one told me," and "It couldn't be helped."

Be Aware of the Political Environment

Make a point of spending time with your peers; schmooze and promote your department's activities and accomplishments. Don't hesitate to create a department newsletter or find other avenues to publicize and communicate your department's contributions. Spend time listening to how others perceive your IT department. Build your own capacity for good communication and don't let fear shut you down. Meanwhile, make sure that your staff gets adequate communication training.

How to Know When Communication Is Good

Measure it. By implementing monitoring tools, you can give yourself a set of metrics and indicators as to how well you are doing on your journey to communication nirvana. These tools do not have to be elaborate. The following key metrics will be good indicators of improvement.

Measure Behavioral Improvements

Have there been changes in the way that IT communicates with customers? Are you getting closer to your customers? Is their perception of IT changing for the better? Is staff morale getting better? One way to find out is to take a poll. Ask staff members to rate morale within the department right now, and ask what they would like to see improved. Tally the results and repeat this simple survey monthly.

Is the blame game less prominent during production control or other staff meetings? This is a strong soft indicator that the teams are starting to gel and work together. Is employee retention improving? Soothing the combative atmosphere created by lack of communication can go a long way toward helping you retain good employees. Is the executive team more supportive and educated on IT projects? Some of these are questions that you need to ask only of yourself. Make sure you do it consistently. Make it part of your daily awareness.

Process Improvements

Ask yourself, "Is good information being created and communicated throughout your department on a timely basis?"

Improvements in IT Business Fundamentals

Customer satisfaction can be simple too. Ask customers to rate each IT support call. In addition, perform a customer satisfaction survey before a project and quarterly thereafter. Other metrics include system up time, average time of trouble ticket closure, and on-time project completions.

▶ Conclusion

The IT department touches every business process and every member of your organization. Creating consistent avenues for accurate and timely information flow is essential, both for information flowing out of IT and for feedback information flowing into IT. That is the essence of good communication practices. Needless to say, good communication practices cannot be possible without good management practices that create consistent, accurate, and timely measurements of IT initiatives. Don't kid yourself: Changing the entrenched practices and stereotypes within your organization is a giant undertaking. So, let me leave you with a few simple ground rules.

First, you as an individual have to buy into the idea of change. You have to believe that there is a real bottom-line benefit to your business in changing your department's and company's bad habits. In the beginning, you may be the lone voice asking people to make these changes in the way they behave and feel. To sustain that position, you have to have a tangible sense of purpose in your effort.

Second, understand that creating the right tools for your team and building more productive habits and perceptions is going to be a process of discovery both for you and for your department. This perspective is essential; it allows you to constantly search for bottlenecks in the process and ask how to improve them. Build the idea of discovery into your approach.

Third, take from this discussion only what applies to you. Your business is unique; apply the advice in this chapter that works for you. Identify the tools you need and get them in place. Give your team incentives to break down stereotypes on both sides of the IT wall. Take personal responsibility for your communication and be committed to improvement. Most importantly, measure your progress. In other words, make it a priority to improve, and check your results against the goals you have set.

Fourth, begin with one specific improvement. From the above discussion, you may rightly believe that moving toward good communication practices for you and your department is a huge endeavor. I suggest keeping it simple. Identify one particular change you can make to improve one specific communication avenue in your organization. Whether it is improving the response time of your help desk or revising procedure and documentation for systems changes, fix one thing you know how to fix. From this success you can expand your initiative. After all, you now have a track record of success in reforming your communication practices.

IT is woven into the very fabric of every modern organization, which means that changing communication practices is a big job. But it is also a chance to have a big impact. From customer support to the CEO, the changes you accomplish can make an immediate difference across the entire business.

IT Organization

by Guy de Meester

Guy de Meester provides special insight into IT organization, within which getting the structure right is an ongoing exercise. First, the successful CIO must assemble the right people with the right technical and soft skills; next, ensure that organizational structure is closely aligned with the way the business is organized and operates; next, establish special relationships with different business units; and finally, monitor key functions to ensure that strategic business processes are properly supported, and keep executive management informed. The successful CIO also needs an external view to ensure that the IT organization manages outsourced activities too.

In this chapter, Guy de Meester discusses:

- *The importance of aligning the IT organization with the business plan.*
- *Types of organizational structures.*
- *Centralized versus decentralized controls.*
- *Establishing guidelines to centralize specific information services like help desk and desktop support, network and system administration, telecommunications support, applications support, and database administration.*

- *The impact of policies and procedures on the organization.*
- *Internet support implications.*
- *The impact of insourcing and outsourcing on the organization.*
- *Metrics and management.*
- *The impact of mergers and acquisitions on the organization.*

▶ Challenges in Determining the Ideal IT Organization

Choosing the right structure for your IT organization is not easy and remains an ongoing process. Certain special challenges within this process are worth the attention.

Follow the Business Plan

Influence of Corporate Officers

It is generally accepted that IT should be aligned with the business and should be a strategic partner in driving business decisions. In many cases, however, the IT organization is seen purely as a utility function providing basic infrastructure services such as network, email, printing, and accounting. Productivity gains provided by more advanced functions such as workflow applications, content management, and B2B applications are not always perceived by executives as adding value.

This basic perception has an enormous impact on how IT is managed and funded; it also affects the way in which IT is viewed by the other departments, how IT is able to add value to the underlying business, and how IT personnel are motivated, especially where it becomes clear that the IT organization is not strategic to the enterprise. The CIO's level of representation is affected at the highest level; important decisions are taken without the input and cooperation of the IT organization. As a result, IT is ineffective, as the organization is constantly in a reactive mode and likely to fail in supporting basic functions. It is time for enterprises to stop considering IT as a pure cost center entirely dedicated to spending money and to realize the benefits of advanced productivity.

Utility Function

There is a legitimate utility aspect of IT. If email, network access, printing, and other basic needs are not met, the IT organization will be judged based on the failure to provide a single function. The IT organization must be structured in such a way that multiple functions can be supported successfully. A maintenance-oriented IT organization is seen as adding low value. A good example lies in ERP implementations that have proven so expensive that the company can no longer afford to add functionality; the entire application staff is required to perform production support, and soon the company sees this group as too expensive, redundant, and of no value. The organization should be structured in such a way that new functionality can be added in a flexible fashion while maintaining production support.

Industry Type

The utility versus strategic debate depends heavily on the type of industry to which the company belongs. Software companies have a tendency to minimize IT organization because the nature of the engineering business provides a false sense of knowledge and security to the main group. If any of the corporate officers has an engineering background, the negatives are compounded and can lead to dangerous miscalculations, putting the entire company in jeopardy.

Hardware and manufacturing companies seem to be more conservative in IT spending, but the IT organizations are at the same time more in synch with the business. Manufacturing, however, relies more heavily on computerized systems and their functional departments are less IT savvy.

This is probably the single largest issue CIOs have to deal with. Successful CIOs will be able to slowly turn the wheels in their favor if they can quickly demonstrate the productivity gains available from their organization. Time is of essence, and corporate patience is extremely limited, especially in down times.

Be the Driver or Be Driven

Depending on the executive management style, the IT organization either drives or is driven. Regardless of being a utility provider or a strategic partner, the IT organization can take the lead in both models. Being the utility provider, however, can generate a sheeplike mentality in which the organization is more often than not driven by events. Breaking out of this model is a challenge for the CIO, because the challenges to the team are not visible and are often quite risky for the team members.

Risk management is the biggest challenge for the new CIO. Organizations do not tolerate risk in this downturn economy, but taking risks is essential to avoid sliding down the traditional path of being a driven organization. Successful risk-taking needs to be rewarded by executive management and shared with the IT organization. The CIO must communicate the risky strategy to both his team and executive management in order to be successful. If neither direction is followed, the CIO will fail.

Risk can be managed successfully by taking good advice and establishing relationships with executive management. Failing in a risky project does not necessarily signify the death of this strategy, but in fact can be beneficial to the success of projects, depending on the risk loss that should have been expected to occur in case of negative output. In short, to be able to drive a more risky strategy to support growing organizations, the CIO needs to take a proactive approach and communicate the strategy not only to upper management but to his team. Such a strategy can be put on hold in downturn times, but some element of risk must remain to avoid breaking the spirit of the IT organization.

▶ Centralized Versus Decentralized Organizational Structure

Once the role of IT in the overall company plan has been determined, the CIO can start thinking globally. She has to make a decision about whether IT services should be run within a centralized or decentralized management structure. This decision may not always be her choice—some companies make this decision at a higher level—but if the CIO has the luxury of making her own choice, she must decide which services should be centralized and which should be local.

This is an eternal debate, and strong opposition can be encountered from regional sites. IT is usually perceived as a local privilege by local sites. Remote employees do not have the global picture; changing attitudes is extremely complicated and can represent one of the CIO's biggest challenges. Passive resistance, local habits that are not fully understood by central management, cultural differences, and culture in the central office are the main factors to consider. Running a centralized organization requires highly flexible people in the central office to understand regional needs. Time zones, awareness of local activities, and sensitivity to the "big-brother" syndrome are elements that IT personnel usually do not handle well. IT personnel are generally extremely capable technical individuals who typically do not like to deal with human sensitivity issues in their busy lives.

The following sections provide some guidelines for centralizing or decentralizing specific information services.

Help Desk and Desktop Support

Local Functions

If policies and procedures are well designed, the core support activities and the style and nature of their responses should be similar throughout the organization. Local support should always have an escalation path back to central second-level support. Equipment purchase and delivery standards should be as uniform as possible throughout the company. (This does not mean central purchasing, as shipping costs may be prohibitive.) Small offices require stronger support people than do central locations where the tasks are more clearly divided and more junior people can be hired.

Influence on Support Team from Local Management

Local management style varies from site to site. The most difficult ones are typically found at engineering sites. Engineers in general have a poor understanding of IT functions and network architectures. They also have basic needs; logon, backup, storage, Internet access, email, and intranet for document sharing are the most common. Any disruption in network activity can have an impact on product release schedules. Relationship with engineering must be particularly well thought out. Sales organizations have a strong need for network access, remote access, and laptop support.

Reporting to Local or Global Management

Reporting can go either way, local or central. As long as the procedures and policies are set by corporate management in agreement with local management, the reporting line should not matter. The biggest danger of having local support disconnected from central policy is when local management changes, or has different views on, the way in which things are handled. As an example, the purchase of nonstandard networking equipment or telecomm equipment can have disastrous results on overall infrastructure.

When local management controls the desktop support function, there can be a huge conflict in setting priorities for the local desktop people. Global projects suffer, and other IT strategic initiatives may fail. While it is crucial that the central IT operations manager manages the expectations of both local IT and management personnel, this role is extremely difficult to assume and often leads to tensions. Where this is the case, the local support function should report locally only; global projects must be driven by executive support, with the resources to implement them supplied by central management. Local assistance should be reduced to a minimum.

Small to medium-sized companies have enormous difficulties in achieving this balance. Local powerhouses well connected to executive staff can undermine global IT strategies. This is an area to which many CIOs do not pay enough attention.

Due to the high visibility of the support function, poor management and misconstrued organization structures can lead to disaster for both the CIO and the whole IT organization. Our best advice is to appoint a particularly strong operations manager with strong negotiations skills who can establish a formal or informal service level agreement (SLA) with local management.

Reporting Structure

Figure 6–1 illustrates the reporting relationship for local support departments in a global company, showing the three types of relationships that should be constantly monitored and reviewed for optimal

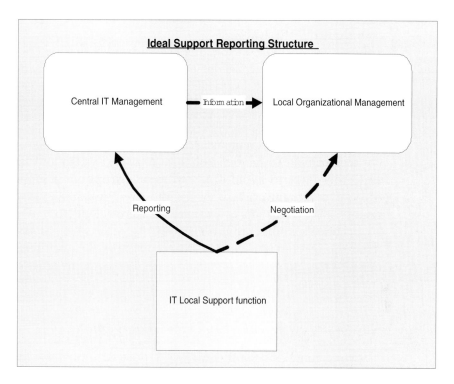

Ideal Support Reporting Structure

Central IT Management — Information → Local Organizational Management

Reporting

Negotiation

IT Local Support function

Figure 6–1 Ideal reporting structure.

results. The relationships between the different groups are the same for most IT departments, but there is some variation depending on the nature of the department. For example, the relationship between the local IT support group and the local organizational management group is one of negotiation. Local support groups have great powers to potentially disturb other users, and it is imperative that any change is negotiated before taking effect. Central management needs to support local IT initiatives by doing the public relations work with the local groups affected.

Network and System Administrator Functions

Local Functions Migrate to Become Global Functions

The network and system administrator functions require special consideration. In smaller companies in which the CIO inherits resources distributed across the globe, the physical location of the individuals is relatively unimportant. Today's technologies allow for remote system management; physical access to devices is required only for hardware failures, and local desktop support can provide that function. The biggest challenge is the trust put in remotely managed individuals to perform the activities in a satisfactory manner; thus, the biggest challenge for the IT operations manager is to establish this trust between himself and the remote people.

Another important challenge to overcome in order to be successful is the requirement to have a global monitoring system and strict policies and procedures to avoid duplication or disruption in services because of poor communication between the sites. A good example is when remote individuals make changes to Active Directory objects in the Microsoft environment without notifying other sites. These disruptions reflect poorly on the entire IT organization. Again, this IT function must be extremely well managed and must gain the trust of executive staff. Only senior operations people can accomplish these ends.

Reporting to Local or Global Management

Network functions should always report to global IT management, with the local IT team reporting on a dotted line to local management for information and coordination purposes when changes are made to the network. Central IT management is responsible for negotiating the changes to the network with local management.

Reporting Structure

Figure 6–2 illustrates the best organizational structure for network functions. We recommend a centralized model only.

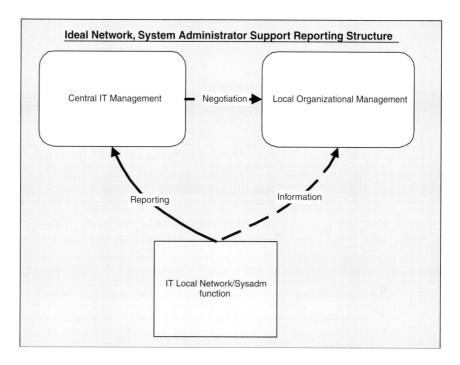

Figure 6–2   Ideal network system administration support reporting structure.

Telecomm Support Functions

Centralized Function from an Architecture Perspective

This is an especially important issue nowadays because telecom equipment is more integrated with data systems. Voice over IP and Unified Messaging are examples requiring careful planning and worldwide support. User maintenance is a dedicated local support function and is often outsourced because remote sites do not have the correct skill sets or the time. The diagrams for both desktop support (Figure 6–1) and network support (Figure 6–2) apply in this regard. Infrastructure design is related to network model, and local support is related to desktop support.

Reporting Relationships

The telecomm people should be associated with desktop functions for day-to-day maintenance and with the network people for infrastructure changes. They should report to the local management for operational matters and to central management for other changes.

Applications Support Functions

Scope of the Applications to Be Supported

Guidelines for this department can vary greatly from organization to organization. Large systems requiring a lot of change management and affecting global functions need to be centralized. Process owners should be distributed across the organization to capture local differences. A strong central business process analyst is required to handle the various and sometimes contradictory requests. To support the systems, the application manager needs to build a strong relationship with the process owners of the various departments as well as with the operations manager. Maintenance weekends need to be coordinated between the two managers to avoid disruptions in services.

Many smaller companies have decentralized systems, such as those for accounting and HR, that do not require many integration points. Centralized support may not always be required and could be counterproductive if the central decision-making process is too slow. In the long run, smaller systems should be either linked together or replaced by globally-accepted systems.

Reporting Relationships

Figure 6–3 illustrates an ideal application support reporting relationship for global systems only. The challenge for central management is to quickly grasp complex business process issues generated by cultural differences or by different legal requirements overseas.

Fast resolution of unusual problems is critical for success in this area. Many U.S.-based companies struggle heavily in providing adequate support to international sites, and this represents a risk and possible lost opportunity for large companies. Local management is frequently exasperated with the inability of central management to support local requirements efficiently and often resorts to building its own application team—with known disastrous effects on the company. Again, this should be a particular concern to the CIO; in building an effective global application support team, he should not abdicate to pressure from local management but rather obtain support from central management.

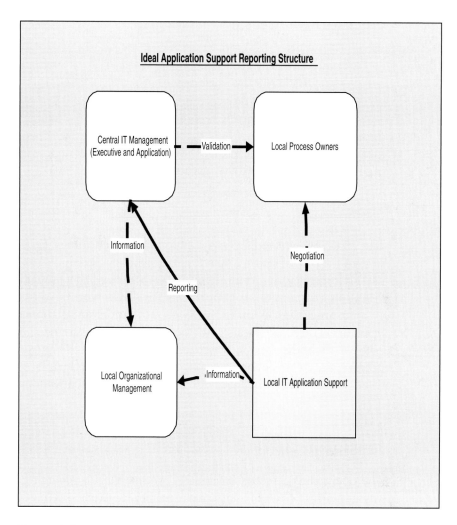

Figure 6-3 Ideal application support reporting structure.

▶ Reflections on Critical Information Systems Functions

This section addresses some common shortcomings of IT organizations. We do not cover the entire spectrum of positions in the IT organization but instead discuss a few critical areas that are extremely important to the CIO.

Operations Director

Strong Management Skills

CIOs who hire weak operations directors have a difficult time being successful. Managing day-to-day operations requires strong technical abilities, lots of diplomacy, and extensive soft skills. Many CIOs focus on determining the overall IT strategy, understanding the business, and setting the technological direction, but are weak in creating a solid organization to support the infrastructure.

Challenges

The challenges posed by rapid changes in technology, constant retention of the operations team, the extraordinary demands imposed by the user community, and diminishing perceptions of the value added by the "plumbing" function are enormous for CIOs who have not grown up in a technical environment and do not understand the needs of the operations director (budget not being the smallest item). CIOs who are able to pick the best infrastructure people are the most successful, because they can devote most of their time to further automation and to enhancing business processes through the application department.

Impact of Support Functions on the Success of the Operations Director

The operations director is directly responsible for managing the day-to-day activities of the IT team. Two particular areas of concern are desktop support and the system administrator function. Typically, these areas require highly skilled technical people not known for their soft skills. The operations director is responsible for educating her team on the culture of the enterprise, how to deal with customers, and how to deal with upper management to provide a buffer for the lower ranking employees.

One of the greatest challenges is the risk of being overrun by one's own people. This happens when strong individual contributors are able to undermine their manager by imposing system restrictions on the user community for their own benefit. Weak or nonexistent standard operating procedures are often at the root of these situations. Users whose work is being affected by ill-guided IT policies and practices quickly find a way to circumvent these obstacles—unfortunately to the discredit of the entire IT organization. Once again, it is important for the operations director to evangelize about the merits of having well-defined support procedures. The CIO should constantly measure the customer's satisfaction through well-defined feedback channels, good metrics, and personal contact with the heads of the functional departments.

Architect Function

The Architect Function Is Required

The IT organization should have either a dedicated architect function or a strong leader responsible for driving systems architecture designs through unbiased rules. The critical architect function is too often overlooked and forgotten, resulting in poorly designed systems.

The architect function within an IT organization often does not exist in the form of a dedicated person but instead is buried within the various functional teams. Projects are often managed with a vertical silo-type mentality. It takes a seasoned IT specialist to view his project from a higher point of view, to understand the ramifications and the impact of the new system on the existing environment. Based on years of experience, it is our opinion that a successful IT organization can be well served by having the architect function explicitly available on both the infrastructure and applications sides.

Location of the Architect Function within the Organization

Embedding the architect function in an IT team is not an easy task. The architect function is the "fun" part for any project manager; each manager thinks he has the Holy Grail and is convinced that everyone else will jump on the bandwagon to embrace his new technology. Too often, the technology is either too new or does not fit in the existing environment, which often leads to disastrous consequences. If the architecture aspect of a new system or project has not been examined in depth prior to implementation, the project is not only risking failure on its own but may bring down other processes or systems. The reanalysis phase should contain a discussion of architecture because, while the actual analysis may discover some flaws once the scope of the project is defined and approved, the momentum is gone by then and a lot of project managers are unwilling to acknowledge the architectural flaws and change course.

Internal or External Resources

Reviewing architectural issues requires the assistance of external resources in most cases. Vendor assistance can be useful but can skew the results due to conflict of interest. Using internal non-dedicated resources may also lead to conflicts, as each project manager will have a tendency to skew the direction toward his technology. If a manager feels that potential conflicts may jeopardize his project, he may simply refuse to collaborate with other functional IT groups. These groups will soon detect that communication is insufficient, and this game can quickly escalate into endless meetings resulting in a dysfunctional IT organization. Scars remain, and the whole process has not advanced the cause of IT.

Database Administrator Function

Scope of Database Administration Function

Database administration is a well-understood function in many IT shops around the world. Discussion is required, however, because many high-tech shops do not necessarily share a common understanding of the scope of this position. In our analysis, we discovered that the database administrator's role is not always understood by other functional departments, and this misconception sometimes leads to a great deal of confusion and tension between IT and the rest of the organization.

The activities of database administrators span the requirements of several IT groups. If the DBA is dedicated to supporting one specific type of system, for example, the ERP System, and this work is being filtered by a business systems analyst, there should be no problem. In many small to medium-sized companies, however, the DBA is directly interfacing with customers who have a lot of unrealistic expectations.

Need to Include Business System Administration Functionality in the DBA's Role

The DBA is often asked to be the guardian of the data. In our view, data integrity is a responsibility shared between the user and the DBA. The DBA must ensure that the system does not corrupt the data and that the needed procedures are put in place to prevent bad data from being entered into the system.

Bad data entry is generally a user issue. The DBA can assist in setting up business rules as defined by the user; the user expects the DBA to perform this function automatically. This is a utopian view from the user community. An experienced DBA can help users go in the right direction, but in the end the business rules have to be set by the user community or by a business system administrator.

The BSA function, if not present, must either be embedded in the DBA function or come from the users. In small companies, this aspect of the DBA's daily work is often overlooked, and if the DBA is supporting multiple groups, it often becomes impossible to properly fulfill the BSA function in addition to the DBA function. To support successful DBAs, IT management should set expectations correctly within the user community and hire the appropriate type of DBA depending on whether there will be dedicated BSA support or not. Small companies should hire administrators with both DBA and BSA capabilities in order to be successful.

Data Cleanup Responsibility

Another misconception within the user community concerns the data cleanup activity. It is often expected that the DBA will perform manual entries to correct bad data that in effect cannot be corrected. Even if it could, DBAs should not have to use their expensive skills in correcting bad data. If data needs to be corrected, the requesting functional department should provide an interface for this based on specific business rules.

Marketing departments are usually not good at defining detailed business requirements, as the people in them are often more artistic and market and consumer-driven than they are analytical. It takes a strong IT team to foster a good working relationship with marketing folks, and the DBA should be shielded as much as possible from the "artistic" behavior of the service requesters.

Reporting Relationship

In light of these two considerations, the DBA ideally reports directly to the application manager in charge of all DBA-related projects, generally including Web, customer service, marketing, and legal projects. If the DBA is required to support systems managed by multiple managers, she should report to the next level up to avoid conflicts of interest. It is also possible for managers at one level to agree on how to share DBAs, and arbitration should be at the next level up when needed.

Database Administrator Positioning in the IT Organization

The DBA function can be extremely tricky to position in the IT organization, and the CIO should pay close attention to determining that this function is being handled well within in his team. The DBA function is crucial because it spans the entire spectrum of IT activities.

Desktop, Help Desk, and System Administration Support

Regular and Executive Desktop Support

A strong support team is the most visible and most essential IT function in a company. The CIO should pay close attention to this team, request appropriate metrics from the operations manager, and reward and promote high performers. The directives coming from the CIO should be clear and crisp, with no ambiguity, when support decisions need to be made.

Many companies maintain, in addition to regular support, an unofficial and nonexplicit function for executive support. This is probably one of the biggest challenges in small to medium-sized companies, because the executive staff often includes the founder or members of the founder's family. We have seen many operations directors fail because little attention has been paid to this detail. Unfortunately, this type of support is a fact of life and will always be required. The CIO, together with his operations director, will have to establish a few rules on how to deal with requests, sometimes unreasonable, coming from the top. If the rules are not clear, the support staff will feel vulnerable and will not operate in the most optimal manner.

Handling Executive Support

Techniques for handling executive support include setting high-level priorities, creating an alliance with someone close to the top, or simply dealing with the requests first, at the expense of the rest of the organization. The last option may be the most practical one in most cases, at least until the management is being replaced or the dynamics of the company's business undergo a radical change. During downturns, it is easier to remind the executive staff that with dwindling resources the support function should be dedicated first to the business interests rather than to their individual needs. This is another area requiring considerable soft skills from the CIO.

Project Management

A Necessary but Often Unwanted Position

The project manager position is more often than not completely overlooked by CIOs. Project management relates more to execution than to strategy and is often left to the lower levels of the IT organization. The danger of failing to openly support good and well-established project management procedures becomes visible during system implementations. Delivering systems and applications on time and within budget requires support at the CIO's level. He should be aware of how project management is conducted in his organization and sufficiently confident that existing procedures and tools will work. Companies just beginning to establish project management practices may have a tendency to go overboard, leading to paralysis in the management of larger projects. The CIO should involve himself in the selection of good project managers, whether they are embedded in existing functions or are dedicated people, to ensure that the right personalities are being chosen.

Project Manager Skills

Generally, project managers should be amiable drivers with great analytical skills. Finding this combination of skills is not an easy task. It is in the CIO's best interests to make sure that his internal recruitment processes include ways to determine these skills. Using external advice is probably the best way to recruit project managers. Using internal resources biases the selection process due to interpersonal relationships; technical experts are often recommended by peers, while soft skills are ignored.

CIOs Need Trusted Project Managers

The project manager function is a difficult one to fulfill, especially in a dynamic environment in which people change positions and companies rapidly. Project managers must have full support from the CIO to be successful. Conflicts should be arbitrated at the highest level as soon as possible. CIOs typically have neither the expertise nor the time to perform this arbitration; when this is the case, the CIO should select a trustworthy person make the decision in his place.

▶ Decisions and Topics Impacting the Organizational Model

There are many varying elements of the environment in which IT operates and many approaches you may consider applying that are worthy of particular consideration in attempting to identify and implement an appropriate structure for your IT organization.

Policies and Procedures: Impact on the Organization

Not enough emphasis can be put on the need to have good policies and procedures in place to foster good IT management. But policies and procedures alone are obviously not enough; feedback mechanisms, excellent metrics, enforcement, and above all executive staff-level support for the policies instituted are also critical.

The CIO's role is particularly important in this regard. The CIO is the promoter, the advocate, the enforcer of the policies and procedures throughout the company. He needs to sell changes and new policies at large and is responsible for getting buy-in from each functional department. To achieve user acceptance of his policies, he will have to spend quite some time negotiating with his team on how to provide the promised services according to the agreed-upon SLA. If the CIO does not have enough resources to support the SLA, he will be unable to satisfy the users' demands and unable to enforce policies. Incredible demands are sometimes made on the CIO in budget-constrained IT organizations.

When enforcement is not feasible, it may be better not to create some policies. The CIO who elects not to have policies due to a resource shortage will need the approval of executive staff. At the same time, he will have to navigate his ship in the fog and risk a collision every time a crisis comes up. Users will scream for better processes and support procedures, while the CIO is unable to supply them.

To change the attitude of the company toward policies and procedures, the CIO must give constant attention to detail and to monitoring of events, make his case based on ongoing support issues, and get peer support from the industry. Bad attitudes often result from bad past experiences; policies and procedures are often associated with more big-brother control and less flexibility by the user community. The very notion of creating policies and procedures stems from the mainframe era. In today's client/server environment in which the users have been able to shake off the restricted environment in which they were previously allowed to operate, it has become difficult to reimpose a minimum of common sense and discipline. Traditionally, users are willing to give control back to IT following integration disasters, budget restrictions, or executive staff mandates, or simply because the technology has become too complex.

Negotiating good policies and procedures with his own organization, peers, and management is probably one of the biggest challenges the CIO faces in today's environment. The nature of the company's business heavily influences the degree of latitude the CIO may have in maneuvering to create the policies. Software companies, for instance, are notoriously bad for CIOs due to the nature of the business. Hardware manufacturers are far better—they are more conscious of security and more process-driven because they are more involved in manufacturing operations.

Roles and Cooperation of Functional Departments

Influence on IT from Other Departments

External influence on how the IT organization is run is rampant is today's world. Everyone in the world pretends to know how to run an IT organization based on the simple fact that they know how to switch on a personal computer. The CIO's role is therefore complicated to the point at which he can find himself in the position of having to justify decisions made on best practices, common sense, or technical factors to senior management from other departments. Once again, this challenge should not be quickly dismissed as a simple one to solve.

Engineering Departments

Engineering VPs naturally trust their engineers. Unfortunately, software engineers are the worst type of customers for IT organizations. They understand system development but have no notion of networks in general, no notion of scalability and stability issues, and little respect for the IT engineers, as they are not "true" developers. Such situations have the potential to create complete distrust between the CIO and the VP of engineering, as the message from IT is not always pleasant to hear on the engineering side. In our opinion, this represents another major challenge for the CIO.

Marketing Departments

Marketing departments are famous for wanting to control "their" Web sites. The technology has changed to the point that Web development is comparable to ERP implementations. Stability, redundancy, 24/7 support, and scalability are common requirements in the traditional application world. In the first years of creating Web sites it was relatively easy for anyone to create great-looking Web pages. Nowadays, with the advent of application servers and database connectivity, the software development needs to be done in a traditional IT change-management environment. Setting appropriate expectations within the marketing team and responding extremely quickly to changing market conditions require close collaboration with marketing program managers.

The CIO needs to develop a close relationship with the VP of marketing. Together, they can have a major impact on improving revenue, as online sales are set to grow in the coming years. It is imperative that Web development should not be done by marketing for the simple reason that Web applications need to talk to other systems within the company. Application integration with CRM or ERP systems, unique customer databases, data mining, and email management all have to be designed by system architects from the ground up. Only seasoned IT personnel can successfully achieve these goals, and the CIO will be the conduit to other departments required to make this happen.

Sales Organizations

Laptop support and remote access are the biggest tasks facing IT functions supporting sales departments. Sales executives must fully support IT, and vice versa, to avoid potential loss of revenue due to malfunctioning equipment.

Sales organizations can heavily influence the IT application department by strongly suggesting the outsourcing of activities requiring its support. One example is the collection of sell-through data from large distributors, which the sales representatives must help IT collect on a regular base. Salespeople generally prefer to outsource this activity, while IT prefers to handle it inhouse for better integration with other systems. Yesterday, outsourcing this activity was difficult; today things have gotten a little better due to the advent of XML-based data exchange technology. Full integration remains a challenge, however, and it will take years before B2B is fully accepted and standards are widely available.

The CIO must ensure that in working with sales, his organization positions itself to be successful, not to take the blame for inaccurate reports due to partial information availability within the company.

Support Organizations

IT can come under a lot of pressure when the rate of business change increases or decreases rapidly. Shared services usually bear the brunt of the changes. Human Resources can have a special impact on IT due to increased hiring or layoffs. Facilities experiencing increased activity require more cabling and network and telecom activations from IT.

Customer support is probably the biggest customer for shared services from IT. This relationship can be difficult; technical support tends to have its own view on how systems and projects should be managed. A wise CIO will rapidly make friends with the heads of these departments to avoid negatively affecting the company's responsiveness to business issues.

Effect of Budget Type on Organization Model

Budget discussions and restrictions shape the nature of the IT organization. In today's world, IT-related functions should all be captured in IT's budget. This simple statement has broad implications. If functional departments are allowed to outsource or insource their own applications, they will eventually outgrow their IT infrastructure. At that point they will request traditional IT help, leading to endless integration discussions, control issues, and eventually loss of productivity.

The CIO should analyze his IT organization based on two factors: budget and services rendered within the budget. If the budget does not allow for some services to be handled by IT, he should negotiate with executive staff on how to reintegrate them or, where this is not possible, be very specific on the support level that can be provided to these "rogue" IT organizations. It is usually bad practice and counterproductive to have, as an example, finance departments running their own little application setup with the help of consultants but without IT's blessing.

The CIO should seek help from the CFO to control IT expenditures across the company and avoid potential crises down the road.

Remote Management and Its Implications

Remote management should be a no-brainer with current technology. The main challenges for the CIO are to ensure that policies and procedures are in place to handle change management. Remote management is different from centralization in the sense that central systems can also be managed remotely. Creating remote support functions to integrate remote sites can be productive; centralized organizations tend to "forget" their edges.

The flip side of this coin is the danger that loss of central control will pose security risks. Change management is also more difficult to achieve, and once again the quality of the operations manager will be tested.

Business Drivers: Impact on the Organization

The CIO has yet another important set of relationships to nurture in his already busy schedule. He should constantly identify and evaluate the business drivers in the company and seek to understand their requirements. These people will typically have a lot of say in how support organizations are structured and funded. Business development, sales, and marketing organizations are important for top-line revenue. Road warriors require special attention.

This invisible user community is too often forgotten by support personnel. The CIO is responsible for structuring his organization to heavily support this particular community. Dedicated functions to support VPN connections and network connectivity in far away places must be built into the IT team.

Internet Support and Implications

Since the late 1990s, almost every company on earth has created its own Web site, not only to promote its products and services but also to sell its goods through the Internet. Traditionally, the marketing department virtually owned these Internet sites, but as the technology has evolved and as Web sites have required more integration with other information systems in the company, the burden of developing applications has fallen on IT or engineering.

Earlier, we briefly discussed the relationship the CIO must foster with the VP of marketing; this section provides a few insights into the challenges faced by IT-based Web teams.

First and foremost, it is extremely difficult to find experts on designing stable and scalable Web sites. The technology is fairly new, and while building static Web pages and managing databases are old skills readily available on the labor market, these up-to-date Web site experts are still in short supply, although the downturn has improved the situation. Meanwhile, revenue can be negatively affected by poorly designed e-commerce systems. With the rapid demise of the various application server vendors, the best way to get good application design expertise inhouse is to hire a software architect who (preferably) was employed by the professional services group of the vendor whose application server is being used in the company. The biggest mistake one could make is to believe that any Java programmer will do for this critical position.

The second critical position in the Web team is the infrastructure manager. This is the person responsible for keeping the Web site up and running 24/7, controlling all change management to ensure that the infrastructure is capable of holding up under new applications and expected increases in traffic. The infrastructure manager will also be responsible for the managed services function for the Web site. Large Web sites cannot be managed by inhouse teams for various reasons; the Web site may be considered too strategic for the company to leave the maintenance responsibility inhouse, or it may be that skill sets required simply cannot be found. In any case, the Web architect and the infrastructure manager need to be working as one team. Ideally, they would not report to one another, but the infrastructure manager could conceivably report to the architect.

The third critical position in the Web team is the overall manager, who is responsible for managing new applications as well as the change control processes used to implement new technology on both the application and infrastructure sides. The Web manager must make sure that both the architect and the infrastructure specialist have been involved in any given situation. The team requires a third, neutral person for three reasons: First, architects are typically insufficiently concerned with infrastructure issues resulting from the introduction of new features or applications. Second, the infrastructure specialist doesn't have the necessary knowledge to assess the impact on the site of newly installed applications. Third, the Web site manager understands the issues surrounding integration with other information systems in the company and acts as the guardian of data integrity and data flow to and from other systems.

Overall, a well structured Web team can improve the visibility and credibility of the IT organization.

Insourcing or Outsourcing: Impact on the Organization

Outsourcing non-core activities can affect the IT organization in many ways. Outsourcing specific services that do not require any integration with internal systems and that can be done more economically through outsourcing makes a lot of sense. When integration is required, however, it is imperative that everyone involved be aware of the hidden costs and the additional vendor management overhead imposed on the IT organization. Small companies with limited cash flow and little access to capital have a tendency to outsource as much as possible. The low upfront cost can be attractive, but usually, after careful analysis, the total cost is higher than expected. Companies with lots of divisive politics and weak upper management also have a tendency to outsource as much as possible to avoid conflicts. These companies are typically more cash rich but find themselves locked in expensive contracts that are difficult to break quickly or cheaply.

The debate over whether to insource or outsource specific information services requires considerable attention from the CIO, who is constantly being presented with the greatest outsourcing solutions by vendors and peers. A seasoned CIO is easily able to justify going one way or another, but a lot depends on his relative dotted-line position within the company.

Metrics and Management

In times of rapid change, it is a great challenge to the IT organization to provide decent metrics showing how efficiently things are done. The CIO should put metrics high on his agenda and automate the collection of meaningful numbers as much as possible. IT managers should always augment their decision rationales with good numbers.

Good metrics alone will not provide perfect service but can help steer the ship in the right direction. People are in general unwilling to provide numbers: They perceive this activity as an intrusion on their privacy. "How do you dare to ask me numbers on how well I do my job?" is a typical response to IT management queries from the lower echelons. The CIO's responsibility is to explain the rationale behind the numbers in a positive light, including noting that good metrics usually benefit an organization by improving processes rather than by replacing people.

Mergers and Acquisitions: Impact on the Organization

The impact of mergers and acquisitions on the IT organization is huge and is the topic of several publications. In this context, it is worthy of mention in order to complete the list of high-impact concerns in creating and managing an IT organization.

The IT Organization in Down Times

The IT organization is in perpetual motion, and its structure is continually changing. During a company's startup time or ramp-up period, certain organizational models work better than others. These models do not work as efficiently, however, in a sustained period of low growth. The CIO must detect the moment at which the IT organization should begin adapting to this new environment. Organizational change management is perhaps the most difficult thing to accomplish due to its sensitive nature. People do not like change in general, and it is rare to find individuals getting excited about change. Nonetheless, the successful CIO possesses the skills needed to make these changes almost transparently, without upsetting the balance of services rendered to the company.

▶ Final Comments on IT Organizations

Determining the right organization for your IT department is an ongoing exercise, fluctuating over time. First and foremost is the need to acquire the right technical and soft skills in-house. Furthermore, in setting up the correct organization, it is important to analyze the overall company's organization to determine what level of risk is likely to be tolerated. The next step is to determine the relationship between the various departments and structure your organization to support the strategic ones. Some companies have a greater emphasis on marketing, others on engineering, and others on finance. The CIO's manager—CFO, COO, or CEO—needs to be informed of how the IT organization is structured in order to provide full support. Outsourcing decisions will flow from this analysis as you identify non-core activities that do not need to be managed in-house.

The CIO has the difficult task of creating an organization based on the reality of the company he works for. Best practices are frequently recommended by peers and in professional literature, but in the end success rests on the ability of the CIO to understand and evaluate the group dynamics of his organization and business. Excellent CIOs will fail if they do not consider the dotted lines between the business drivers and mold their IT organization accordingly. It is equally important for the CIO to successfully communicate his strategy and to explain why the IT group is being structured the way it is.

Governance

by Danny Maco

Danny Maco tells the following story:

> One afternoon, around twelve years ago, I was in a discussion with someone in my engineering group. I was trying to get approval to load a newly released software application, something called email, on the local engineering server (our company's only server at the time). The engineer voiced a common opinion within the group that "a company our size has no use for such an application. We can get along just fine communicating with faxes and face-to-face conversations...." The software went in anyway, and if I had returned to the same individual six months later to request that he remove the application from his desktop, I would have been threatened with my life.

Maco also recalls a story he heard relating to Bill Gates. Gates claimed that while attending regular meetings early in his career, it became apparent that certain individuals repeated specific phrases so often, it would be much easier if they were to assign a number to each phrase. This way, the sheets could be distributed before the meetings, and instead of tolerating long orations, individuals could simply recite a sequence of numbers, thus substantially shortening the length of the meeting.

If you have not yet assigned a number to the sentence "A company our size has no need for…," eventually you will want to. Whether the discussions are related to software or hardware standards, security policies, service level agreements, or any other governance initiative, the same argument will be put forth.

The point that must be made during these discussions is that what a company is now is less important than what a company plans to be. For a business to be successful, it must grow; in order to grow, it must be proactive in establishing the proper infrastructure to support that growth, whether it is in the form of hard infrastructure (networks, systems, and so on) or soft infrastructure (decision-making bodies and policies). If executed or implemented properly, things that seem nominally necessary at the time of the decision ultimately end up being integral components in the company's ability to perform its daily operations.

In this chapter Maco explores:

- *How governance provides a "soft infrastructure" that facilitates decision making.*
- *How governance allows daily operations to function with minimal supervision while allowing the CIO to focus on strategy and vision.*
- *How governance facilitates communication throughout the organization.*
- *Why successful governance is about building consensus.*
- *How governance typically addresses two dimensions.*
- *The types of governance models that exist, and why the "right" model is determined by the context—a specific company at a particular point in time.*

This chapter may appeal to a slightly different reader than some of the other chapters in this book. I believe it will appeal less to the seasoned CIO, for example, who has worked in many different environments, and more to the individual who is moving through the ranks to become a CIO or to the CIO who is working in a rapidly expanding company environment. My experience comes not from working within multiple organizations for short periods, but from being part of a single organization for 13 years. This has given me the opportunity to see an IT function evolve from a sparkle in the mind's eye to a multinational, globe-spanning system of networks and services.

Various sources give examples of many different governance models. While it is important to be aware of these models and to have access to them, it is equally important to search for insights on *how* to govern successfully regardless of the model. If you are not successful in applying a given model to your real-world organization, your governance diagram will serve as little more than an interesting wall decoration. This chapter tries to identify some key factors inherent in this achieving this objective.

I hope that both this chapter and this book will provide some peace of mind to those moving into this type of position. The role of CIO is not an easy one. I remember thinking many times, early on, thoughts like, "I can't believe that nobody has dealt with this situation before," "Am I crazy for my position on this?" and "Are we the first ones to ever try this?" There is comfort to be found in realizing that the challenges, obstacles, reactions, and perceptions you encounter while performing this role are usually not unique to your environment.

Many analogies are used in this chapter, in part to help transfer ideas to the reader, but more importantly, in the hope that the analogies can be helpful to readers in their efforts to convey concepts to their user communities. As the chapter on communication points out, communication problems are often not the result of bad intent by either party but instead are simply due to the absence of a common language. Analogies can help bridge these gaps.

▶ The Paradox of IT

The beauty of being involved in the IT industry is that the technology and activities surrounding it permeate everything. Everything a company *does, is,* or *knows* flows through its information systems; information, with its underlying technologies, is the glue that helps tie together every function within an organization. Information is a language that is becoming common and universal, that lives in a pervasive form in every industry and discipline that exists. Indeed, the way we live our lives, and for some of us, even the ability to live, is intimately entwined with developing information technologies.

The paradox, however, is that when you are trying to provide general insights or "how-to" recipes in this field, these same wonderful attributes can be the source of great frustration. There is an infinite number of dynamic environmental factors within companies that make generalizations difficult. For example,

- Level of expertise in IT matters among user communities throughout the company.
- How technically-oriented the company is in general.
- Whether IT technology is integrated into the company's products.
- The company's degree of appreciation for the benefits of IT.
- Experiences the company has had with IT in the past.
- Maturity of the IT group within the larger company organization.
- The phase of evolution the IT group finds itself in.
- Infrastructure that already exists.
- Size of the company.
- How distributed the company is.

The list goes on. When you combine the variables associated with technology implementations, business environments, and social/cultural practices, hard and fast rules are the exception. The only way to cohesively channel this concoction of energetic forces is through governance.

▶ The Role of the New CIO

It is commonly accepted that a CIO's value to an organization comes from the ability to bridge the gap between information technology and business. Not so long ago (at least I would like to think so) it was rare to see any reference to information technologies in the *Wall Street Journal*. Then, over the course of perhaps a year, a transition occurred; I realized that it had become almost impossible to read an article in the WSJ *without* seeing a reference to information technologies.

At this point, the role of a CIO took an irreversible new direction, and the mandate of the new breed of CIO became to effectively use 3D glasses—one eye peering through the color of technology, the other through the color of business management—to describe the future for all. No longer are the skills of the technologists sufficient; the new CIO must also master the skills inherent in managing businesses and people.

Governance, one of those newly required tools, has little to do with either technology or business per se. Rather, it is a social construct, something we have collectively created and, to varying degrees, accepted as a way to channel our collective activities and interactions toward productive output.

▶ What Is Governance?

Excerpts from Dictionary.com and Webster-Merriam define the term "to govern" in the following ways:

- To exercise continuous sovereign *authority over.*
- To rule over without sovereign power and usually without having the authority to determine basic policy.
- To *manipulate.*
- To *control,* direct, or strongly influence the actions and conduct of.
- To exert a determining or *guiding influence* in or over.
- To hold in check; *restrain.*
- To serve as a precedent or deciding principle for.
- To control the speed or magnitude of; regulate.

In more practical terms, in our context, governance accomplishes three primary things. Governance should create a soft infrastructure that:

- Facilitates decision-making processes.
- Supports daily operations and functions with minimal supervision, allowing the CIO to focus on strategy and vision.
- Provides an organizational infrastructure to facilitate communication throughout the organization as a whole.

The third item is absolutely mandatory and cannot be stressed enough. It is interesting to note that beyond the entire chapter devoted to communication, every chapter in this book includes some reference to the importance of enabling and effectively utilizing communication in order to succeed. A well-executed governance model can help make that happen.

▶ Successful Governance

We have defined governance, but what makes governance successful? If you were to ask someone on the street to read the formal definitions previously given, with terms like "authority over," "manipulate," "control," "restrain," and "regulate," you would likely see the beads of sweat beginning to form and veins starting to swell. Imagine the thoughts that run through the minds of users, managers, and colleagues whenever you discuss IT governance. As any business professional knows, you must understand your customers, and understanding that these negative perceptions exist is a good first step.

Successful governance is not about control; it is about having and using the means to build consensus. This is a very important point that can completely change your perspective on how to approach problems. If you move forward with a plan in an attempt to control the environment, you are likely to fail. This becomes particularly true as the complexity and scale of an organization increases.

Luckily, people tend to be much more willing to be convinced or to share in a decision than to be controlled. Therefore, if you change your objective from trying to control your environment to trying to build consensus within it, you will often encounter reduced resistance and increased cooperation. Remember that even if you succeed in controlling an individual or group, resentment usually lingers, and your targets will patiently await the opportunity to return the favor.

The ability to build consensus has other side benefits. I remember, as a child, seeing cartoons in which the tiny ball of snow rolls down the hill and spontaneously expands into a giant snowball. I have tried this on hillsides time and again, but the snowball always seems to get smaller instead of bigger. My only consolation is that this principle does seem to apply within the context of an organization. If you can provide compelling information to key individuals, you can watch as the people who could potentially halt a project become your advocates, creating a human snowball with momentum that can be quite powerful. The reduction in the effort required is really quite striking when you are successful in initiating this phenomenon.

Governance naturally involves politics. These days, many people shy away from the term "politics" because it is often confused with polemics. We also tend to grimace at the thought of being labeled politicians, but politics by definition is the art or science of governance. In the chapter on the Tao of IT Leadership, my colleague refers to the advantages of being a diplomat, which perhaps is a more accurate term. Politicians, if nothing else, understand the importance of relationships as the means of getting things done within an organization.

IT governance requires leadership in order to function. This concept seems obvious, but is often neglected. As CIO, you *must* be a leader. The bodies within your governing model must be seen by the organization as groups that can make tough decisions—and then follow through. By its very nature, the IT function exists within a turbulent and contentious environment. Your people need someone who will shelter them while they do their best work and provide direction in a sea of opinions. A CIO must be able to provide leadership at the executive level, understanding the business objectives and providing strategic guidance as to how information technologies can help reach those objectives.

Above all, a CIO must be trustworthy. This is different from saying a "CIO must be trusted"; being trustworthy makes trust itself a foregone conclusion. A CIO must work hard to earn the trust of both his staff and his colleagues. Without trust, nothing else described in this chapter can fall into place.

▶ Skills to Help You Govern

Any professional who wants to succeed in his or her work needs to develop a suite of skills. Listed below are skills and attributes that, if mastered, can help you govern more effectively. Many of these concepts are elaborated on further in other chapters.

Earn trust: This is the first on the list because it is the most important. Too many people start a new position as CIO believing that the title itself bestows trust and respect. It does not. Trust must be earned.

Enable communication: Governance's highest potential value is to serve as a soft infrastructure to facilitate communication throughout the organization. Make sure the lines of communication you put in place are always bidirectional.

Define and communicate a vision: During most complex, long-term projects, there are times when the stakeholder will see nothing but seemingly disjointed chaos. At such moments, the ability to communicate a final vision is all-important. This vision gives people the strength required to endure necessary pain until the objective is reached.

Listen: Many of us have lost this skill. I have seen situations in which individuals were dead set against a view but allowed themselves to change their position upon being listened to. Often, actively listening to the parties involved can cause obstacles to give way to solutions, even when positions don't change. People want to believe they are being heard and understood.

Cultivate influence: Guiding influence is another powerful concept. IT governance often involves affecting the actions and behavior of individuals and groups you have little if any formal authority over. As a result, you must often rely on your informal influence on others.

Make your initiatives and ideas infectious: One way to initiate the human snowballs is to find ways to make people excited about your ideas, so they in turn will share them with others. This allows your ideas to be spread on your behalf. In essence, make your proposals and initiatives infectious. A fascinating book by Malcolm Gladwell titled *The Tipping Point: How Little Things Can Make a Big Difference* expands on this idea.

Foster transitions to self-governance: Governance requires a large investment of time and can divert the energies of IT resources whose skills are best used elsewhere. The best way to minimize this workload is to always try to transition centralized governance into self-governance. Work to educate the organization, so that people within it understand the importance of your policies and become not only capable of governing themselves but willing to do so.

Maintain your integrity: There are many times when the approval of an initiative has nothing to do with "understanding the numbers" or "getting the concept." More often than not, your people and peers will accept risk and take blind leaps because they trust you. Mistakes will be made, deadlines missed, but whatever happens, take care to always keep your integrity intact; it is the key to your support.

Improve your social skills: As previously stated, governance is a social tool, which naturally requires social skills. Actively work on these abilities as you would any other skills. Train on techniques for improving them.

Verify information: Before you act, get your facts straight. Check, double-check, triple-check. Never assume.

Build consensus: Human snowballs again. Resistance and differences of opinion are expected in all cultures, corporate or otherwise. Where opposition to your ideas, beliefs, or initiatives exist, it can seem like this resistance may be insurmountable. But if you are able to focus on building a consensus, and your cause has merit, you will often find that a strange thing happens: Time becomes a friend, and over time, people naturally want to be part of the majority. Be patient and let that momentum do some of the work for you.

Start governance at home: Lead by example. Make sure your people can live with the policies being set for others, and live by them religiously. Don't be fooled by the misconception that "people won't notice if we bend the rules a bit within our group." You can be sure they will notice and will discuss it with others. Negative communication spreads through an organization as fast, if not faster, than positive communication.

Pursue education: There is no better opportunity to build momentum and plant the seeds of self-governance than through education. Full-blown education initiatives are fine, but remember that every single time you or one of your people comes in contact with someone, it is an opportunity to educate. I remember a speaker at a Gartner Group Symposium using the analogy of the way in which gas diffuses itself within a confined space. If you have a bottle full of a clear gas and introduce a blue gas at the mouth of the bottle, over time this blue gas will distribute itself throughout the entire bottle. You can understand this phenomenon by imagining the gas molecules as active spheres constantly bumping into each other, imparting bits of energy to each other each time they make contact. This is a wonderful way of describing how you can work to distribute ideas, concepts, and initiatives through an entire organization.

Practice patience: Remember that most knowledge is not common knowledge; you must work to make it common knowledge. Go out of your way to help transfer knowledge, and accept that learning usually requires repetition and patience.

Network informally: This is last but not least; it is very important. Informal networks are the communications that pass among friends, next to water coolers, via informal emails, and so on. Recognize the power of informal networks; tap into them and *listen*. They are incredible sources of feedback. If you can't personally monitor such networks, make sure there are people in your group who can. While working for a company that literally spans the globe, I have been amazed at how much information fails to reach its destination through formal communications, and how much detailed information is passed along informal networks, information which more often than not "isn't supposed to be common knowledge."

▶ Typical Governing Bodies

Regardless of the governance model you choose for your organization, there are some basic components that are included in most models. These concepts are also expanded upon in Chapter 1, "Within and Beyond: Understanding the Role of the CIO." You may see many different names assigned to these bodies, but their functions remain essentially the same.

Executive Level Management Committee (ELMC): The highest operational decision-making body in the organization (beneath the board of directors), this body provides the following benefits:

- An opportunity for the CIO to be exposed to overall business decisions, strategies, and issues.
- A venue for providing high-level IT project status.
- Direct access to those empowered to decide on strategic priorities and to commit required resources.
- A venue to enable the CIO to communicate and provide education on technology issues which affect the organization.

– An opportunity for the CIO to act as liaison between the committee and the IT organization.

Operational Information Steering Committee (OISC): A high-level group that may be a subset of the ELMC, this body is generally a cross-section of the primary functional groups within your organization. OISC members must have the authority to make decisions regarding resources within their respective functional areas. This group's role must be explicitly defined, and it must try to operate under that definition at all times. The OISC provides the following benefits:

– A conduit by which relevant IT-related information can flow from the executive level to operational levels, via the CIO.
– An opportunity for functional stakeholders to participate in the decision-making and prioritization processes.
– A pathway for bidirectional transfer of information to the lower operational levels of the functional groups via the functional stakeholders.
– A venue for group education on information technology issues.
– The ability to assign priorities and perform conflict resolution at the operational level.
– The structure of this group can be scaled up or down and used efficiently at different levels throughout the organization among business units, divisions, even down to a project level. The factor that varies most drastically among different organizations is the answer to the question, "Who participates in these groups, and how is the structure imbedded in the organization?" This depends directly on the organization itself, but basically the IT governance structure should follow the model used by the overall organization, as determined by its corporate culture. In other words, distributed models do not typically work well in a centralized organizational culture, and vice versa.

Information Systems Management Team (ISMT): The organization that manages IT resources. This body provides the following benefits:

– Bidirectional communication between the CIO and lower level IT operations via IT operational directors.
– Bidirectional horizontal communication between IT operational directors.

– Bidirectional horizontal and vertical flows of information between the user community and the CIO via the IT organizational structure.

▶ Considerations Related to Governing Bodies

I am a firm believer that the CIO should be part of the ELMC. The more integral information technologies are to the core business, the more important this concept is. Some might suggest that it is sufficient for the CIO to be a member of an OISC, particularly when a subset of the ELMC resides on the OISC, yet there are distinct functional differences between the two groups that relate to the value brought by the CIO's participation.

By participating in the ELMC, the CIO is able to *receive* information related to the overall operations, decisions, and strategies associated with the organization. This information in turn allows the CIO to proactively integrate these considerations into an overall IT strategy and provide feedback on potential issues or opportunities that are recognized.

An OISC, on the other hand, is primarily oriented toward information technology agendas from which information is *presented* by the CIO and OISC members for consideration. If the CIO participation goes no higher than the OISC, the organization must rely on ELMC members to bring all relevant information to the CIO. Unfortunately, this does not typically happen, in which case the company's business strategy and information technology strategy have a high probability of diverging.

Some IT executives fear that when an OISC exists, IT decisions may become mired in a decision process conducted by a group whose members who do not have the needed technical background. This is usually not a problem with the existence of the group, however, but instead a problem with its mandate. For this reason it is important that the role of the group be explicitly defined, and that the CIO makes sure the body operates within these parameters. Deliberations on details that are not within the scope of the group's defined mission should never reach the table.

▶ Operational Governance

Standards and cost containment are two commonly discussed topics in the area of operational governance. Standards are probably the most commonly used form of operational governance—and the most controversial. I am a strong believer in the benefits of standards. They provide tangible benefits that are fairly straightforward to quantify (some are mentioned below for reference) but there are also intangible benefits involving synergies which, while more difficult to quantify, are actually more significant.

Consider geometric progression, a powerful concept that refers to the ways in which the effects of a given event can propagate and compound each other, and thus how a small change can have a disproportionately large long-term effect. Many of you might be having déjà vu with chaos theory, but let's explore a simplified practical example.

Some standards practices are justifiable through simple mathematics. Most have benefits that increase geometrically with scale and number of locations; others can provide benefits to even single-location enterprises. On the surface, hardware standards generate an advantage through the ability to leverage larger volume discounts with vendors.

Now let's look one layer deeper at one sample hardware component, the printer (the same model can be used for servers, network infrastructure components, and so on). We define two different scenarios under which a company's environment contains one hundred printers. Under the first scenario, you have ten different brands being used, each with its own consumables and on hand spare parts. Under the second scenario, you have two brands.

You have calculated that, based on service and delivery lead times, you need to have four consumables on hand for each printer brand in order to satisfy the terms of your SLA. We will assume a cost of $200 per consumable. Under the first scenario, you have $8,000 ($200 x 4 x 10) tied up on shelves as consumable inventory; under the second, this figure is only $1,600 ($200 × 4 × 2). Under the second scenario, however, the number of on hand units would probably need to increase, let's say to eight, plus we'll add two more to further improve response times, costing us $4,000 ($200 × 10 × 2).

Now a difference of $4,000 may not seem like a big deal, but look what has taken place: We decreased our costs by 50 percent, thus freeing up capital for better uses within the organization, and at the same time increased our quality of service. In large organizations, cost reductions of 20 to 50 percent can add up to large sums of money. (What volume of sales would be required to have the same effect on the bottom line?)

Let's look one level deeper. Assume the repair of each printer requires a unique set of skills. How many more resources need to be found, coordinated, and funded under a ten-model scenario than under a two-model scenario? Now, another level deeper, where do these resources get support when they run into problems where they lack either the expertise or available resources to solve? This compounding effect can have a significant impact on resources.

Another example shows how the qualitative factors related to synergies and best practices can begin to make contributions. Assume four company locations (within the same geographic area to keep it simple). These locations are similar in size and operations. Each has a network infrastructure, an ERP system, and a CAD system.

Under the first scenario, which we'll call S1, each location has its own unique and autonomous set of systems. Under the second scenario, S2, all locations have common network infrastructure, ERP and CAD systems. We'll assume all resources are internal, just to make the math simple. Let's compare the scenarios:

- **Required resources:** Under S1, all locations have systems with unique characteristics. One individual is needed for each system at each location, a total of 12. Under S2, one full-time individual is required at each location, while two CAD specialists and two ERP specialists can roam to support all four locations, for a total of eight—a reduction of 33 percent.

- **When a problem exceeds the skills of an individual at a specific location:** Under S1, since all locations have unique skill sets, there is no choice but to use outside resources, resulting in higher consulting costs. If these individuals are new to the environment, there are additional costs associated with "bringing them up to speed." Under S2, there is a higher probability that a solution can be found by joining multiple internal resources from multiple locations with common skill sets.

- **When multiple simultaneous problems exceed the capacity of a given location:** Under S1, outside resources are required, as described in the previous paragraph. Under S2, there is a high probability that resources at multiple locations can be pooled for short periods of time to address such fluctuations in demand.

The concept of building an environment within an organization in which common skill sets perpetually compound each other is a powerful one. Only within such environments can the benefits of best practices be fully realized. Individuals who make the extra effort to build their skill sets find expanding demand and opportunities throughout the organization that would not otherwise exist, and the increased level of internal contact and interaction helps build a greater sense of community and connectedness within the organization.

Further, governance of an environment that lacks standards tends to put in place controls that discourage discovery and exploration, because much potential activity of this kind is not productive. For example, if you have five individuals within an organization using five different development tools, and each of them is delving deeply into the capabilities of their favorite, a large amount of time and energy is spent debating the virtues of each, dealing with data incompatibility issues, and so on. In a standards-based environment, on the other hand, there is no reason to discourage exploration; even those individuals diving into the deepest, most mundane capabilities of the tool are investing time in a task that can ultimately spread benefit across the entire organization (as long as good communication mechanisms are in place). In fact, isn't this the definition and application of "best practices"?

The second common topic in operational governance is cost containment. IT initiatives that report reductions in operational costs often meet a lukewarm reception, given the significance of the savings involved. Sometimes it is useful to make a comparison between the cost-cutting initiative and a product sale that would produce the equivalent benefit. Since cost reductions contribute directly to the bottom line of an income statement, they compare quite favorably to product sales when margins are included. In other words, a legitimate hard cost reduction of $100,000 has the same effect as a $200,000 sale at 50 percent margin—and for the majority of companies, 50 percent margins are a dream. Most operate at margins between 10 percent to 30 percent, which means that the $100K savings has the same effect as a $333K to $1,000K product sale.

▶ Creating a Governance Model for Your Organization

It is important to remember that governance does not just happen. Rather, you create it—above you, around you, and below you. One basic concept and one basic question, in combination, can serve as the basis for the development of any governance model.

The basic concept says that there are two distinctly different processes that need to be supported by the governance structure. The first is the strategic decision process: Who (which body) decides what is going to be done? The second is the operational process: by what means are the chosen actions executed?

Once this concept is established, it must be followed by the question, Where in your organizational structure does the strategic decision process end, and the operational process begin?

Ideally, strategic decision making (not to be confused with operational decision making) is completely independent from the operational mechanism. These processes should be seen as two black boxes: The first spits out strategic directives, the second executes them. The power in this is that it allows each to operate and evolve autonomously without detrimentally affecting the other. For example, in designing my organization, I set this boundary between the CIO level and the regional IT director level defined just below it. My objective was to enable the operational organization (regional director and below) to function independently of a specific CIO (ouch!); in this way, the organization could accommodate a change in the source of strategic direction—a new CIO, or even a transition from a CIO to a strategic decision committee—without negatively impacting normal IT operations.

In this model, strategic decisions were made at the corporate executive level based on inputs from business area managers and subsidiary general managers. These directions would then flow through the CIO to the IT regional directors, who would work together to decide how to execute the directives and would do so utilizing the appropriate operational groups.

Another important aspect of your developing model is the role of governing bodies. Previously, I gave some typical examples of these. In defining the role of these groups or deciding which should exist in your organization, you need to ask yourself, "How is this body going to provide the support I need to be successful?" This may sound a bit self-serving, but helps convey the point that governance is a tool you put in place with specific objectives.

Potential considerations regarding the establishment and role of a governing body include the following:

- Does it help establish the legitimacy of IT-related decisions and initiatives?
- Does it properly distribute the responsibility and accountability for decisions and project results?
- Does it create high-level stakeholders who have strong interest in the projects' success, in part because they share in the benefits and recognition of projects?
- Does it establish an important venue for education at the executive or intermediate level?
- Does it build a formal and informal communication infrastructure that can help support initiatives and provide important feedback mechanisms?
- Together with other such bodies, does it operate in conformance with existing corporate culture? Are the bodies dynamically established, centralized, distributed, and/or multifunctional as is appropriate to the culture? This alignment is essential for proper governance.

As implied, the first thing you must do before deciding which governing structure to put in place is to take a hard look at the existing organization. (There are some great hints on what to look for in Chapter 3, "The First 90 Days").

It is no secret that implementing improvement on any scale involves the execution of change. You must therefore honestly evaluate the company/organization and its ability to absorb change, then plan and execute accordingly. Beware, though—it is easy to convince yourself that you can force accelerated change through the organization "for the good of the company." Your efforts may appear to be successful at first, but resistance to change is like an elastic band that stretches under pressure but (unfortunately) often snaps back with less-than-pleasant results. The king in St. Expury's well-known book, *The Little Prince*, says, "If I ordered a general to change himself into a sea bird, and if the general did not obey me, that would not be the fault of the general. It would be my fault." The king claims always to be obeyed because his commands are always reasonable.

The Gartner Group has an excellent document that helps establish steps for evaluating an organization's ability to change.

▶ Putting a Governance Model in Place

Any large project seems overwhelming as long as you view it in its entirety, and putting in place a governance model where none previously existed is no different. I remember one of my first engineering professors telling us, "Break it down. Break the problem down into manageable parts. Focus on solving all the components, and you will find that the overall problem will end up solving itself."

Ask yourself, What *must* be under control in the next six months? What *would be realistic* to have under control in the next six months? What do you want to get under control in the next year? What, if left unchecked, will do the most harm in the next six to twelve months? Prioritize accordingly.

Try to look at the execution of your governance program as a long-term investment. I have heard it said that when Michelangelo was asked, "How is it that you are able to carve an angel out of solid stone?" he replied, "I do not carve an angel out of stone, I simply remove from the stone all that is not angel." Implement your governance model with this in mind. Have a clear picture of what must be in place for your plan to be successful, execute as best as you can, then work with people one-on-one to find solutions that can help remove obstacles to the plan's completion.

Look at the final hurdles as opportunities to educate and build consensus. Remember that in the long run, the individuals you are going up against who seem frustratingly obstinate right now may provide you with crucial support for future projects.

I remember two specific cases in which I ran into what seemed like insurmountable opposition in trying to execute an initiative. (Actually I remember many, but will limit it to two for demonstration purposes.) In one case, it was determined that the global group would standardize on the NT operating system, but one location favored its existing OS2.

When it became apparent that this subsidiary was not going to change its mind in the near term, the project went forward anyway. Over time, as presentations were given and discussions were shared, it became increasingly difficult for that subsidiary to explain why it was the only one in the group not following the standard. Additionally, individuals at that location began hearing more and more through the informal communication networks within the organization about the benefits of using the standard. In the end, the subsidiary came to its own decision that perhaps it was a good idea to adopt the standard operating system. I also experienced an almost identical sequence of events related to network topology standards.

▶ Managing Expectations for Governance

Work within the realm of reasonable expectations. Be firm and hold to your convictions, but expect exceptions and have a plan for dealing with them. Live by the 80/20 rule. Appreciate the value of getting as much of an initiative in place as you can then working with the exceptions and unanticipated anomalies.

You may find it easy to get frustrated when you see that the structure and policies you have put forth are not being fully adopted or accepted, but the important thing is not to give up. There will always be those who question the value of putting governance structures in place, and will jump on the opportunity to criticize such attempts. Take heart in knowing that nothing in life spontaneously assembles itself into a perfectly functioning system.

As an illustration, I recently visited my newborn nephew. You look down and see a little human body, but it certainly does not operate like one. The head rolls one way, the arms another, and the legs bend in some third direction. Clearly this little person is never going to get up off the ground. The reality is, of course, that within a relatively short time, this same little body will be performing feats of motion that seem to defy physics (much to the chagrin of his mother).

The point is that even after all the components of your governance program seem to be in place, it will take some time for the structure to fuse and work smoothly. There will be things you didn't anticipate, there will be people who forget or go around the procedures—hang in there.

If your plan and objectives are good ones and you keep the communication lines open, things will come around. It is easy to bend under pressure and retreat from an initiative, but remember that a project that is not followed through will always be thought of as a failure. Always have faith in yourself, and keep moving forward until you reach a finish line.

Another analogy I like is highlighted in *The Tipping Point* [Gladwell, 2000, 2002], which takes up the invention of the fax machine. The discussion points out that the annual sales of this item were initially anemic but after time reached a point at which they shot up exponentially. This change occurred not because of improvements to the technology, which remained basically unchanged, but rather because a certain level of infrastructure had to be in place before the value of the invention could be realized. After all, there is not much value in owning a fax when no one else does; it is only when "most" people own a fax that it becomes useful. The book identifies this as one example of a "tipping point"; a snowball effect then follows because now "everyone must own a fax" to have the basic communication capabilities of their peers. This analogy can also be useful in explaining why some projects, such as executing a governance plan or even implementing a worldwide intranet, require a "curing" period.

▶ How Much Energy Should Be Committed to Governance?

The question of what resources should be devoted to governing your environment is a good one. While the point may seem obvious, it is important to recognize that governance is an administrative function. As such, the resources used for its execution must be minimized.

When looking at all available resources—time, money, people, and so on—it is useful to look and think in terms of available capital. In the IT world, such capital can potentially go into one of two specific categories: innovation/production or administration/maintenance.

Innovation/production includes those activities that either advance the capabilities and efficiencies of the overall organization or produce products that materially enhance and enable the organization's function. The benefits of such activities may either focus internally or deliver benefits externally, directly to customers or vendors. Maintenance/administration includes those activities needed to sustain the required infrastructure, system functions, support of product, and so on.

Both categories are equally necessary; the IT function cannot properly operate if either of these two components is missing. The difference lies in how these two categories are managed and the resulting outputs.

Let's go back to the concept of capital. Investments made in the area of innovation/production bear interest, which compounds itself. In other words, the benefit brought forth by a truly enabling application or initiative replicates itself in an exponential way. Investments made in maintenance/administration, on the other hand, have flat returns. They are necessary and useful, but rarely reap compound benefits. There may be arguments about which category things like support services, help desk, and so on fall into, but the underlying concept remains the same.

Based on the above, and given that there is always a fixed amount of capital, a CIO must minimize the percentage of capital used to provide the required administration/maintenance activities, and maximize the percentage used for innovation/production activities and initiatives. As such, your governance structure must use minimal but sufficient resources to reach its objectives and perform its functions.

▶ Evolution of Governance

Everything evolves. For example, companies evolve: They begin as an idea, gather funding, operate as an R&D-centric organization, and then evolve into one that focuses on manufacturing and eventually on field service and support. IT organizations also evolve. For example,

1. No coordinated IT effort exists.
2. Various individuals at independent locations assume the role of managing IT assets, usually in addition to other responsibilities.
3. An individual is given "official" responsibility for IT assets and activities. Such IT managers (one-man IT departments) may exist at multiple locations, operating independently.
4. IT managers are allowed to hire resources.

5. Autonomous "islands" of systems and information, and the need to coordinate them, are recognized. Often a harmonization project is initiated.

6. The benefits of full coordination are recognized. A director-level position is established, responsible for crosscompany or global activities.

The new IT organization begins its evolution as an integrated group.

Sound familiar? Governance too must be dynamic. The challenge is that this requires you to walk a fine line. On one hand, the changing environment demands the continuous reexamination of processes. On the other hand, you must be careful to always give governance structures sufficient time to take hold before tossing them out for new ones; if you fail to do so, a well-executed plan can suddenly be perceived as nothing but chaos. It takes time for people to learn and operate under new policies and procedures and new responsibilities. Remember to execute change at a pace that can realistically be absorbed by the organization.

As an example, when our global intranet was being developed, we went through a number of distinct transitions. Initially, while our internal IT group was learning Web development skills, and we were trying to establish a reliable infrastructure, governance was put in place to tightly control access to the development environment. Over time, as our methodologies, understanding, and internal skill sets began to mature, value was seen in allowing different functional groups within the company to develop their own sites and integrate them into the intranet, and governance was changed to allow this new model to function smoothly. As individuals were chosen and trained to understand the important policy issues, and to take responsibility for their functional groups, we were also successful in making the transition from a resource-intensive central governance program to a self-governance environment.

If possible, try to work with both the business strategic plan and your IT strategic plan to map out an appropriate timeline and identify the significant "change events" required to achieve your objectives. In this way, you can quantify the pace at which these changes will need to be absorbed, and establish milestone dates on which governance components must be in place and functioning.

▶ Mistaken Uses of Governance

Unfortunately, governance can be a double-edged sword; there are just as many ways in which it can harm you as there are in which it can help you. Here are a few things to watch out for:

Throttling: Being a new CIO can be a bit unnerving. As reiterated throughout this book, it is not an easy job in the best of circumstances. With so many demands, changes in business environments, and changes in available technologies, it may at times seem as if a whirlwind is spinning around you, and you may feel the urge to say "Wait! Put all of these things on hold until I can deal with these other issues."

Resist this urge. If you use governance purely as a throttle for activity, your organization will be seen as a bottleneck. This is different from prioritizing projects and resources, which of course is a genuine need. In the latter case, be sure to use your high-level governance bodies to help share in prioritization processes and responsibility, following up with communication throughout your organization about the decisions that have been made.

Hypocrisy: As previously discussed, governance starts at home. Let's face it: The adoption of new procedures, policies, and standards does feel restrictive and confining. People do not like to be told they can't do something. Even so, if you do a good job of communicating, people will understand the value and make the sacrifices.

Nothing, however, will take the wind out of your initiatives' sails faster than the perception of hypocrisy. Before issuing policies and standards, be sure to discuss the initiative with your people. Let them know that they must follow the same restrictions as are being required of all others. If anything, in fact, they must be more diligent in their adherence; after all, they are setting an example.

It is perfectly reasonable for individuals or groups to occasionally deviate from policies in order to perform their jobs; for example, a research group may need to run a new operating system, security analysts may need access to "hacking tools," and so on. Whatever the exceptions, make sure they are reviewed, discussed, and most importantly, communicated openly throughout the organization before being executed. This will help to minimize potentially embarrassing and damaging misunderstandings.

Governance for governance's sake: I had a roommate in college who was studying landscape architecture. As he worked on a design for a large project, I wondered if he ever reached a point at which he felt like arbitrarily inserting trees and bushes just to fill empty space. He responded by passing on something his instructor had said: "Never place anything in a design unless it has a specific reason for being there." I believe governance should be executed under the same principle. When you place controls in your environment, design your governance plans around your objectives to ensure that only those elements that are required are included. Not only is this good common sense, it provides you with sound rationales when confronted by individuals who may feel you are simply building a personal empire.

▶ Effect of Acquisitions on Governance

Okay, you finally have in place a finely tuned governance model; operations are running like a well-oiled machine. Out of the blue, your company makes one or more acquisitions that threaten to contaminate the utopia you have achieved with nonstandard equipment and contrary methodologies. In addition, you have the CEO reminding you that it is absolutely imperative that this integration goes smoothly.

What now? First of all, if you are asking this question after the acquisition has been made, you are already behind the eight ball. Traditional wisdom concludes that since the cost of IT integration of two companies is small compared to the cost of the overall acquisition itself, such matters may be addressed after the agreement has been made. While this is true in pure mathematical terms, it is important to ask which one factor is most often the main contributor to the failure of a merger. The resounding reply will always be the inability of the two corporate cultures to merge and assimilate.

Here is where lack of planning related to the integration and the governance surrounding it can have fateful impact. I have seen CEOs threaten to resign if they are not allowed to purchase their preferred brand of server. I have seen key people threaten to leave the company over new software standards. IT issues can affect the entire organization.

Before we can examine ways to minimize these problems, we have to understand the psychology behind an acquisition. You have a buyer who has found an undervalued company and negotiated a low price. On the acquisition side, you usually have a group of people in a transition team who may or may not have a long-term interest in the company but have been given significant incentives to reach aggressive short-term financial objectives in order to show a quick return on the initial investment.

The deal is completed, budgets and objectives have been established. Now the acquiring company wants the systems of the acquired company integrated. A naturally anxious group of people in the acquired company is told that responsibilities and standards are going to change. Unbudgeted expenses that negatively impact the financial objectives will be incurred by the acquired organization for things like standard servers, updating expired licensing, WAN connectivity, and so on.

In this scenario, something is going to pop, and the fallout could impact the success of the merger itself. What can be done to minimize these negative impacts?

- Before any acquisitions occur, create a corporate standard relating to systems integration policies for acquired companies. Which systems must be integrated and how soon after the merger? Which systems can wait to be integrated? It does not matter whether full integration or minimal integration is the policy; what is important is that the policy is fully understood by all parties within the acquiring company.

- At the highest level, if the CIO resides on the corporate executive committee, he or she should be able to have enough advance knowledge of the potential purchase to plan accordingly. If not part of this body, he or she must be made aware early on in the process.

- Make sure that capable IT personnel are part of the due diligence team.

- If incentive schemes are used for a transition team within the acquired company, define a smooth system transition as one of their objectives.

- Make sure to develop a comprehensive cost estimate of the work required during the due diligence process, which can then be discussed during negotiations.

- Make sure policies are communicated during the negotiation process that identify which entity is responsible for which expenses and communicate what will be expected of the acquired company related to labor and cooperation.

- If standard policies are going to be relaxed for the acquired company, communicate this to the personnel of the acquiring company along with the reasons why. Reinforce the fact that for existing employees there is no change in policy. This will help minimize people trying to use the allowance accorded to the new company as justification for not following the established policies.

- If significant changes are going to occur on the side of the acquired company, make sure an officer of significant position and reputation communicates the importance of cooperation and the reasons for the changes.

- In the end, the fewer the surprises introduced into this environment, the more smoothly the process will go.

▶ Summary

A properly designed governance structure is closely analogous to a physical infrastructure, whether in systems or social terms; it is the framework that supports the overall ability of an organization or any social entity to function. The amount of care and foresight that is invested in its design and implementation has a direct impact on the long-term success of the overall organization. Great attention should be focused on creating a structure that enables and promotes communication throughout the organization.

Above all, neither the CIO alone nor any one group can successfully execute governance. This is a collective effort that requires the deliberate support and collaboration of the entire executive team. Without the support of upper management and key operational leaders within the organization, no governance model will succeed. This support must be vocal and active. If conflicting signals or even indifference is sensed within the organization, formally or informally, your overall efforts are likely to fail regardless of how well you have designed your model. For this reason, you must do everything you can to build this support and maintain it.

Chapter 8

Architecture

by John Dick, Holly Simmons, Maureen Vavra, and Steve Zoppi

John Dick, Holly Simmons, Maureen Vavra, and Steve Zoppi provide the following anecdote to describe the CIO's architectural reality today:

Joe Marketing VP: *Hi, Bob. Just wanted to let you know that our sales and marketing division has purchased the XYZ CRM solution to fulfill our strategic goals for this coming year. I wanted some time with you to discuss how we get our software set up for our marketing and sales folks. Do you have time tomorrow?*

Bob CIO: *I am concerned that I was not included in the decision to purchase this software. There are many things to consider with respect to our architecture, and we need to understand what is required to implement and support the product. What are you planning to use this software for?*

Joe Marketing VP: *Oh, you know, CRM stuff. This is the best package on the market today. I'm sure you'll be able to get it working easily.*

Bob CIO: *Joe, were requirements written up for this? Was a technical review of the software performed?*

Joe Marketing VP: Requirements? We had several demos and decided that this product would best meet our needs. The XYZ salesperson can hook you up with some techie guys from their company. I'll get you the contact information.

In this chapter the authors provide an introduction to enterprise architecture and discuss:

- *The practical steps necessary to create an architecture strategy.*
- *How to avoid the pitfalls frequently associated with architectural planning and implementation.*
- *How investing time up front in defining a successful architecture avoids frustration and expense later in the process.*
- *Why architectures should not be developed using a pure product development approach.*
- *Why it is important to focus the architecture on customers and users and the processes that enable their success.*

▶ Are We Having Fun Yet?

Being a CIO in today's environment is a tough job. Vendors target marketing, sales, and customer support executives to sell their enterprise solutions, frequently resulting in a sale without any involvement from the IT organization. In their efforts to keep the sales cycle short, vendors are happy to avoid the difficult, technical questions raised as part of a genuine product evaluation. Unfortunately, the business users do not typically understand the potential architecture, implementation and support issues, and do not ask all of the pertinent questions, thus resulting in a decision based on only a fraction of the necessary information.

What is most difficult is that the CIO is the one left holding the bag when this happens, taking responsibility for making the solution work. Vendors enjoy lauding their product as straightforward to implement, easy to integrate, and simple to support. They even claim that their product solves your enterprise architecture problems for you, but the reality is that these products are simply a point solution behind an enterprise architecture smoke screen. The CIO and the IT organization must expend a great deal of effort figuring out how to make it all work harmoniously together.

A CIO career is truly not for the faint of heart. Architectural challenges abound, what with varying standards, technology, integrity, and scalability that can leave you with a hodge-podge of incompatible equipment, software, and data. But this is part of the challenge and opportunity for a CIO. You and your team have the opportunity to identify what works and what does not work, and there is always a great deal of change and variety in the technologies and available solutions. You are getting paid to play with new technology and solve interesting, although difficult, architecture problems. Appreciate the challenges and rewards ahead of you.

▶ Overview

Our focus in this chapter is to provide you, the CIO or technology manager, with a "walking tour" of enterprise architecture. Our intention is not to provide a detailed reference manual for implementing an enterprise architecture strategy, but instead to offer an introduction to enterprise architecture, a practical outline of the steps necessary to create an architecture strategy, and advice on avoiding the pitfalls frequently associated with architectural planning and implementation. Whenever possible, references to other sources of helpful information have been included.

We define enterprise architecture, or target architecture, as the framework that encompasses your corporate data, network, infrastructure, security, and applications, providing a foundation to support the needs, processes, and information of the business. While traditional definitions of the term *architecture* focus on the design and building of structures, this same concept can be applied to enterprise architecture. When building a house, your foundation must be implemented with care, since every component of the house relies on it. Your enterprise architecture is your foundation, requiring stability and flexibility gained only through careful planning and design. Similarly, a shoddy house foundation can result in a structure that is unstable, that cannot be expanded or added on to, and that is in many cases unfit for living. The same is true for poor enterprise architecture. Careful planning that incorporates the need for future growth or change allows your organization to avoid costly replacement or being left with an inflexible, inefficient, high-maintenance foundation.

As a CIO, planning your architecture ensures future viability and a solid return on your technology investment, as well as job security. Planning allows you to minimize downtime, eliminate technical incompatibilities, and enforce smooth operations; it also assists you in controlling your staffing plan and costs.

In short, when it comes to planning your technology architecture, the "pay now or pay later" principle applies. Invest your time up front in defining a successful architecture to avoid frustration and expense later in the process.

▶ The Classic Architecture Approach

In this chapter, we discuss various ways to develop and maintain your IT architecture. Most organizations use a formal method to do the initial development and make significant updates two or three times a year. The underlying persistent blueprints, standards, and procedures must be assigned owners, updated as needed, and published widely so that internal resources as well as vendors are aware of them.

In an area such as architecture, it is essential to build a foundation of organizational understanding regarding the need for standards. This may be a real challenge in a shop that is heavily into departmental computing. To accomplish this task you may need to establish or reverify principles for major internal IT processes, articulating why you need a formal architecture in a group setting, so that key technical leaders in your organization (and any others which impact your environment) buy in. Beyond that, policies—definition and decree of your key ones—are the true infrastructure of architecture and should represent what your organization believes is needed and is willing to live by and enforce. Policies are particularly critical in the data and security areas, as these set the proper foundation for everything else.

In general, the classic approach requires that you start with an end state vision statement of what your organization wants to put into place for architecture. These frameworks can be borrowed from various sources, but should be tailored to your own needs. It's all about explicitly stating that your future direction is a layered, component-oriented model, based upon industry standards whenever possible, rule- and API-orientated, and as open as possible. You ultimately will be developing a target architecture based on business need, assessing your current state against that target, and building a migration plan to get there.

Most classic approaches today rely on a formal system, such as the Zachman framework or Whitemarsh knowledge worker framework and various tools or methods. The idea is to create a common model at the business level and cascade top-down to specific layer definitions and the standards needed to support these.

The Zachman framework, for example, was created by John Zachman in the late 1980s and is shown in Figure 8–1.

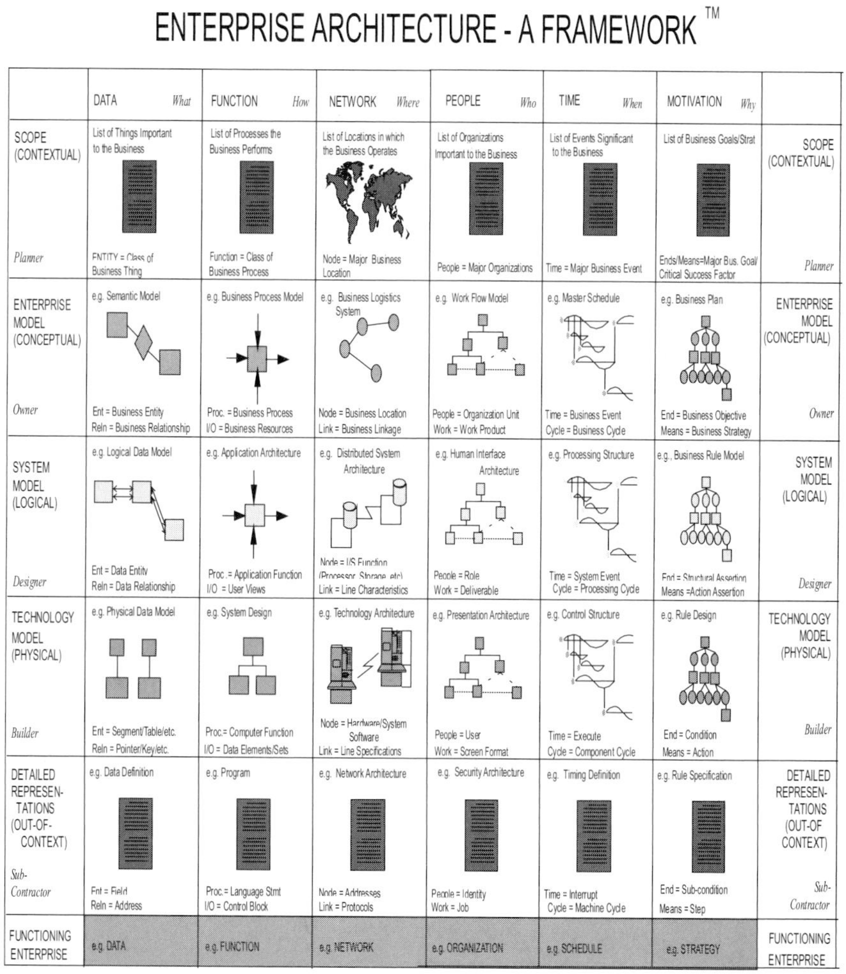

ENTERPRISE ARCHITECTURE - A FRAMEWORK ™

John A. Zachman, Zachman International (810) 231-0531

Figure 8–1   Enterprise architecture framework.

Zachman was a senior engineer at IBM at the time; his framework, which has stood the test of time, is intended to straightforwardly depict an enterprise model for an organization. It shows the designs or documents that represent the intersection between the roles in the system design process—that is, *owner, designer*, and *builder*—and the product definitions—that is, *what* (material) the system is made of, *how* the system works (process), and *where* the components are relative to one another (geography or network). The Zachman framework a useful logical tool in understanding the extent to which your enterprise is made up of multiple subsystems that interconnect.

Whatever models or methods you choose, your organization must have the structures, tools, and supporting processes needed to view individual IT projects in an enterprise-wide manner, thereby ensuring integration of:

- Critical data.
- Key applications.
- Enforcement of corporate policies—security, controls, data privacy.
- Common service levels.
- Unified user/interface to facilitate intuitive use of systems.
- Viable product development (if that's what you do).

▶ Enterprise Architecture Overview

Figure 8–2 provides an overall view of the relationships within an enterprise architecture.

To consider any architecture apart from its business context is to miss the point of what you, as CIO, are trying to accomplish. Your goal is to focus your architecture on accomplishing a business objective. You are generally not developing this architecture as a pure product development engineer might, but are rather driven by an enterprise business need generated by a requirement to sell product through a business channel that includes sales, marketing, finance, customer service, operations, product delivery, as well as human resources functions. The actions of these groups result in a revenue flow and profitability calculation for the company.

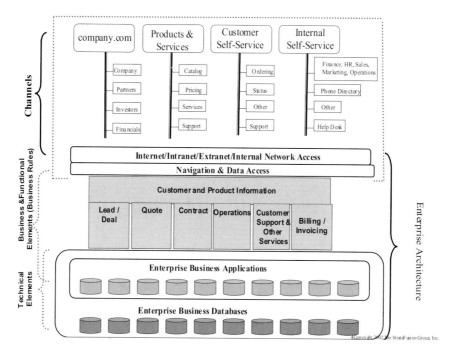

Figure 8–2 Relationships within an enterprise architecture.

For this reason, your architecture is a melding of business channel considerations that generates a set of business rules, which in turn create a functional roadmap by which the delivery and support functions of your enterprise provide value through products or services. These business rules also drive a set of physical technical elements that actually operate the technology component of your company's product or services delivery, support, and accounting processes.

The business channel portion is the key starting point of your architectural quest. Here is the definition or recognition of your company's actual delivery proposition to the market. This section is not focused on internal functional organizations, as a traditional approach might dictate, but rather on the ways in which product or services are delivered and those transactions are communicated to your customers, and eventually to your internal enterprise processes. The focus of your architecture therefore becomes not your finance, engineering, or manufacturing organizations, but your customers and the processes that directly support their success.

Once your channels and general information delivery requirements are identified, the business rules or functional roadmap portion of your architecture can begin to take form. Many IT organizations start this phase by focusing on functional organizations, not business channels. They are therefore distracted from the true value they can deliver by the "requirements" of a functional organization, which are important and certainly relevant to that organization and possibly the enterprise. These requirements, however, may be business processes that do not truly support the channels they think they support, but rather add potentially administrative overhead to your enterprise. This overhead may not actually be part of the essential channel delivery function and therefore is probably not as valuable a target for technology investment or return on investment (ROI).

By maintaining focus on your key channels, you can determine key functional business rules and processes that deliver value to your customer, yet still allow for proper accounting of their transactions with a minimal amount of overhead. Yes, this does mean that some functions may be better left unassisted by expensive technology, but isn't that appropriate?

After you have identified your key channels, derived from them your key business rules, and developed a functional roadmap, you are ready to start addressing the technical elements that constitute the heart of your enterprise architecture.

Necessarily, this process starts with your network infrastructure. In today's world, the Internet and associated Web technologies create the window into your enterprise for customers and even for internal users of your systems. For this reason, Internet, intranet, extranet, and browser-driven access to your information systems have more recently dominated the focus for your network infrastructure.

Also integral to creating this window is the architectural component that deals with the navigation and data access element of your architecture. This layer, which is intimately connected with your fundamental network structure and feeds into your business rules and functional roadmap processes, should produce controlled, consistent look-and-feel and access into your applications and database architectural layers.

The final layers of your technical architecture are the heart of the business rules and logic and implementation of your functional roadmap, the applications and databases that direct, store, and manage the specific functions of your business. Based on channels, business rules, and business processes, these technologies—whether custom developed or purchased from vendors—form the heart of your systems. Integral to these layers, but architecturally separate, are the enterprise application integration (EAI) components and inter-enterprise components, which provide the pathways that allow disparate applications and databases to interact, enabling the business channels and functional roadmap.

The next few sections explore each of these layers in more detail.

▶ Planning for an Enterprise Architecture

Enterprise architecture may not be the most obvious contribution of the IT organization, but it is integrated into many aspects of the business. As a CIO, you must be aware of and able to plan for these interdependencies when budgeting, resourcing, or calculating your return on investment, or even as part of your daily operations and internal processes.

Aligning IT with the Business

While IT is a support organization, it also has a strategic role in defining and driving technology decisions to support the business. This role cannot be fulfilled by IT in a vacuum, but instead should flow directly from corporate goals or objectives.

Assuming the executive team is defining the direction and needs of the company, and each business unit is interpreting what these mean in fulfilling its objectives, it is the CIO's responsibility to plan for sustaining systems support, focusing on strategic IT needs such as infrastructure growth or systems to improve efficiencies. In addition, the CIO drives the translation of the business needs into technology needs, providing a check and balance to the business units in an organization, helping to avoid investment in technology that may become shelfware—never implemented, or even worse, implemented but not used. As part of this analytic process, IT must also define what architectural changes or additions are required. This is imperative in determining the current and future architecture plan as well as determining budget and staffing requirements.

As discussed in Chapter 11, aligning the architecture with business strategy and processes is essential. The obvious follow-up to this is that every major business change must initiate a reexamination of your IT architecture for impact—the more formal, the better. The chart in Figure 8–3 is helpful in this regard.

IT Strategic Planning Process

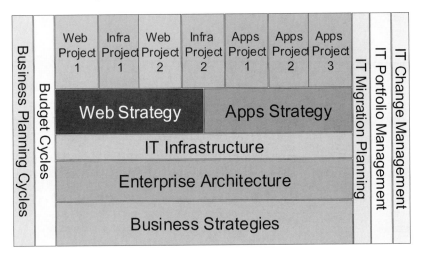

MWV 7/12/02 V1.0

Figure 8–3   IT strategic planning process.

The key is to ensure that all the vertical processes on the right side of the chart include architecture in some form or another. Migration planning should be a direct result of establishing your target architecture, the project portfolio should be managed by the architecture and have a project methodology that supports it, and change and configuration management processes must incorporate architectural planning at the logical and implementation level.

Whatever architectural models and associated processes you adopt in IT, they will have ongoing value only if they keep that link to the business. To have integrity, these architecture models must themselves be standardized and integrated enterprisewide, and *they must be observed by all new initiatives and projects if you want to sustain a strategic direction.*

This link is critical to keep in mind, yet we all forget or ignore it regularly. Here are some hints to help stay on course, and to mitigate the damage if you don't:

- Don't make the initial architectures, policies, rules, and processes so involved and difficult that no one will follow them. Link them to the business culture.
- Pay people to stay in touch with industry direction and incorporate that knowledge into your plans.
- Set up architectural reviews early in project lifecycles and allow course corrections when new information indicates they are appropriate.
- In setting up your architecture, follow industry models and standards whenever you can (and if you have to wait 6 months to do so, wait); rolling your own and retrofit are hard work and make your direction tough to anticipate, and it's much harder to integrate packages.
- Set the goals of the target architecture 6 to 18 months out so that new projects can anticipate what's coming.
- Have a migration plan for noncompliant systems and use it as a "plan B" to retrofit the renegades that sneak by your standards and get implemented.

Another, more organizational way of looking at the IT planning process, including enterprise architecture planning, is shown in Figure 8–4.

Budgeting for an Enterprise Architecture

Defining requirements for or changes to your enterprise architecture should be an integral part of the IT/business alignment process. Your major architecture costs are identified, as are specific cost drivers that determine the options available. The chosen options for your budget will depend on corporate growth plans, acceptable risk factors, and finding the best fit for your organization. The whole process can be daunting, but ensuring that each initiative is analyzed will help to avoid excluding key items from your budget.

In addition to the architecture costs associated with the business unit plans, the IT group must also analyze its own strategic plans for costs that need to be included. This process assumes that your IT organiza-

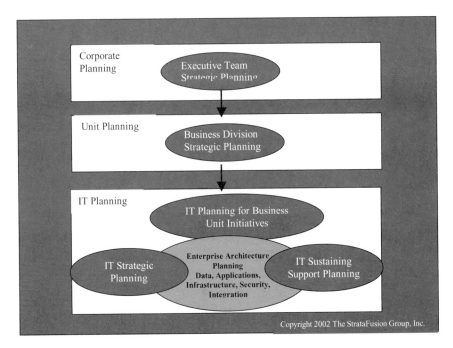

Figure 8–4   IT planning process.

tion has a current and future architecture strategy in place, and that both sustaining and forward-looking initiates are addressed. Again, the options can be analyzed and specific costs associated with the budget.

Completing these steps will take you past the first hurdle. Compiling this information is not easy, but it is necessary in order to avoid what can frequently seem to be hidden costs.

The second hurdle in the enterprise architecture budgeting process is obtaining buy-in for the proposed budget. A well-thought-out budget plan in which each cost is tied to a corporate initiative is easier to justify and can streamline the budget approval process. It is important to clearly articulate that any strategic initiative with architecture requirements must be funded in full; in other words, the company cannot choose to back the business initiative without supporting the IT initiative behind it. Architecture expenditures are frequently viewed as optional due to lack of understanding of their purpose. The information you collected in the first part of this process, in addition to ongoing education, will assist in communicating the importance of supporting the architecture budget. For more detailed information regarding the IT budget process, see Chapter 13, "Budgeting."

Structuring an Organization to Support Your Enterprise Architecture

Defining, developing, and maintaining an enterprise architecture is a big job. In spite of this, many companies tend to neglect the importance of having employees who specialize in enterprise architecture. Frequently, CIOs rely on application developers who understand the intricacies of developing software but do not have a firm grasp on the entire technology picture and the interdependencies between applications, database, network, security, and infrastructure.

This is not to say that a developer is incapable of defining a successful architecture, but instead to stress that enterprise architects are senior contributors with a wide and varied background in technology. In developing or maintaining a solid architecture, it is worthwhile to invest in architects who have the proper set of skills. An architect's role is not based just on technology knowledge, but also on strategy and leadership, since it frequently involves not just defining but also evangelizing the solution.

A CIO may face a challenge in justifying architects on his staff. When headcount is already limited, or there is not a need for a full time architect, this role can be filled or supplemented by other internal staff or consultants, but there is some amount of risk associated with this approach, and the CIO must weigh the options. By not hiring at least one experienced architect, who perhaps can share other duties in the organization, a CIO may be putting his company's architecture at risk. Relying on technical staff with a limited background may save budget in the short term, but being shortsighted or not able to analyze potential architecture issues can lead to costly fixing or replacing later in the process, entailing great expense and frustration.

When bringing in consultants, it is important to focus on the level and breadth of their experience, and it is frequently necessary to hire multiple consultants who are specialists in one particular area such as security.

Establishing an architecture group—even if only one person—is critical to creating a balanced IT organization. For reasons similar to those for separating development and quality assurance, architecture should be separate from development or infrastructure. Having your development group test final code before providing it to the customer is not a successful approach, and in the same way, having development personnel drive architecture design is pulling them away from their core competency of application design and development.

As shown in Figure 8–5, which depicts a typical IT organizational structure that separates each entity to provide a system of checks and balances, your architecture group should be integrated across your IT organization. The architect should be involved in the early stages of design with the program management group to focus on software or tool evaluation and high-level information or application design, and to gain involvement in driving standards, policies, and procedures. Additionally, interaction with development, QA, and infrastructure should occur regularly to focus on integration, security issues, code reviews, and general research and development.

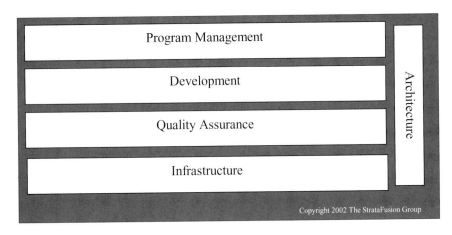

Figure 8–5 IT organizational structure.

Architectural Review and Fit Assessments for Systems, Technology, Major Changes

Once you have architectural models and standards, you can assess all significant new proposed projects against them for fit. Most organizations do this at least twice in the project lifecycle: once at project initiation, to determine the technology scope, fit, and infrastructure requirements, and later to review more formalized logical designs prior to development and infrastructure build. Here are some tips for these reviews:

- Make architectural review or pre-review a requirement for any IT project approval (watch for packages).
- Have formal lifecycles and/or methodologies requiring the production of standard documents that become part of your overall architectural model.
- Use an internal team of IT experts—it helps to develop people.
- Review against your standards, and revise them if they don't work.
- Reward both compliance and innovation.
- Watch for "pilots"—they can become ingrained and hard to extract.
- Use the team to evaluate and make recommendations on the architecture migration plan.
- Respond to changing needs by viewing noncompliant architectural requests as a signal of such change. Several rejections of similar requests could mean you have a major gap in your model or infrastructure—use this to justify and fund upgrades.
- Communicate architectural review information as an early warning to the change and configuration management processes.
- Periodically use the team to evaluate and make recommendations on new technologies or business direction.

Change Management at the Meta and Operational Level: A Critical Success Factor

Change management and the activities of release and configuration management are significant marks of maturity in an IT organization. Ad hoc and uncontrolled change in the environment threatens production service level agreements (SLAs), causes chaos in development and can wreak havoc with your architecture.

This is especially critical in the later phases of large projects when workarounds may show up as solutions to poor design. It is the operational, project-related decisions that critical people make on the fly that truly enable you to sustain and advance a viable strategic IT direction.

Your best technical people can, just by trying to do their jobs properly, introduce disconnects that can completely derail your strategic direction.

Use the change management process to protect your architectural investment. Proper release management review steps and environmental testing can identify noncompliant technology. The implementation of these processes effectively puts a wall around your production environment and forces changes to go through the proper lifecycle in which architectural fit can be assessed.

▶ Component Architecture

This section introduces the concept of multitiered, integrated-component architecture. This layered concept consists of:

- Network access (Internet/intranet/extranet/internal).
- Navigation and general data access.
- Customer, channel, and product processes, usually depicted as business rules, and a functional roadmap.
- Enterprise application integration tools and interfaces.
- Enterprise business applications and databases.
- Interenterprise integration tools and interfaces.
- Outside enterprise business applications and databases with which your systems interface.

These layers form the primary units of your multitiered, integrated-component architecture and can be looked at in two parts: the functional architecture or roadmap and the technical architecture. Each of these layers is described in more detail in the following sections. For now, suffice it to say this concept can be depicted in many ways but the components remain much the same. Figure 8–6 shows the relationship of a functional roadmap and a multitiered, integrated-component technical architecture and provides a basis for further discussion.

The key point to understand is that the functional architecture, or roadmap, and the technical architecture are distinct and different units that can be developed separately, but must be brought together in the

Figure 8–6 Business channels.

overall architecture to insure business synchronization. The key integrating layers, in order of importance and impact, are:

1. Enterprise applications
2. Enterprise databases (included in the diagram with enterprise applications)
3. Enterprise application integration (EAI)
4. Interenterprise integration
5. Navigation and data access

The functional components of the architecture determine the implementation of the technical components, and therefore must be understood first. These rules must be uniquely identified, then incorporated knowingly and carefully into the five areas above, according to the priority depicted.

That means that the majority of these rules should be first of all contained in the enterprise applications layer. Once you have placed all those possible or technically feasible in that layer, you can then utilize the enterprise database layer for those business rules that are best kept there, such as some data architecture design and modeling items, denormalization, data warehousing, stored procedures, or triggers clearly not appropriate to the applications layer.

The EAI and interenterprise integration layers should contain only those rules that govern the transportation of information from one application, database, or enterprise to another within the enterprise, and should not include any functional business rules. The navigation and data access layer should be limited to only those rules that impact data access and presentation to a customer (such as what information is displayed). Any attempt to actually process or modify information in the presentation layer must be avoided; graphic delivery of the required information is all that it should address.

Overview of the Functional Roadmap

The functional roadmap, expressing the business rules, is the most important part of your architecture. Without these definitions, you can't know how to implement the technical portions. You will be making many implementation decisions during the technical portion, but ideally these will be largely configuration and data handling decisions; they should not decide how the business is to be run. This does not lessen the importance of these decisions, but if you find yourself deciding how the business should operate in the technical architecture, a problem is rapidly developing.

The roadmap (see Figure 8–7) does not contain technical terms or tools identifying where functions occur, such as in an ERP or CRM system, but rather focuses on the business process itself, identifying data points and flows to standard business processes, not organizational departments. Simply put, it is the flowchart of your business, starting with customer identification, and ending with the delivery and accounting of the value provided. It is the "what" and procedural "where," but not the technical "how." That comes later.

A good functional roadmap has four important attributes:

1. It is driven by the relationships between the business channels discussed earlier and actual business processes which deliver to those channels. These are best depicted graphically in flowchart

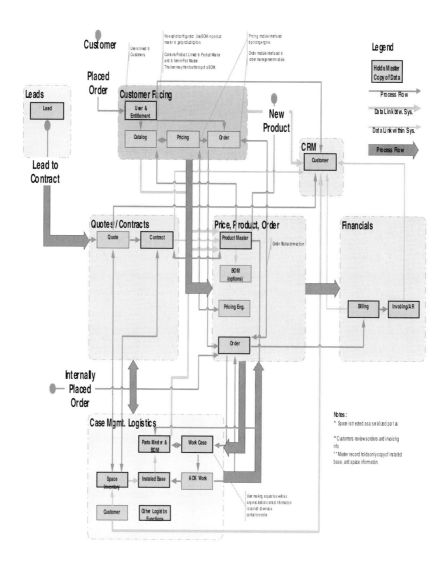

Figure 8–7   The functional roadmap.

manner as shown above, starting with the larger overall processes such as quotes, lead generation, or customer service, and then drilling down into each of those processes in enough detail to establish data points and information flow.

2. Its major components are those that procedurally or functionally drive the business, such as order to cash or product master maintenance. These components are definitely not organizationally identified departments such as sales, operations, or finance but rather are the actual key processes driving the business channels.

3. It includes the data points, units, or types needed to identify the "what"—the actual information content.

4. It identifies the actual data links required and the specific data points that are linked or exchanged and identify the information flow, exchange, or integration of the identified data.

It is also important to follow some of the traditional forms of data modeling to make sure you are doing such things as collecting the data—particularly the master data—once and in one place only, being careful not to duplicate data in multiple locations or collect it twice in two different ways or in the wrong process.

The functional roadmap is usually broken down into multiple maps associated with each general process of the overall map. These general processes may then be further broken down into specific data points, data flows, and presentation to be implemented by the technical toolsets applied. Without this crucial yet often bypassed piece of the architecture, the technical implementation phase is at best difficult and risky, and at worst futile. Unless you know what you are technically implementing, or what problem you are trying to solve, you are most likely doomed to failure.

The next section discusses several other examples of the functional roadmap.

Drilling Down in the Functional Roadmap

This section provides an example of a drill-down section of the previous overall functional roadmap to illustrate what the next level might look like for a given process. As an introduction to some architectural ideas, this chapter unfortunately cannot complete your roadmap for you, but rather shows why you need one, what one might look like, and how it is critical to your overall enterprise architecture.

Figure 8–8 shows the product master maintenance process, and reflects a real world process.

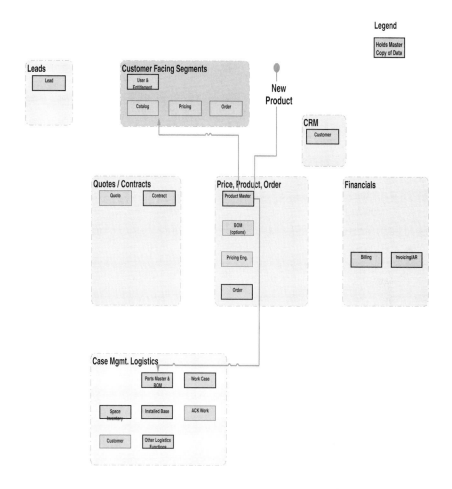

Figure 8–8 Product maintenance data process.

This process can be clearly traced from its location within the overall diagram, which indicates its relationship and integration with the other major customer channel supporting functions. Note especially that:

- The master locations for information are clearly identified.
- The required information flows are articulated.
- The subfunctions, and their relationships to the other functions within the product master process, are clearly identified.

This diagram can then be used to facilitate specific, most likely tabular, identification of required data points and flows, which can be turned into a configuration, setup, or development specification for use by your technical architecture and eventual implementation plan.

Another example of a drill-down section is the order to cash and logistics process, again based on a real life example (Figure 8–9).

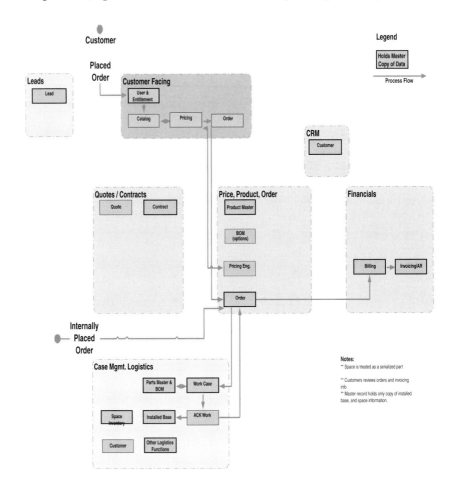

Figure 8–9 Order to cash and logistics data process.

This particular business function represents a solution for a company selling tangible products, utilizing a best-of-breed application approach. Key to the solution is pricing of the tangible item relative to the logistical location, which drives the invoice creation and the collection of cash. Retrieval and processing of the data from the correct application must be designed carefully, to ensure that the business user community does not enter the same information in more than one step or process.

Figure 8–10, again based on a real life example, although similar in appearance to the previous two, defines a unique and important component, that of the data integration links.

This component is critical to your functional roadmap and must be included in all roadmaps. It specifically defines the flows and integration of your data points throughout the process(es), and while portions are incorporated in other diagrams, this one should contain all of the required integration and be able to stand on its own in showing the flows and integration of the required customer channel processes.

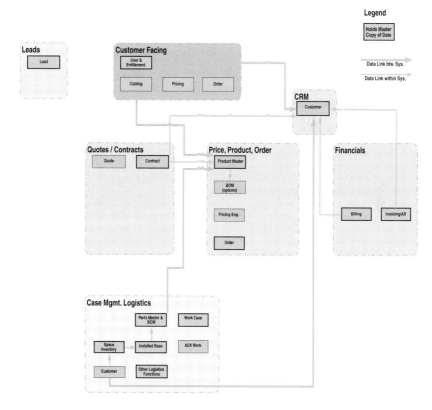

Figure 8–10   Data integration links.

▶ Multitier Architecture, Layer by Layer

Having completed our discussion of the functional roadmap, we now define and discuss the layers of the multitiered, integrated-component architecture portion of your enterprise architecture. See Figure 8–11.

Figure 8–11   Business rules and functional roadmap.
Copyright 2002 The Strata Fusion Group, Inc.

Before we continue, it is important to again briefly emphasize the importance of the relationship that exists between your technical architecture and your functional roadmap. Together, these two constitute the multitiered, integrated-component architecture, which will deliver direct product value to your customer via the defined business channels and will also provide the processes and accounting necessary to control and operate your enterprise.

These two major portions of your enterprise architecture are symbiotic in their relationship and must exist together. If you have one without the other, you either have a technical infrastructure without clearly defined business rules, logic, and technology processes, usually resulting in increased overhead and maintenance and therefore poor cost efficiency and (most likely) ineffective customer channel delivery. Or you may have a good functional roadmap with a flawed or inappropriate technical infrastructure, again impacting costs and effective customer channel delivery.

The business rules and their expression in the functional roadmap provide the logic and flow pattern for the technical portion of the architecture, which constitutes the nerve pathways resulting in the delivery of information and products to your customer channels. The total neural pattern and flow constitute your multitiered, integrated-component enterprise architecture.

In the following sections, we diverge into a series of discussions around the technology layers of the architecture and their interrelations with the whole. These sections are not intended to constitute a technical treatise on each layer, but rather to discuss the major technological layers primarily in relation to the whole, while demonstrating the importance and uniqueness of each.

The Network Access Layer

Our excursion into the technical portion of the multitiered component architecture begins with the network access layer, shown in Figure 8–12.

Internet / Intranet / Internal Network Access

Figure 8–12   Network access layer.
Copyright 2002 The Strata Fusion Group, Inc.

The network access layer is often most associated with those technologies that create the Internet, intranet, extranet, and general internal access networks of your enterprise. Some of the distinguishing characteristics of this layer include:

- Physical data communications access into and out of the enterprise, such as DS3, T1, VPN, and collocation resources.

- Firewalls and DMZs, which define and defend the perimeters of the enterprise, usually a combination of software and server/network hardware tools.

- Routers, switches, and other network devices, which provide intelligent routing of information in and out of the enterprise.

- Network cables, network interface cards, and wireless access units, which create the physical topology of your network.

- The browsers and other software data access components that actually control the presentation and physical access logic of your desktop and portable computer units.

- The transparent security of this layer via addressing schemes, port IDs, and operating system roles and responsibilities, which are more transparently applied than in their own layers.

- Although not addressed in any detail in this chapter, the computer units themselves, which provide the personal tools to obtain, retain, and interact with information from the enterprise architecture at a personal level.

In today's world, especially with the advent of the Internet's Web-based technologies, the network is the glue that holds all the other layers together. There are, essentially, no business rules involved in this layer, nor should there be. When operating properly, the network access layer should be transparent to the using community, but without it each unit of the enterprise architecture becomes an "island of independent computing," and most likely little to nothing works at all.

This is the first layer that you encounter in any enterprise, but as we have explained, it is also the most technically self-sufficient layer. Business rules and functional roadmaps have minimal impact on this layer, which is deeply immersed in the purer technologies of TCP/IP, ports, topology, network addresses, switches, and firewalls.

Some key considerations regarding this layer include the following:

- No business rules should be included here. This is the most purely technical portion of your multitier component architecture.

- A significant portion of your front-line security is included in this layer, and its capabilities should be coordinated with the security capabilities of the navigation and data access layer of your overall system security plan.

- This layer is often forgotten in the planning surrounding your enterprise architecture. Remember that this is the physical doorway in and out of your architecture; if the door does not open when appropriate, or is too small, you have no architecture, only a wall or inadequate funnel.

- Make sure your technical designs account for the capabilities and limitations of this layer. Some critical considerations include the volume of data transported; geographical distances transited, particularly for distributed database access or update;

inadequate telecommunications bandwidth and/or bottlenecks; and single points of failure.

- Efficient database modeling and access schemes minimize long seek times and large, complex searches.

We will not spend a great deal of time on this layer, other than to emphasize its importance; while critical to architectural success and the "beating heart" of information communication, it pretty much stands by itself in the multi-tiered, integrated-component architecture.

The Distributed Data Access Layer

The distributed data access layer (see Figure 8–13) can be viewed as an integrated portion of the network layer, but for purposes of understanding the multicomponent technical architecture, we examine it as a separate layer. This is useful because this layer provides the presentation and common user interface (UI), which enable navigation and entitlement, as well as aspects of globalization, security, workflow, and persistence that are impacted by certain portions of the business channels, business rules, and functional roadmap.

Figure 8–13   Distributed data access layer.
Copyright 2002 The Strata Fusion Group, Inc.

This distributed data access layer, especially when looked at from the Internet, Web, or browser interface perspective, controls the look and feel of what a user sees, the initial navigation whereby she chooses and moves among application toolsets, databases, and the presentation of data from these toolsets. Here, the more visible security of passwords and sign-on methodologies is applied, and requests for transactions or information are initiated.

Some business rules are applied at this layer, mostly related to the functions of navigation and entitlement, but such application should be limited to these functions. The more complex rules of transaction, data integrity, data integration, and reporting must be assigned and maintained within the other layers, for example, in enterprise applications and databases. It is important that this layer utilize that information for the fundamental presentation, navigation, and entitlement functions, but the process of business rule structuring and adherence should occur within those tools and technologies. A common mistake, particularly in predominately Internet-based systems, is to incorporate and integrate these rules into the navigation and data access layer. This almost universally results in a vast and complex duplication of capability and design, which is more appropriately inherent in the application, database, and integration layers of the architecture and produces systems that are not only difficult and expensive to maintain, but also serve the enterprise poorly.

This understanding is one of the keys to success and, most importantly, flexibility in enterprise architecture. If you develop your navigation and data access interfaces properly, future incorporation of application and database changes become much easier. If you embed or duplicate functional and business rules within this layer, you end up with considerable duplicate effort and as a result significant complexity and cost into reacting to business condition changes. If you do not carefully utilize change control or document the locations of such duplications, then you can easily cause your systems to be nonfunctional, with little data integrity.

With the advent of Internet/Web technologies such as the browser and a large assortment of Web server, application, and emerging Web services tools, many of the traditional limitations surrounding this layer have disappeared and been replaced with almost too many alternatives. The new power of this layer, which started with the client/server age and came to near full fruition with the advent of the Web, makes it a true ally to the CIO in the difficult task of common user access, standardization, and information integration. Revolutionary tools, unheard of just a few years ago, exist today to perform these functions, making this layer one of the most powerful advantages for systems in the last five to ten years. Admittedly, it presents some new complexities and a learning challenge for technology professionals, but one can hardly imagine a world in which such tools are no longer available.

Navigation and data access, when coupled with the next layer—enterprise applications integration (EAI), sometimes referred to as "middleware"—truly provides today's enterprise with a powerful one-two punch in responding to the enterprise integration challenge. And when you add some of the emerging inter-enterprise integration techniques discussed later in this chapter, the CIO now has some truly significant tools in his battle to provide solid business systems information to his enterprise.

Initially, small enterprises generally resolve their EAI issues with direct, point-to-point coupling of application and application integration. Once an enterprise has several integrating enterprise applications such as ERP or CRM, or multiples of each, it begins to find that point-to-point solutions are no longer sufficient or are becoming too complex for application interfaces. When an enterprise begins to require multiple interfaces among several similar or related applications, it becomes necessary to consider purchasing, or under some unique circumstances developing, a more robust and standard EAI layer.

Many of the standard market EAI tools can be purchased and—depending on the requirements of your enterprise architecture, especially if these are more complex—can reliably be used in a somewhat standard fashion to integrate your enterprise applications and databases. These tools can, however, be expensive and are often complicated to implement due to what really becomes a more custom implementation, more cost-intensive than originally perceived. Every effort must be made to utilize standard implementations of these products to keep configuration costs and complexity down to minimize follow-on maintenance costs.

As we have said, an alternative, as long as your EAI requirements are relatively simple, is to utilize point-to-point solutions, at least initially, perhaps in a combination with carefully architected and thought-out use of your navigation and data access layer to facilitate the sharing and interfunctional use of enterprise application information. In some cases, the newer business process management and emerging Web services tools may also be of assistance. This sophisticated approach to combining point-to-point solutions with solid and flexible navigation and data access layer design can hold off the potentially more expensive EAI tool purchase and implementation for a considerable period of time. You must be careful, however, to ensure that the design of the navigation and data access layers is mindful, flexible, and well documented, and also to plan thoughtfully ahead for the potential implementation of a more standard EAI toolset before your architecture becomes too unwieldy, significantly complicating or decreasing the time available to implement a more standard approach utilizing purchased tools.

The development of this layer of your multitiered, integrated-component architecture is probably the most important for the growth of your enterprise, as it experiences increased complexity in becoming a larger company. Be very careful to consider your strategy for this layer well before you need it and to proceed cautiously and thoughtfully down this path. Although generally transparent to your user community, this is a key area that can successfully simplify and standardize your EAI issues or conversely can make your enterprise architecture extremely expensive, overly complex, and less dependable than what today's powerful tools are capable of delivering.

The strides technology has achieved in the last five years in EAI technology is nothing short of amazing, and can be of significant benefit to you as a CIO, and to your enterprise architecture.

The Applications and Database Layers

We now discuss the functional and business heart of your multitiered architecture: the enterprise business applications and database layers (see Figure 8–14). These two layers, by design, should provide the majority of your business rules. We have noted a couple of potential exceptions to this in the implementation of your navigation and data access layer and your EAI layer, but it is important to emphasize again that these should be exceptions to the overall the rule.

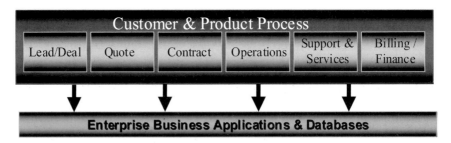

Figure 8–14   Applications and database layer.
Copyright 2002 The Strata Fusion Group, Inc.

The business applications layer contains almost all of the design encompassed in your functional roadmap and associated business rules. In most enterprises, this layer consists mostly of purchased applications—ERP systems such as SAP and Oracle applications and CRM systems such as Siebel—and your business intelligence and knowledge management systems, such as SAS, Business Objects, Cognos, and reporting tools developed inhouse. In some cases, internally developed applications that support unique business functionality are also included. Extraction, transformation and loading (ETL) tools, which also contain business rules around the aggregation of data, reside in this layer as well.

The functional roadmap and business rule requirements are and should be best contained within this layer, since the applications themselves derive their capabilities from the configurations and implementation approaches driven by the functional roadmap. These applications then become the heart of your business process environment and channel processes. Here the traditional business functions such as finance, operations, customer service, sales, and marketing derive their basic functionality form the business channel-driven functional roadmap. Together, the functional roadmap and traditional business organizations drive the configuration of applications to match not their structure, but rather the processes they support.

The database layer usually contains almost all of the rest of your functional roadmap and business rules technical implementation, but only as it supports the applications layer through such mechanisms as stored procedures, database triggers, and the fundamental capabilities of a relational data model. In addition, your data warehouses reside in this layer. The key to success within this layer is a solid, well-thought-out relational data model for your applications based on sound relational concepts supported by good table design, careful key selection, and effective indexing. Through these mechanisms, supported by effective stored procedures and database triggers where appropriate, you provide solid support to your applications layer where the majority of your business rules reside.

It is worth emphasizing that the only business rules that should be included in your database layer are those that directly support and are tightly coupled with the application through significant added functionality or effective design. While business rules should be limited in this layer, effective data modeling techniques should be used.

This layer also incorporates the data marts and data warehouses that support the analytical, business intelligence, and knowledge management portions of your enterprise architecture. These databases, usually in a denormalized state and sometimes updated en masse on a regular basis, have their own rules, usually uniquely identified for each warehouse via a data model supporting its specialized capability. In this sense, these constructs must have business rules associated with them, but since by definition they are reorganized duplicates of already maintained data, the real key is to have a well-documented data model that is based on channel-driven business rules and identified in the functional roadmap. In that sense, they are not truly a duplicate set of rules but rather a supplementary set that is appropriate to this layer.

The concept of an enterprise data warehouse has been discussed over the years. It is an unusual organization that can support and sustain such a large effort across even a small enterprise. Although data warehousing and its attributes are beyond the scope of this chapter, it has been our experience that starting with focused data warehouses or data marts on a smaller, more distributed scale can provide focused value more quickly than trying to create a single large enterprise warehouse.

The Interenterprise Integration Layer

The last layer we discuss in the technical portion of the chapter is the interenterprise integration tools layer (Figure 8–15), which provides other enterprises with organized access to and information flow in and out of your enterprise. In this sense, this layer is similar to the navigation and data access layers previously discussed, but it is directly targeted on the exchange of information between your enterprise and another. In the context of the Internet and Web infrastructure today, this is the home of your extranet and associated tools.

Figure 8–15   Interenterprise integration.
Copyright 2002 The Strata Fusion Group, Inc.

Chapter **8** | Architecture

Some of the key priorities for this layer include the following:

- Ensure that it is physically but not logically insulated from your other layers.
- See to it that your security strategy isolates and controls access from this layer to your internal systems.
- Utilize standard interfaces to or from this layer, using standardized approaches such as XML or EDI transfer, or a data access transfer layer developed inhouse and similar to those discussed for the UI-associated layers.
- Ensure that information transfers are carefully thought out, standardized to preclude duplication of access methods, well documented, and under change control.
- Less is always better than more.
- Think flexibly in regard to systems, because these interfaces will be changing and will probably need to support multiple enterprises, most likely with different requirements.
- This layer will support its own set of interface business rules and its own data integration roadmap, but should be a subset of, or dependent on, the internal business rules and associated functional roadmap that constitute the master set. You definitely want to have a clear line of demarcation between your internal systems and these internal feeds, with clear separation and precise transaction tracking incorporated as basic concepts in their development.

From an architectural standpoint, this is clearly a tool layer. Any applications operating in this layer must focus only on the extraction, data exchange transformation, and actual transmission of interenterprise data and on applying well-documented business rules that are directly related to those processes only. Aside from transaction logging and associated functions, database storage and subsequent enterprise use of information from this layer should be discouraged.

▶ Developing a Strategic IT Portfolio

As previously discussed, IT must develop its own strategy, not only partnering with the business units to support their initiatives but also determining what projects are necessary to support growth, improve efficiencies, and (in some cases) move the company to the status of a market leader or technology innovator. Review and assessment of the current architecture, from both functional and technical standpoints, is key to defining an architecture roadmap and formulating a solid technology portfolio from which to operate and extend.

After understanding and developing a functional roadmap and multitiered, integrated-component architecture, the final step is to develop a technology roadmap and portfolio that identifies the specific technical tools you will utilize to deliver ongoing solutions for your business channel requirements. This creates your blueprint and strategic portfolio of the technology tools that will run your enterprise, see Figure 8–16.

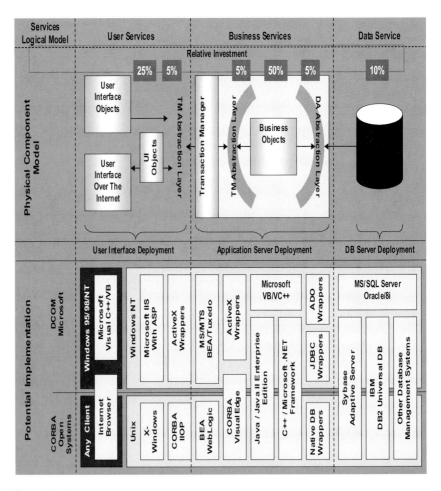

Figure 8–16   Technology roadmap and portfolio.

A well-rounded technology roadmap and portfolio is the foundation of any effective architectural blueprint. Figure 8–16 shows a graphical model describing a typical range of services required for a global client-server architecture. The model is not intended to be exhaustive or definitive, but must be sufficiently robust to address the majority of interoperation, development, and deployment needs faced by the organization. Although this model is predicated on a three-tier architecture, it can (and should) be extended into a full services-based architectural roadmap, including an overlay of the four basic operational services: transaction management, messaging, directory services, and security services.

At the 30,000-foot level, the creation of such a chart can be leveraged in multiple ways. Providing application developers, architects, and management with a consistent view of the application architecture becomes an extraordinary advantage when introducing new applications into the portfolio. The ability to organize the incoming applications' features into their logical strata can also give light to potential incompatibilities or highlight rough spots in application rollout and integration. For the implementation of units of work or functionality (according to commonly accepted object-oriented design principles), the chart can facilitate a walkthrough of the target environment.

At the 10,000-foot level, when this chart is fully completed and documented, it helps the program management office, engineering groups, architects, and coders understand the interrelationships of the products they are producing and the frameworks into which they must fit. It is also extremely helpful as a tool to manage the reassessment and attrition of the "tools repository," which tends to become littered with unused parts over time.

At the 5,000-foot level, the chart is of significant value when starting the process of specifying projects of any kind. Because the architectural blueprint can be used as a checklist guide to the overall implementation of new technology or iterations of existing technology, there is less likelihood of an architectural oversight due to a lack of understanding of the existing environment. While it may seem unlikely, it is not uncommon for organizations of all sizes to encounter significant oversights when performing preliminary application design, only to discover that a critical component was overlooked in the infrastructure portfolio. For example, it is quite common to overlook the value of directory or messaging services when architecting applications. The tendency is to take the simplest design approach of "letting the database do it all," but in reality, this is a poor substitute for a scalable architecture.

There are other helpful reference elements in this form of architectural blueprint. The computations of relative investment represented at the top of our chart have been derived as an average from approximately 300 software engineering organizations, but these numbers (or their projected values) can change drastically depending on the specifics of the project. Also of note are many elements seen in the "Potential Implementation," which can cross various boundaries. Note that Microsoft's tools are seen in the user services and business services layers, whereas the Sun Microsystems (Java) tools are largely relegated to the business services tiers. The increasing competition between the two foundation framework players (Microsoft .NET and Sun Java in this example) makes it extremely difficult for an architect to maintain purity in the final implementation. The .NET framework has potential, as of the time of this writing, to limit Java's significance in physical delivery models whose implementations use Microsoft operating systems in the application concentrator (business services) tiers as well as the client delivery tiers where browser-only clients are not viable.

The identification of a technology roadmap and portfolio, which flows from the functional roadmap and multi-tiered, integrated-component architecture, all derived from a sound understanding of business channel process requirements, provides the technically astute CIO with a powerful and sustainable platform that will significantly contribute to his company's productivity and profitability, not to mention to his own career.

Strategic Outsourcing

by Bharat C. Poria

Every CIO is likely to face the challenges of outsourcing at some point. Outsourcing involves special relationships between IT and external organizations that provide services—services that critical business processes often depend. Successful CIOs must therefore ensure that these special relationships are properly managed and controlled. They need to understand the different types of outsourcing and their advantages and disadvantages.

In this chapter, Bharat Poria explores situations in which outsourcing can be beneficial to the IT organizations. He describes what outsourcing is and the options that exist. In particular, Poria discusses:

- *Key drivers of outsourcing.*
- *Understanding the company's strategies and their impact on outsourcing.*
- *Various outsourcing options.*
- *Aligning outsourcing with company goal and objective.*
- *The importance of fully understanding the services provided by outsourcers.*
- *Key elements of outsourcing.*
- *Role of service level agreement (SLA).*

- *Balancing insourcing with outsourcing.*
- *Simplifying the outsourcing process.*
- *The importance of ensuring that key knowledge is retained by the IT organization.*

▶ Understanding Outsourcing

At some point in a CIO's career, he or she is likely to face the question of whether to outsource—by choice or through inheriting an outsourced environment. In the latter case, the outsourced relationship may be working, at best, but is more likely limping along or broken, or the outsourced vendor may even be managing the customer.

Typically, business is moving so fast that project requests come in at a pace that the IT group cannot handle—and by the way, the users requesting the work needed it done yesterday. IT has neither the budget nor people to review or analyze these requests, not to mention implement them.

Another common scenario involves support staff becoming overwhelmed by the number of support calls coming to them, with service levels dropping as a result, and before you know it, user confidence is at an all time low. As a result, IT as a group gets a bad reputation and is blamed for not responding to user demands in a timely fashion.

Before any tactical plans are put into effect, it must be clearly understood what outsourcing is about: the whys, the whens, and the hows. The CIO must also understand the company's overall strategies and views on outsourcing and the potential impact this decision can have not only on the IT organization but on the company as a whole in terms of morale, effectiveness, financial options, and long-term or short-term goals across departments.

In its simplest form, outsourcing involves having work done by non-company staff. The decision to outsource can be brought about by a number of factors within the organization or as a result of forces beyond the control of the organization.

In general, outsourcing is understood to involve some work that is sent to another company to be performed and is then, in the ideal world, completed, tested, and integrated back into some program or system.

In reality, the topic is quite broad and cannot be measured only in terms of a project or program. To outsource, among other things, means to understand what services are available, who can do it, where can it be done, how quickly can it be achieved, and at what price.

▶ Elements of Outsourcing

The elements involved in outsourcing within an IT organization are quite complex. When deciding to outsource, the CIO must be clear about which level of service is being addressed. The following elements can be defined to make the process easier:

General Information Technology Services Market

- Contracting.
- Consulting.
- Systems development.
- Integration of business systems.
- Integration of infrastructure.
- Information technology management.
- Production maintenance and support.
- Infrastructure support (such as data center, network, security, administration, Web).
- Education and ongoing training.

Related Services

- Business process IT-enabled services.
- Offshore business process (remote services).
- Service providers (IT utility, ASP, BSP, ISP, xSP).
- Specialized services (such as call centers, help desk, technical support).

Armed with these categorizations, the CIO can start to narrow down the options available in deciding exactly what needs to be strategically outsourced, what can stay internal, and what can be achieved in a hybrid fashion.

Options for Outsourcing

First, let's step back and determine what outsourcing really means and what options exist to execute a strategy. Outsourcing, like all things in IT, has many facets. The following are some possibilities that exist:

- Onsite support.
- Offsite and offshore.
- Offsite and onshore.
- Functional support.
- Program or project support.

Before making any decisions to outsource or execute a tactical plan, the CIO must understand what parameters are driving him or her down this path, what outcome is expected, and what timeframe is being addressed. Quite obviously, by the time these questions are being faced, it is already reasoned that:

- The internal IT organization cannot handle the workload facing it.
- The cost to perform the service internally is unacceptable.
- Time is of essence.
- Internal resources do not have the expertise or experience.

In reality, the driving forces behind the decision whether to outsource in some manner clearly include the need to:

- Gain knowledge inhouse, whether it be process, domain, or technical in nature.
- Move to a new set of technologies and/or complement existing technologies.
- Improve service levels.
- Add to existing staffing levels quickly.
- Address operational, functional, or technical shortcomings.
- Return the focus of inhouse staff to core competencies.

- Accelerate benefits by rapidly implementing services or projects.
- Reduce costs in a specific functional area.
- Reduce capital costs.
- Reduce repetitive operational costs.
- Enable business strategies and or transformations.

Armed with one or many of these reasons, let's explore what each outsourcing option means. It is also quite reasonable to expect any one or multiple combination of these options to be chosen when looking at a strategy. Quite often a one-size fits all solution simply does not exist, no matter how badly the outsourcing vendors may want the CIO to believe it.

Onsite Support

Onsite support is also referred to as consulting or contracting. The key differentiator is that a consultant is there to provide guidance and/or options without prejudice and has a much broader understanding of the business, the technical and functional environments, and the work to be performed but may not necessarily be the subject technical expert. The contractor, on the other hand, is there to perform a certain defined task as the subject technical expert.

By definition, this work is performed at the customer's premises and is typically located with the project, program, or functional team for a set period of time. Staffing methods can vary from hiring independents to hiring a team, either independently or from a professional organization directly.

One of the pitfalls with this option, especially in the United States, is the classification and treatment of the consultants or contractors with respect to the privileges of regular employees and the length of time they are contracted for. If a consultant is treated like an employee of the customer, for instance, in control of his or her hours and vacation schedules, the U.S. Internal Revenue Service recognizes this and attempts to have the customer withhold taxes. With this interpretation, legal cases have been brought forward (and won) by consultants who, after contracting for a number of years with one customer, claimed they were owed the same entitlements (bonuses, stock options, share of profits) as regular employees, based on the new tax definitions.

To address this concern, some companies have instituted policies whereby a consultant/contractor can be contracted only for a certain period of time and cannot be rehired back for a defined period of time as well, ranging from six months to a year. Other strategies have been to have the consultant form a legal entity such as a corporation; payment is then made to the corporation directly as opposed to the individual. A consultant or contractor who is working multiple contracts at the same time is more clearly of independent status as well.

The advantage of hiring in this category is that it can indeed fill some short-term needs, costs will be at market rate, and the customer has flexibility to terminate the contract as and when required as long as terms and conditions set forth in the contract (which are generally quite liberal) are met.

Offsite and Offshore

Offshore services became popular starting in the 1990s. Partly driven by cost, the need to develop solutions quickly, and the availability of technical resources in cheaper English-speaking economies, it became a viable option. Although cost savings of 70 percent and sometimes 90 percent over onsite support were promised, only rarely did those percentages materialize. Savings can be gained, however, if the project is monitored and managed correctly.

This option can be quite uncomfortable the first time, and for that reason many CIOs choose not to go down this path, which is a shame. The global economy is here to stay; companies are conducting business globally; borders and boundaries are being broken with the availability of 7/24 infrastructures. Offsite and offshore is one more weapon the CIO should strongly consider having in his or her arsenal.

There are some strong perceptions and myths that still exist today when the words "offshore outsourcing" are first tossed around. The perception is that going offshore will mean large job losses in the IT organization, wages will remain frozen, and there will be social turmoil both internally and for customers facing the outsourced vendors. The reality is quite different, however. Offshore is not a slam dunk; not everything will or can go offshore, not all companies will be successful (although the trend will be irreversible), constraints will still remain in terms of business processes, technology, and cultural aspects. The constraints that exist can actually be turned into opportunities to leverage services in the future.

The offshore option can be used in a number of, but not in all, scenarios. It should be considered favorably when:

- Time is of essence.
- 7/24 hour availability is advantageous.
- Requirements can be well defined and will remain relatively stable.
- Cost of the program or project is an issue.

The overall maturity of this option can be broken down into the relative maturity of several aspects, listed in Table 9–1.

Table 9–1 Maturity Aspects

Aspect of Offsite and Offshore Outsourcing	Maturity
Software or application support and management	High
Software redesign	High
Development of legacy/custom systems and applications	High
New application development	High
Knowledge of package applications and software	Medium
Business intelligence	Medium to low
Software and engineering design	Medium to low
Enterprise application integration	Medium to low
Business process outsourcing and call centers*	Low
Data center services and infrastructure support*	Low
* Some larger companies are actually setting up their own call centers and data centers in offshore locations, in which case the level actually goes from low to high. Employees in these call centers or data centers are typically not outsourced but are regular, full-time employees of the company.	

Assuming that offshore is the answer and the CIO wishes to proceed down this route, it now becomes important to develop an element of trust between the customer and the offshore entity. Does that mean you can simply throw things over the wall and expect magic to happen? Of course not; the CIO is still accountable to ensure that goods are delivered in the time promised and that excellent project management skills and people communication skills are developed to ensure successful completion.

Once you have decided that this is a viable option, how do you go about initiating the next steps? More often than not, speaking with other CIOs, vendors, and customers will elicit a list of a number of offshore firms that service this area. Contact a few of them and have them talk about their successes and failures, types of projects, base cost structures, organizational structure, and what makes them successful. The best ones will have representation close to the customer site and their own network infrastructure. They should also have local resources as well as offshore development centers.

In the ideal situation, the offshore party has technical and functional representation at the customer site where requirements are validated before the project is sent offshore. The customer also has a staff member at the offshore site to clarify any issues that arise and to assist in quick decisions so as not to halt progress (this step is often missed). The offshore organization is then responsible for delivering a product that meets the specifications and that also involves full quality assurance before handoff to the customer. The customer's staff member at the offsite location is also in constant touch with the program/project team and is notified of any functional change so that the offshore site can react accordingly to any decision requests.

Offshore organizations do have elements of risk. A major one involves communication between the two parties: How good are the verbal skills, written and spoken, of the staff that will be interfacing with the customer? This issue must be addressed early on. Is the offshore entity just delivering to the requirements given, or are they functionally savvy as well? If they spot a problem, will they simply continue to work to the requirements, or will they bring the issue to the client's attention immediately for resolution? When there is a difference of opinion, what is the conflict resolution process? These are all questions that must be ironed out before a contract is signed, negotiated, or entered into.

Many global companies are going one step further and have either already developed or are developing their own offshore centers, primarily to take advantage of lower local costs, the availability of resource talent pools in a specific region, and the global tie-in infrastructure (telecommunications, Web, power) that is available. Not only have technology-based companies taken this strategy in stride, but organizations with heavy customer support requirements are also going down this path. Those companies that have large technical development projects have extended their own offices into the offshore economies and have either built or acquired to take advantage of this scenario. Extending even further, some global companies have now set up customer support centers at these locations, with Web or phone infrastructures routing unknowing users to one of these centers behind the scenes.

The one black cloud over this option is and will always be the political and economic instabilities of the countries involved. With terrorist activities on the increase and possibilities of sabotage, companies still cannot take this option as its single end-all solution. When opting for offsite, offshore services, this possible problem must be a prime consideration, and the risks must be weighed equally with other alternatives.

Offsite and Onshore

For offsite service, onshore is easily a more comfortable option than offshore, but not necessarily the best for what needs to be achieved. The option has some merit, but not necessarily from a cost standpoint. One of the main reasons that we contemplate offsite options in the first place is to get some leverage with respect to cost, but in any westernized country, we have already lost the resource cost battle in comparing onshore to offshore.

Offsite but onshore really means outsourcing to another organization within the same country or region. The benefit is that the development or work to be done is removed from the customer, thereby saving the cost of infrastructure to support the work effort.

This option can be used as a stepping-stone for some CIOs to eventually go the full offsite, offshore model, as processes can be tried out and ironed out. This onshore option can also be used as an alternative to onsite consultants.

Some outsource companies offering this solution tout the lower regional cost in various parts of the country, but be aware of shared resources; the lower cost may be derived from the outsourced resource working multiple projects, when they should be working on one customer's project. In the case of technical infrastructure staff (such as database administrators, system administrators, or system operators) this practice may be acceptable, but if deadlines are not met, it will be hard to prove whether the resource was actually working the requirements and what led to the delays.

This does become a viable option for the large companies that may have multiple divisions served by a corporate-owned IT organization, where the money stays within the corporate entity but not necessarily within the division that spends it, and where it is quite likely that each division is responsible for its own P&L and hence has options to source at its discretion. Because it is perceived the money stays within the corporate body, cost may not necessarily be the driving factor when facing the outsource decision. If the IT arm has a location nearby and can provide the services offsite, this may become an attractive alternative to either onsite or offshore sourcing, depending on the work to be performed.

Functional Support

Functional support in this context means to outsource an entire function. On the infrastructure side, this could include help desk, network management (data/voice), server operations, administration support (database/system administration), firewall management and support, or any other infrastructure function peculiar to the company. On the business application side, it could include application support, application development, Web content management, or again, any other business application function peculiar to the company.

Outsourcing of an entire function or service has its own set of advantages and disadvantages. Each CIO has to weigh the options pertaining to his or her own corporate culture, needs, and requirements, taking into account the corporate political climate and what changes are needed.

Reasons to outsource at a functional level are generally driven by a number of factors, such as:

- Internal group is not experienced (technical or customer service).
- Rapid expansion makes it difficult to keep up with requirements.
- Service cost reductions are sought.
- Entirely new function is created and required immediately.

Considering any of these factors, the CIO has to assess the situation and the potential impact it will have on the current staff both within and outside the organization. This is a decision that should not be taken lightly: It impacts the entire organization. Questions external to the IT organization *will* pop up: If IT outsources the help desk, for example, people in manufacturing, shipping, receiving, and other departments will wonder if they will be the next to be outsourced. On the other hand, the reverse is sometimes true: If the IT group has not performed to user expectation, a decision to outsource a specific function may be seen as a positive step.

Some companies have outsourced the entire IT function, some have outsourced small pieces, and others use a hybrid model. There is no right or wrong model; it all varies depending on the company's culture, whether it sees IT as a strategic or operational group, its long-term goals, whether it is considered important to keep knowledge inhouse, temporary cost-saving strategies, and so on. Whatever the reason, careful thought and consideration must to be given when deciding to outsource an entire function.

The current climate has seen deals in which functions are outsourced with 10-year fixed contract terms, including heavy penalties for cancellation in the earlier years. These deals are structured with favorable terms in the near future but high costs thereafter. IT is not a fixed world, so although a scope may be set initially for the terms of the contract, there is generally out-of-scope work that has to be done, which is where the outsource provider makes its margin. Conflicts arise out of badly written agreements that set an expectation by one side and that is not fully understood or defined by the other. Beware of agreements and service levels set by the vendor; these generally have the vendor's best interest at heart.

Contracts for this category are generally geared to provide service at defined service levels and can operate under a generic service framework. However, most customers do not have the measurement tools to challenge the provider's service level numbers. This leads to situations in which user expectation is not being met, but all the statistics coming back from the provider hit the marks. Such a scenario can be a CIO's nightmare in the making.

Outsourcing also does not guarantee that service will improve; there have been a number of cases in which the A players have been brought in initially, then quickly replaced with B and C candidates.

The overall message is that if a function is outsourced, be prepared to manage the relationship as with any outsourced work. Manage the provider and don't let the provider manage you or your staff. I had a situation in which the provider's account manager would come to me repeatedly and ask why I did not see them as a partner; after all, they did all the work, they supported the account, and they maintained the infrastructure and responded to situations as necessary. My response, very simply, was as a working partner yes, but as an account, no. I paid them for all the time they put in, they billed me for out-of-scope work, and there was no risk on their part. The day they came to me with a solution that saved me, the customer, money to the detriment of their own revenue was the day I would see them as a partner—and not until then.

One other big area of contention is over response versus resolution. The vendor always tends to discuss response time, whereas the customer is really interested in resolution time. The difference? Response means the provider will get back to the customer within a designated timeframe without any expectation of problem resolution, whereas resolution means the problem has to be *actually solved* within a set timeframe or service level. The normal vendor response when negotiating this is, "We cannot give a resolution time because we don't know the problem, and it may be unrelated to us." How should the CIO answer? "That's fine. Give us fixed resolution time with a percentage fudge factor"—that is, the goal of having, say, 80 percent of calls resolved within, say, two hours, with the understanding that the other 20 percent may go over this service level. Of course, the CIO has to have tools and processes in place to measure this—such tools should be in place to measure vendors anyway.

When selecting your functional support provider, remember that his or her entity will become an extension of the IT organization and as such will also carry your business knowledge.

Is all functional outsourcing bad? When technology moves so fast in your organization, training often comes as hindsight. IT staff may not be able to keep up with the pace; hence an external organization may be the answer, especially when it has a talented and varied resource pool to call upon at a moment's notice.

Good opportunities to outsource at a functional level include situations in which:

- The function is not strategically important.
- The function requires 24/7 support and no internal resources.
- The function is not within the core competence of the IT group.
- The location is too small or geographically challenging to support.
- Experienced resources are not available internally.

Outsourcing strategically in this area may also be a politically savvy move for a CIO, especially if the internal IT organization has been badly beaten by its customers—for whatever reason and whether fairly or not—and confidence is low. When this is true, it may make sense to bring in an external party to desensitize the situation and redirect attention away from internal IT staff. If taking this drastic route, careful consideration must be given to how an exit strategy is worked out for current staff in this function. It's quite possible that the external provider can take over current functional staff in this area or provide work for them elsewhere, especially as the staff itself is generally not to blame, regardless of the perception outside of the IT organization.

Program or Project Support

A project or program has been thrust upon the IT group, and internal resources are either not available or not appropriately experienced. When this happens, one option is to have the work outsourced by a contracting or consulting company, which can range from one of the Big 5 (KPMG, Deloitte & Touche, Accenture, and so on) to smaller "boutique" firms serving the same area.

In general, the Big 5 firms are business-savvy, have the functional resources, may be lacking in technical resources (but can get them via subcontracting), and are primarily focused on delivering the solution. As such, they come with a price tag beyond the independent consultants and contractors, and way beyond offshore entities.

Although the larger consulting companies generally take on projects based on time and material, there have been instances in which they have bid a fixed price based on the project scope, although this is rare unless they have also been involved in the project scope phase itself. Be aware that in the fixed-price scenarios, the real cost will come with scope creep and any changes that come along with scope creep that are defined as any work that was not specifically agreed to in the contract.

On a longer term project, it is guaranteed that the final product will never be limited to 100 percent of the original scope. The longer the project time, the greater the chances of changes; after all, business conditions can change quickly with considerable impact to any projects or programs that are being implemented. The need to adapt to these ever-changing situations quickly becomes a change management issue, including how to "park" and manage change during the development and implementation cycles.

The larger consulting organizations also take these opportunities to expand their services into other aspects of the business. Once they understand the business, it does not take a stretch of the imagination to see how they can assist in other areas, and indeed this may be an opportunity the CIO can take advantage of. Any areas that are weak in terms of business, process, technology, or process flow are usually pointed out quickly, especially in the larger programs, which may create a real challenge in managing the scope of the original project. It would be far better to park these issues to be tackled at a later stage or initiated through a different channel. This allows the CIO to again entertain competitive bids at a later point in time and does not make the incumbent the de facto vendor.

The smaller consulting houses are generally cheaper than the Big 5 firms, but may not have all the needed resources or experience to carry out the task at hand, as much they promise. This shortfall, however, may not be a big risk, as they can overcome this by contracting the help of consultants who are then presented to the customer as part of the consulting company. Former Big 5 partners, managers, or consultants have indeed started a number of consulting companies, and the business knowledge risk is therefore mitigated in terms of experience. The CIO in this instance is really getting the benefit and experience of a Big 5 player at a much lower cost and maybe minus the tools and processes, but gaining a team that can make decisions rapidly and adapt more quickly to the needs of the ever-changing customer climate.

Another factor to be considered is the customer's own physical infrastructure. Does the facility have room for a team to come onsite? Typically, consulting companies like to have dialup access. Does the facility support dialup? How many outgoing lines are available? Is there enough desk space for the team members, or will they operate out of conference rooms? Where will needed private interviews with business-level staff take place? Are there enough conference rooms or private offices to allow this? There are many other factors and physical limitations that should be considered; some will be highlighted before the contracts are signed, and others will come to light afterward.

It all comes back to the level of risk acceptable to the organization. In all instances, the infrastructure must be in place to support a consulting team coming onto the customer's premises, and access to required key staff must be made available ahead of time. This is a game of time and money in which the burden is on the CIO's organization.

▶ Conclusion: Trends and Opportunities

When we think about outsourcing, there are no defined best practices or magic pills that can be taken to ensure 100 percent success. By weighing all the factors and options presented and then taking a course of action suitable to the particular situation, the CIO can remove at least some element of risk.

In reality, if time is of the essence, it comes at a cost. If you have the time, then you can negotiate a better position. Cost is defined in ways particular to the company and as a relative number, which in the end can be measured in terms of return of value. Value can be regained over time, but can you wait that long? Market conditions may change, and it can be for the better or worse; the CIO must understand not only the business value but also the duration of the proposition when deciding which option to take.

As a trend, outsourcing is an option that many businesses are now considering heavily. Others that have already outsourced are bringing some levels of services back inhouse. Again, it all goes back to cultural fit, company politics, and past experiences in this realm.

In the area of business process, trends include:

- Movement from tactical and transactional processing to strategic and transformational outsourcing.

- Outsourcing from single process to multiple processes though a general contractor that can act as a solution integrator.

- The emergence of business process players in the offshore model as supply chain services get more global in nature without business boundaries.
- The convergence of Internet, application, and business process service providers, and the emergence of IT utility providers supplying multiple services. The latter will grow significantly as CIOs look to find players that can service their needs as a "one-stop shop" without involving multiple partners.

The evolution of outsourcing can be drawn simplistically, from low complexity to high, as follows:

- Outsourcing started with contractors and consultants working onsite.
- Then came onsite project and program teams.
- In the early 1990s onsite, offshore relationships started forming.
- In the mid-1990s offshore development and projects became common.
- In the late 1990s offshore data, development, and call centers formed.
- The early 2000s heralded collaboration of services across regional boundaries.

This evolutionary model can still be used today for the companies that have yet to engage in strategic outsourcing. The easiest and simplest way is to start from the top and work down as experience is gained. But strategic thinkers recognize the value of collaboration and are willing to take the steps necessary to get to the collaborative stage quickly. In some instances, they may already be there with their internal structure without recognizing the true value of such an environment. Gartner Dataquest also recognizes this and classifies these steps as stages of complexity of service delivery on the horizontal axis and the persistence of services on the vertical axis (Figure 9–1).

Looking at the opportunities that result, the offshore model clearly needs technologies to emerge on a more global scale to enable:

- Extension of enterprise and portal applications.
- Virtual enterprise integration as businesses become more distributed.

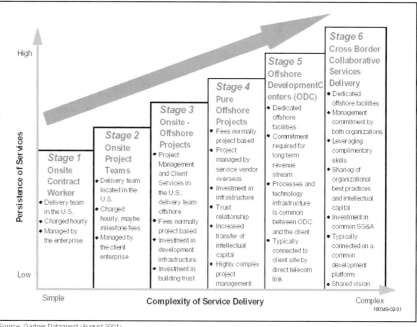

Figure 9–1 Evolutionary stages in offshore models.

- Far greater communication and collaboration across the information chain.
- Global access to systems, including stronger and more reliable security.
- Content structure and management as the Web creates more documents.
- Digital asset control and rights management as assets become more global.
- Web services.
- IT utility and grid computing.
- Business and IT monitoring tools, including remote management.

CIOs and employees must still be aware that even if a decision to outsource has been made, the following considerations still apply:

- Businesses must retain key employees to act as "watchdogs" for the business as the need for vendor management increases. The need for effective vendor management cannot be overstated in the context of IT outsourcing.
- Retained employees require new skill sets and training.
- There is far greater employee exposure to global cultures, languages, interactions, and ways of doing business.
- As internal staff compete with outsourced partners, they must adopt new technologies, tools, architectures, and processes. Separating the skill sets expected of an employee versus the outsource partner is also required.
- As the need for global business processes evolve, so must new standards and methodologies for distributed development and implementation. A new category of staff that manages these resources is needed.
- Solution aggregators will evolve, the general contractors will act as the one-stop shop, and hence the skill sets will simply move from one organization to another.
- Offshore entities will also establish onshore presence to be closer to their customer. People who are knowledgeable in the business aspects of the customer and can work directly with the customer (with customer facing qualities) will be required.
- Employees responding to downward cost and wage pressures must acquire higher value roles and acquire skills beyond current or normal technical levels.
- Soft skills that must be acquired include project leadership and teamwork, communication and documentation skills, tolerance and understanding of global cultures, and patience in dealing with people of multiple ethnicities.
- Hard skills that must be acquired for software development include understanding methodology, processes, procedures, and architecture, and developing design specifications. Other necessary skills include business (both industry and function) as well as particular domain expertise.

IT Workforce

by Dean Lane

The Marine corporal came to a halt in front of Lieutenant Lane's desk and snapped to attention. Slightly irritated by the interruption, Lieutenant Lane glanced up and asked, "What is it, Johnson?" Corporal Johnson began to explain why he needed time off later in the day. The Lieutenant stopped him in mid-sentence, because Johnson always had a reason for needing time off. "Corporal, I have already heard every excuse you have to offer on this subject! Go away and come back when you are prepared to give me a legitimate reason, one that I have never heard before, and I will consider your request." About 30 minutes later, Johnson again snapped to attention in front of Lieutenant Lane's desk. "Okay, Johnson," Lieutenant Lane said, "why do you need to have the afternoon off?" Without hesitation, he said, "Well sir, this afternoon my wife is going to get pregnant, and I'd like to be there." Lane felt like Ralph Cramden from The Honeymooners as he threw his index finger skyward and shouted "Out! Get out! Take the afternoon and don't let me see you until morning."

The Corporal Johnsons of the world are what make being a manager in a technical environment such an enjoyable challenge. As you make your way through this next section, you are given the keys to making people work with you and not for you. We all want employees who are self-motivated and anticipate the task. This chapter provides insight into how to motivate a technical workforce, but more importantly, how to get them on your side so that your every move is not questioned or contested. When a detail is missed or something is not exactly right, they will move in a positive manner to keep things on a proper track.

In this chapter Dean Lane discusses:

- *How to make people work with you, not for you.*
- *How to motivate a technical workforce.*
- *The best way to avoid workforce problems and retain key technologists.*
- *Understanding the business's goals and objectives.*
- *Defining the role of technology.*
- *Linking IT staff activities and technologies to the business's goals and objectives.*
- *Addressing the special training needs of IT staff.*

It is redundant to say "business" and "change" in the same sentence when referring to any industry or marketplace. And so it is when considering the IT workforce. There are times when the job market affords an individual greater bargaining power and independence and other times that are more advantageous to the businesses. We can recognize the harvesting of situational benefits by either the individual or the business unit. Importantly, and on the other side of the scale, is the continuance of best practices.

A business utilizing enterprisewide computer systems requires IT professionals who have varying competencies. The traditional skill sets of systems administrator, database administrator (DBA), and developer are a good starting point. However, applications software stretches the required abilities to include an understanding of how the business operates and what software adjustments (setups) are required for proper functional integration as well as how the software and business will interact. To satisfy this requirement, we need yet another skill set—that of the systems analyst.

The demand by the business for increased efficiency coupled with the need to employ IT professionals who possess enhanced skill sets creates an employment environment that fluctuates with the ebb and flow of the economy.

Regardless of the job market, having skilled employees leave a company is a less than desirable circumstance. We must then pay the costs associated with recruiting new associates or perhaps pay high consulting prices. In some cases we may find ourselves having to do both.

So what's a business to do? Avoid the whole mess by retaining its key technologists.

▶ Five Basics for Retaining IT Professionals

On first reading, you may think that the concepts presented here seem rather simple. After all, volumes have been written about, and everyone has been exposed to, the topics of training, communication, leadership, environment, and motivation. However, you should accept the challenge of considering each topic on its own merits as well as how it should be integrated with the other topics. For example, what is (or should be) the relationship between communication and leadership, or motivation, within your own company?

You may be thinking that these seem like the basics. In fact, they are the basics. We can be successful in retaining our employees as part of high-performance teams by reaffirming, applying, and expanding on the basics and by maintaining their proper balance.

Training

IT personnel in general covet training. Training is valued much more highly by IT professionals than by those in other fields. Since existing technology changes rapidly and new technology is constantly being introduced; training is essential to keeping one's skill set current and therefore marketable. An employee with a well-maintained skill set feels confident and employable.

Make training a part of each employee's goals and objectives. There is no better way to communicate your commitment to training. Training requirements must be very specific and not vague objectives that never seem to be accomplished. One of the tricks to planning training for an individual is to approach and resolve it like any other issue. Begin with the desired state: What do you want this employee to be able to do after the training curriculum is complete? The answer will assist you in determining what is needed to achieve your goal of training an individual employee.

To be fully trained on a topic may require that an employee be enrolled in multiple courses and training sessions. Training is available from many sources; vendors and consulting firms are valuable sources, as are independent consultants. Therefore, a comprehensive training plan should be developed for each individual employee. Developing individual training plans for each employee might seem like a large task, but it can be simplified by asking the employees to list the training they think they need to maintain or improve their skill sets. One standard rule always found in corporations is to make certain that training undertaken is job-related. This is necessary to achieve the desired result as well as to justify the cost of the training. Obviously, a company is not in business solely to provide training for its employees. There is the need to ensure that the necessary work of the company is accomplished.

Once individual training plans have been developed, they should be reviewed for commonality so that any economies of scale can be leveraged. (For example, if all employees need "fixed assets" training within a specific software package, perhaps an onsite course should be arranged.)

Training comes in many forms and should always be viewed from the standpoint of the desired end state. From that perspective, the following is a list of different pieces that can be combined to reach that end state, each contributing to the overall training of an employee:

- Half-day seminars (often provided at no charge).
- Vendor sales calls discussing future directions.
- Magazine subscriptions.
- Conferences.
- Lectures.
- Expositions.
- College courses.
- Specialized training courses.

- Visits to other divisions or companies utilizing the same technology.
- Researching an issue or module/product.
- Being teamed with a knowledgeable consultant.

Sometimes the best way to learn is to teach; to provide instruction to a group of people, much preparation is required. The instructor must be organized in terms of what is being presented and must also have comprehensive knowledge of the content. This probably means hands-on activity within the company's own system to do the research, resulting in a course of instruction that is specific to the company's current situation. The effect is quite positive, as most employees can then identify with and relate the training to their everyday work life.

Technical training received by an employee can be leveraged by ensuring that the knowledge gained is transferred to other employees. Aside from reinforcing what has been learned, this activity has the added benefit of making the trained employee feel good. (Hmmm, imagine feeling good while performing a task that provides value to the company.)

Technical training is often a dilemma for an organization because although it is necessary, it also represents cost, including the price charged for the class, the associated travel and living expenses, and the opportunity cost of taking an employee away from the tasks he or she needs to accomplish.

If you are a manager or supervisor, it is up to you to enlist upper management's support to achieve the desired end state. If you are an individual contributor or a "worker bee," it is up to you to help foster the learning environment.

You can have immediate impact in the area of training by utilizing internal resources to increase an employee's knowledge about the processes or issues facing a company. By reserving the first half-hour of staff meetings for training and developing a schedule in cooperation with other departments, you can enable the most knowledgeable person associated with a given process to provide 30 minutes of useful instruction.

Some choose to schedule these training sessions in a sequence that reflects real-world occurrence. This strategy might see a topic of "New Product Development" in one week, followed by "Bill of Material" in the next, and so on. Others organize by functional area; such a schedule might present "Invoicing" one week and "Vendor Check Cutting" the next.

Communication

Many people who have chosen careers as technologists find that a large part of their communication is with a machine rather than another human being. Companies believe that communication, both written and oral, is so important that they include it as a requirement in job descriptions. Some even have it on their annual evaluation forms.

Communication is vital to employee retention. The flow of information must be bidirectional, with some regularity. If this is not the case, how will the manager or supervisor even know that there is an issue, let alone what to do about it? To cover this topic prior to the arrival of the next millennium, we restrict ourselves here to communications between supervisor and employee.

Too little attention is paid to the definition of "effective communication." Often, when a convincing memo is written or an audience is captivated by a powerful presentation, it is said that effective communication has taken place. While this may be true for that particular occurrence, communication with our employees can be evaluated only as the sum total of all contact, or lack thereof, that we have with them—measured by the changes in their behavior that the communication was intended to effect.

You can communicate with employees by many methods, and each should be used to enrich the communications link between employees (usually not an issue), between managers and their employees, and between the company and its employees.

To make effective use of various communication methods, you must first understand the elements of communication. More than one book has made reference to the following four elements, which must be present for communication to be possible:

- Message—An idea, concept, or some other form of notification.
- Transmitter—Someone or something that originates and sends the message.

- Receiver—Someone or something that gets the message.
- Medium—The means or vehicle by which the message is sent.

Note that the presence of these four elements does not guarantee that communication will occur or be effective. To quickly illustrate this point, picture a manager telling his staff in a meeting that on Saturday they must begin planning a software upgrade. At this point, we have all four elements present. The *transmitter* was the manager, the *message* was to begin planning the upgrade on Saturday, the *receiver* was the manager's staff, and the *medium* was the spoken word.

The two missing elements that can verify whether communication has occurred and was effective are *feedback* and *action*. In the above example, if the meeting adjourned with no further communication, feedback did not occur. If on Monday, however, the manager discovers that the upgrade planning was started on Saturday, then that action makes it obvious that the communication occurred and was effective. It is a good practice to follow up on action and at the very least on feedback.

The circumstances surrounding the communication medium can enhance the message being sent. Imagine a singing telegram: ⊷*Your sister Pearl is dead*⊶. While a singing telegram may be a fun and effective way to deliver some messages, it is important to ensure that the medium utilized is appropriate to the message being sent. Aside from singing telegrams, some ideas on other effective forms of messages and mediums that can be implemented with little planning and almost no cost follow.

Employees always appreciate recognition of an anniversary date with the company. Even if this is an employee's first or second anniversary, the occasion is a good opportunity not only to recognize service, but to praise employees for the work that they have been doing. A one-page letter of three paragraphs works best. The first and last paragraphs can be standardized to discuss the state of the company and the future of the company respectively. The middle paragraph should be used to personalize the letter by choosing something that has been successful because of the employee's involvement.

Birthday wishes from the boss are always a welcome communication when done tastefully. A simple email at the beginning of the day provides the sentiment. Additionally, when the employee runs into the boss later that day, the opportunity arises to briefly exchange pleasantries that are not work-related.

Staff meetings are the old standby and should always be held with regular frequency (same day and same time). These meetings are extremely important, not only to communication, but to leadership, environment, and good chemistry as well.

Another effective method of communication is the 10-minute stand-up meeting. This type of meeting can provide a quick update of what has occurred over the last day and may also be used to outline expectations for the next day. This is an excellent time to praise an employee in front of peers. Short meetings such as this can also be used as abbreviated awards ceremonies.

The "skip level meeting" is an outstanding mechanism for a supervisor to communicate with the employees of his or her direct reports. The purpose of these meetings is for small groups of employees (five to seven) to meet with their bosses' boss. Such encounters are not intended to undermine anyone's authority; when used properly, in fact, they can assist the management team in resolving issues before they become exacerbated.

A last communication method worth mentioning is the "management by walking around" concept. Making the rounds (daily) to exchange a few words with each employee serves a number of purposes and spills over into other areas discussed later in this chapter. Daily rounds assist the manager in developing an employee's review and help ensure that the review, even if only provided annually, is not a surprise to the employee. The amount of time to be spent with each individual will work itself out; not every employee must be seen every day.

Leadership

Managers and leaders who have had to choose between saying "follow me" or "take that hill" may not learn anything in this section. Social climbers may not either, but for different reasons. Leadership means "guiding or conducting in a certain course, or to a certain place or end, by making the way known, or showing the way." Sometimes leadership means directing with authority, and in those situations, actions by a leader should be so strong and distinct that people automatically follow.

Employees look for and need leadership. They want to be guided or have the way made known to them. This does not mean that an employee wants to be told exactly what to do and when to do it.

Leadership or management style has always had an effect or impact on employees. As a manager, you have many situational predicaments to tackle; an employee's attitude is reflective of the leadership you provide in doing so. The character that you display is what employees will sit in judgment of or follow. Nobody wants to work for a screamer.

Being a feared, short-term, on-the-edge, moving and shaking "taskmaster" may appear useful when the company is experiencing a crisis, but even if it is, how will employees ever get anything accomplished during normal times? We should never forget that things must get done, but the discussion is leadership and not task completion. Too frequently, people who can bully others into doing something, but are without leadership qualities, attempt to redefine management and leadership. To provide leadership, IT managers must meld their understanding of the company's goals and objectives with a definition of the role technology plays in that plan and link these directly to the activities expected of the employee.

All managers and leaders will agree that some degree of planning is necessary. The depth with which a plan is developed is completely dependent upon the organization. Imagine trying to do a conference room pilot without first attempting to define what needed to be tested. Chaos would soon reign, and the complexities associated with thoroughly testing the technology would become overwhelming.

Having the employee participate in planning is always possible at some level, but communicating how the employee's assignment fits into the high-level plan is often overlooked. Leaders should avoid falling into the trap of believing that the employee knows how his or her individual contribution will assist the company or department in meeting its goals. Besides, this is five minutes of conversation that will provide the guidance and stability that employees seek. Should any leader risk *not* spending that five minutes? Once the employee knows what is in store over the next quarter and year, and how she fits within the plan, she will begin to support that position, perform the necessary detailed planning, and attempt to achieve the desired results.

Keeping the work organized for the DBA, system administrator, and other technical associates is paramount to retaining your technology employees. The employee must be kept busy with meaningful work. To handle certain times when workflow is ebbing (usually because something required is not yet available), the leader must plan ahead.

The importance of documentation is common knowledge, as is the fact that most IT organizations are behind in this portion of their responsibilities. If the manager consistently stresses the importance of documentation, the stage is set for two events. First, when the workload is down, the manager can direct that work be performed on documentation. Second, since it has been given a degree of importance, it will not seem such a lackluster task.

As the leader, you play many roles. As the supervisor, you must ensure that a productive and motivated team is being maintained and that the right project is delegated to the right person. There are times when you must delegate and empower others to get the job done. You must be able to turn over entire tasks with confidence.

There are also times when you must turn employee conflict into productive action. This may mean handling difficult people and situations for a win-win result and will require utilizing more than one of your leadership capabilities. There may be still other times when you must become a worker on the team. One example might be a manager who jumps in at the appropriate time and writes a specification for a developer. This action will enhance your leadership position because it saved the analyst time and made the developer more productive by allowing him to get to work much sooner.

The organization of your employees will also be a factor in retaining them. Don't be afraid to assign titles such as Technical Lead or Team Leader of Manufacturing Modules. Of course, such titles must reflect not only the employees' positions, but also the actual job content they fulfill. Having more prestigious or important-sounding titles should not offend anyone.

A leader is only as good as the team he or she creates. The better the team, the more will be accomplished—and the less time required.

Environment

Titles were discussed in the previous section, but not the appropriate structuring of an organization to accomplish its task(s) and the resulting effects of structure on the people involved. It is important to look at the approach to *process*—that is, how the task is accomplished, including how people relate to each other and the interpersonal dynamics that occur.

Any IT shop will find itself somewhere on the managerial grid shown in Figure 10–1. This grid has been adapted and modified from *The Managerial Grid* by R. Blake and J. Mouton.

Absentee Manager: Does the bare minimum in terms of visibility and exerts just enough effort to get required work done. The management style is to stay out of trouble and not make waves. This manager is about making resources "appear" busy and will merely put people on a job. There is little consideration for skill sets because the manager allows people to do the job, or not do the job, as they see fit. This can lead to great difficulty with the applications as well as with the functional end users.

Cruise Ship Director: This style values people more than the accomplishment of the task and provides security, comfort, and ease for

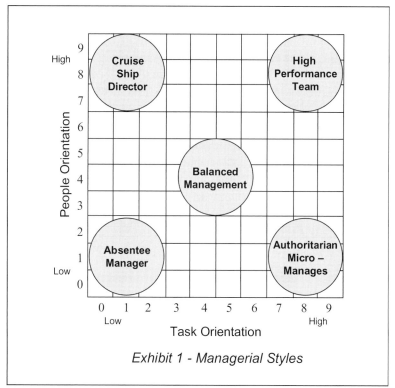

Exhibit 1 - Managerial Styles

Figure 10–1 Managerial styles.

employees. It provides thoughtful attention to the needs of people for satisfying relationships and leads to a comfortable, friendly, organizational atmosphere and work tempo. Employees in turn will be intensely loyal and therefore will accomplish their jobs without undue coercion or pressure. Care must be taken here to ensure that goals are established and that employees understand what is expected of them and feel as though they are making progress both as individuals and as a team.

Authoritarian Manager: This style is characterized by a low concern for people and a high concern for producing. As long as everyone agrees with the boss, there won't be a problem. However, employees are asked to buy into the underlying assumption that they are truly subordinate and inferior to the boss, and obedient performance is the watchword. It is implied that deviation from the above will result in retribution up to and including termination. Choosing or allowing this scenario will definitely result in high employee turnover and its associated costs on all fronts—dollars, morale, productivity, and customer service.

Balanced Management: This style of management balances the maintenance of morale with the need to complete work, using a different mode than the others of addressing the conflict between task and people. The cruise ship director resolves this conflict by siding with the people, while the authoritarian manager doesn't care about the people and so prefers to side with the task, and the absentee manager, if even aware of the issue, withdraws from the battle and doesn't attempt to address the conflict. In contrast, the balanced manager realizes that people know they must get their jobs done and so assumes a "half and half" position of attempting to balance the needs of the employees and the need to get out work. This can be effective, especially when the manager is adept at shifting the balance to fit the situation. For example, during an upgrade period, more focus might be placed on task while empathizing with the employees and helping them to see light at the end of the upgrade tunnel.

High-Performance Team Management: This style is qualitatively and quantitatively different from the other four in that the others make the basic assumption of an inherent distinction between the needs of the individual and the needs of the organization. The high-performance manager lives and breathes the belief that the needs of the organization and the needs of the employee can be integrated by involving people in making decisions about the strategies and conditions of work. The basic goal here is to achieve high productivity and high morale. This is obviously the best place to be if employees are to be retained.

Notwithstanding the above, it has been my experience that management is highly situational, with the current circumstances often driving the requisite management mode. In other words, while it is generally desirable to strive to be a high-performance manager, the situation may require an authoritarian style until the environment changes sufficiently to warrant another approach. This is particularly true in turnaround situations.

This situational condition can also hold true at the individual employee level; some people require a more hands-on management style than others. Effective management of the IT workforce occurs when the management mode aligns with—and stays aligned with—the situation being managed.

Motivation

The difference between *vocation* and *avocation* is one letter, but oddly enough, this addition does not create an antonym or opposite. These two words are related and are key to understanding motivation. *Vocation* is most often associated with occupation or profession; if an individual is extremely motivated, it may become a pursuit or calling. *Avocation* is thought of as a pastime or hobby, but again, depending on the intensity, may become a sideline or side interest. The difference, then, is that one is work and the other is play. Employees are self-motivated when they enjoy what they are doing. In order for a manager to motivate an employee, the question of how to enjoy work as much as play must be answered.

Mark Twain captured the essence of this in his book *Tom Sawyer*. As punishment for something he has done, Tom is assigned the task of whitewashing a fence. As Tom stands there, not very motivated, with paint brush in hand, a friend arrives on the scene and asks him to go fishing. But Tom says he doesn't want to because he's painting the fence. The friend is incredulous and says, "But ain't that work?" Tom replies that he's having a great time and soon convinces his friend that painting the fence is actually fun. The friend wants a turn with the brush, but Tom hesitates, saying that while this is fun, the end result is extremely important and must reek of excellence. Over a short period of time, a group of friends who have paid for the privilege of painting the fence is assembled, and the task is accomplished in a fraction of the time, leaving Tom free to go and see his best friend—Huck Finn.

Tom's original task was to paint the fence white, not to see Huck. But he was clever enough to present this task as both fun and extremely important. He had to do some "selling," but this was overcome based on the relationship and trust that Tom had with the people whom he wanted to paint the fence for him.

This scene is directly applicable to an IT shop. There are many ways to "sell" a task that needs to be accomplished. Motivating employees is an everyday task, but not every employee must be motivated every day. Additionally, some employees (self-starters) may seem to require less attention than others, but don't fall into the trap of impoverishing that employee. Everyone has an ego and likes to receive feedback. Listed below are seven possibilities that may help motivate employees in different situations and circumstances:

1. Explain the longer range reason(s) why a task must be undertaken. Sometimes it is helpful to show that while this task seems small or meaningless, it is a building block for other activities. Perhaps it is a gating item for other dependent tasks. This is certainly the simplest and most straightforward method of motivating an employee. As a coach or mentor (to all of his or her direct report employees), the leader/manager can help the employee develop the innate capability to discern such reasons on his own. Over a period of time, the employee will learn to recognize the impact this particular task will have on the business. Once the employee harnesses this ability, the next logical step is to learn to prioritize those activities that have a greater impact. Eventually, return on information technology (ROIT) will take on a whole new meaning.

2. Evangelize the value or importance of what the employee is doing, even if only with the employee. This is effective in making an employee believe that the current task she has undertaken is the most important activity occurring at the company. While many tasks are important, some are less visible and therefore have a higher likelihood of going unnoticed or unattended to by managers. Functional users always want to obtain the result of

the task at hand. Typically, it is the functional user who generates the requirement upon which the employee is working. Taking the opportunity to evangelize the importance of a task while the employee is together with the functional user may create some excitement and synergy related to the task.

3. Explain how the completion of this task will make for a happy functional end user. This is a good motivator for those employees who are service-oriented and also works well for employees who are image- or reputation-conscious. Because enterprise requirements planning (ERP) systems are integrated packages, actions taken by employees are visible to the functional end user (quite possibly in many disciplines). Positive reinforcement upon task completion will make it that much easier to motivate the employee the next time this technique is be used.

4. Make the completion of tasks a game or form of competition. This can be accomplished in many ways. A few examples include issuing a challenge that refers to how quickly this or a similar task has been accomplished in the past; indicating that completing this task by a given date will reap a reward; and providing the information that another company took five months to do the 10.7 upgrade, while we're scheduled to do it in three. Care should be exercised with this technique, as the manager does not want to pit one employee against another in a negative fashion or create any other form of unhealthy competition.

5. Appeal to employee professionalism, or ask that a task be accomplished to maintain a standard. This approach is in the gray area as to whether it has enough positive effects. Improper presentation of this concept could leave the employee thinking that there is no good reason to be undertaking this particular task. Certainly professionalism and a sense of pride are positive, and if maintaining the standard is contributing to the overall strength of a position or capability, then it is also viewed as a good thing. When this approach is used, therefore, care should be exercised to ensure that the employee sees the result as a positive contribution.

6. Clarify that performing this task now will make life easier or more efficient later. This motivational scenario attempts to sell short-term pain for long-term gain. This is further down the fun scale and definitely has some negative connotations. What is being sold here is "let me tell you how wonderful things are

going to be," which requires that the manager be a skillful salesperson, since the benefit is deferred and gratification is not instant, but could be postponed for quite a while.

7. Identify the task as something that is not fun but must be done. This is the "It's a dirty job, but somebody's gotta do it" scenario. While at first glance this appears to be a negative scenario, it does have positive points if presented correctly. For example, if an employee is the only logical person to complete the task, it can be sold as "You're the only one who can do this job, and it's lucky for the firm that it has an employee such as you with this capability." If the job requires that more than one person be assigned, this can also serve as an excellent team building element.

No matter which scenario the manager is presenting, the sell must ring true. When we talk of "selling" something to an employee, we are talking about packaging the truth (that is, that a task or tasks must be completed) in a manner that is acceptable to the employee.

▶ A Can-Do Attitude Cannot Be Beat

When you are "down on somebody," it is too easy to forget that almost everyone has a high opinion of himself or herself. Some may be more humble than others, but the book *In Search of Excellence* [Peters, 1988] cites a psychological study in which a random sampling of male adults were asked to rank themselves on their ability to get along with others, and all participants ranked themselves in the top 10 percent. Hold on, because more than 25 percent of the participants were so humble that they ranked themselves in the top 1 percent of the population. Other extracts from the study show that when asked about leadership, 70 percent rated themselves in the top 25 percent of the population, and on the athletic ability front, 60 percent thought they were in the top 25 percent of the population.

The lesson here is to take advantage of this innate opinion that people have of themselves. Set goals that not only can be met but exceeded. If goals are set so high that only 60 percent of the employees meet their goals, do the other 40 percent feel as though they have failed? The employees must be helped to think of themselves as winners.

When employees are asked to do self-evaluations, they tend to be hard on themselves. However, they also tend to act in accordance with the image that they have of themselves, which is more in line with the previously mentioned study. If the employee believes himself to be well regarded and trusted, he will work hard to maintain or perpetuate this image. All of the things that can be done to foster this belief—public recognition, title changes, delegated authority, spot awards, simple compliments, certificates, commendations, and of course raises—play an important role in how an employee sees himself and thus in how productive he will be.

An employee must be someone who can be trusted and relied upon, because the composite of the individual employees reflects the overall quality of the operation. If you see eye-to-eye on priorities, share a similar approach to problem solving, and have good rapport, you will generally click together and confidence will grow.

Modern-day managers have figured out the balance and hierarchy of the decisions that are appropriate to manage employees in a participative manner. Employees will surprise their management if given the opportunity. Most importantly, when employees are positioned for success, they will work exceptionally hard to show that the manager is doing the right thing in this positioning.

▶ Conclusions

Experience is the best instructor, and if you are a faithful student, the lessons learned will always be with you. Employee qualifications, including properly managing technical personnel, are always a necessity in the IT field. In any particular IT shop the same principles apply, but the stakes have been raised. It is paramount that executive management has the right leadership in place. This is a cardinal truth. It's just too easy for an employee to walk down the street and begin his or her next job.

Training and an understanding of the influence it can have upon the IT employee cannot be overstated. In some cases, training may be the single most important item that an employee considers when taking, leaving, or remaining in a position.

Open and honest communication is the fuel that makes things happen. Employees are as capable as anyone else of determining when they are given the straight scoop. The grapevine is alive and well wherever there is a population of employees. Be proactive, communicate with your employees, and take charge of the influence that the grapevine may exert.

Leadership comes in many forms but boils down to one's ability to have others follow or in some manner perform the activities desired. To have a leader, there must be respect. To have a follower, there must be respect. The leader may have to trust and respect first. In the Army's Officer's Guide of 1894, the following quotation can be found: "Enlisted men are stupid, but they are sly and cunning, and bear considerable watching." To practice leadership under that pretense will leave little time to actually lead.

Without a leadership or management style, any given IT shop will still have an environment, but it is difficult to know what that environment would look like. Leaders do not leave the environment to chance but rather create the environment in which they and their employees operate. This is probably the biggest value-add item that a manager can contribute.

The seven techniques of motivating employees provide guidelines only; motivation of an employee more often than not is situational. Good managers, who know their employees, can be extremely effective at triggering an employee into action. Managers accomplish this either by inspiring an employee or by using one of the other techniques.

A can-do attitude is a contagious thing yet must be ignited by someone or some group. Being creative in thought and "off the wall" in discussion costs nothing. Employees should be trusted associates and view their manager as an "honest broker" between themselves and the company.

Strategic Planning

by Maureen Vavra and Dean Lane

With extensive strategic planning experience, Maureen Vavra underscores the importance of thinking strategically. Strategic planning is an essential skill. CIOs are playing a greater role in corporate planning because critical business processes rely on the IT infrastructure.

Strategic planning cannot be done in isolation. As Dean Lane points out, successful CIOs have a unique ability to integrate strategic planning with other key skills, such as project management and leadership.

This chapter explores how to align and integrate strategic business and IT plans, and describes various planning approaches, models, and methodologies. Vavra and Lane discuss:

- *Why planning skills and strategic thinking are more valuable than published plans and strategic roadmaps.*

- *How successful CIOs are able to develop an understanding of business goals and key processes.*

- *How to develop a common framework for thinking and "building the muscle" to effectively respond to constant challenges.*

- *How strategic business and IT planning can operate as a system.*

- *Models for strategic IT planning and how to implement them.*

- *Why and how setting priorities and managing the project portfolio should be done strategically as well as tactically.*
- *How to set priorities and align them with the annual budgeting process.*

When I was working in telecom in the late 1980s, I ran a large development division in customer records processing in the usual reactionary manner. My district teams were in love-hate relationships with marketing over new billing products, and all of us were working weekends trying to comply with contradictory CPUC and FCC mandates. Additionally, we were pushing QA and QC so our developers wouldn't screw up the 11 million bills we generated monthly, while observing budget rituals and headcount tallying matches in the unique manner of public utilities.

At that time, companies still launched large teams to prepare for major projects, and so strategic planning for a new revenue-generating initiative got started—in a separate division staffed with several bright new district managers and a host of analysts. They studied customer preferences and trends, economic forecasts, competitive position, sales volumes, the regulatory climate, our own strengths and weaknesses, and made enough graphs, pictures and slides to fill three conference rooms. They developed plans and proposals, held regular steering committee meetings, and gave executive presentations. For six months this went on, and some excellent planning was done, but the business couldn't seem to get on with sponsoring the changes.

Then the corporate (and probably regulatory) priorities changed, and some of the ideas that had been studied became compelling. I was moved to head the division and asked to come up with an implementation plan within a month, reorganize the division for action, and get the thing moving. Until that point, my definition of strategic leadership had consisted of checking to be sure each of my districts looked far enough ahead to find separate long weekends for their major system conversions. Fortunately for me, an excellent foundation *had* been laid, and this talented group knew enough about the strategic options for us to put together a solid plan for the three-year effort needed. Adding direction, urgency, and some movers and shakers to the mix got us kick-started properly.

That experience convinced me of the importance of being *able* to think strategically about my company—having the tools and the information in hand before the need arose. I think planning strategically for IT in business involves both a key skill and a knowledge base that must be kept current. In addition, these must be augmented with practical implementation experience and project management skill to be effective. If we have all that, we are conditioned for the "career opportunities" that suddenly emerge when market or competitive conditions provide a catalyst.

▶ Chapter Profile

This chapter takes the position that although published plans and strategic roadmaps are useful, planning skills and the capability for strategic thinking have the most significant value to the CIO, both personally and within the IT organization. To quote another leader, "In preparing for battle I have always found that plans are useless, but planning is indispensable."[1]

The chapter discusses the CIO's role in corporate planning and reviews survey results from the members of our Community of Practice (CoP) regarding how they choose to use their expertise to influence their corporations in business planning. It includes an overview of how business strategic planning and IT plans operate within a system, and various approaches to setting strategic goals and objectives are outlined.

The chapter also surveys the biases and approaches of several planning models as they pertain to IT and suggests that external resources be consulted for detailed planning methodologies and templates. There are also references to the budget and architecture chapters.

Several planning checklists are provided as well as a section on managing to plans and milestones. The chapter emphasizes the importance of setting priorities and managing the project portfolio in a strategic manner, and it suggests methods for prioritizing multiple projects in alignment with annual budgeting.

The chapter concludes with a "big picture" slide that discusses how planning interrelates at various levels and how metrics and feedback loops contribute to the effectiveness of the process.

---

1. Dwight D. Eisenhower, *The Columbia Dictionary of Quotations,* 1993, 1995, Columbia University Press.

The CIO's Planning Role within the Business

As CIO, you work actively in two planning domains, and these complement one another. At the executive level, CIOs are usually members of the senior team, called upon to provide input and judgment in strategic planning efforts and key business decisions, particularly those that involve infrastructure or technological change. You also lead strategic planning for Information Systems.

The title Chief Information Officer has certain implications relating to expectations regarding what you bring into the executive meeting room to improve the quality of plans made. By the very nature of the job, CIOs have wide and timely access to information, metrics about performance and the effectiveness of processes, and a broad view of the business and its requirements for its systems. Your company will benefit if you build an organization that monitors key pulse points of the business and stays informed of major changes, shifts in emphasis, opportunities, and risks. This information is vital to good planning.

CIOs are also called upon, often with the CTO, to provide direction about the opportunities and pitfalls represented by new systems, approaches, and technical advances, as well as acquisitions that involve technology. To support this, architecture teams and senior technical resources must stay conversant with technology advances in germane areas.

Fulfilled properly, the CIO's position as the leader of strategic planning for IT can provide a constant source of the up-to-date information needed to perform these executive roles proactively. Correspondingly, you must have systems plans within your shop.

This chapter does not tout the virtues of the bound, finished IT strategic plan. If you end up with a formal plan at all, that is a bonus, but it is not essential. That ultimate finished plan can be a formidable task and the weight of it a barrier to what absolutely *must* develop: an understanding of business goals and key processes coupled with a habit of strategic thinking about IT at all organizational levels.

On both counts, the most important product of strategic planning is creating a common framework of thinking and "building the muscle" for effectively responding to the constant challenges. CIOs and IT teams must be poised to react strategically when faced with a business imperative that demands systems innovation or a pure technical opportunity—and you cannot predict when those challenges will show up.

Therefore, a strategic approach to the tactical work of doing the day-to-day job is what's important: the infiltration of directional thinking in our organizations so that business analysts, applications developers, and systems engineers—the people who do "real work"—know what the direction is and what imperatives are critical to sustaining strategic thrust.

▶ Business Strategizing

Follow the Corporate Strategic Plan?

One of the reasons I don't emphasize the formal IT strategic plan is that most of us in the CIO CoP have not seen consistency in the requisite formal business planning within our organizations. In an internal survey of the CoP membership performed in late 2002, I found that less than 40 percent of us have worked in corporations in which formal business plans were maintained.

Judy Armstrong, CIO of Benchmark Consulting, comments, "I think the least valuable planning tool is a formal documented strategic plan. My reason is that it changes often due to many factors, and as long as you have a regular planning process, executive session follow-up, and the measurements and budget implications in place, that should be enough documentation."

We all see a much higher incidence of regularly scheduled business planning sessions that generate less formalized strategic direction but produce long-term action items, and we value this most highly. Next most useful to our CIO group is strategic business planning, which occurs as a component of regular executive committee meetings.

As Judy mentions, flow-through of strategies to budgets and key corporate measurement systems are important, but our group found those follow-up measures to be even less prevalent as by-products of planning than the formal plans are. A warning message is clear from this: *If strategic direction warrants heavy expenditure in new or renovated systems or infrastructure, you must take steps to ensure that the impact is reflected in the capital and long-range budget forecast.* It might be handy, too, to see that there are measurements in place to drive the right behavior and quantify success.

Later in the chapter, we explore various planning methodologies and how they work for both corporate-level planning and the creation of IT-specific roadmaps. But first, let's delve more deeply into what happens in those executive sessions that chart strategic direction and what we are expected to bring to the table.

How CIOs Influence Strategy

The survey mentioned earlier also asked the CoP membership to rate ten activities in terms of their strategic importance to the CIO's role in business today and how they choose to influence their corporations as they compose plans or make key decisions. The group assigned the order of importance to the activities listed in Table 11–1.

Table 11–1

1. TIME TO MARKET OR CYCLE TIME REDUCTION, AND AUTOMATION TO ACHIEVE THIS.

2. SPONSORING DATA/INFORMATION AS A CORPORATE RESOURCE

3. COST REDUCTION (FOR EXAMPLE, TCO EMPHASIS, ERP, HELP DESK SOLUTION COST CONTAINMENT).

4. BUSINESS PROCESS DEFINITION VIA CREATION OF BUSINESS MODELS AND RULES.

5. USING TECHNOLOGY AS A STRATEGIC BUSINESS DRIVER; FINDING OR SPONSORING THE "KILLER APPLICATION"

6. FOCUS—PORTFOLIO MANAGEMENT, ARCHITECTURE DIRECTION, STANDARDIZING TECHNOLOGIES.

7. INNOVATION, R&D, PREPARATION FOR TECHNICAL BREAKTHROUGHS OR COMPETITION.

8. CHAMPIONING METRICS AND CORPORATE PERFORMANCE TO KPIS.

9. ACQUISITION DECISIONS OR SUPPORT AND INTEGRATION OF MERGERS.

10. OUTSOURCING RECOMMENDATIONS.

These results should be viewed in the appropriate context of economic cycles. The survey was taken at a time of significant downturn, one that has severely impacted our CoP companies in the Silicon Valley.

Given that, the emphasis on cycle time reduction and cost reduction are not surprising. Cycle time and processing efficiency have been consistent opportunities for IT to value-add, so the relative rank could be expected to hold up in flush or lean years. In better times, the cost reduction activity might slip down a few notches in favor of higher placement for business process improvement, which is often related to cycle time, or "killer apps," R&D, or acquisitions.

What is heartening is the high ranking we continue to give to the importance of viewing data and information as a corporate resource. Most of us agree with Jim Cates, CIO of Brocade, when he says, "If corporations do not master the effective use of business intelligence applications, they will be destined to wander inefficiently among the piles of automated data being created in their environments." This topic gets more in-depth coverage from Jim Cates in Chapter 16, which discusses the Ladder of Business Intelligence (LOBI) model.

The list of 10 activities is a useful one to test within your company and as the business climate changes. You may need to build capability in your organization or refresh your own knowledge of these areas as priorities fluctuate.

Systems Planning and the Business

If you think of the word "system" in the sense of "solar," your position as a CIO is optimal. You have a view of the critical operational and functional systems, a request list that describes most of the business priorities for change, and access to data that measures application and business performance. In addition, your planning and portfolio management processes are vitally linked to those of the business.

The IT strategic planning process linkages diagram in Figure 11–1 depicts the dynamic environment that the CIO can leverage—various business aspects and activities that interconnect and potentially contribute to sustaining a strategic approach to systems. We refer to it in several of our discussions to align subjects and approaches, because it is the synergistic view of all these components that provides your best opportunity.

The center elements are tangibles—articulated business strategies and models, architectures, core infrastructure, application strategies, and, ultimately, discrete IT projects that achieve those strategies in the form of tangible deliverables: production systems. The model works when

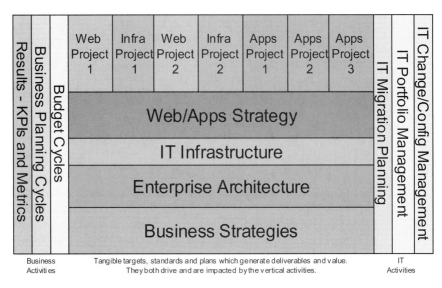

Results - KPIs and Metrics	Business Planning Cycles	Budget Cycles	Web Project 1	Infra Project 1	Web Project 2	Infra Project 2	Apps Project 1	Apps Project 2	Apps Project 3	IT Migration Planning	IT Portfolio Management	IT Change/Config Management
			Web/Apps Strategy									
			IT Infrastructure									
			Enterprise Architecture									
			Business Strategies									

Business Activities   Tangible targets, standards and plans which generate deliverables and value. They both drive and are impacted by the vertical activities.   IT Activities

Figure 11–1   IT strategic planning process linkages.

foundational business strategies and architectures are defined and mapped so that the upper-level strategies and funded projects can set clear goals and scope, which achieve the direction stated in the lower boxes, usually in a series of 6- to 12-month increments.

The vertical components of this dynamic represent ongoing processes and cycles that constantly affect the center elements. On the left, quantified results, business plans, and budget cycles have a clear influence on all the center elements, though not necessarily at a "bottom-up" level. They can cut across the strata. For example, a budget reduction can unfund a key project, regardless of its importance to overall business goals or to other projects underway. Similarly, a business plan that introduces new technology or an acquisition can blow your architecture infrastructure wide open. The survival of your strategic work in IT depends upon your ability to anticipate, adjust, and rework the center model to realign with major changes. You and your key people must understand how this all fits together, and your understanding should influence how you perform several IT functions, such as architectural planning, budgeting, and business case management for projects impacting IT, as well as how project lifecycles are managed.

The right-side verticals, which become more operational in focus as you look further to the right, represent IT internal processes that you must have in place in order to evolve and control systems. These work alongside the business-oriented verticals and support them. IT migration planning moves your platform to target architectures and systems via sequenced implementation of key projects. Portfolio management ensures that your spending is the proper mix of investment (development or implementation of key packages) and maintenance, and is measured against goals. Finally, change and configuration management control quality, and protect the production systems from chaotic implementations that can disrupt service levels and customer satisfaction.

Departmental IT Models

There is a certain amount of "departmental computing" in every organization now, especially with the proliferation of intranets, simple-to-use Web authoring tools, and automated publishing. This is healthy and enabling for the organization if it is managed within the venue of the IT guidelines. A planning challenge associated with your IT architecture and standards function is to set up appropriate principles (especially in reference to data stewardship, security, and SLAs) to bound departmental computing and to determine when an application can cross from departmental to systemwide in scope. In polite circles, this is sometimes associated with the notion of herding cats.

IT Plans in a Technology-Oriented Company

If you are the CIO of a technology-oriented company that is heavily involved in hardware or software manufacture, distribution, or consulting, you have a unique set of opportunities and challenges. Because there tends to be significantly more IT capability spread all over the organization, this environment can look like departmental computing gone mad, with servers and systems spun up outside the production environment in "R&D mode." The resultant configuration and security issues may well fall to your department to resolve, so it is better to work with these efforts in the planning stages, to set boundaries and allocate roles and resources. The problem will be finding out about them soon enough.

In general, the more open everyone can be about end goals, the better. As CIO, you have legitimate concerns if systems are being developed that will ultimately affect your production environment; if this is the case, you'll want them to follow some level of internal standards and produce deliverables that can be checked against architectural and other requirements. In fact, you may want to jointly plan for environments to support these systems from the beginning and allocate your own resources to ensure technology transfer.

If your business is creating systems or software that has no bearing on your internal environment, a more hands-off approach can be taken, and you'll need to pick your battles. Don't forget possible software linkages to your corporate CRM, user registration, help desk, and accounts payable systems; however, as these e-business interfaces are often touchpoints, your systems must eventually accommodate.

Finally, one way to operate proactively in a technology-oriented company is to serve as a beta customer for your own products. This allows you an early view into internal technology research, development, and marketing roles, and affords your team the opportunity to see if things are as "transparent to IT" as is usually advertised. It also builds a solid bond between these corporate technical resources and offers a career path for some of your "stars," who will remain eternally loyal.

▶ Approaches to Setting Strategic Goals and Objectives

There are various documented approaches to planning, many supported by highly academic models. We discuss a sampling here. Most of the better-known methods are useful and offer the advantages of existing templates to reuse, published books and articles, trained consultants who can help, defined metrics, and existing models or benchmarks for comparison.

These methods may be used for corporate planning as well as planning at the department level. This means that you may see (as inputs to your plans and architecture models) documents from various planning methodologies coming from the executive level or from a key business unit, which has a strategic mission and goals that require IT support. In many cases, that information provides ground-level strategies for the IT systems roadmaps that you create. Of course, many of these tools are equally useful for the initial steps of planning for systems, too, and you may elect to use some of them internally.

It is important for you to be aware that each method views the IT function slightly differently, and there are imbedded biases. Be sure that the planning process is not making assumptions about IT that misrepresent your organization or its value. Most planning tools pinpoint the customer interface as a key component but must also regard the underlying systems and infrastructure that support customer contact with equal value *and must sustain their service levels.*

It is essential to tie IT architecture and infrastructure planning to the deliverables of formal or informal corporate planning initiatives. They provide you with clear statements of sanctioned direction with the expectation of action and formal project initiation.

Traditional Models

Traditional strategic planning includes organized processes for developing mission and goals; external and internal analysis; environmental scans and resource audits; developing objectives and strategic actions; developing action plans; implementation; monitoring; and updating. Some aspects of the processes and activities that follow are present in any planning effort. See Table 11–2.

Visionary strategic planning is oriented toward a desired end state, consensus on establishing a vision of that, strategic action development and action assessment, evaluation, and implementation. It is a top-down model that deals authoritatively with the type of indecision many corporations face at one time or another: Alice's quandary in Lewis Carroll's *Alice in Wonderland* is instructive:

- "Would you tell me, please, which way I ought to go from here?"
- "That depends a good deal on where you want to get to," said the Cat.
- "I don't much care where—" said Alice.
- "Then it doesn't matter which way you go," said the Cat.

Economic development planning is oriented toward economic development or reaction to economic circumstances. Units include starting with the economic base, analyzing current economic development efforts, identifying SWOTs (strengths, weaknesses, opportunities, and threats), inventorying programs and projects, setting priorities, strategic action ranking, project/program analysis, and strategic action

Table 11–2   Strategic planning.

VISION AND MISSION STATEMENT
Identification of the vision and mission is the initial step of strategic planning. The vision identifies the reasons for the organization's existence and the "ideal" end state that it aims to achieve; the mission identifies key goals and performance objectives. Both are defined within the framework of the company's philosophy, and are used as a context for more focused goals and strategy development and assessment.

GOALS, STRATEGIES, and MEASURES
Focused long-range goals, preferably framed in "what by when" terms, are key to achieving the mission. These should be clear and actionable, and lead to the formulation of strategies for achievement. Metrics should be identified—both Key Performance Indicators for measuring goal achievement and performance, but also measures of *directional movement* when strategies require this.

ENVIRONMENTAL ASSESSMENT
Analysis of the external and internal environment— the SWOT analysis (described later)—is a good tool for organizing internal data. The environmental scan, performed within the framework of a tool like scenario analysis, produces information about an organization's external environment (economic, social, political, demographic, legal, technological, and global factors), the industry, and organizational factors.

GAP ANALYSIS
This is an evaluation of the difference between the vision and desired end state and the current position. It sets the stage to develop specific strategies, plans, and timelines, as well as allocation of resources to close the gap and achieve the desired goals as measures define them.

MIGRATION PLAN
The actual plan, usually a series of projects with prerequisites clearly identified and sequenced deliverables that are intended to achieve the mid-term goals identified by the gap analysis. Includes resource plans, budget requirements, and a vehicle for portfolio-managing the key projects that are on the critical path to achieving the goals.

BENCHMARKING
Measuring and comparing initial plans, results, performance, operations, practices, and aspects like TCO against those of other organizations helps establish operational objectives or identify "best" practices. This process can also jumpstart planning by providing a reference point for setting strategic goals and targets as well as implementation timelines.   It is especially useful if the comparison is with a competitor.

implementation. It includes a number of suggested model forms for use.

Situational Analysis: The SWOT Model

SWOT analysis identifies factors that may affect the organization's performance and achievements. The SWOT model is based on identifying strengths and weaknesses internal to the company and delineating external threats and opportunities. The model represents information in a way that makes it convenient to think about critical success factors and core competencies that have strategic value. SWOT is an effective tool for balancing internal and external factors in strategic planning.[2] A sample result is shown in Table 11–3.

Table 11–3   Sample SWOT analysis,

STRENGTHS	OPPORTUNITIES
1. Customer satisfaction with services 2. High product quality 3. New product time to market speed 4. Capital reserves high 5. (IT) Internal call center highly efficient 6. (IT) Scalable systems	• Related products/services – expand to leverage reputation • Expand service model • Acquire related businesses – supplier?
WEAKNESSES	THREATS
1. Supply chain weakness, inventory shortfalls 2. On time delivery <75% at peak times 3. High personnel turnover 4. (IT) Connectivity and system issues serving APIA business	• Market vulnerability at peak times – sales losses • External service providers acquiring our staff/customers • APIA vulnerable to competitive sales and services providers

---

2. Andrews, 1980; Christensen et al., 1982; in Mintzberg, p. 36–37.

Critical Success Factors

The Sloan School of Management first proposed this method of identifying the key goals of strategic business units and units of measurement for establishing achievement. Critical success factors (CSF) are by definition *the objectives that must be met to achieve success—and only those*. Developing and honing them is an excellent way of achieving focused goals and of clarifying what is important but not essential.

One CSF is unlikely to be enough, as it will be too generalized. A right-sized group of CSFs is the minimum set of necessary and sufficient goals your enterprise (department, group, project) must accomplish. Best is three to five; you should be able to remember them, though it is also great to post them on the wall so that staff members see tangible statements that help prioritize amidst the firefighting.

Value Chain Analysis

Value chain analysis is an approach created by Michael. E. Porter in his book, *Competitive Advantage,* and it is still in use today.[3] The method is related to contemporary models for analyzing business processes, especially the business process reengineering (BPR) approach, though it is not as formal and detailed. This model identifies what is most valued by customers and who provides it. The approach involves analyzing data and looking at the product and service the customer receives in terms of which people and systems provide skills (or add value) at all levels of the product research, development, sales distribution, and service cycles. The idea is to determine what serves the customer best and develop or leverage those skills. This is therefore a customer-oriented model of assessing core competencies, which can include systems.

Porter's value chain method states that an enterprise's activities can be divided into nine generic types, five of which are considered primary for creating a product or service, marketing it, and delivering it to customers. The other four activities are support activities that cross between the primary activities; *technology services are typically classified as support.*

---

3. Porter, Michael E., *Competitive Advantage: Creating and Sustaining Superior Performance*, 1985, Free Press.

Value chain analysis places a premium on primary, direct customer interface activities—a key perspective to grasp pragmatically, as it often causes IT to be viewed as a cost center to be minimized. There is nothing wrong with this; it forces the business to evaluate whether expensive systems (and proposals to upgrade them) are worth the cost. A good foundational enterprise architecture will minimize the likelihood of misunderstandings here, as the requirement for customer support services and critical infrastructure will have been substantiated.

Scenario Analysis and Impact Assessment

Scenario analysis and impact assessment is not a formal planning method but rather a technique to allow for the discussion of various scenarios that can affect any aspect of planning, a process to assess their likelihood and impact, and identification of what plans should be in place or what changes are needed to accommodate these. It is fun and interesting to the people who participate and a good way to get alignment on business drivers and responses to them. I tried it years ago, doing planning with a group of operational directors in the insurance business. I couldn't get them to commit to any directional statements, but it turned out they would make prognostications if I let them assign a *likelihood* to their scenarios.

This technique started with an Excel spreadsheet, and I have seen it refined into a full database for information collection, including entry screens. No matter how you collect the information, you are using this vehicle to document possible situations that will impact the business. Examples include economic forecasts, geographic moves (factory relocates from South America to Canada), increases or decreases in sales volume, and regulatory setbacks.

Ideally, a group of business people gathers and brainstorms possible short scenarios in one or more of the category areas. The scenarios are rated in terms of their likelihood and risk, or impact; people are encouraged to surface all possible options, even though many may be of low likelihood. A typical spreadsheet will have eight to twelve categories, with four to ten scenarios in each category. Once the scenarios are articulated, they are assigned business owners who validate the likelihood, assess the risk/impact further, and perhaps segment the impact into broader analysis categories in terms of both severity to certain business segments and immediacy to the business.

The scenarios can be good news or bad, so this is not a disaster planning activity, though it can be used as such. In most companies, doubling the number of customers would be just as much a strain as halving the number of them, so good news can still have a huge impact that must be anticipated. The basic technique is the same as that used for disaster recovery planning: Assess the level of risk and impact, and determine the viability and advisability of preparation versus reaction.

Ultimately, the scenario planning process drives back into action plans to deal with the various business aspects identified, and this returns to a more formal planning method. The scenarios can be revisited every six months or so to identify what has changed, how good the predictive capabilities of the participants are, and how well responses to scenarios worked.

▶ IT Planning

Importance and Value

Figure 11–2 conveys the path from business focus areas, usually via goals or CSFs, to IT infrastructure and functions that are defined as key systems components. IT projects are initiated to build or enhance these components, and these projects should result in measurable business impacts. This is a representation of how strategic business plans impact IT planning and delivery.

The resulting IT plans are drivers for future IT architecture, investment plans, and organization. They set (or acknowledge) the tone and priorities of your shop—strategic, tactical, or reactionary—and allow you to strive for changes and activate steps to get there. Properly done, your plans stage and allocate resources to major projects, focus on delivery with key performance indicators (KPIs) agreed upon up front, and provide guidelines to measure progress.

It is also important to address day-to-day business requirements in this planning process—including funding for maintenance and sustaining support—and make sure these are part of your KPIs by tying them to SLAs.

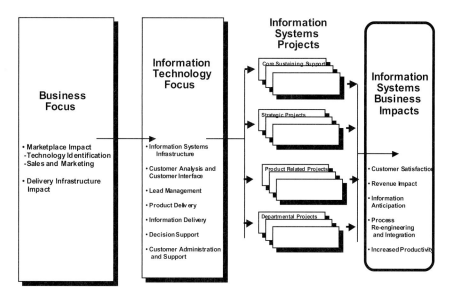

Figure 11–2   Information technology initiatives.

Plans Your IT Organization Must Have

It doesn't matter who does these or how they are derived, but you must have documented and filed high-level plans to cover:

- Business recovery and resumption.
- Capacity plans to ensure SLA management for basic business functions.
- Technology plans, to minimally include
  - Ongoing security compliance.
  - Network evolution.
  - Approaches for (mandatory) upgrades of commercial packages.
- Year-over-year project budgeting.

IT Planning Checklist

Table 11–4 provides a checklist of specific aspects you should be sure to address no matter how you do IT planning.

Table 11–4   IT planning checklist.

1. INTERNAL VS. EXTERNAL FOCUS—IDENTIFY SPECIFIC DRIVERS

2. MAJOR CORPORATE GOALS—AND YOUR OWN

3. MAJOR CUSTOMERS' OR SPONSORS' CRITICAL IMPERATIVES

4. KPIS—COST, CYCLE TIME, COMPETITIVE ADVANTAGE

5. COST OF IT AS A PERCENT OF REVENUE AND TCO

6. ECONOMIC PRESSURES—YOUR BUDGET

7. ARCHITECTURE AND MIGRATION PLANS

8. YEAR-OVER-YEAR PROJECT PORTFOLIO

9. SERVICE LEVELS AND BUSINESS SERVICE GUARANTEES

10. GLOBAL BUSINESS STRUCTURE AND NETWORK IMPLICATIONS

11. ACQUISITIONS AND MERGERS—CURRENT AND POSSIBLE

12. EMPLOYEE GROWTH AND RETENTION

▶ Steps to an IT Plan

Plan to Plan

IT planning will go by the wayside unless it is integrated into the day-to-day workload. This means enabling your organization to both plan and follow through. To accomplish this, you must:

1. Establish realistic objectives and deliverables for your IT plan, keeping in mind any critical drivers you must satisfy.
2. Choose a method and tools. Many of the techniques mentioned in the section "Approaches to Setting Strategic Goals and Objectives" can be modified for use in IT planning.
3. Set timelines (work in maximum 3-month delivery cycles) and stage some quick wins.
4. Allocate resources and accountabilities for delivery and upkeep of the plan itself.
5. Prioritize this process appropriately for your organization and the user community, and tie planning goals to that level.
6. Ensure that corporate sanction and funding are formalized for the approved plan.
7. Determine which planning documents must be maintained and updated—be realistic about it.
8. Prioritize the plans and efforts you do sanction.
9. Set up status reporting and a regular review cycle.
10. Reward progress.

Critical Soft Components

Other chapters of this book cover subjects that are germane to the planning function, and marketing and communication are key subjects to address. Whatever your corporate culture and how you approach it, be sure your plans are a key component of the information you choose to disseminate.

There are aspects of planning that are especially critical for IT work, and stakeholder management and user group interfaces are among them. Your team should identify internal and external stakeholders and their interests, build key relationships, and ensure that they are connected to the informal information flows. Other areas where user interfaces make a difference include:

- Individual project scoping and goal definition.
- Business process definition and rules.
- Requirements management.
- Implementation planning.
- Acceptance testing.
- Communication.

Clarity on organizational assumptions—which may evolve—is also vital. As you create the IT plans, be sure you know the long-range corporate model, especially in terms of outsourcing and any planned acquisitions. You may be making assumptions regarding what you will manage internally and what will be outsourced in IT, and these tactics should be explicit. The extent of decentralized or departmental computing should be agreed upon formally as well, as this will impact your organization significantly.

Finally, delivering on plans requires that your organizational infrastructure have the skill sets, positions, resources, processes, and maturity to follow through. At some point you'll need to ask yourself, "Can we do this?" and assess whether you have prerequisite organizational changes to make, training or experience needs, and whether you should consider waiting until your organization is ready or going outside for help.

Drivers for Change

Your corporate business strategies are the key drivers for all planning, and some statement of these, or identification of CSFs, must form the foundation of IT planning. If there is no formal company strategy source, you must extract these (or a subset that impact IT) from the less formal processes and validate them. Systems evolution is no different than any other kind.

It's not the strongest of species that survive, nor the most intelligent, but the ones most responsive to change. — Charles Darwin

The best way to be responsive to change in IT is to see it coming. Sometimes this is referred to as "picking up minimal cues." You could also define change catalysts and get your stakeholders to help. The following are potential categories for scenario analyses that might identify requirements for system changes, infrastructure reinforcement, or deployment of new technology:

- Market changes.
- Economic drivers.
- Business direction.
- Technical climate, advancements.
- Political, governmental, legal influences.
- Company style and culture.
- Security concerns.
- Disaster recovery plans.
- Acquisitions or divestments.

Migration

Under the traditional planning model, the migration plan was a basic component. Migration has become fundamental to planning for IT in the past 10 years and is seen as a technique for mapping systems evolution, with all of its implications for factoring in embedded and legacy processes, systems and data, and the bridges required to allow for controlled change. The basic requirements are a well-thought-out statement of the target environment, a current system assessment, the gap assessment, and a set of migration goals and incremental steps. Chapter 8, "Architecture," provides much more detail.

In IT planning, your migration strategy and goals are important because they define the level of resources and priority you will place upon systems evolution, and this may well impact the amount of bandwidth you have remaining to address other imperatives—making it all the more important that your target IT environment is already closely aligned with business goals.

Developing an Ongoing/Evergreen Plan

How well you are able to follow through on your planning efforts depends a lot on your business and IT culture. There will be constant pressure to pull resources from long-term objectives to satisfy short-term needs. Executives often manage this with organizational solutions such as isolating new development. Your directors will often need to utilize project management techniques for scope control and issue management.

Balancing IT/architecture against business goals is not a trivial task, and there are many similarities to playing bridge. Work with your partner, get to know and understand his or her style, communicate about the cards you've been dealt, and think ahead. You'll play a lot of rounds.

You also need to use your influence to remind the business of its priorities when your teams get conflicting direction from some great "new idea" that conflicts with resource allocation. Then you must either clarify and explicitly revise course, or you must change prioritization input. Key times when these issues tend to arise are at budget cycle and new major project initiation.

Milestones for Applications Portfolio Planning and Project Management

This section deals with preparatory steps that many of the other chapters in the book use as a basis for action. The more you take into account and include rated activities, integrate planning across disciplines and organizational groups, and establish checkpoints, the better.

In the long run, the success of your planning is measured by how well action plans are executed, and a good feedback loop that tracks successes and misses is critical to improving the process. We wrap this chapter up by discussing how it all fits together, but first, let's discuss in some detail another critical activity that brings the budgeting process together with planning—setting priorities for projects.

▶ Setting Priorities

Once you and your team have completed IT planning, there is still a need to ensure that your strategic directions and your user/client priorities are managed together to provide a balanced set of deliverables for the business. In some circles, this is called project portfolio management, and the executive staff members actually rate themselves on how well they held to their commitments to fund strategic work. To prepare the executive teams to evaluate major work proposals and set priorities for IT project funding, we must first do some "good staff work." At a minimum, questions such as "How much will each project cost, to develop and TCO? and What are the risks, benefits, efforts, disruptions, consequences of not doing it?" must be answered.

Putting Things in Context

Once the IT strategy has been defined, an iterative process begins in which it is linked to the budget and the amount of dollars available for IT expenditures. The vision and direction for the IT department may extend far out into the future, but from a practical standpoint, an 18-month tactical plan is all that is needed. Figure 11–3 presents a sample project list.

Prioritized Project List					
Incremental Spending					
			Aggregate		
		Project	Total		
Priority	Project Name	US $K	US $K	Notes	Priority
	Total Possible Project Submission		12,373		
19	Reporting Project Phase III	625	12,373		Pend
18	Marketing Project	1,250	11,748	Requirements very high level - target late in 2nd Half	Pend
17	LMS Project phase ii	90	10,498	not committed	Pend
16	E-Commerce interface	750	10,408	Rosetta net - advances interop strategy	Med
15	New OEM Partner Project	500	9,658	external funding after requirements compl - may be next year	Med
14	Knowledge Management System Phase III	590	9,158	External customers access	Med
13	CRM Project	2,400	8,568	improved configurator + proposal generation	Med
12	ERP project	3,035	6,168	New version - deferrable to next half	Med
11	CMS Project phase ii	550	3,133	increase the number of web sites - project continuation per plan	Med
10	LDAP Project phase ii	1,150	2,583	Offshore development - needs 60 days lead - licenses and env req	High
***********	Current Cutoff line			***	*
9	Central warehousing project	-	2,583	Assumes reimbursed at 100%, prereq to Reporting Project	High
8	2 new UNIX servers, 10 NT servers	228	2,583	Prep for CMS and LDAP environment changes - Migration Plan	High
7	New product release	300	2,355	May target for launch - web and sales support	High
6	Continuation of SFA upgrade project	950	3,005	2.3 Million committed thru 2003 - full allocation for this year	High
5	Application Enhancement Project Budget	700	2,055	Budget for ERP enhancements per user committee	High
4	Temporary resources for new Web requirements	250	1,355	Assumes Portal Project moves ahead - staffs thru July	High
3	Upgrade capacity of current servers and consolidate	350	1,105	Capacity plan forcasts need in May	Critical
2	Mandatory changes per Feb audit	530	755	File # 2720-1 - apps and software	Mandate
1	Regulated data privacy changes	225	225	Per legislation in Europe Dec 2001 - required by July 2002	Mandate

Figure 11–3   Project prioritization list.

Good Staff Work

The project list in Figure 11–3, which shows projects ranked bottom-to-top from 1 to19 in order of importance, shows a priority column that reflects the criticality of projects. The distinction between discretionary and nondiscretionary projects is not a new one. At some companies, the terms "must have" and "nice to have" are used. Regardless of the terminology, projects can be categorized, at the lowest level, into those projects that *must* be undertaken and those that may not. On the sample list, projects that are prioritized as *mandate* or *critical* are considered nondiscretionary and are ranked as the top three to be completed.

Nondiscretionary projects are required because the consequences of not completing the effort are known and will have a severe negative impact on the business. One example is any change in regulatory requirements that affect the business; in our example there is data privacy legislation that requires business compliance. Y2K, regardless of the hype associated with it, was an example of a nondiscretionary project. Capacity planning can also identify nondiscretionary projects.

Discretionary projects are just that—efforts that, while important or desirable, may be forgone if necessary. This means that there are discretionary dollars that must be applied (or not applied) to make these projects occur. Executive management must be involved in these decisions. Dividing the projects into those that are required and those that are desired is the first step at prioritizing all of the proposed projects.

Rough Order of Magnitude (ROM)

For the most part, executive teams are aware of business and corresponding IT needs at the project level. What we need to assist them with is a thumbnail sketch of the undertaking—the major steps, the risks and benefits, and an approximation of what the cost is going to be. Figure 11–4 shows a simple form that can be completed for each project on the project list.

Some executive teams may want more finite information in the form of an ROI and the opportunity costs—or a full business case, though this is normally done in the project lifecycle. If this is the situation, you may find it better to conduct that analysis on the top of four or five projects—after you have determined if each is a must have and the approximate level of effort (cost) associated with each project.

PROJECT DESCRIPTION	MAJOR MILESTONES
Implement Learning Delivery system to build and deliver virtual classes, conference calls, web meetings, and other e-learning events. Implementation target is 18 months from Project Initiation	• Project scope and approval • Publish RFP • Vendor Screening/Evaluation/Selection • Architecture Review • Implementation • Training • Go-Live
BUSINESS BENEFIT Creates dependable, cost-effective, scalable solutions that offer all learners rich distance learning experience to expand their knowledge in the way that works best for them. Cite savings and revenue generation expected. **DEPENDENCIES/RED FLAGS** Project budget, Resource & skill sets, Technology	**LEVEL OF EFFORT / COST** • 100 hrs ERP Interface • 300 hrs Build Learning • 100 hrs Customization • Estimated Licensing , Time & Materials (500hrs X hrly rate = $$$$ • Total Cost of Ownership annual or per user •FTE Support required

Figure 11–4   Project prioritization template.

The reasoning behind performing the discretionary versus nondiscretionary and ROM steps first is that the executive team may elect to forgo the ROI on certain projects if they are nondiscretionary or of great importance to the business—*or are a key step in the strategic plan*. In this way, the process of prioritization itself helps the organization to manage with a long-range view.

High-Medium-Low and Variations

As with most things, the Pareto principle (the 80/20 rule) is useful in this process. With my sponsors' and clients' help, I rate my IT projects and make recommendations *before* I take them to the executive committee for review, but you can rely on the fact that the executive team will determine its own ranking for every project under consideration. I never send in anything that I've ranked low, so medium is the bottom level that stays open to review. Often, however, I leave projects that are in deferred or "pending" status on the lists to keep them on the radar screen for future consideration. I also use the list and the notes on it to provide memory joggers about prerequisites, links to long-term migration plans, and related strategic corporate goals.

Once the executive team has this list, some (nondiscretionary) projects will be quite simple for them to rate, and these will receive a high ranking and get funding. Many projects will be subject to discussion and review before a list of ordered priorities can be developed. Ranking by the executive team may be accomplished individually or in a meeting. There are tremendous advantages to holding a meeting to arrive at the preliminary rankings; a meeting takes less time and follow-up. However, this is not the primary reason for recommending a meeting as the better of the two processes. The real value is that in a single meeting, the executive team will bring information to the table that will help other executives arrive at a better decision and build understanding.

There will also be a group of projects in the middle (usually referred to as the gray area). These projects will require a process to reach a final determination on whether to undertake them. While the executive team meeting may reduce or narrow the number of projects that fall into this category, the "rack and stack" method will help bring great clarity.

Rack and Stack

In our previous example you see a "dollarized" list of projects that have been identified as those that must be completed. The executive team has indicated the important projects (both discretionary and non-discretionary) in this example.

Because the dollars are incremental on the list, we can look up the list to see the funding levels needed to undertake each incremental initiative. In our example (Figure 11–3) the cutoff was drawn just past the

$2.5 million line. It is when funding levels are determined that this final list is so critical, because as you can see on the prioritization list, the amount of discretionary project funding draws the make-or-break line across the list and determines what work actually gets approved funding based upon the priorities established.

This may not be the final iteration, because when projects do not "make the cut," the executive team will have some discussion and debate surrounding how to accomplish specific projects. It is important to note which specific projects are being considered, as they represent the most important of the lower priority projects. Another common occurrence is to trade projects; by taking a higher dollar project out of the running, two less costly projects may be undertaken. If additional funding is allocated, the bar rises.

It is not unusual for this list to remain volatile all year long, as priorities change and the economic picture fluctuates in a corporation. Many of the projects on such a list may need preparation work and some level of attention before they reach the stage at which a business case is ready and the effort launched, and you will have to decide how much R&D you can afford to spend. IT organizations can use the list as a way of "seeing things coming" and allocating scarce resources wisely, based upon strategic cues, the political climate, and real dollars available. This can be livened up by singing along with the last line of an old Willie Nelson song, which warns that "If you've got no more money, honey, I got no more time."

▶ The Big Picture and Feedback Loop

To conclude, I'd like to use a picture to tie together the most important aspects of planning and associated processes that we have talked about in this chapter. The framework and arrows in Figure 11–5 show how a clear vision and properly framed strategic goals influence everything that goes on in a business, creating a climate that casts light on every level of execution.

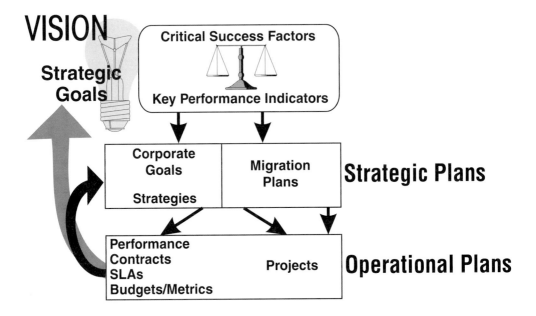

Figure 11–5 Strategic/operational planning vectors.

Most closely aligned to that vision are CSFs and KPIs for business success, and these balanced drivers set the framework for all the strategic planning the business undertakes. At the Strategic Planning level of the diagram is a box containing Corporate Goals and Strategies, which drive all aspects of lower level operational plans and execution (both day-to-day operations and projects), and Migration Plans, which tend to use the project framework in implementation.

Thus, the Corporate Goals and Strategies box on the left of the Strategic Planning level has vectors into day-to-day operations, such as performance, contracts, service levels, and associated budgets and measures. Those activities generate results and information that must feed back into the strategic and higher level of planning; remember the importance of analysis of strengths and weaknesses, value chain execution, and organizational capability to the core strategic planning process. The project execution box must feed back metrics into the upper levels as well, because the success rate, true delivered (as opposed to advertised) scope, and adoption of those projects tell you what rate of change you are actually capable of sustaining.

This is a tidy model to review from an IT perspective at a minimum, because asking for that feedback and assessing how the pieces are working together can be a healthy, ongoing monitoring activity that keeps you closely involved with the workings of planning and builds the strategic muscle in your organization.

IT Infrastructure Management and Execution

by Joe Feliu

Joe Feliu notes that the life of the CIO is anything but predictable. Here's a brief example:

> *It was a quiet Thursday morning as I was checking my stock portfolio on Yahoo! and calculating my early retirement date. I had worked hard over the first few months as CIO, launching several key strategic initiatives—becoming a business partner with the influential few who lead the company, developing a strategic vision/mission for IT, and embarking on the "vital few" projects that would make the company successful in the marketplace. I admit it, I was feeling pretty good about the likelihood that our IT team would have a positive impact on the business and on our customers. Then, the phone rang. It was the vice president of facilities. He was irate; his email wasn't working, as he put it, "...for the third time in a month!" Being the good CIO, I promised to look into it immediately.*

> *I called my help desk director and asked her to get the problem fixed. Within minutes the phone rang again. This time it was my trusted peer, the vice president of manufacturing, who was upset that the morning pick lists were all wrong. This costs the company money, so I became personally involved. I called my team together, found out what hap-*

pened during the prior night's job runs, and launched the all-too-familiar Herculean effort to get the problems fixed as quickly as humanly possible. By the end of the day, I was breathing a sigh of relief as I just finished answering the last "nasty email" and felt reasonably confident that the production environment had stabilized. That was, until the next morning, when the phone rang and . . ."

In this chapter Feliu discusses the key elements of the infrastructure management that all CIOs must address, including:

- *Why a framework can be a powerful tool in organizing your approach to infrastructure management and execution.*

- *The three perspectives of the IT environment: operations, applications development, and human resources.*

- *Key operational elements, including asset management, capacity planning, change management, disaster recovery planning, high availability, problem management, security management, service level agreements, and vendor management.*

- *Key elements of applications development, including programming practices, project management process, and systems development life cycles.*

Although the scenario described in this chapter's introduction may seem extreme, it is unfortunately far too often the norm. The lesson is quite clear—all the effort spent on strategic activities will be for naught unless the tactical elements are well managed. (I assure you, for me it was a lesson I will never forget.) Further, the successful CIO knows full well that this can be accomplished without having to become the tactician. Rather, the challenge is to know *what* needs to be done and *when*. The *how* should be left to those directly responsible for the tasks.

In this chapter, we provide a framework to help the CIO ensure that the necessary components of the IT operating infrastructure are being managed appropriately by his or her staff. We hope to drive home the simple point of this chapter: that the day-to-day execution of the fundamental tasks of IT can be an asset and not a liability to the success of a CIO. As you read further, you will learn what we believe are the essential components of operating the organizational IT infrastructure.

The Operational Framework

The framework is organized into three major topical areas: operations, development, and human resources. Specific areas of focus are listed within each topic area, as shown in Table 12–1.

Table 12–1   IT Infrastructure Management Framework

Operations	Development
Asset Management	Programming Practices
Capacity Planning	Project Management Process
Change Management	Systems Development Life Cycle
Disaster Recovery Planning	
High Availability	**Human Resources**
Problem Management	Company New Employee Orientation
Security Management	Managing Staff Performance
Service Level Agreements	Training & Staff Development

For each focus area, we provide the following:

1. Description—What are the essential elements of the topic?
2. Benefit—Why is the focus area important?
3. First Steps—What can you do *now* to get started and show immediate results?
4. Example—A real-world implementation of the principles.

A word of caution: The framework presented here includes a broad itemization of areas of focus. For each organization, the priority and "order of attack" will vary. These depend entirely on the nature and size of your business (a large manufacturing company will require ERP high availability, whereas a small company with a highly mobile sales force will need to place high emphasis on reliable remote access); on the existing IT infrastructure you have deployed (desktop standardization will be a high priority for companies with aging desktops and laptops); and on the availability of funds for projects (under budget constraints, projects such as problem and change management can be undertaken immediately with minimal incremental cost). Regardless, each brief "First Steps" section highlights some specific initial tactics to implement the concepts described in previous sections.

Pragmatically, we suggest that a CIO perform a readiness assessment in which he or she reviews each key area of the framework presented in this chapter. This can be done quickly and will highlight key opportunities for improvement.

For example, the CIO could call a meeting of his or her direct reports and review the topic heading for each section in this chapter. Signs of trouble will include no clear ownership of problems, blank stares, or arguments about whether these items are really important. Alternatively, a comprehensive review can be performed by an independent third party (the top IT consulting firms are prepared to conduct such reviews). This approach is recommended if substantial funds will be required to remedy the deficiencies noted in the assessment.

In either case, we recommend that an assessment not only be a priority for you now, but also be performed periodically as a "health check" on the effectiveness of the IT organization.

Focus Areas in Operations

Asset Management

Description

Asset management is the process of procuring, tracking, and disposing of any IT software or hardware component. This includes managing all vendor relations for hardware and software maintenance and licensing to ensure that they are current, viable, and cost-efficient. Managing the IT assets of the company may seem a rather straightforward administrative task; it is not.

Defining the term *asset* provides some insight. Do you tag and manage individual plug-in cards for every PC in your inventory, or do you just track the PC? What about tracking wireless devices? With the emerging power of over-the-air data synchronization, key corporate information such as customer contact information and confidential emails regularly appear on your employees' smart phones. Without managing the "disconnected" devices, how can you know when devices, potentially containing highly sensitive information, are lost? This issue is exacerbated when you consider that many employees purchase their own devices and even their own remote access synchronization services.

Further, the information gained when tracking assets can form the foundation for other processes, such as configuration management and desktop standardization. The essential components of a good asset management process are:

- A repository of IT assets.
- A data collection methodology that spans asset acquisition through disposal (incorporating as much automation as possible).
- Active links to supporting processes, such as those mentioned earlier.

Advanced asset management systems may include features such as usage/metering to assist in license management and direct links into budgeting/financial systems.

Benefits

Asset management is an operational imperative, primarily for financial accountability, and further supports other essential processes as mentioned above. Those of us who lived through the Y2K challenge learned the value of an accurate asset management process. Absent such a process, we were faced with initiating an organization-wide inventory of assets, a costly and time-consuming effort.

First Steps

If you are concerned that the information assets of the organization are not properly managed, we suggest you take the following steps:

1. Determine the key resources of the organization (for example, high-cost items of hardware and broadly used software products).

2. Evaluate maintenance and software license status for these items (there is a good chance that this step will yield substantial opportunity for cost savings). Renegotiate contractual terms where appropriate.

3. Undertake a longer term program for asset tagging and tracking (but ensure that the level of asset tagging is not extreme, such as tracking sub-components in PCs).

Example

As part of the asset inventory effort, we recommend that the following data be collected on hardware elements within your infrastructure:

- Department
- Physical location
- Accountable contact person and phone number
- Description
- Manufacturer, model number, serial number
- Date acquired
- Product cost
- Cost center billed
- Asset control number

Capacity Planning

Description

Capacity planning is the process of identifying and planning the future resource requirements of the IT infrastructure. A successful planning process ensures that IT resources are available just before they are needed—a just-in-time approach to resource management. Typical resources include CPU, memory, disk, I/O, bandwidth, database, and environmental support resources (power, cooling, space, and so on).

In order to be effective, the capacity planning process must obtain accurate information on business growth needs. Often, it is driven by the corporate business planning and budgeting processes. The CIO must see the capacity planning process as an opportunity to be proactive in anticipating needs enough in advance that they can be met without going into "crisis mode."

Benefits

Hardware and software expenditures are often the most expensive elements in the IT budget. Having an effective capacity planning process reduces costs to the barest minimum required to run the IT infrastructure. An experienced executive knows full well the difference in the leverage he or she has with a vendor when there is adequate lead time to plan for long-term deliveries; asking for a costly server immediately because of a performance impact can be interpreted as a "blank check" by a vendor. Further, proper capacity planning ensures that infrastructure components are available before there is a negative business impact. Investment in procedures that accurately predict infrastructure needs will make for a far less reactive IT function.

First Steps

To launch an effective capacity planning process, begin by taking the following actions:

1. Identify the key components under stress in your environment (for instance, storage capacity).

2. Take the time to perform a single point of failure (SPOF) analysis to identify those areas that may be particularly vulnerable in the event of an unanticipated failure.

3. Establish performance thresholds at which replacement is required (such as percent of available storage in use).

4. Put monitoring tools in place to detect when these thresholds are reached.

5. Take action to reduce usage of the resource (for example, purge files to clear up space) or acquire additional resources (for example, increase available storage capacity).

Example

A sample long-term capacity planning process is shown in Table 12–2.

Table 12–2   Long-Term Capacity Planning Process

1. Monitor and collect performance data daily for following:
    - CPU Utilization
    - Disk I/O
    - Disk Usage
    - Swap Rate/Memory Utilization
    - Network Utilization
    - LAN & WAN Network Utilization
2. Obtain Application and Network growth (demand forecast) in the areas of:
    - New functionality/Release
    - Number of Users/Concurrent users
    - Users growth by Region
    - Volume by transaction types
    - Batch growth
    - Database growth
    - Additional network requirements/load
3. Perform capacity modeling and analysis
    - Trend Analysis
    - Run Simulation model
    - Graph Capacity vs. Forecasted Demand
    - Identify when additional capacity is needed
4. Identify specific hardware capacity and reliability requirements for:
    - CPU, Memory, Storage, Network, Voice, and Voicemail
5. Analyze alternatives and determine recommended course of action
    - Define alternatives to meet business needs
    - Assess cost of each alternative
    - Decide on best configuration
6. Provide Capacity Upgrade Proposal for management review and approval
    - Cost analysis
    - Selection and approval process
7. Generate, Publish, and Implement Capacity Upgrade Plan
    - Place PO with Vendor
    - Obtain hardware; install hardware and related software
    - Conduct acceptance test & obtain release approval
    - Release to production
    - Implement feedback loop to ensure ongoing process improvement

Change Management

Description

When you perform a root cause analysis of IT service interruptions, one cause stands out above all others—an incorrectly made change to the IT production environment. There may be an adverse affect resulting from a set-up that was done a year ago and is now encountering a new condition for the first time. Or, the planning of two projects may be correct, but when combined an interface may have been overlooked. Imperfections in the IT production environment can occur in a number of ways.

Immediate results ensue when a rigorous change management process is implemented. This process is easy to put in place, but it is more difficult to obtain buy-in from all involved. All stakeholders must participate; typically, representatives from all infrastructure groups and select key customers make up the change management committee. This team meets periodically (weekly is appropriate in most cases) with the sole purpose of reviewing the prior period's changes to the production environment, assessing their success, and reviewing the changes of the upcoming week (and beyond) to ensure that all necessary planning and coordination has taken place. The change management process is typically led by someone from the QA or operations management team, usually the person heading up the Production Control function.

When major systems changes (either hardware, software, or applications) are introduced into the production environment, a "go live" meeting should be held in addition to following the normal change management process. Essentially, this entails a formal meeting, prior to implementing the change, in which key stakeholders review the readiness of their respective functional areas. The moderator of this meeting, typically the project manager for the major change being introduced, should obtain the explicit agreement of all stakeholders to proceed with the change; any stakeholder has the right to "stop the production line." It is advisable to have senior executives from the IT group and from business units affected in attendance at this meeting. Using this forum ensures a greater sense of personal accountability for delivery and avoids after-the-fact second-guessing of the decision to go live.

Benefits

There are two primary benefits to a rigorous change management process. First, communication of changes is enhanced, and when working properly, all who should be aware of a change are notified and have a chance to provide input into the change. Second, should the change not work as planned, an immediate identification and back-out procedure is predefined, minimizing the impact of the error. In addition, all changes can be fed into dependent infrastructure processes, such as disaster recovery planning and asset management.

First Steps

If there is no formal change management process in place, take the following steps immediately:

1. Identify a management owner to champion the process.
2. Inform all impacted areas of the new change management process. (Initially, there may be delays in implementing changes as a result of the greater planning inherent in the process.)
3. Start small by having only a subset of the infrastructure group (perhaps the help desk, network, and systems administration groups) participate in the first phase.
4. Establish a written process using the guidelines mentioned above and the form provided in Figure 12–1.
5. Launch a weekly meeting to review changes to the infrastructure made during the prior week as well as those planned for the coming week.
6. When the process is working effectively, expand to other components of the infrastructure and ultimately to the application development and customer stakeholders.

Example

A sample Change Management Request form is shown in Figure 12–1.

Production Change Request (PCR)

Date: *Date the form is started*	**Who to contact** (include pager, cell or home phone#): **Developer:** *name and contact info* **QA Engineer:** *name and contact info*			
Change Requester *Person requesting the change*	**Phone #** *Requester's #*	**Project Title** *Project Reference Name*		**Change Control #** *Obtained from the Change Control Manager*
QA Engineer *Specialist assigned to complete the PCR for Requester*	**Phone #** *Specialist's phone number*	**Pager #** *Pager and cell phone number*	**Proposed Date & Duration** *When to start and how long the change will take to complete*	**Proposed Time** *When the change will be implemented*
Business Benefits: Describe business benefits resulting from change.				
End User Impact: Describe downtime and functionality of change from end member perspective.	*What will the end member see as the change is being implemented? What is the impact to the current system as it is modified?*			
Summary of Change: Describe for technical peers. Attached Release Check List, or project plan. Include Prerequisites to the change.	*Detailed description of the change. Attach sheets as required and specify the attachment in this block. Is this a fix of a previous error? Add any prerequisites that must be in place before the change can be performed.*			
Risk Analysis & Contingency Plan: What happens if change fails and what is recovery plan?	*Detailed statement of the risk to doing the change. Detailed statement of what will have to occur if the implementation of this change is not successful. Where are the backup tapes, other hardware, or technical expertise that will return the system to the as-before condition?*			
How will members and management be notified?	*Details on the notification process and proposed text for that message.*			
***Approvals** Print Name Signature Date*				
Immediate/Functional Manager				
Change Control Manager				
Customer Support				
QA Manager				
Other Manager / Vendor Rep				

Figure 12–1   Change management request form.

Director of Product Support or QA *Circle the applicable one*			
QA Verification			
QA Engineer			

QA Test results:
Was the testing completed satisfactorily? Who did the testing?

Released to Production

Date:	Time:	Print Name:	Signature:

Upon Completion of Change
Final Review of Project

Comments(Satisfactory/failed, details):
What happened? Was the implementation completely satisfactory? Did the implementation go perfectly? Is the system that was changed up and running perfectly?

Production Installation Sign-Off

Date: *Date/time of change*	Print Name: *The installation/change implementer*	Signature:

Manager of QA

Date:	Print Name:	Signature:

Figure 12–1   Change management request form (continued).

Disaster Recovery Planning

Description

Disaster recovery planning (DRP) is an essential component of an IT services portfolio. DRP involves implementing a technology infrastructure to support business needs before, during, and after a disaster. This planning effort attempts to reduce the risk of exposure to an acceptable level by ensuring a cost-effective capability for resuming essential business operations in the event of a major business interruption.

DRP is a subset of the broader discipline of business continuity planning (BCP), which is focused on ensuring the continuance of business operations over and above technology operations. For example, bringing up the accounts receivable application is a DRP responsibility, while ensuring that necessary staff, documents, and procedures are in place is the responsibility of BCP. Typically, the finance department leads the BCP effort and the CIO leads the DRP effort.

It is important to remember that the traditional natural disaster (such as storm, earthquake, flood, and so on) accounts for only 3 percent of occurrences of major data loss, according to ONTRACK Data Recovery. Hardware failures and human error account for over 75 percent of these occurrences. A highly reliable backup and recovery capability is an important foundation for a successful disaster recovery plan. Backing up and restoring data and programs must be considered a core competency of IT.

Benefits

Due diligence as a senior executive mandates that a DRP be in place for any size organization. Perhaps the best way to understand the benefits of DRP is to reflect on the lessons learned from the September 11, 2001, disaster. Here is a summary of the findings:

- Testing of disaster recovery plans critical.
- Communications plans essential.
- Chain-of-command contingencies needed.
- Need for voice and voicemail systems recovery underestimated.
- Key info on desktops not backed up.
- Paper still widely used and vulnerable.
- Mismatch of business requirements and BCP plans.
- Key personnel dependency underestimated.
- Cell phone plans inadequate.

First Steps

If your organization does not have a DRP, take the following actions:

1. Approach an executive, most likely in the finance department, to partner with you to ensure that the IT assets of the organization are protected.
2. Launch a small team to develop an initial plan (see the sample outline for a DRP below). If you have no one on staff with experience in DRP, we suggest you find a consultant to provide guidance to the team.
3. Identify the major applications that support key business functions.
4. Ensure that backups of critical data are performed reliably.
5. Develop a plan to use either external resources (for example, a vendor such as SunGard to provide a "hotsite") or excess internal equipment capacity in the event of a disaster.
6. After this initial plan is in place, launch a more comprehensive DRP for all applications, and then expand this plan to a broader BCP for your organization.

Example

Figure 12–2 provides an outline for the essential components of a DRP.

High Availability

Description

The operations of a complex IT infrastructure demand that the IT executive understand expectations for system, network, and services availability of both internal and external customers. Availability requirements depend fundamentally on the customer's tolerance for downtime, which can be expressed informally or in a service level agreement (formally). It is the CIO's job to determine the "threshold of pain" that the business can stand. Having too robust an infrastructure is an unnecessary cost, but having too weak an infrastructure can result in dissatisfied customers and, ultimately, less effective business operations and lost revenue.

DISASTER RECOVERY PLAN OUTLINE

- Recovery Plan Overview and Specifications
  - Purpose and objectives of the Plan
  - Description of personnel assignments and responsibilities
  - Summary of recovery actions

- Disaster Alert/Assessment Activation Procedures
  - Recovery management initial notification
  - Senior management notification
  - Disaster verification and assessment
  - Disaster Recovery Plan activation and recovery personnel notification

- Disaster Recovery Management Procedures
  - Recovery operations management
  - Recovery operations control
  - Departments support coordination

- Resumption of Processing and Operational Service Procedures
  - Establish operations at alternate or backup locations (if cost effective)
  - Recover and reconstruct essential data and information
  - Activate backup computer facilities
  - Activate backup communication and network facilities
  - Activate essential processing and operational services
  - Activate end user interface and services

- Facility Restoration Procedures
  - Activate damage assessment and salvage actions for buildings, equipment, software, data, information and supplies
  - Repair and reequip the damaged site
  - Reactivate the restored site

- Activate vendor support

- Computer Center Disaster Level of Services Statement
  - Identify the level of services that would be provided following a disaster occurrence that impacts the computing capability of the enterprise.
  - This statement of service should be included in a Service Level Agreement (SLA) developed and published for each major user of the computing services offered by IT.

Figure 12–2   Essential components of a DRP.

A systems/service-downtime impact analysis is an economic analysis of the impact of systems and service interruption. The best approach to conducting this analysis is to start by identifying the SPOFs within your IT infrastructure. This will indicate where there is inadequate redundancy to assure continued operations. With these vulnerabilities understood, your team can develop strategies to eliminate the critical SPOFs. A basic format for such an analysis is provided in the example that follows.

Once the costs associated with these mitigation strategies are estimated, a rather straightforward economic analysis can be performed which assesses the cost versus the impact of downtime on your product and service offerings. Presenting this analysis to senior management in your organization will enable them to make an informed judgment on the level of spending it will take to achieve specified levels of availability.

With a clear expectation of availability in hand, the challenge becomes to establish 24/7 automated monitoring and alerting systems at critical points in the IT infrastructure to ensure your ability to achieve these standards. Today, tools are available to identify component utilization, performance and for all the mature elements of the IT infrastructure. Of course, there is a tradeoff to be made. The most desirable situation—having monitoring and alerting available for all services on servers, all network components, and all application processes—is prohibitively costly. So, where do you draw the line?

Unfortunately, one size does not fit all. If your firm is developing equipment that monitors the vital life signs of seriously ill patients in a hospital, then you can clearly cost-justify a substantial monitoring and alerting investment. However, most CIOs are faced with the need to strike the appropriate balance. Thus, it is imperative that you include in your SPOF analysis the elements of the monitoring/alerting systems that will be needed to achieve the availability levels that ultimately emerge.

Whatever the level of redundancy and monitoring you decide to implement, we strongly recommend that you procure an integrated environment for your operations staff to use. The theoretical optimum is a single, virtual console that captures all alerts and employs enough intelligence to alert the appropriate staff with enough advance notice to minimize customer impact. Of course, this is much easier said than done. However, there are excellent tools today (such as the HP Openview family of tools) that provide pragmatic solutions.

Benefits

The primary benefit of establishing explicit, business-based availability levels is to ensure organization-wide consensus on the appropriate amount of resources to be allocated to keeping systems and services up and running. Having an effective automated monitoring environment will cost-effectively enable you to minimize the service impact of a significant component failure in the infrastructure. (If you haven't launched a systems/service-downtime impact analysis for your company's critical infrastructure components, we strongly suggest you do so.) By implementing automated monitoring at strategic points within the infrastructure and developing threshold alerting in advance of a service interruption where possible, you are taking a huge leap forward in achieving a cost-effective, high-availability IT infrastructure.

First Steps

Take the following steps now to improve availability of the IT services you offer:

1. Perform a SPOF analysis on critical components in your IT infrastructure.
2. Develop a strategy for each SPOF to eliminate, or at least reduce to an acceptable level, the associated risk.
3. Develop costs associated with each redundancy strategy and the business impact associated with a given service interruption.
4. Present to senior management an economic analysis associated with implementing redundancy for key areas of impact (look for the "low hanging fruit").
5. Implement monitoring and alerting (preferably by purchasing third-party tools, but using some form of scripting if necessary).

Example

A sample format for an SPOF analysis is shown in Figure 12–3.

Problem Management

Description

The ability to effectively manage a service interruption from initial identification to resolution has long been an important capability of every IT organization. As the systems we run increasingly become part of the core business, however, an effective problem management process is essential. The purpose of this process is to identify an event that

SINGLE POINT OF FAILURE ANALYSIS

(TIME REQUIRED TO SWITCH TO REDUNDANT EQUIPMENT/SERVICE)

	Transparent Switch			Switch in Seconds			Switch in Minutes			Switch in Hours			Switch in Days		
	Today	Future	Cost	Today	Future	Cost	Today	Future	Cost	Today	Future	Cost	Today	Future	Cost
NETWORK															
Routers															
Loc 1	y/n	y/n	$	y/n	y/n	$	y/n	y/n	$	y/n	y/n	$	y/n	y/n	$
Loc 2															
...															
Hubs/Switches															
Loc 1															
Loc 2															
...															
WAN Links															
Link 1															
Link 2															
...															
SERVER															
NT															
CPU-Board															
CPU- Power Supply															
Memory															
Storage															
I/O Channels															
Network Connection															
UNIX															
CPU-Board															
CPU- Power Supply															
Memory															
Storage															
I/O Channels															
Network Connection															
Other Server Types															
CPU-Board															
CPU- Power Supply															
Memory															
Storage															
I/O Channels															
Network Connection															
VOICE/PBX															
Main Processor															
Remote Nodes															
Voice Network															
Voicemail System															
Facilities															
Power															
Air Conditioning															

Figure 12–3   SPOF analysis.

results in a missed expectation, ensure that appropriate resources are allocated to the event, track the progress of the resolution process, facilitate appropriate communication throughout the event, and ensure that organizational learning takes place in an attempt to prevent the recurrence of the problem. Most often this responsibility rests with the help desk function within an IT organization.

Here are three essential elements of an effective problem management process.

- **Problem Logging and Tracking:** A formal system that tracks the problem from start to resolution, gathering the necessary information to ensure that appropriate communication and organizational learning can take place. There are many tools available that handle the entry and tracking of problems (such as those from Remedy Corp. and Clarify Corp.) and that assist with the problem analysis and reporting tasks.

- **Root Cause Identification through Corrective Action:** An analytical view of the event to determine the root cause of the problem(s) and what can be done to prevent recurrence. This step is often omitted, which is the primary cause of repeating problems. With regard to the scenario that opens this chapter, for instance, I could be certain that similar events would occur unless I instituted a rigorous prevention process. To instill a root cause/corrective action mentality within the IT organization requires some work, but the benefits are manifest and can occur quickly. Figure 12–4 presents a simple one-page form, the Service Interruption Report, that facilitates this process. For extended outages, a more formal "post mortem" process should be followed in which all major stakeholders convene shortly after the resolution of the event and walk through the Service Interruption Report form.

- **Problem Reporting and Communication:** A structured process for notifying stakeholders of the progress of the problem resolution from start to finish. Use the help (service) desk as the communication focal point, enabling the technicians to focus on resolving the problem. With today's tools, online status reports are the way to go. Periodic reporting (daily, weekly, and monthly) is essential to support the management of the IT function. Event tracking logs contain a wealth of information about core problems experienced with the IT infrastructure and its use. Tracking trends in trouble tickets provides a wealth of information and should be a key metric for a CIO in evaluating IT performance.

Service Interruption Report
(SIR)

Originator _____

Outage Date _____

Problem Number _____

System/Application _____

Total Outage Time _____

I Problem Description
(Define specifically what happened, include all pertinent dates, start time, end time, etc.)

II Describe the Fix
(Describe what was done to restore the service, include who was contacted & when)

III Root Cause Analysis
(State why the problem occurred by identify the basic root cause and select the root cause category which applies)

Hardware:	Applications Outages:	Operating System:	Network Interface Cards:
Memory boards	Oracle	Backup Tool	FDDI
Backplanes	SAP	Network Service Failure	Hubs
I/O	Peoplesoft	3rd Party Interfaces	Routers
Power Supplies	Application A	Monitor Hangs	Ethernet/LAN
Bus Converter	Application B	UNIX	Other:
Disc Drives:	Application C	Facilities:	Remote Access Srvr.
Disc Mechanisms	Applciation D	Power	Web Service A
Power Supplies	Application E	Air Conditioning	Web Service B
Controllers	Processes & Procedures:		Vendor A
Tape Drives:	Patch Process		Vendor B
Tape Mechanisms	Migration to Prod.		Vendor C
Controllers	Problem Mangt.		
Tape Media	Capacity Planning		
	Configuration Mangt.		
	Change Mangt.		

IV Corrective Action Taken

(Explain what actions have been or will be taken to prevent this from happening again)

V Follow-Up
(Describe the follow up steps, if any, to ensure that the root cause analysis was performed and the corrective action was effective)

Figure 12–4   Service interruption report.

Benefits

The benefits of problem management are well known to any experienced IT executive. They include:

- Improved quality of service.
- Reduced downtime and risk.
- Anticipation and frequent prevention of system outages.
- Earlier and more effective responses to system outages.
- Information provided to other processes, such as asset and change management.
- Enhanced communication with stakeholders during an outage.

First Steps

If problems seem to recur in your infrastructure, here's an opportunity for you to instill a culture focused on rooting out their causes and ensuring they will not recur:

1. Insist that the management team enforce a policy of providing a root cause analysis/prevention write-up for each event that results in a service impact to IT's customers (see the Service Interruption Report form, Figure 12–4).

2. Post these write-ups on a shared resource so that IT staff and customers can review them.

3. Ensure that each write-up is reviewed in the periodic change management meetings, or institute a production management meeting with the express purpose of reviewing them.

4. Measure and display aggregated results over time.

Example

Templates for outage notification (both scheduled and unscheduled outages) are provided in Figure 12–5.

TEMPLATE FOR SCHEDULED OUTAGE ALERTS:

From: Smith, John
Sent: October 27, 2003 4:42 PM
To: *appropriate distribution list*
Subject: SCHEDULED OUTAGE ALERT – *reason here @ dd/mm hh:mm* Pacific Time

DESCRIPTION:
This section briefly describes the nature of the problem and the necessity for the outage. It also summarizes the systems affected, the expected duration, and the date and time outage will begin including the following date information day, month ddst beginning at hh:mm am/pm Pacific Time. This section also lists the Change Control number for the Change Request document (e.g., This outage is Change Request Number XXXX, (Title)).

START TIME: dd/mm/yy hh:mm AM/PM (Pacific Time)
END TIME: dd/mm/yy hh:mm AM/PM (Pacific Time)

SHORT-TERM SOLUTION:
Some outages occurring during normal business hours impact services. This section will describe any workarounds that users can use until full services are restored.

SYSTEMS AND SERVICES AFFECTED:
The following system(s) and service(s) will be unavailable during the scheduled outage:
* *List of all systems and services affected by the outage...*

If you have any questions, please call the **Responsible Director/Technician at yyy-yyyy**.
****

TEMPLATE FOR UNSCHEDULED OUTAGE ALERTS:

From: Smith, John
Sent: October 27, 2000 4:42 PM
To: *appropriate distribution list*
Subject: UNSCHEDULED OUTAGE ALERT – *reason here @ dd/mm hh:mm* Pacific Time

DESCRIPTION:
This section briefly describes the nature of the problem and why it occurred to the extent that this information is available. It also summarizes the systems and customers affected, the expected duration, and the date and time outage will begin including the following date information day, month ddst beginning at hh:mm am/pm Pacific Time.

START TIME: dd/mm/yy hh:mm AM/PM (Pacific Time)
END TIME: dd/mm/yy hh:mm AM/PM (Pacific Time)

SHORT-TERM SOLUTION:
Some outages occurring during normal business hours impact services. This section will describe any workarounds that users can use until full services are restored.

NEXT UPDATE:
This section provides users with information regarding the next update should the outage be prolonged.

SYSTEMS AND SERVICES AFFECTED:
The following system(s) and service(s) will be unavailable during the unscheduled outage:
* *List of all systems affected by the outage....*

If you have any questions, please call the **Responsible Director/Technician at yyy-yyyy**.

Figure 12–5   Outage notification templates.

Security Management

Description

Security is a huge topic and presents a host of challenges to the CIO. Just as you become confident that one security vulnerability has been addressed, another arises. This state of affairs will not change in the foreseeable future. So, what is the CIO to do? There are five management steps that each CIO should be taking to minimize risk:

1. Appoint a security officer or security committee. Depending on the culture and size of your organization, establish a single point of accountability for all information security matters.

2. Establish and communicate an information security policy. It is imperative that the information security position of the company be documented and communicated throughout the company for practical and legal purposes.

3. Conduct a security risk assessment to define the current state of security readiness. Identify key vulnerabilities and develop a plan of action to address each.

4. Implement standard security processes, procedures, and tools including:
   - Intrusion detection systems
   - Firewalls
   - Robust backup and recovery systems and processes
   - Rigorous update of applications and operating systems with latest security patches
   - Trained security technicians
   - Access authentication—use strong password access to all information, systems, and facilities (smartcards, public key infrastructure, and biometrics where needed)
   - Encryption
   - Virtual private networks
   - Antivirus software
   - Periodic security audits

5. Champion an organization-wide security awareness training program. Remember, the weakest link in most systems is the human factor. Bruce Sneier states it well in his book *Secrets and Lies: Digital Security in a Networked World*:[1]

Social engineering bypasses cryptography, computer security, network security, and everything else technological. It goes straight to the weakest link in any security system: the poor human being trying to get his job done, and wanting to help out if he can."

Benefits

Protecting the security of the company's information assets is a core responsibility of the CIO. The fundamental principles of asset protection apply, and often the CIO is the cornerstone for the protection of the critical intellectual property of the company. As with any other technology responsibility, cost justification is an issue. Those of us who have experienced major security breaches, however, know full well how costly a "security event" can be. Make security one of your top priorities.

First Steps

Begin your new emphasis on security using the following steps:

1. Appoint a security officer or security committee.
2. Develop and publish an information security policy.
3. Launch an abbreviated risk assessment initiative and take corrective actions on key vulnerabilities.

Example

Figure 12–6 shows a sample template for a server security audit.

---

1. Sneier, Bruce, *Secrets and Lies: Digital Security in a Networked World.* John Wiley & Sons, August 2000.

SERVER SECURITY AUDIT

System Name/Type/Administrator: Although the primary unit for this assessment is a server, some system classes such as desktops and HR security are not server specific. The Systems Name, Type (e.g. Novell, NT, Unix, etc.) and Systems Administrator must be included for each server. A class of servers may be included on one form; in this case, place the name, type, and systems administrator for all servers in these sections.

System Class/Audit Area details the specific item to be audited or commented on.

Level indicates relative importance of item.

      A = Business Critical – Must be complied with for legal or other business reasons. If not 100% compliant, explain in comments with expected compliance date.

      B = Region or Business unit may make determination of critical nature. If compliance is needed, explain in comment area with expected completion date.

      C =Compliance is advised, but not required. Comment as necessary.

Compliance - indicator of percentage of compliance of each item that is currently in place. To the degree possible, objective and verifiable measures be used to determine compliance level.

Comments - include any explanatory comments as desired.

Note: for all Level A items for which there is not 100% compliance, include the date when 100% compliance will be achieved.

Location: Headquarters		Assessed by: Jane Doe		Date: 6/12/2003
System Name: SAP				
System Type: Unix Systems				
System Administrator: John Smith				
	System Class/ Audit Area	Level	Compliance	Comments
1.	Servers – Physical Security			
1.1.	All servers are maintained in a physically secured location	A	100%	
1.2.	Access to server location monitored and logged	B	100%	
1.3.	HVAC is adequate for all servers and systems at location	A	100%	
1.4.	UPS for all critical systems	A	100%	
1.5.	Fire suppression systems adequate for server location	A	100%	Upgrade scheduled-9/03
2.	Servers – Logical Security			
2.1.	Procedures documented and implemented to manage Supervisor Accounts	A	100%	
2.2.	Procedures documented and implemented to manage concurrent user connections	C	100%	
2.3.	Procedures documented and implemented to ensure user passwords are unique, of a minimum length, and are required to be changed periodically	B	50%	Procedures in final review; will be implemented by 10/03
2.4.	Server console access is restricted	A	100%	
2.5.	System login auditing is enabled and audited	B	100%	
2.6.	The number of invalid log-on attempts are limited	B	100%	
2.7.	Inactive users are logged out after a specified period of time	C	0%	To be completed-10/03
3.	Desktops/Workstations – Physical Security			
3.1.	Procedures documented and implemented to secure the hard drive of portable computers	B	100%	
3.2.	Procedures documented and implemented to recover data from terminated employee systems	B	100%	
3.3.	Cable-security device provided for all portables	B	30%	To be completed-12/03
3.4.	Intrusion detection seals provided on all workstation case housings	C	100%	
4.	Desktops/Workstations – Logical Security			
4.1.	Power on password initiated for all portables	B	100%	
4.2.	Screen-saver passwords enabled on workstations	B	100%	
4.3.	Individual logins required on networked workstations	C	100%	
5.	Data – Physical Security			
5.1.	Redundant physical drives for all critical data file systems	A	100%	
5.2.	Procedures documented and implemented to verify drive physical integrity	B	100%	
6.	Data – Logical Security			
6.1.	Procedures documented and implemented to ensure encrypting of sensitive data	B	100%	
6.2.	Procedures documented and implemented to ensure integrity of locally stored data (e.g. server backup)	A	100%	
6.3.	Procedures documented and implemented to ensure latest release of anti virus software is running in real time on all servers	A	80%	To be completed-8/03
6.4.	Procedures documented and implemented to ensure all desktops are running anti-virus software	B	100%	

Figure 12–6   Server security audit.

Service-Level Agreements

Description

The operations of an effective and efficient enterprise-wide computing capability, whether provisioned inhouse or outsourced, demands that expectations between provider and client be well documented. Such a document is commonly referred to as a service-level agreement (SLA), and requires buy-in and formal approval by both the provider and the client. Of course, most CIOs are both providers and consumers of services, so we need to give SLAs to our internal/external customers as well as expect SLAs from our providers. The SLA spells out the responsibilities of all stakeholders, the levels of service to be expected, the scheduled environment/system downtimes, and the consequences (such as penalty payments) of not meeting the agreed-upon expectations.

Overall ownership of the SLA rests with the provider. The SLA should be seen as a living document, closely tracking the changes that take place in the operational environment.

Benefits

An operation in which expectations are clearly defined in a mutually agreed upon SLA enjoys the following benefits:

1. Higher customer satisfactions, as expectations are clearly defined and performance against those expectations can be objectively measured and presented.
2. A common understanding of roles and responsibilities both within and outside of the IT group.
3. A common communication system between provider and client for interfacing with the data center operations function.
4. Clear identification of the implications of service levels not being met.

First Steps

If SLAs are not in place in your organization, take these steps:

1. Identify your key service providers and establish SLAs with them immediately.
2. Identify the key services you provide to internal customers and establish SLAs with this group.
3. Depending on the nature of your business, consider establishing SLAs with external customers to whom you provide service; this

can help provide an objective, metrics-based foundation for performance evaluation.

Example

An example of an SLA outline is provided in Figure 12–7.

SERVICE LEVEL AGREEMENT

TABLE OF CONTENTS

I. INTRODUCTION
    A. PURPOSE
    B. SCOPE
II. DURATION OF AGREEMENT
III. SERVICES RESPONSIBILITY MATRIX
    A. PROVIDER
    B. CLIENT
IV. OUTAGE SEVERITY LEVELS DEFINED
V. SUPPORT SPECIFICATIONS
    A. HARDWARE
    B. SOFTWARE
    C. NETWORK
VI. CHANGE MANAGEMENT PROCEDURES
VII. PROBLEM MANAGEMENT PROCEDURES
III. SCHEDULED SERVER DOWN TIMES
    A. BACKUPS
    B. PERIODIC MAINTENANCE
IX. PERFORMANCE COMMITMENTS
X. KEY CONTACTS
    A. PROVIDER
    B. CLIENT
XI. ESCALATION PROCEDURES
APPENDIX A - DEFINITIONS

Figure 12–7 SLA table of contents.

▶ Focus Areas in Development

Programming Practices

Description

Is programming an art or a science? This debate, dating back to the early days of software development, still makes for good water cooler discussion. What is generally accepted, however, is that certain standard operating procedures in the development and maintenance of software are essential to the effective operation of an IT organization.

What constitutes programming best practices? This is a broad topic, which depends heavily on the languages and operating systems that exist within your infrastructure. An in-depth discussion is beyond the scope of this book, but certain fundamental concepts apply across most environments, from basic code design to the release management process that transitions code to the production environment. The "Example" section that follows provides a comprehensive set of topics for you to consider in constructing your programming practices and standards document.

Benefits

The seemingly countless benefits you can derive from developing and enforcing good programming practices include:

1. Increased maintainability resulting from less complex, more readable, and more reusable code.

2. Greater programmer interchangeability as standards are followed.

3. Improved productivity, resulting in more timely delivery of higher quality code.

4. Fewer "surprises."

5. Improved communication among development teams and with customers.

6. Reduced-volume, higher quality rework.

First Steps

If there are no standard programming practices in place in your development group, take the following actions:

1. Convene a team of senior developers willing to engage in a standards/practices effort; if facilitation is needed, contract with an expert in the field.
2. Select a small number of high-impact standards/practices to start—typically, we suggest you start with naming and coding standards along with formal code reviews—and have the team document and disseminate them.
3. Ensure that management enforces the standards/practices.
4. Systematically expand the effort.

Example

Perhaps the most comprehensive categorization of software development practices is included in the IEEE Software Development Professional Certification examination specification. Figure 12–8 includes these categories along with their relative weighting in the examination.

Project Management Process

Description

Although projects occur throughout all organizations in the IT group, application development projects tend to exhibit the most urgent need for a documented project management process. Business literature is replete with case studies of projects gone wrong, and careers are sidetracked as a result. If your organization exhibits any of the following symptoms, make an effective project management process a high priority:

- Approved initiatives out-of-sync with business needs.
- Key business-enabling projects not implemented.
- Requirements and costs not well defined/understood.
- Project surprises (dependencies, unknown commitments, and so on).

I. Business Practices and Engineering Economics (3-4%)

    A. Engineering Economics
    B. Ethics
    C. Professional Practice
    D. Standards

II. Software Requirements (13-15%)

    A. Requirements Engineering Process
    B. Requirements Elicitation
    C. Requirements Analysis
    D. Software Requirements Specification
    E. Requirements Validation
    F. Requirements Management

III. Software Design (22-24%)

    A. Software Design Concepts
    B. Software Architecture
    C. Software Design Quality Analysis and Evaluation
    D. Software Design Notations and Documentation
    E. Software Design Strategies and Methods
    F. Human Factors in Software Design
    G. Software and System Safety

IV. Software Construction (10-12%)

    A. Construction planning
    B. Code design
    C. Data design and management
    D. Error processing
    E. Source code organization
    F. Code documentation
    G. Construction QA
    H. System integration and deployment
    I. Code tuning
    J. Construction tools

V. Software Testing (15-17%)

    A. Types of Tests
    B. Test Levels
    C. Testing Strategies
    D. Test Design
    E. Test Coverage of Code
    F. Test Coverage of Specifications
    G. Test Execution
    H. Test Documentation
    I. Test Management

Figure 12–8   IEEE Software Development Certificate examination.

VI. Software Maintenance (3-5%)
   A. Software Maintainability
     B. Software Maintenance Process
     C. Software Maintenance Measurement
     D. Software Maintenance Planning
     E. Software Maintenance Management
     F. Software Maintenance Documentation
VII. Software Configuration Management (3-4%)
   A. Management of SCM Process
     B. Software Configuration Identification
     C. Software Configuration Control
     D. Software Configuration Status Accounting
     E. Software Configuration Auditing
     F. Software Release Management and Delivery
VIII. Software Engineering Management (10-12%)
   A. Measurement
     B. Organizational Management and Coordination
     C. Initiation and Scope Definition
     D. Planning
     E. Software Acquisition
     F. Enactment
     G. Risk Management
     H. Review and Evaluation
     I. Project Close Out
     J. Post-closure Activities
IX. Software Engineering Process (2-4%)
   A. Process Infrastructure
     B. Process Measurement
     C. Process Definition
     D. Qualitative Process Analysis
     E. Process Implementation and Change
X. Software Engineering Tools and Methods (2-4%)
   A. Management Tools and Methods
     B. Development Tools and Methods
     C. Maintenance Tools and Methods
     D. Support Tools and Methods
XI. Software Quality (6-8%)
   A. Software Quality Concepts
     B. Planning for SQA and V&V
     C. Methods for SQA and V&V
     D. Measurement Applied to SQA and V&V

Figure 12–8   IEEE Software Development Certificate examination (continued).

- Staff, not management, making strategic decisions.
- Slipped due dates and project cost overruns.
- Duplicate or unclear project roles and responsibilities.
- Project processes and procedures defined but "gathering dust."
- Project resources overcommitted.
- New project initiative-generation process a mystery.
- Frequent emergencies—reactive mode is SOP.
- Extensive rework late in development process.
- Overlapping or duplicative projects.

The challenge is to implement a process that fits the organizational culture and provides early warning of impending problems so that timely and appropriate action can be taken. The basis for the process is a project methodology, most often expressed in terms of a systems development lifecycle (see the following section). Such a methodology works equally well for infrastructure and applications development efforts. With this methodology in place, project success rests on the adequacy of the project control process used by the project manager. Figure 12–9 provides the key elements of an effective project control process. Look for these features in your process, particularly the rigor of the change-control subprocess.

Benefits

A rigorous project management process is a necessity. Here's what it does for you:

- Provides a common language for cross-functional communication.
- Integrates actions of all stakeholders.
- Identifies problems early so that corrective action can be taken.
- Minimizes rework.
- Provides a framework against which to assess project changes.

First Steps

If your organization has not instituted an effective project management discipline within your organization—if projects are started and not

<u>**PROJECT CONTROL PROCESS**</u>

I. Definition
    A. A process in which constant comparisons are made between actual and planned deliverables and due dates, and action taken as appropriate. The Project Manager owns this process

II. Key Elements of Project Control
    A. Tasks are decomposed into a Work Breakdown Structure, attempting to define the lowest level of self-contained work
    B. Tasks are assigned owners and due dates in a Project Plan
    C. Project Plan provides the framework for tracking tasks
    D. Task completion should be validated, with feedback given to the worker
    E. Communication to all stakeholders of project progress is essential and should be frequent

III. Managing Project Change
    A. Initiate
        - Change Board created to manage the change process
        - changes may come from any stakeholder
        - perform initial evaluation/approval to discard ideas without management approval
    B. Evaluate
        - assess resource and schedule implications
        - prioritize changes based on established set of criteria
        - decision made to proceed, queue or reject change
    C. Implement
        - project manager schedules approved changes
        - project manager informs stakeholders of revised dates/deliverables

IV. Responsibility Matrix
        - Specifies the responsibilities of all stakeholders in the project
        - Three levels of involvement for each task
            >> Own a task
            >> Work on a task
            >> Review deliverable of a completed task
        - Attempt to minimize tasks with shared responsibility
        - Example:

Task	P.M.	Team	User	Network	Operations ......
1	O/W		W	W	
2	O	W			W
3	R	R	O		
4	R		O/W		R
5	W		R		O

Figure 12–9   Project control process.

PROJECT DOCUMENTATION

A. Project Workbook – a comprehensive catalog of all project documents (electronic and hard copy)

  1. Project Definitions and Scope

    a. Project Description - several sentences defining the key characteristics of the project (what is the project purpose and outcome?)

    b. Business Purpose - several sentences describing who is the customer, and the fundamental business reason this project addresses. (Why should senior management find this project worth doing?)

    c. Project Scope - several sentences describing the extent of the impact of project. (What customers, resources, geography's, etc., will be impacted?)

    d. Project Approvals – project acceptance and signoff

  2. Project Plan

    a. Project schedule - include a Microsoft Project Schedule (or equivalent)

    b. Project Team and Roles - provide a project responsibility matrix (see III.D.)

  3. Project Budget

    a. Budget Plan - provide details for the capital and expense expenditures

  4. Project Implementation

    a. Status reports - include copies of all periodic project status reports.

    b. Project Change Logs - include copy of a documented log of all changes made the scope of the project.

    c. Change Board Minutes - include a copy of the minutes from the Change Board Meeting in which the project "go live" date is announced.

B. Status Reports

  - Effective tool for managing project expectations

  - Should be sent to all stakeholders

  - Should be produced periodically so that stakeholders expect its arrival (either monthly or weekly, depending on duration of the project)

  - Ensures consistent and comprehensive communication

  - Essential components of the status report

    >> Brief overall opening statement of status of project

    >> Describe what has transpired during the last reporting period

    >> Describe what is expected to transpire over next reporting period

    >> Identify specific issues to be brought to management's attention

Figure 12–9 Project control process (continued).

completed, for example, or time/cost estimates are regularly missed—take the following steps:

1. Search through your senior staff to identify a resource with expertise in project management (use external resources if necessary).

2. Have the individual you identify document a project management process, with components similar to those provided in the previous example, tailored to the culture and development processes in your group.

3. Quickly institute project phase reviews (tied to your systems development lifecycle) to ensure that current projects do not get far off track while you are implementing the more formal project management process.
4. Consider creating a "competency center" consisting of a small number of experienced project managers who can be allocated to projects as they arise.

Example

A sample high-level project plan covering the technical aspects of the implementation of a major system is provided in Figure 12–10. In practice, each task in this plan would be expanded into numerous subtasks, typically of several days in duration. Further, this project plan would constitute a subset of a broader plan, including the complementary business-related activities involved in the successful implementation of any information system.

Systems Development Lifecycle

Description

A systems development lifecycle (SDLC) is a methodology that defines the steps necessary to successfully conduct a software development project. The methodology may be an established product (such as the Rational Unified Process) or one developed inhouse, and should accommodate projects of all sizes, including both applications development and infrastructure projects. Further, the adopted methodology should be able to accommodate the need for rapid deployment projects. The SDLC should explicitly specify:

- Discrete phases with "go/no go" criteria.
- Formal reviews at critical phases (for example, design review).
- Role and responsibility definition for all participants.
- Communication structure such as meetings, reports, and so on.

Benefits

Experience has taught us that no software development project should start without a well-defined SDLC in place. Following the methodol-

	Task Name	Task Duration	Start Date	End Date	Task Dependency	Task Owner
0	I.T. Infrastructure Readiness Plan	247 days	6/9	2/10		
1	Obtain Project Signoff (**Inception** Phase)	1 day	6/9	6/9		Sam
2	Generate Detailed Project Plan	5 days	6/10	6/15	1.1	Sam
3	Define Technical Requirements (**Requirements Phase**)	16 days	6/15	7/1	1.2	Sam
4	Conduct Technical System Design (**Design Phase**)	31 days	7/1	8/1	1.3	Steve
5	Plan Production Support Strategy (**Begin Development Phase**)	20 days	10/28	11/25	1.4	Howie
6	Complete Quality Assurance System Site Preparation	5 days	8/8	8/12	1.4	Steve
7	Complete Production System Site Preparation	10 days	8/10	8/21	1.4	Steve
8	Define and Implement a Printing & Spooling Strategy	54 days	9/25	12/23	1.4	Mike
9	Assess and Install a Storage System Strategy	35 days	9/18	11/7	1.4	Mike
10	Define and Implement a Backup/Restore Strategy	46 days	11/7	12/23	1.9	Joe
11	Identify and Implement High Availability Capability	89 days	8/15	12/19	1.4	Shelton
12	Define and Install a Disaster Recovery Plan Strategy	89 days	8/24	12/30	1.4	Shelton
13	Define, Implement and Train - Operations Management	101 days	8/25	1/26	1.4	Brenda
14	Assess and Install Sufficient Network Capacity	76 days	7/15	11/25	1.4	Brenda
15	Implement Production System Management Capability	65 days	10/2	12/22	1.4	Glenn
16	Define and Implement Desktop Management Strategy	58 days	11/26	1/23	1.4	Glenn
17	Assess Production Readiness	2 day	1/23	1/24	1.16	All
18	Conduct Go Live Meeting—Sign Off for Production Cut Over	1 day	1/24	1/24	1.17	All
19	Production Cut Over	1 day	1/25	1/25	1.18	Bob
20	Execute Post Go-Live Activities (**Begin Support Phase**)	12 days	1/26	2/10	1.19	Sam

Figure 12–10   High-level project plan.

ogy ensures that appropriate phase reviews occur, that roles and responsibilities are clearly defined, and that expectations can be managed in a structured way. Typically, the SDLC is closely aligned with the general project management methodology within your organization. If your organization has a methodology, ensure that it is followed. If not, institute one immediately.

First Steps

If your organization has no documented SDLC, take these steps:

1. Convene a team of senior technical/management staff from your development group.
2. Charge the team with defining or acquiring an SDLC based on a set of specific requirements developed for your development team. For example, if you develop code only in Java, an SDCL uniquely tailored to Java is appropriate, but if you typically implement packages and discourage native code generation, other tools would be a better fit.
3. Create a project plan for the implementation of the selected SDLC, starting with a single development project and expanding to all future projects.

Example

Figure 12–11 provides a high-level overview of a five-phase SDLC that can be implemented quickly. In fact, this model was implemented in a small company within one month. Note that phase deliverables are illustrative rather than comprehensive.

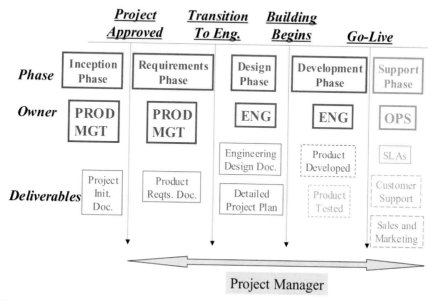

Figure 12–11   System development life cycle overview.

▶ Focus Areas in Human Resources

Company New Employee Orientation

Description

Although the responsibility for new employee orientation typically rests with the human resources function, this orientation provides a key opportunity for IT to communicate its policies and standards to the rest of the organization. If your HR group hasn't started a new employee orientation process, partner with the head of HR to put one in place as soon as possible. If your company has an orientation process in place, be sure that the IT agenda is presented at some point in it, preferably by an IT person.

Handing out materials to be read at leisure by the new employee has minimal value. Instead, develop a presentation on the mission of IT, on your internal standards, and on the "how-tos" of email and other corporatewide applications. Go even further and have every new employee sign a security policy statement.

Benefit

Capturing the attention of the employees is a difficult problem for IT in any organization. Perhaps the best time to reach employees is during orientation, when their attention to corporate policy is likely to be at its greatest.

The degree to which a CIO can influence the behavior of the rest of the corporation is very much dependent on the culture of the organization. When I worked for a federal agency, I was able to enforce standards across the organization. When I worked for a startup in Silicon Valley, however, individual autonomy was the rule; "standards" was a bad word. The key benefit of reaching employees early in their tenure is the ability to influence their usage of information resources in a way that both reduces your support costs and ultimately increases their satisfaction with your service.

First Steps

If your organization does not have an employee orientation program in place, take the following steps:

1. Approach your HR peer and lobby hard for a program that includes IT.
2. Develop a presentation that briefly outlines IT's role and communicates the essential elements of your infrastructure that you want new employees to know about.
3. Arrange for a senior IT staffer to make the presentation at each new employee orientation session.

Example

Figure 12–12 presents a recommended agenda for a new employee orientation meeting:

New Employee Orientation IT Agenda

- **OUR MISSION AND VALUES**
- **OUR ROLE - WHAT WE DO**
  - **Services**
  - **Products**
- **HOW WE DO IT**
  - **Infrastructure**
  - **Methodologies**
  - **Standards**
- **HOW YOU CAN HELP**
- **QUESTIONS?**

Figure 12–12   Recommended IT agenda—new employee orientation.

Managing Staff Performance

Description

IT is not a good career choice for those who like calm, quiet, and order. Every day presents new challenges, and learning to live with pressure is an essential requirement for success. How can a CIO focus staff on the key projects and day-to-day activities that lead to a high-performance IT organization? This section covers two tools that have proven effective in varying settings.

Most organizations have some form of performance management system in place, often tied directly to compensation. (Our favorite approach is a management by objectives program, which ensures that employee performance is compared directly to measurable objectives.) In IT, however, the formal corporate performance evaluation program is not enough.

How can you align the efforts of the entire organization to work as a team toward accomplishing your primary objective of delivering high-quality services to customers? We recommend using the IT Customer Expectations Matrix approach, a simple, one-page statement of expectations for the delivery of service to customers. The IT Customer Expectations Matrix includes explicit identification of customer groups, statements of their expectations, and metrics that define success. Evaluating performance against these metrics ensures that the IT team is meeting the stated expectations. This tool also serves as an excellent communication mechanism, from your IT organization straight to your customers. A sample form is provided in the "Example" section that follows.

Often it is the "small stuff" that leads to the highest level of customer satisfaction—the devil really is in the details. Establishing expectations within your organization for the day-to-day behaviors that lead to an excellent customer service reputation is a challenge.

Here is another straightforward approach that leads to results: Define a set of IT business practices, in collaboration with your management team, that forms a baseline of business behavior for your entire organization. The focus should be on those areas that matter most to your customers: staff responsiveness and availability. Be sure to align these behaviors with the fundamental processes defined earlier in this chapter, such as change and problem management processes, service interruption reports, outage notification processes, and so on. Figure 12–13 is an example of an IT business practices document.

IT Business Practices

1. Each workday, we will listen to voicemail at least at the beginning of each day, between noon and 1:30PM, and at the end of the day. Voicemails requiring a response will be responded to within 24 hours after receipt. If a voicemail relates to an urgent matter, response will be immediate.

2. Voicemails will be cleared so that the "voicemail box full" message will never be received by a caller.

3. We will read all emails at least once each day. Emails requiring a response will be responded to in not less than two working days.

4. An extended voicemail absence greeting will be left when out of the office for one day or more.

5. The out-of-office email feature will be used whenever someone is out of the office for more than one business day.

6. Cellulars and pagers should be kept operational (e.g. batteries charged) and available at all times.

7. All commitments made will be kept or renegotiated before the expected due date.

8. An Unscheduled Outage Notification will be sent by the [responsible party] to affected users using the standardized format immediately upon becoming aware of the outage. A follow-up message will be sent immediately after service has been restored.

9. A Scheduled Outage Notification will be sent by the [responsible party] to affected users using the standardized format at least 3 days prior to the scheduled outage. A second notification will be sent a minimum of two hours prior to the outage on the day of the event using the same standardized format.

10. For each production outage, a Service Interruption Report (SIR) will be completed by the technician accountable for the resolution of the outage within 24 hours of the event. If the root cause and/or prevention are not known within 24 hours, the form will so indicate; a revised form will be completed once the required information is available. If the root cause is not resolved within one week, the technician will escalate to his/her manager.

11. An attempt should be made to resolve all issues at a peer level. Escalation should be made to management only if peer level resolution cannot be achieved.

12. Punctuality for meetings is expected.

Figure 12–13   IT business practices.

Benefit

The benefits of the two approaches discussed in this section are in the identification and communication of key expectations for organizational success. Coupled with an objectives measurement program, these tools become a powerful foundation for improved organizational performance.

First Steps

Supplement your organization's existing performance management program with the two approaches mentioned above. Here's how to begin:

1. Ask each of your direct reports to define the "critical success factors" for their organizations and for IT as a whole (no more than five).

2. Convene a meeting of your direct reports in which your team defines the most vital factors and uses them to generate an IT Customer Expectations Matrix defining customers, expectations, and corresponding measurements.

3. Work with key internal and external customers to calibrate the matrix.

4. Communicate the matrix to your staff.

5. Put measurement and reporting in place (for both customers and staff).

6. Gather your direct reports for an IT business behaviors brainstorming session; start by identifying no more than five critical behaviors.

7. Communicate to your staff in an "all hands" meeting that these behaviors are now the norm in IT.

8. Expand the IT business behaviors list by adding one behavior a month (but keep the document to one page, at the most).

9. Review the IT business behaviors list at each management meeting and institute the measurements needed to determine whether your organization is meeting these expectations.

Example

Figure 12–14 contains a sample IT Customer Expectations Matrix.

IT Customer Expectations Matrix

FUNCTIONAL GROUP	CUSTOMER	EXPECTATIONS	MEASUREMENT
Systems Admin. Support	External Customers	Ext. DB & Systems Availability	>99.99% Availability
	External Partners	Ext. DB & Systems Availability	>99.95% Availability
	Internal Users	Email Availability	>99.9% Email Availability
		File & Print Services Availability	>99.9% Local/>99.5% Remote
		Int. DB & Systems Availability	>99.5% DB & Local System Avail.
Networking Support	External Customers	Ext. Network Availability	>99.99% WAN Availability
	Internal Users	Data Network Availability	>99.9% Availability
		Voice Network Availability	>99.9% Voice/Voicemail Avail.
Applications Support	Finance/Sales (ERP)	ERP Apps Availability	>99.95% Apps Availability
	Project Support	Delivered Systems	Within 15% of time/$ plan
	Existing Sys. Support	Response to Problems	Lo Priority - Within 4 hours
			Hi Priority - Within 1 hour
Customer Support	External Customers	Accurate & Timely Response	>98% Accurate/90%<48 Hrs. Old
	Internal Customers	Immediate Access to Sales Rep	>95% of Inquiries w/in 1 Hr.
		Help Desk Support	>85% Tickets Closed w/in 24 Hrs.

Figure 12–14   IT customer expectations matrix.

Training and Staff Development

Description

How often have you heard this platitude: "Our employees are our most important asset"? How do you give real meaning to this now highly overused statement? To be credible to your employees, you need to exhibit a genuine commitment to their professional growth while at the same time remembering that you are not running a training organization.

Achieving this balance is not that hard. Actually, the key to success is keeping it simple. The essential elements of a development plan are clearly tying training and education to business objectives, defining and obtaining mutual commitment to specific actions, and following up periodically on the commitments made. In practice, you will find that some employees who have complained about not being given the opportunity to develop their skills are actually not living up to their end of the commitment. Over an extended period of time, those who are committed to developing their skills make themselves evident.

Benefit

An effective training and development strategy:

- Provides a clear statement to employees that you are interested in and committed to their professional growth.
- Focuses on the mutual commitment between employee and employer necessary to make career development a reality.
- Enables predicable budgeting of training costs.
- Provides for feedback on the efficacy of training.

First Steps

If you do not have in place a formal training/development program, take the following steps:

1. Develop a program for training and development using as the foundation a form similar to that provided in the "Example" section that follows (we recommend you keep it simple).
2. Ensure that adequate funding is available to carry out the program.
3. As the senior IT professional in your group, consistently and visibly assert your commitment to the program.
4. Ensure that support for the program is part of the management evaluation process for your management team.

Example

A sample individual development plan template is provided in Figure 12–15. Note the simplicity of this form. In reality, it is a tool to achieve a basic agreement in which the employee and his or her manager agree and commit to one another that the development plan is feasible (for instance, funding will be available) and that the end result is mutually desirable.

INDIVIDUAL DEVELOPMENT PLAN

NAME: _____John Smith_____   **DATE:** __5/5/2003_

ORGANIZATION: _____Operations_____

MANAGER'S NAME: _____Jane Doe_____

PERIOD COVERED: _____ 1/2/2003 – 12/31/2003 _____

    I.   **TRAINING/DEVELOPMENT OBJECTIVE(S):**

Obtain a formal networking certification
Improve project management skills
Improve competency in technical writing

    II.   **TRAINING/DEVELOPMENT PLAN:**

Training/Development Activity	Expected Completion Date	Actual Completion Date
1. Identify networking certification courses	2/17/2003	2/12/2003
2. Complete coursework	7/10/2003	
3. Obtain network certification	12/1/2003	
4. Cross-train with Joe on Project X	4/17/2003	5/1/2003
5. Identify CBT course on technical writing	9/20/2003	
6. Successfully complete CBT course	11/15/2003	
7.		

EMPLOYEE SIGNATURE: _____ **DATE:** _____

MANAGER SIGNATURE: _____ **DATE:** _____

Figure 12–15   Individual development plan.

▶ A Closing Comment

In a few pages, we have attempted to capture the essential elements in making your IT infrastructure a true asset for you and your company. Of course, it is never quite that simple; what we have outlined here serves as a foundation on which you can build. By now, you recognize how interdependent many of the processes are and how they form building blocks for a comprehensive operations strategy. Our hope is that we have defined the key elements that will enable you to create such a strategy and help you in leading your organization to success.

13

Budgeting

by Bob Denis, Maureen Vavra, John Dick

> *Bob Denis introduces us to the perils of budgeting:*
>
> Hi, my name is Bob and I am a budgetholic (this word can be found in the dictionary of "Bobisms"). I have been clean for nine months but lately have fallen; this time of year is very difficult and emotional for me.
>
> Most managers go through this for the three months or so prior to the next fiscal year. I remember my first promotion to management level as if it were yesterday. "Congratulations on your promotion, Bob," said my boss, Guy, as he walked me to the new office on Wednesday morning. "Bob, this may seem a bit unfair, but I need a first-pass budget for your department by Friday," Guy went on, to which I replied, as we all do, "No problem," using my household budget as a reference point for budgeting (measured in minutes, not days).
>
> That was a life-impacting experience, as Guy made me go through nine iterations between Friday morning and the following Monday morning. Lucky for me, Guy wanted me to succeed, so he spent the time to make me understand the value of budgeting. I learned a career-saving lesson from Guy that applies to all management levels—critically so for CIOs and soon-to-become CIOs.
>
> Tip: When starting a new CIO assignment, upon completing the mandatory "meets and greets" of the first day on the job, find the budget and

get oriented. Use the budget as a guide to identifying and programming changes needed to tighten alignment with the enterprise strategy and economics.

Bob Denis, Maureen Vavra, and John Dick bring more than 50 years of collective experience to this chapter on budgeting—one of the most important aspects of any CIO's career. They discuss:

- *How to approach budgeting for success.*
- *How to simply break down the elements of a solid budget.*
- *The role of relationships in budgeting.*
- *Useful budgeting metrics.*
- *The budget toolbox.*
- *A simple budget process flow.*
- *Budget philosophy.*

It is important for a CIO to have a philosophy around budgeting. More important is that the philosophy be aligned with other members of the senior management team. Some philosophies that you may see include:

Budgeting is a necessary evil. This philosophy reduces the overall impact IT can have on improving the health of a company. This approach can lead to companies that feel IT is not a major component of their competitive front, a conservative approach that might result in tight spending, few to no projects, and largely a sustaining-only environment. If this philosophy inhabits the entire enterprise, the CIO may need to boldly but carefully evangelize the value of change, persuading the executive team of the value of IT as a competitive weapon and a change stimulus. This can be a difficult situation, but quite rewarding if a turnaround is achieved.

The budget is the Bible. This means tight monitoring of all major spending categories and little to no flexibility in adjusting for changes in major influencing factors. Although the budget components might be well planned, forcing a budget to survive for a full period of 12 months with little flexibility can lead to mediocre results in energizing the enterprise. If this is the way of the enterprise, you must work on relaxing this boundary so you gain the flexibility you need to react appropriately. Keeping executives abreast of trends in external influencing factors is one way to address this. Another is to take advantage of opportunities created by significant changes in the enterprise (acquisition, divesting, reorganization, a new product line launch, a new line of business) to revisit your budget and propose necessary adjustments to make the change a success.

The budget is a guide. This looser definition implies flexibility, but too much of it over the course of 12 months can lead to overreacting to changes that do not necessarily critically impact the success of your enterprise. This philosophy can result in major overspending in one or several areas of IT. If managed well, this approach is a good one; allow corrections based only on major changes in influencing factors.

The budget is an opportunity to influence change and support overall corporate direction. This means the IT budget is considered an investment, not a cost. A budget stemming from this philosophy is usually balanced and filled with corporate and line of business (LOB) strengthening projects, a very healthy approach. Adjustments are made for significant changes in influencing factors and in harmony with the rest of the senior management team. This is the most effective in our opinion.

Overall, the budget is a significant aspect of managing for success, but it is only one of many. Be serious in defining and using it in balance with the other aspects of successful IT management such as people, internal and external relationships, organization, and technology.

▶ Building Blocks for a Strong Budget

The following are some important elements in building an effective budget process:

Having a budgeting philosophy: It is important to know the rationale behind the budget: Control? Change? Conservation?

Investment justification (the ROI thing) and planning: A solid planning phase with clear budget impact statements, using a solid justification for the investments and attracted yearly expenses, is a necessity. (See Chapter 11 for more on planning.)

Building support for investments: The CIO can recommend investments within the IT "plumbing" domain. For all other investments, build the necessary support between the LOB and corporate function primaries.

An enterprisewide architecture: It is difficult to build a structure without a blueprint. This is your reference point for all adds and changes in the infrastructure, and it is simply a must.

Simplified view of the budget: Typically, people need to know about large expenses and major changes year over year. They also need to know the rationale behind the investments and their impact on the budget. Avoid getting lost elsewhere. Avoid getting too deep in details.

Review, acceptance, and signoff of initial budget and of all significant interim course corrections: Any major change impacting budgets (plus or minus) should be reviewed and ratified by the executive team at least.

Review of previous years' actual spending (two years' worth is enough): History has good value for adjusting ongoing expenses and for normalizing ratios. Make good use of it.

▶ Relationships and Budgets

The long and short of it is that a strong relationship with the executive team and the rest of the executive management members is critical to successful IT management, budgeting being just one aspect of that success. Solid budgeting relies on enlisting the team to support critical investments (strategic or sustaining) and getting their endorsement when significant budget adjustments (up or down) are required.

One way of accomplishing this is to link projects that represent major budget initiatives to specific enterprise or LOB goals and objectives, and then demonstrate how those links benefit and can be tracked back to the business goals. An example of how this might be done is shown in Figure 13–1.

In this diagram, business-focused initiatives are tracked through IT goals to IT systems projects and back into business impacts, thus completing a loop that enables LOB executives to see how they benefit.

Information Systems Initiatives

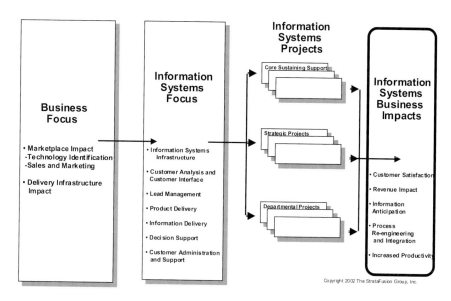

Figure 13–1 Information systems initiatives.

The strength of the relationship is usually based on the CIO's credibility in managing budgets and projects during his or her tenure as an executive. Managing bad news is critical to credibility; waiting until the last minute to inform the executive team of cost overruns and/or major deliverable delays can be career-limiting and certainly tarnishes your credibility. This is all just common sense. The best advice we have is to leave your ego outside the office when it comes to managing IT investments and expenses; it is a humbling yet rewarding experience to perform well in this area.

In some companies, there exists an IT leadership group, usually composed of representatives from the LOB and the corporate function groups. This group is tasked with issuing IT investment recommendations to the executive team, who are more than likely to endorse them. IT often co-chairs these groups, but *the leverage comes from getting consensus among the group on investment priorities*. This approach is often slower to produce decisions but does help in gaining acceptance, thus easing implementations. Although this can be a test of patience for CIOs, maintaining composure and good relationships with all members of such a team is highly advised.

Figure 13–2 reflects these relationships. The process of determining buy-in on a budget requires support from senior staff and your IT users. You can accomplish this through the empowerment of users via an operational planning layer that includes them in the prioritization process and the strategic participation of the senior staff, which reinforces LOB participation and gives them "ownership" of the results.

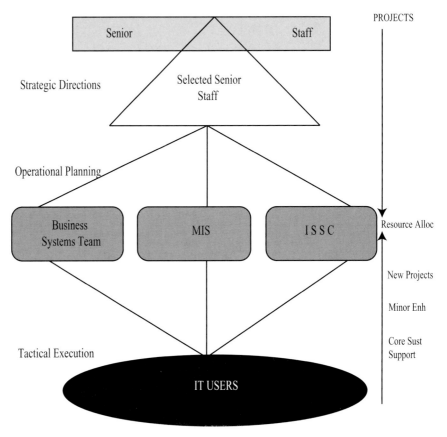

Figure 13–2   Project flow and resource allocation.

▶ Budget Feeds: Significant Influencing Factors to Consider

Significant influencing factors are clustered in two major categories: corporate factors and IT environment factors.

Corporate Factors

Geographical coverage (local, domestic, international on some or all continents): Infrastructure complexity and costs go up substantially in a multilocation setup, even more so if multicontinental, especially in locations in which infrastructure and support services are much less developed.

Size (small, medium, large, mammoth): The more users, the more complexity and costs. The logical breaks differ between companies, but you can always tell when a barrier has been broken. Anticipating the growth steps just before they happen is an art to develop.

Trajectory (growth, as in investing or mergers and acquisitions, versus decline, as in cost reduction or divestment, versus holding, as in cost containment, flat revenues, or majority market share): The budget philosophy adopted is almost directly related to this factor. Be wary of overbuilding your infrastructure when targeting meteoric growth; it is easier to adjust IT expenses up as revenues are coming in than it is to reduce IT expenses if revenues fail to match expectations.

Business type (tangibles, services, e-commerce, traditional): Most companies within a particular industry group have similar cost structures. The smart CIO keeps abreast of the trends and the major shifts affecting his or her business sector.

Enterprise business organization architecture: The organization of the enterprise can have a significant impact on the budget and on project investments: single versus multiple lines of business, centralized versus decentralized corporate services (such as finance, manufacturing, planning, information services, human resources, research and development). Each permutation comes with its pros and cons from IT management and budget impact perspectives. (See chapters 8 and 11 for more on enterprise architecture and planning.)

IT Environment Factors

Systems availability expectations: Must be 24/7—but there are shades of 24/7. The closer to full 24/7, the more expensive, with the last four hours of the 24 logarithmically more expensive.

User support expectations: Online 24/7; what are the repair time expectations? Again, shades of 24/7 with increased expense in the last four hours.

Systems response time expectations: Subsecond response on transaction and R&D systems? Any subsecond expectation costs dearly—weigh the value before jumping to such tight expectations.

Security: Spam, virus, intrusion detection systems, encryption—at what levels? Overinvesting in this area can be expensive and complex to manage. Consider a balance of investments in protection and service restoration.

Access: From anywhere in the world at all times? Connectivity and access redundancy to ensure no single points of failure and access at all times is expensive. High-availability technologies (such as ATM and Frame) are also expensive. Research the amount of time you can afford to be out of access before it negatively impacts the business.

Makeup: Is your IT shop "buy" or "make"? Do you need more developers or more business analysts? Consider the need to fund and maintain development environments and whether to increase engineering change controls, rollouts, and documentation.

- Are your application users advanced or traditional? An engineering environment requires more skilled IT personnel.
- Are your IT organization and budget management centralized or decentralized? Since some cost is typically incurred in a decentralized model, ensure that the IT organization is *in synch with the enterprise business organization architecture.* If the enterprise is decentralized (including major decision making), centralizing IT is probably going against the fabric of the company.
- How are data and voice responsibility allocated (or not)?
- Significant outsourcing versus insourcing? Outsourcing entails management overhead and may be more expensive, but the pros (such as a more flexible staffing model or specialized skills) may be worth it.

- Do you have an enterprisewide technical architecture? You are flying blind without it. You need a reference blueprint to build something solid.
- What kind of network architecture are you using? More advanced technologies (VPN, VoIP, and so on) are expense savers overall but require technical skills to configure and maintain the environment.

Legacies from prior commitments and budgets: Are multiyear projects in progress? Are multiyear equipment and services leases in force? Are outsourcing contracts active?

These lists of influencing factors are partial, and you should amend any factor deemed a major influence in your business context. Writing down your list of influencing factors is what is important. You may consider weighting these factors for complexity of the environment involved; this can be useful during the justification portion of the budget process.

▶ Partitioning Your Budget

IT budgets are stated in two types of dollars: capital expenditures and expenses. Capital expenditure is cash that is treated differently, in financial terms, from operating expenses. Simply put, capital expenditures create assets that are consumed over periods of time. Examples include implementing a new ERP system or expanding the capacity of a storage area network. From a financial reporting standpoint, cash is reduced during the build/acquire phase, with a resulting commensurate increase in the capital asset; for example, pay $1,000 for a component, and the value of your assets goes up by $1,000. When the asset is put into production, a "useful life" and "residual value" are estimated based on financial reporting rules. The difference between the cost of the asset and the residual value is divided by the useful life in months, and that amount, called depreciation, is charged to expenses every month that the asset is in service. The theory is to align the expense of the asset with its useful life.

Expenses represent cash outlays for goods and services that are consumed in the period in which they are acquired. Examples include employee salaries, electricity, and copier paper. Consult with your CFO for a deeper understanding of the differences in financial reporting treatment in your organization.

Capital Expenditures

The capital expenditure budget is probably your most important tool in enabling change. CIOs are evaluated on their accuracy in estimating capital expenditure dollars in projects; a deviation of plus or minus 10 percent is usually an acceptable performance, with 5 percent approaching heroism. Capital expenditures usually include purchases of the hardware and software (including licenses) required for implementation projects and the related professional services implementation fees (for consultants, offshore development, and so on).

Capital expenditure dollars are allocated to a depreciation schedule (between three and seven years, with the bulk in the three-to-five year range), and a depreciation line is entered on your expense budget as soon as a portion or the entirety of the new capital project is officially in service. The impact on the expense budget is important to recognize, as it can be significant. Capital expenditure typically does not include "maintenance and updates" annual fees, nor does it cover end-user training fees; it does, however, cover training for the implementation team.

A final note on capital expenditure money: Some or all of it may be eligible for R&D tax credits depending on the custom nature of the project. Review with your tax primary to ensure you take advantage of this corporate tax feature.

It is important to track capital spending (quarterly at a minimum) if only as a good project management practice, but also for sound business reasons. Remember that capital expenditure is "cash," and the company may have bank covenants limiting its cash outlays quarter-over-quarter until its cash position improves. Work closely with the CFO to understand this impact and adjust project spending accordingly. One way to help bring relief to a cash crunch from an IT perspective is to consider leasing as much as makes sense of a new project's equipment, perhaps even selling existing in-service equipment to financial companies willing to lease it back to you over a decent period for a favorable rate. Application packages are also included in assets that should be considered for leasing.

Capital Expenditures for Large Projects

Dealing with mega projects spanning multiple budget years can be a challenge and one that really boils down to good project management, specifically tying deliverables to capital expenditures in each budget period. Realizing that some deliverables can run over into the next budget year, you need to make the necessary adjustments to compensate in the new budget year.

Here's a tip: The smaller your time intervals for meaningful deliverables, the easier the challenge of managing multiyear projects. We recommend logically slicing deliverables to no more than three months elapsed time, ideally a single month. Deliverables of less than one month for mega projects can, however, become a management burden. Be careful about getting too granular; thrashing details that bring little value to the project or enterprise can give you a false sense of control.

Strategic Versus Sustaining Capital Expenditures

The difference between strategic and sustaining capital expenditures can be simply explained as follows: *Sustaining investments* are those that keep the infrastructure operating at your advertised availability and performance targets. We are talking about the "two 9" to "six 9" targets and the 5/8 to 7/24 coverage periods. The closer to 24/7 at 99.9999 you want to be, the higher your yearly investments in this area. Potential investments include:

- Redundancy galore.
- End-of-life replacement.
- Expansive disaster recovery and business continuity plans.
- Complex network analysis and security tools.
- Sophisticated backup equipment.
- Technology conversion projects.
- Asset management.

You may find it useful to further divide sustaining expenditures into "survival" and "maintenance" for normal operations. This will ensure at least the network security and connectivity investments typically found in the survival category are retained.

Strategic investments can be initiated by LOB, corporate functions, or both. They are usually based on increased revenues, increased efficiency and productivity, business process reengineering initiatives, increased customer loyalty, and integration of mergers and acquisitions. From a pure IT perspective, this area also includes research into technologies and applications for potential future sponsoring by the LOB and corporate functions, as they would best determine the value. Items in the strategic list include:

- Typical core systems implementations: ERP, CRM, PDM, APM, OSS, billing, and so on.
- E-business: B2B, B2C, partner sites, and so on.
- Online employee self-services: expenses, timesheets, stationary orders, and so on.
- Data: knowledge, intelligence, and intuition projects.
- Network: voice over IP, wireless, and productivity user devices such as PDAs and handhelds.

There might be value in further splitting strategic investments into "growth" and "breakout." This helps in securing breakout investments, since they are usually mega projects that typically require investments across multiple years.

Prioritizing Capital Expenditures

Another approach to deciding on capital expenditure investments is to assign a *priority* to each investment proposed. The priority is a combined representation of the ROI and the risk of not doing (which is sometimes difficult to assess in ROI terms). We tend to limit the priority scale to values, as follows:

1. **Absolute Must.** Includes security, legal, regulatory, end-of-life equipment; typically externally mandated, that is, you really have little or no choice. Simply stated, if you are under tight capital expenditure and/or expense budget constraints, the cutoff is drawn here.

2. **Highly Desired/Business-Critical.** Includes short-term "break even" (less than six months), significant short-term "return to top or bottom line" less than months), and mega projects

already in progress. Most priority-2 items are approved for budget year funding under normal revenue growth projection conditions. Typically, the cutoff for funded projects gets drawn here.

3. **Wanted.** Valuable, with a longer return term (more than 12 months). Typically, these projects get funded only if there is capital money remaining, if resources are available, and if revenue projections are fairly secured. They may find their way to priority 2 or even priority 1 in subsequent budget years.

4. **Nice to Have** Given available bandwidth in people and money, there is a good return on these projects, but typically the ROI has more intangibles. Unlikely to be funded in this budget year; might go up the priority list in subsequent budget years. It is important to have some projects in this priority, as it helps to better calibrate the higher priorities.

Another possibility in prioritization is to continue on the theme discussed above and track the projects back to the business goals and associated resources. This might be as easily done by major category, as shown in Figure 13–3.

A more tactical approach that can be effective, particularly in small to mid-sized organizations using a budgeting philosophy that is conservative in its focus on business benefit, justification, and ROI, is depicted in Figure 13–4.

The message here is for the CIO to apply some dimension to project candidates, such as category and priority, to indicate the rationale for inserting these project investments in this budget year.

Figure 13–5 is a sample *executive summary of proposed investments.* We include both dimensions of classification and priority. This is a good demonstration of the CIO's ability to understand the business conditions and economics influencing the budget as well as the technology response the CIO is expected to provide. Capital expenditure proposal and management is a major area that can make or break a CIO's career; it requires serious attention.

This summary includes totals by priority, by category of investment (hardware, software, and professional services organizations, or consultants), and by attracted expenses for the budget year (depreciation, maintenance, and services).

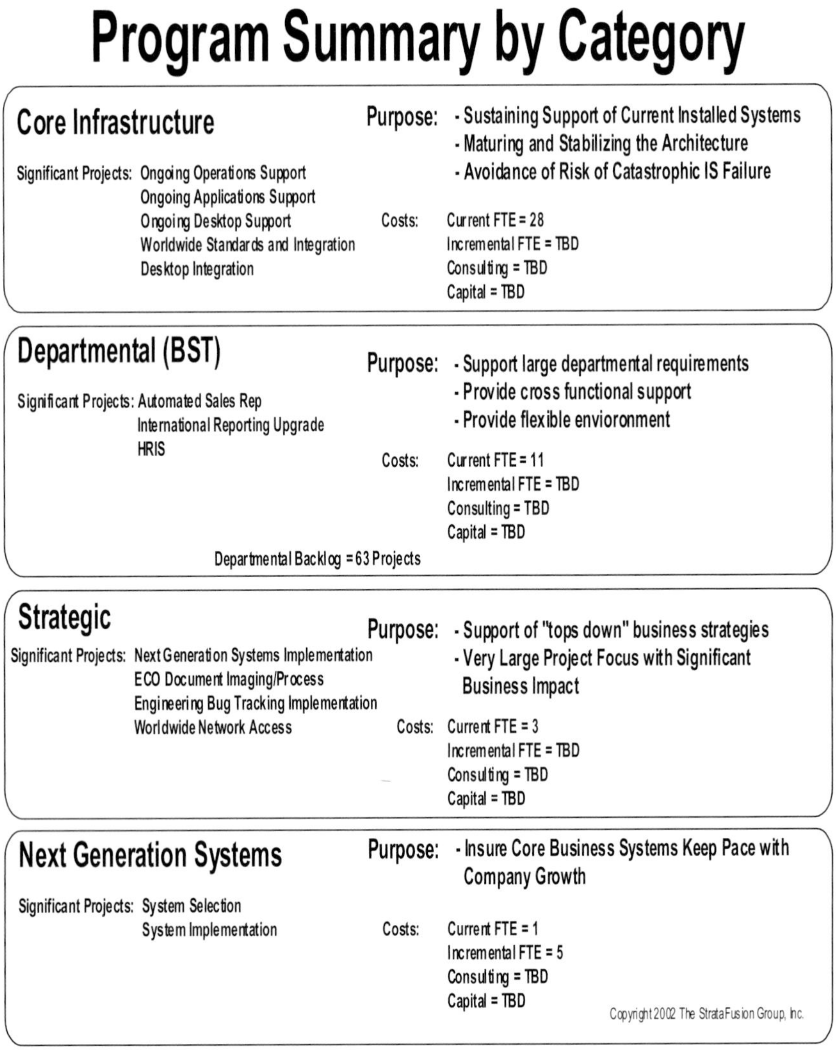

Program Summary by Category

Core Infrastructure

Significant Projects: Ongoing Operations Support
Ongoing Applications Support
Ongoing Desktop Support
Worldwide Standards and Integration
Desktop Integration

Purpose: - Sustaining Support of Current Installed Systems
- Maturing and Stabilizing the Architecture
- Avoidance of Risk of Catastrophic IS Failure

Costs: Current FTE = 28
Incremental FTE = TBD
Consulting = TBD
Capital = TBD

Departmental (BST)

Significant Projects: Automated Sales Rep
International Reporting Upgrade
HRIS

Purpose: - Support large departmental requirements
- Provide cross functional support
- Provide flexible envioronment

Costs: Current FTE = 11
Incremental FTE = TBD
Consulting = TBD
Capital = TBD

Departmental Backlog = 63 Projects

Strategic

Significant Projects: Next Generation Systems Implementation
ECO Document Imaging/Process
Engineering Bug Tracking Implementation
Worldwide Network Access

Purpose: - Support of "tops down" business strategies
- Very Large Project Focus with Significant
Business Impact

Costs: Current FTE = 3
Incremental FTE = TBD
Consulting = TBD
Capital = TBD

Next Generation Systems

Significant Projects: System Selection
System Implementation

Purpose: - Insure Core Business Systems Keep Pace with
Company Growth

Costs: Current FTE = 1
Incremental FTE = 5
Consulting = TBD
Capital = TBD

Figure 13–3 Program summary by category.

Data entered in the "in-service month" is used to modify the depreciation based on the predicted "in-service" date of the project; if a project goes in service next year, enter zero here and reenter the line in the next budget year with a note on the capital that has already been spent. Depreciation is calculated in this case on a three-year basis for hardware and a four-year basis for software and related implementation professional services. Maintenance is calculated in this case at 18 percent per year, 25 percent for software; maintenance is further adjusted

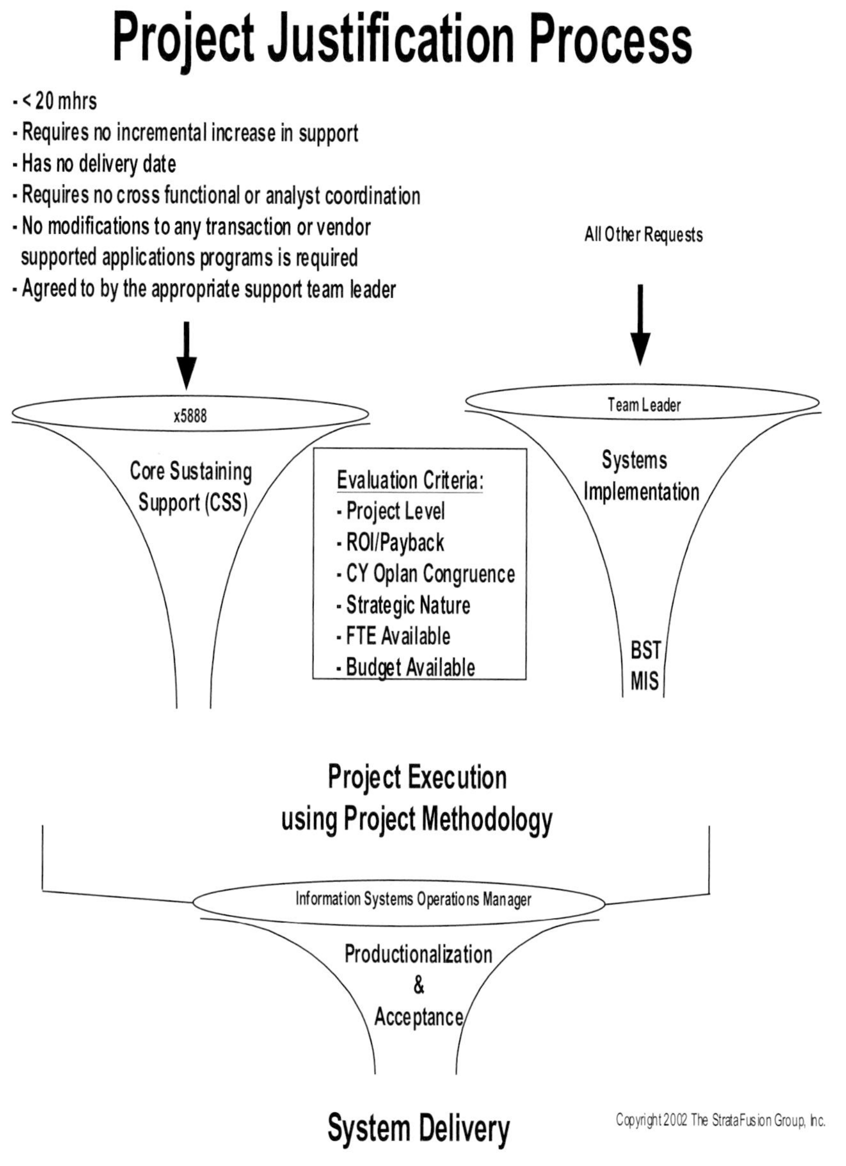

Project Justification Process

- < 20 mhrs
- Requires no incremental increase in support
- Has no delivery date
- Requires no cross functional or analyst coordination
- No modifications to any transaction or vendor
  supported applications programs is required
- Agreed to by the appropriate support team leader

All Other Requests

x5888

Team Leader

Core Sustaining
Support (CSS)

Systems
Implementation

Evaluation Criteria:
- Project Level
- ROI/Payback
- CY Oplan Congruence
- Strategic Nature
- FTE Available
- Budget Available

BST
MIS

Project Execution
using Project Methodology

Information Systems Operations Manager

Productionalization
&
Acceptance

System Delivery

Copyright 2002 The StrataFusion Group, Inc.

Figure 13–4   Project justification process.

by a starting factor, in this case set at .75, meaning most purchases will
happen in the first two quarters of the year. One could open different
columns of data to capture the exact start of maintenance to increase
accuracy; for this summary level of presentation, the adjustment factor
is sufficient. The data entered in the yearly services column (connectiv-

ALL values in $KUS	Investment hw	Investment sw	Investment PSO	In-Svce Month	Deprec. sw/hw	Yrly Mtce *Adj Factor	Yrly Service	Svce	2003 Cap $	2003 Exp $	Priority	Cat
ORACLE												
RFC's Enhancements			$ 100	2	$ 23	$ -		0	$ 100	$ 23	2	Str
SQL Tool (Toad)		$ 25		1	$ 6	$ 5		0	$ 25	$ 11	3	Mtce
Financials		$ 100	$ 200	1	$ 75	$ 19	$ 12	0	$ 300	$ 106	1	Str
Oracle Barcoding		$ 30		6	$ 4	$ 6	$ 12	0	$ 30	$ 22	4	Mtce
ORACLE technology licenses		$ 80		2	$ 18	$ 15		0	$ 80	$ 33	2	Str
Incentive Compensation		$ 5		3	$ 1	$ 1		0	$ 5	$ 2	2	Str
Treasury		$ 50	$ 25	9	$ 6	$ 9	$ 6	0	$ 75	$ 22	3	Str
Additional Licenses		$ 100		3	$ 21	$ 19	$ 6	0	$ 100	$ 46	3	Mtce
Web Order Status			$ 50	6	$ 7	$ -	$ 6	0	$ 50	$ 13	2	Str
Data Warehouse												
Balanced Score Card (BSC)		$ 50	$ 50	9	$ 8	$ 9			$ 100	$ 18	2	Str
Alerts and notices	$ 15	$ 50	$ 10	6	$ 12	$ 11			$ 75	$ 23	2	Str
DashBoard		$ 10		9	$ 1	$ 2			$ 10	$ 3	3	Str
IWR and Alert Servers	$ 10			3	$ 3	$ 1			$ 10	$ 4	3	Mtce
Others												
Forecasting & Planning				12	$ -	$ -			$ -	$ -	3	Str
Nextlinx upgrade	$ 5	$ 150	$ 50	6	$ 30	$ 29			$ 205	$ 59	3	Mtce
Customs Reporting	$ 15	$ 100	$ 100	3	$ 46	$ 21			$ 215	$ 67	3	Str
Network & Servers												
New apps	$ 30			3	$ 8	$ 4			$ 30	$ 12	2	Str
End-of-life	$ 50			6	$ 10	$ 7			$ 50	$ 16	1	Sur
Security												
PKI server	$ 20			1	$ 7	$ 3			$ 20	$ 9	1	Sur
PKI key manager		$ 25	$ 50	6	$ 11	$ 5			$ 75	$ 16	1	Sur
TOTALS	$ 145	$ 775	$ 635	5	$ 298	$ 165	$ 42		$ 1,555	$ 504		

	HW	SW	PSO	~ Mth	DEPR	MTCE	Yrly Svce		TOTALS BY GROUPING		
Priority 1 & 2 ONLY	$ 115	$ 310	$ 460	4	$ 180	$ 74	$ 18		$ 765	$ 277	ORACLE
Priority 3 & 4 ONLY	$ 30	$ 465	$ 175	6	$ 117	$ 91	$ 24		$ 790	$ 227	Others

Calculations Parameters:			By Category	2003 CAP $	2003 EXP $				
						$ 445	$ 147	P1	4
Hardware Mtce	18%					$ 440	$ 125	P2	7
Software Mtce	25%		Str	Strategic	$ 1,040 / $ 321	$ 640	$ 211	P3	8
HW depreciation period	3		Mtce	Maintenance	$ 370 / $ 142	$ 30	$ 22	P4	1
SW & PSO depreciation period	4		Sur	Survival	$ 145 / $ 41	$ 885	$ 272	P1 + P2	11
Adjustment factor for partial year	0.75								

(Count: for Others / P-groupings)

Figure 13–5 Executive summary of proposed investments.

ity, subscriptions, and so on) completes the bulk of expenses for projects.

Notice that there is a subtotal for priorities 1 and 2 combined; this is in anticipation that this will become the minimal approved list, making it easier to sum the results. For mega projects spanning over this year's budget, we reenter the project with a comment (red corner in some cells of column A) and enter the values for this year. We do intend to improve the accuracy slightly, but it is 95 percent accurate, plenty good for budgeting purposes.

Expenses

The following items constitute what is most typically referred to as "the budget." The major categories of budget expenses are:

Personnel

- Salaries and benefits (including hiring fees and bonuses)
- Training and education
- Travel
- Morale
- Staff-related depreciation
- Temporary help/consultants
- Miscellaneous (space, telecom, and so on)

Hardware

- Depreciation
- Maintenance
- Repairs
- Leases

Software

- Depreciation
- Maintenance
  - Customer support
  - Updates
- Repairs
- Leases

Services

- Leased lines
- Outsourced network services
- Security services
- Applications service providers (ASPs)
- Miscellaneous (transport, courier, periodicals, and so on)

The following sections provide rationales for each of the items in this list.

Personnel

Salaries and benefits are obvious. You know where to get the actual salaries for regular full-time employees, and the controller can help you determine what ratio to use to capture the benefits (usually 30 percent of the base salary). For new hires, any public domain salary report contains the high-low for a given job description, and you can simply add the benefits; added expenses are usually a one-time fee for the hiring agency (up to 30 percent of the hiring salary) and a hiring bonus payable to the new employee at specific anniversary date(s).

Training and education is probably the most important people investment. We use the rule of $500/day including expenses and plan for a minimum of five days of development per year per person. Think of it as five out of 220 days, or a 2 percent time investment in keeping skills current. This number needs adjustment if the IT infrastructure is using more new technologies. It is good practice to track training, seminar, and conference days for each of your employees as well as any personal education time spent on business-relevant subjects. We do this, review the information monthly, take action where appropriate, and report on it at the end of the year.

Travel should be considered separately. Since many companies are geographically distributed, IT staff are often asked to travel for new installations or repairs. This can amount to a significant expense and may justify a local permanent hire at a break-even point, which makes the expense more visible. This category could be roped into the miscellaneous line if direct visibility is of no value.

Morale is a contentious item used in some companies. However, we believe it is essential to the proper functioning of the IT group. It certainly should be placed into the miscellaneous line. The important message is to plan a certain amount of group-bonding (team-building) activities to keep the energy level and overall participation at their highest. For budget planning purposes, we suggest an average of some $500 per head for the year. In more progressive companies, the activities tend to be more elaborate; try to keep a per-head view of this investment in your people.

IT Staff related depreciation includes furniture, personal computers, workstations, desk servers, test equipment, and so on. Again, we recommended that you develop and apply a ratio based on the typical cubicle configuration for your IT folks.

Temporary help and consultants, as a talent alternative, charge between two and four times what you pay a permanent employee. However, there are clear instances in which this approach makes for a wise investment:

- For large implementations (such as ERP, CRM, and so on) involving a "bubble" of work.
- For highly technical initial implementations such as security packages, new network technologies, and the like.
- For reengineering initiatives in which the internal bias is removed and best practice is preached by specialists.
- For assessments of the technical or operational health of the infrastructure, the organization, or the environment in general.
- For feasibility studies for which subject-matter experts' knowledge is required.

Although the instant value is high, without a transfer of knowledge into the IT organization, much or most is lost in sustaining the change or implementation past the initial effort. Make sure that the IT organization can support the results of these efforts. Some organizations, with an avid thirst for change and leading-edge technology, may want to consider an ongoing entry in the operations budget for some percentage of their workforce count to come from outsiders (hopefully under 15 percent unless outsourced managed services are used).

Another increasingly popular form of external resources is offshore development. If you are a "make" shop, this can be an attractive approach to many somewhat generic projects, by which we mean integration and reports type of work and operations automation as opposed to product related work. For the latter, you need control and assurance of confidentiality with regard to the goods produced (code). Again, there is overhead in managing these arrangements, but the value to the IT shop and the enterprise makes it worthwhile.

Miscellaneous expenses should be managed by establishing a ratio over your headcount base and applying it across the budget period covered.

Guard against putting too much in here; a fat miscellaneous line will negatively affect your credibility as a business manager.

Hardware

These categories are fairly standard:

Maintenance in hardware typically runs 15 to 20 percent.

Depreciation occurs over two to seven years, depending on the item. Use a budget tool that allows the insertion of new hardware in a specific month and calculates the monthly depreciation based on the entered depreciation period.

Repairs should include relatively little if you cover all your hardware with original vendor maintenance. (This practice is highly recommended, at least for the critical servers and all network elements.) Establishing a solid third-party service contract covering repairs and upgrades is a viable alternative but can lead to trouble if vendor personnel are not certified for all the equipment providers you use.

Warning: Saving a few dollars on maintenance is a dangerous game to play unless the company is willing to live with the possible consequences of business downtime due to system unavailability.

> **Tip:** For critical equipment (such as network switches and routers and servers used for business transactions or customer interactions), it is generally more advantageous to replace the equipment at the end of its depreciation period than to keep on paying maintenance on it and "stretching" its useful life.

For critical equipment, you might want to invest in "hot" redundancy. If under budgetary constraints, standardize on a family of servers and maintain "cold" standbys that you can quickly insert in the event of a crash or can pick for parts on a needs basis.

Leases of hardware are an attractive alternative that you should carefully consider. Pros include

- Preserves cash for more business growth-oriented investments.
- Predictable monthly expense hit on the budget.
- Forces the discipline of turning over end-of-life equipment.
- Usually includes full maintenance and support built into the deal.

Cons include:

- A bit more expensive over the life of the lease than the original purchase price; nowadays, the leasing premium is around 10 to 12 percent, with good deals still existing in single-digit percentages for some equipment.
- Requires action at the end of the lease (extend lease; new lease/ new equipment; buy for $1, at fair market value, or at predetermined value).
- Can get complicated in the case of vendor or leaser bankruptcies; cover yourself in the Terms and Conditions (T&Cs) of the leasing contract.

Negotiating a lease can be complicated. Using reputable IT infrastructure equipment vendors who offer leasing options is generally safer and easier to deal with.

> **Tip:** Perform a detailed review of the terms and conditions, particularly the fine print. Work closely with the corporate counselor for best coverage. In the absence of a corporate counselor, we recommend the use of an attorney specializing in contract ratification or an experienced broker.

Software

Budgeting for software can be complex, since it is highly dependent on the contract terms negotiated and the nature of some of the projects on which the software will be used.

Depreciation is simple enough in that you determine the useful life of the software purchased (three to seven years, usually four years for enterprise software, three years for others). If the software is part of an overall implementation project for which consultants are engaged, their fees are normally included in the depreciation over the same period as the software. All other project related nontangible expenses (training, travel, and so on) are entered directly in the budget for the year incurred.

Maintenance is at the heart of the software budgeting complexity. Vendors vary on how they approach this, and at the moment there are no set definitions of types of licenses, which largely drive maintenance.

The bottom line is that this is all negotiable at the time of contract, which can have a major impact on the budget if rushed or overlooked.

Aspects to consider in negotiating software maintenance include the following:

- In many cases the maintenance percentage goes into the customer service bucket, so the P&L is under a different managing executive; the sales representative has little or no power over this part. You may need to deal directly with the service organization to receive more favorable terms.

- Maintenance is often broken into two types: software upgrades and technical support; each type has its own percentage setting. We recommend software upgrades as a must. Technical support can be avoided if you have enough experience and expertise on staff and the vendor offers a fee-per-support call service feature. You are exposed, but the savings may justify it depending on your comfort with the inside knowledge or if the software is not on the list of critical applications.

- If using the fee-per-support call option, attempt to include a clause in the contract providing a credit back for expenses incurred by calls resulting from bugs in the vendor software. It might also be worth negotiating a partial inclusion, like coverage for a preset amount for a predetermined period, usually equal to the implementation plus three months live.

- Some vendors are covering their increased costs in customer service by building in an annual increase, typically in percentages, and applying a cap over a predetermined period. Ensure clear understanding of these terms, or negotiate this out altogether, as it can have a significant incremental impact on your budget for years to come; maintenance fees can run more than 30 percent over time if this is overlooked.

- Some vendors' maintenance fees are based on the number of users; typically, they use a sliding scale approach under which the fee per users diminishes with the number of licenses in use. This scheme makes for a lot of ambiguity and unpredictability in your budget. We recommend negotiating this out in favor of a flat rate-based approach.

Repairs, as an expense category, is used mainly in cases in which IT has opted away from technical support maintenance and is using the fee-per-support call option, usually set at a predetermined rate per hour with a minimum number of hours charged per call. Also consider using this category for consulting fees for the purpose of repairing software that is not on maintenance. It is prudent to count on two four-hour calls a year for assistance where the applications are stable and under predictable usage.

Leases of software are becoming more popular for the same reasons provided for in the hardware paragraph. Monthly distribution for leases should be managed separately in this category.

Services

Leased lines are the Telco and Internet service provider (ISP) connectivity lines to the Internet or private networks. Although this is a single account in the budget, we strongly recommended that you keep a detailed accounting of the monthly charges by facility, by circuit, and by provider, as this can get complex over a large number of locations and more so if international circuits are involved. One alternative is to turn this management task over to a brokerage firm responsible for provisioning and providing you with unified, detailed billing; they are often worth their management fee.

Outsourced network services include network management fees (onshore or offshore) that typically represent a flat rate for an entire network or a monthly rate per network node under monitor contract. The flat rate is simplest; divide your contract by 12 to give you the expense line result. This type of contract has thresholds for the number of nodes changed over a defined period, with consequent rate adjustment. The per-node monthly charge method is a bit more complex to keep track of but ultimately gives you more granular control over the costs. In either case, aim to get a detailed monthly bill for all charges from your provider(s).

Also use this budget bucket to collect your equipment collocation fees (such as for Web servers), fees for value-added networks (VANs) such as Electronic Data Interfacing (EDI) transparency nets, and any other network-type services subscriptions.

Security services are a collection area for virus protection and spam filter subscriptions, private key infrastructure (PKI) key management services, network security audits, network intrusion audits, security equipment servicing (card readers, fingerprint readers, retina scanners, and so on), and other related expenses. We prefer to differentiate these from standard network services for better visibility of security costs; arguably this category could be rolled into outsourced network services.

Applications service providers covers the monthly fees for total ASP services (ERP, CRM, and so on), Web (e-commerce) storefront services, mail and collaborative, and other metered or flat-rate user applications services provided by entities outside the corporation. Again, the contract is of crucial importance, as it sets the distributed monthly fees for a determined period of time.

Miscellaneous is a collection bucket for the rest of your expenses. This should be less than 1 percent of a well-constructed budget.

Headcount Budget

This is an interesting area that could fill a book on its own. Much has been written on proper project planning. There also exists plenty of literature on establishing functional staffing based on ratios. This section focuses on the operating and functional staffing aspect rather than on project staffing.

The best approach we have found is to use ratios for most functions and plot your target staffing based on an aggressiveness scale. For example, the normal help desk technician to user count could be 1:100, whereas an aggressive ratio to squeeze expenses would be 1:200, which you could choose to manage at 1:150 to remain at an aggressive ratio. The potential consequences of this decision should be captured and presented to the executive team for endorsement.

For business analysts, you may elect to have solid coverage on critical applications and minimal coverage on noncritical applications, compensating as needed by making more effective use of vendor support. In any case, document the rationale in the executive team presentation. The same goes for your DBAs, network people, server team, voice team, and so on. The key is to establish ratios and explain the coverage and exposures.

▶ Ratios and Operating Metrics

This section covers some measurements you can use to make sure your budget is well constructed and aligned with your business.

IT Spending as a Function of Revenues

This has become the ultimate question to answer, as posed by the executive team and potentially the board of directors. Table 13–1 best represents my response:

Table 13–1 IT spending as a function of revenues.

Fraction of Revenue	Consequences for IT Organization
<.01	IT Poverty ... the infrastructure will collapse if this level is sustained for long.
.01-.02	Difficult corporate environment in which to make IT a success partner ... few sustaining projects, little to no strategic investment.
.02-.03	Healthy zone for manufacturing companies. Good blend of strategic and sustaining initiatives. Good balance of funding from LOB and corporate functions. This range is considered the "sweet spot" for most established successful companies.
.03-.06	Ideal zone for companies using IT as a competitive weapon. Strong funding from LOB and corporate functions. Usually contains some revenue-driven projects.
.06-.15	Very aggressive IT investments; very high depreciation, maintenance, and external services fees. Traditional companies operating at this sustained level of expenses justify most of the investments in terms of revenues generated, *and* hit the mark. This level is also seen in high tech startups in the buildup years; careful here, as many companies go bankrupt due to overbuilding of IT infrastructure too early in their evolution.
>.15	On a suicide course ... code **blue** unless this is under control!!

The guidelines in Table 13–1 express a commonly held view among CIOs operating in supply-chain type companies. Engineering and research-based companies, possibly pure services companies, and perhaps others will deviate from the numbers above. For example, for companies in the Internet services space (e-commerce), using IT to *directly* drive revenues, the related labor, equipment, and services expenses should be separated from infrastructure expenses required to run the enterprise. Arguably, direct revenue-driven expenses could be assigned to cost of goods sold (COGS). Without this separation, such companies can reach upward of 20 percent of revenues in IT expenses; with the separation, the operational budget may fall more nearly into the norms.

The key is for the CIO to remain tuned in to prevailing spending ratios for the enterprise's general industry group. This understanding can generate strong support for, or correction of, the IT spending level and positively reinforce the credibility of the CIO in the eyes of the executive team.

Other Useful Ratios and Metrics to Consider

The following items are aimed at getting a handle on IT personnel expense drivers to help normalize the operations budget or detect early signs of a major shift in influencing factors.

Dollars per megabyte of equivalent bandwidth. Consider overall, by region, by service provider.

Dollars spent per long distance call. It might be worth regionalizing, at least per continent. Compare with other companies with similar demographics.

Dollars spent per cell phone. Going to flat rate with maximum minutes free simplifies this.

Number of help desk user requests per week/per month. Annotate this chart with significant changes in user population served.

Number of desktops/laptops, per population group or overall. There will be different ratios for engineering (2.3), manufacturing (.75), corporate office (1), and sales (1.25). Important in predicting workload and technology turnover investments.

Cost-based metrics. TCO per user on desktops and laptops (consider depreciation, maintenance, help desk, and so on); TCO per ERP transaction user (consider maintenance, DBA, business analysts, help desk portion, and so on).

Benefit-based metrics. These are ROI metrics, typically stemming from projects, but how often do we go back to the original justification to assure ourselves of the return? Many payload or cost metrics have a companion benefits metric. For example, increased bandwidth at the same or lower expense can be translated into engineering time returned to the enterprise, while increased server performance throughput can translate into increased revenues if it is used in the partner or customer service realm. Creating benefits-based metrics is well worth your time—just another avenue for better communication with the rest of the executive team.

▶ A Simplified Budget Generation Process

Now that we have defined a working philosophy for the budget, explained capital expenditure and expense budgeting, and reviewed the various budget buckets, let's put this together in Figure 13–6.

The timing of the budget process is of some importance. For the capital expenditure portion, if the company has an annual strategic meeting involving LOB and corporate function primaries, the IT investment plan and profile should fall out of that session within, say, two to four weeks. If not, we recommend creating an IT investment review in which the CIO proposes investments based on their business sense for the audience (executive team minus the CEO) to debate and eventually ratify. Based on a January to December budget timeline, this should take place in an August to September timeframe.

The normal operating budget process can operate independently of, but in parallel with, the capital expenditure process during the same August to September period. During October and November, merge the expenses impact of the new investment profile, targeting the final release of the IT budget for no later than the end of November.

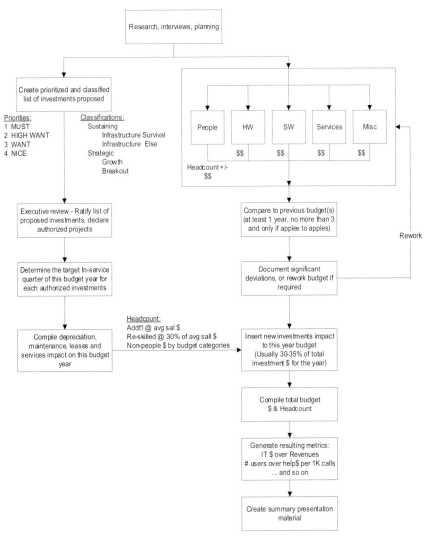

Figure 13–6 Simplified process flow diagram.

▶ Managing the Budget

Managing your budget typically means tracking spending, comparing it to monthly, quarterly, and yearly targets, reporting on significant deviations, and issuing corrections when a significant change is encountered. Simple enough, and a major component of the CIO's credibility. Here are some guidelines to help you avoid becoming a CIO casualty:

- If managing within 5 percent of budget targets either way, simply and quietly go on about your business.

- If managing under budget by more than 5 percent but within 10 percent, work with the LOB and corporate function primaries to find areas in which this budget excess can potentially help them.

- If managing at 20 percent or better under budget by midyear, you will be called a "sandbagger" (or worse) unless you explain thoroughly and return the excess over 10 percent to the IT controller or CFO. Headcount fluctuations or late project implementations are the usual causes of such significant deviations. Beware: You will most probably be under scrutiny when creating the next year's budget.

- If overspending by more than 5 percent but under 15 percent, be well prepared to explain the causes and generate remedial action immediately.

- If spending more than 15 percent over budget, you are exposed to the CIO terminal virus. Serious attention is required; this can be a critical test of the strength of your relationships with the rest of the executive team *unless* they were preconditioned for this possibility.

These guidelines apply to project spending as well as to the operations budget, but scrutiny of the latter is usually much closer.

Managing project budgets involves different complications. Conditions affecting company revenues and earnings can drive the executive team to revisit the project list and make cut decisions—the "you've got to know when to hold, know when to fold" axiom.

Postponing or eliminating projects yet to begin is relatively straightforward. Before interrupting or stopping projects in full flight, consider the cost of shutting down a project as well as the cost of reactivating it if there is expressed intention to complete it at some point in time; these costs typically amount to 10 to 30 percent of the original estimate. Consider a project as a jet engine: When you turn the engine off, it needs to wind down over a period of time to get to a complete stop, and when you turn it on again, it winds up to full power over a period of time.

If a project has passed two-thirds of spending or deliverables, stop or cancel it only under severe financial downturn conditions; the chances of ever completing that project are slim, as the people involved may not be around anymore or may have been reassigned to other full-time jobs. If forced to interrupt a project with intentions to restart later, make sure enough time and effort is spent in securing the environment (specs, software, hardware configurations, status of deliverables and financials, and so on) in a "vault" before reassigning the resources.

▶ The Budgeting Toolkit

Anybody involved in budgeting must be literate in spreadsheet, presentation, and word processing technologies—in that order. No rocket science here. Intermediate to advanced spreadsheet knowledge is particularly useful. If the enterprise uses a more advanced budgeting tool, you can work directly in that environment or use the spreadsheet package and upload the results.

Spreadsheets to Maintain

Investment portfolio (multiple sheets): Proposed for the year (see the discussion of strategic investments in the section "Capital Expenditures for Large Projects"); ratified by the executive team; actual spending versus proposed for the ratified list.

Purchase order tracking: Tracking different worksheets for software, hardware, consulting services, data telecom, voice telecom, subscriptions, and a summary.

Personnel training tracking: One sheet with specific classes, seminars, and events attended by each employee; another summarizing technical, professional, and personal time in days spent on education per employee.

From an operations perspective, we use a workbook containing all major expenses that generate a purchase order or receive an invoice for IT services. The IT expenses planning workbook is copied to create the tracking workbook for the budget year, in which actual expenses and related details are entered per purchase order required or generated. The IT expenses planning workbook is a copy of the tracking workbook from the previous year, edited with new information as required.

Figures 13–7 and 13–8 show two worksheets compiled from individual worksheets containing the details of all purchase order transactions into IT accounts worldwide. There is a worksheet for each category of expenses represented on the monthly view worksheet. The detailed worksheets capture reference information; money; anniversary dates; lease, maintenance, and services fees, and the same information for previous year; responsible department number, and other useful data. The monthly, quarterly, and annual planning and tracking summary sheet follows in Figure 13–7.

The project proposal list workbook contains detailed worksheets for each project and summarized for discussion and ratification with the executive team. This overview summary sheet is shown in Figure 13–8.

Type	JAN	FEB	MAR	APR	MAY	JUN	JUL	AUG	SEP	OCT	NOV	DEC	Cum Total
H/W(<25K)	$ -	$ 8,877	$ 1,550	$ 2,398	$ 3,615	$ 15,320	$ 2,318	$ 6,669	$ -	$ 3,198	$ 8,723	$ 11,084	$ 63,752
H/W(>25K)	$ -	$ -	$ -	$ -	$ -	$ -	$ -	$ -	$ -	$ -	$ -	$ -	$ -
HW Leases	$ 4,721	$ 4,721	$ 4,721	$ 4,721	$ 4,721	$ 4,721	$ 4,721	$ 4,721	$ 4,721	$ 4,721	$ 4,721	$ 4,721	$ 56,657
Subtotal:	$ 4,721	$ 13,598	$ 6,271	$ 7,119	$ 8,336	$ 20,041	$ 7,039	$ 11,390	$ 4,721	$ 7,919	$ 13,444	$ 15,805	$ 120,409
S/W(<25K)	$ 30,335	$ 8,535	$ 31,774	$ 12,187	$ 17,732	$ 10,457	$ 28,433	$ 2,640	$ 6,380	$ 14,293	$ 44,194	$ 30,755	$ 237,715
S/W(>25K)	$ 68,100	$ 68,100	$ 68,100	$ 68,100	$ 68,100	$ 68,100	$ 68,100	$ 68,100	$ 68,100	$ 68,100	$ 68,100	$ 68,100	$ 817,203
SW Leases	$ -	$ -	$ -	$ -	$ -	$ -	$ -	$ -	$ -	$ -	$ -	$ -	$ -
Subtotal:	$ 98,435	$ 76,635	$ 99,874	$ 80,287	$ 85,832	$ 78,557	$ 96,533	$ 70,740	$ 74,480	$ 82,393	$ 112,294	$ 98,855	$ 1,054,918
Consult:	$ 1,967	$ 1,967	$ 1,967	$ 1,967	$ 1,967	$ 1,967	$ 1,967	$ 1,967	$ 1,967	$ 1,967	$ 1,967	$ 1,967	$ 23,600
Com:	$ 69,283	$ 69,283	$ 69,283	$ 69,283	$ 69,283	$ 69,283	$ 69,283	$ 69,283	$ 69,283	$ 69,283	$ 69,283	$ 69,283	$ 831,396
Phone:	$ 1,600	$ 1,600	$ 1,600	$ 1,600	$ 1,600	$ 1,600	$ 1,600	$ 1,600	$ 1,600	$ 1,600	$ 1,600	$ 1,600	$ 19,200
Subscriptions:	$ 920	$ 920	$ 920	$ 920	$ 920	$ 920	$ 920	$ 920	$ 920	$ 920	$ 920	$ 920	$ 11,040
Depreciation	$ 18,333	$ 18,333	$ 18,333	$ 18,333	$ 18,333	$ 18,333	$ 18,333	$ 18,333	$ 18,333	$ 18,333	$ 18,333	$ 18,333	$ 220,000
Subtotal:	$ 92,103	$ 92,103	$ 92,103	$ 92,103	$ 92,103	$ 92,103	$ 92,103	$ 92,103	$ 92,103	$ 92,103	$ 92,103	$ 92,103	$ 1,105,236
Total mthly:	$ 195,260	$ 182,337	$ 198,249	$ 179,510	$ 186,272	$ 190,702	$ 195,676	$ 174,234	$ 171,305	$ 182,416	$ 217,842	$ 206,764	$ 2,280,563
Quarterly:			$ 575,845			$ 556,483			$ 541,214			$ 607,021	$ 2,280,563

Rolling expenses

Type	JAN	FEB	MAR	APR	MAY	JUN	JUL	AUG	SEP	OCT	NOV	DEC
H/W(<25K)	$ -	$ 8,877	$ 10,427	$ 12,825	$ 16,440	$ 31,760	$ 34,078	$ 40,747	$ 40,747	$ 43,945	$ 52,668	$ 63,752
H/W(>25K)	$ -	$ -	$ -	$ -	$ -	$ -	$ -	$ -	$ -	$ -	$ -	$ -
HW Leases	$ 4,721	$ 9,443	$ 14,164	$ 18,886	$ 23,607	$ 28,329	$ 33,050	$ 37,771	$ 42,493	$ 47,214	$ 51,936	$ 56,657
Subtotal:	$ 4,721	$ 18,320	$ 24,591	$ 31,711	$ 40,047	$ 60,089	$ 67,128	$ 78,518	$ 83,240	$ 91,159	$ 104,604	$ 120,409
S/W(<25K)	$ 30,335	$ 38,870	$ 70,644	$ 82,831	$ 100,563	$ 111,020	$ 139,453	$ 142,093	$ 148,473	$ 162,766	$ 206,960	$ 237,715
S/W(>25K)	$ 68,100	$ 136,201	$ 204,301	$ 272,401	$ 340,501	$ 408,602	$ 476,702	$ 544,802	$ 612,902	$ 681,003	$ 749,103	$ 817,203
SW Leases	$ -	$ -	$ -	$ -	$ -	$ -	$ -	$ -	$ -	$ -	$ -	$ -
Subtotal:	$ 98,435	$ 175,071	$ 274,945	$ 355,232	$ 441,064	$ 519,622	$ 616,155	$ 686,895	$ 761,375	$ 843,769	$ 956,063	$ 1,054,918
Consult:	$ 1,967	$ 3,933	$ 5,900	$ 7,867	$ 9,833	$ 11,800	$ 13,767	$ 15,733	$ 17,700	$ 19,667	$ 21,633	$ 23,600
Com:	$ 69,283	$ 138,566	$ 207,849	$ 277,132	$ 346,415	$ 415,698	$ 484,981	$ 554,264	$ 623,547	$ 692,830	$ 762,113	$ 831,396
Phone:	$ 1,600	$ 3,200	$ 4,800	$ 6,400	$ 8,000	$ 9,600	$ 11,200	$ 12,800	$ 14,400	$ 16,000	$ 17,600	$ 19,200
Subscriptions:	$ 920	$ 1,840	$ 2,760	$ 3,680	$ 4,600	$ 5,520	$ 6,440	$ 7,360	$ 8,280	$ 9,200	$ 10,120	$ 11,040
Depreciation:	$ 18,333	$ 36,667	$ 55,000	$ 73,333	$ 91,667	$ 110,000	$ 128,333	$ 146,667	$ 165,000	$ 183,333	$ 201,667	$ 220,000
Subtotal:	$ 92,103	$ 184,206	$ 276,309	$ 368,412	$ 460,515	$ 552,618	$ 644,721	$ 736,824	$ 828,927	$ 921,030	$ 1,013,133	$ 1,105,236
Total rolling:	$ 195,260	$ 377,596	$ 575,845	$ 755,355	$ 941,626	$ 1,132,328	$ 1,328,004	$ 1,502,237	$ 1,673,542	$ 1,855,958	$ 2,073,799	$ 2,280,563

Figure 13–7   Monthly summary sheet.

	Mtce	Lease	Totals
Hardware	$ 63,752	$ 56,657	$ 120,409
Software	$ 1,054,918	$ -	$ 1,054,918
Sub-Total	$ 1,118,670	$ 56,657	$ 1,175,327
Subscription	$ 11,040		$ 11,040
Communications		$ 831,396	$ 831,396
Phones		$ 19,200	$ 19,200
Consultants	$ 23,600		$ 23,600
Total	$ 1,153,310	$ 907,253	$ 2,060,563
Depreciation	$ 220,000		$ 220,000
Grand Total	$ 1,373,310	$ 907,253	$ 2,280,563

	1999	2000	2001	2002	Weekly (2002)	Month @ 4 wks	Month @ 5 wks
Depreciation Reference	$ 700,000	$ 700,000	$ 500,000	$ 220,000	$ 4,231	$ 16,923	$ 21,154
Other Non people expenses	$ 1,700,000	$ 1,800,000	$ 2,000,000	$ 2,060,563	$ 39,626	$ 158,505	$ 198,131
People expenses (Sal, Ben, Trav)	$ 1,000,000	$ 1,000,000	$ 900,000	$ 1,000,000	$ 19,231	$ 76,923	$ 96,154
Facilities	$ 126,041	$ 54,412	$ 300,000	$ 350,000	$ 6,731	$ 26,923	$ 33,654
IT Budget Totals:	$ 3,526,041	$ 3,554,412	$ 3,700,000	$ 3,630,563	$ 69,819	$ 279,274	$ 349,093
Minus allocations out to divisions	$ 2,000,000	$ 2,000,000	2000000	$ 2,000,000	$ 38,462	$ 153,846	$ 192,308
Remains in corporate IT bucket	$ 1,526,041	$ 1,554,412	$ 1,700,000	$ 1,630,563	$ 31,357	$ 125,428	$ 156,785

Figure 13–8 Overview summary sheet.

Reports Healthy to Generate (From a Budget Perspective)

- Project-related financials should be reported as a function of project progress reporting.
- From a pure budgeting perspective, report on major category deviations of greater than 5 percent and keep a running log for the year. Any deviation at or over 10 percent will probably need some deeper explanation, so be prepared.

- The selected operating metrics (some discussed earlier) should be presented monthly to the IT people and at least quarterly to the executive team—more frequently if they are under some amount of heat.

- The year-end report should contain a section for the investment progress summary (including finances) plus a section highlighting budget deviations and significant changes in influencing factors.

▶ IT Expense Distribution

This is a controversial topic in many companies, and yet, if the budget has the blessing of the executive team, there is support for the overall spending level. This largely stems from the fact that the CEO/CFO team wants to see the businesses pay fairly for the services they receive from corporate. In companies where there is only one LOB, this is quite simple, of course. For companies with multiple LOBs (full profit and loss responsibility), it can become an issue. There is no simple answer to this dilemma, but it is essential that the CIO take an active role in determining a fair repartition of the expenses to each business. The days are over when we took total IT expenses and charged back based on LOB revenues. A blend of metrics is required to help work this challenge at the LOB general manager level as opposed to the CEO/CFO level.

In the case in which LOBs are granted dispensation or reductions of their fair calculated value of allocations (corporate sponsoring for good business reasons), this must be discussed and agreed upon at the executive team level to eliminate bickering behind the scenes. Avoid cutting special allocation deals one on one with executive members; get it all ratified by the entire executive team.

It is good practice for IT-related invoices to be routed directly to the consuming LOB as long as the accounting code (reflecting IT spending) is correct; this maintains the visibility of IT while payment initiates directly from the LOB. Some metrics to consider with shared resources include:

Applications: Volume based (transaction, lines, overall cost), per named user.

Network: Cost per named user per site.

Voice: Get detailed billing, direct charge, and subscribe to a communications brokerage firm.

Granularity of allocations flowing to the lines of business can become complex. However, if it is required to get an accurate reading of their profitability, establish the necessary calculation tables and have dedicated staff responsible for producing the correct charge backs at the end of fiscal periods. This can become nonproductive if too granular. An example of one possible approach is shown in Figure 13–9.

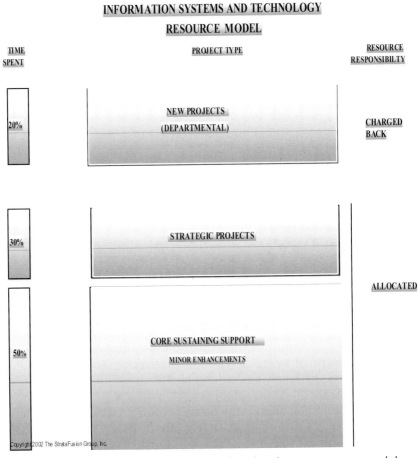

Figure 13–9   Information systems and technology resource model. Copyright 2002 The Strata Fusion Group, Inc.

Using this approach, you might want to allocate certain costs back to the business using a rational algorithm such as business analyst time spent, specific project benefit for departmental or LOB projects, or applications usage. Such mechanical schemes as square footage are useless; avoid these. In the case of projects that can be identified to specific lines of business, it is almost always advantageous to identify them specifically. Note that the proportions represented in Figure 13–9 are quite adequate.

▶ Conclusions

Budgeting is an exercise in common sense. Adjusting IT expenses to revenues, buying off the shelf if product provides the required functionality, keeping an eye on the critical influencing factors, keeping the executive team involved and informed, and treating the budget as a change agent all help you successfully manage the IT shop to be viewed as a solid piece of the foundation from which the company pursues its goals.

Remember, relationships with the IT controller and the CFO are two career-enabling relationships within which you should work to build credibility.

Philosophical: An ounce of planning will save a pound of trouble later on.

Humor: Some slightly twisted definitions of the word BUDGET are

- Best Utilization (of) Dollars Gains (you) Extended Tenure.
- Bungled Use (of) Deaneries Grants (you) Early Termination.
- Beflubbered Use (of) Dough Gleans Excessive Tribulation (this one came from way South).

Marketing the Value of Information Technology

by Judy Armstrong and Steven Zoppi

Having departed the practitioner's role (for a while) and joined the ranks of IT industry analysts, I discovered an interesting and unexpected demand on my time. I began receiving calls from CIOs whose careers were in jeopardy because their team's value (and by association, their value) had been brought into question by the other business leaders. After about an hour of forensic dialog about how this situation evolved, I was alarmed to conclude that there was an emerging epidemic of highly effective organizations and leaders whose value had been completely overlooked because of the lack of problems. They had been waylaid by the perception that "Everything works, so you guys must not be doing anything," swiftly followed by the "What have you done for me lately?" yardstick. While I concede that I am slightly oversimplifying the circumstances, the reality of the situation was that those worried CIOs had actually done something wrong—they hadn't properly marketed their products to their internal customers. Their reward for a silently efficient and low-defect operation: a negative perception of their effort and productivity.

In this chapter Judy Armstrong and Steven Zoppi discuss:

- *How the IT marketing effort is related to communication, quality, consistency, and high interaction.*
- *The importance of managing expectations.*
- *Models for planning a marketing campaign.*
- *PEST and SWOT analyses.*
- *The importance of business value chains and IT value chains, and how they are related.*

This chapter serves as a sourcebook of ideas in marketing your organization's strengths and weaknesses. There are no "silver bullets," and not all of the concepts presented here will be appropriate for all organizations, but the ideas should be sufficiently illustrated to enable you to apply them to your challenges.

One of the basic challenges to all marketers is understanding the problem. In the *Dilbert* comic strip by Scott Adams, the "pointy-haired manager" interrupts the title character with the following monologue:

> (Pointy-haired manager): I put together a timeline for your project. I started by reasoning that anything I don't understand is easy. Phase One: Design a Web architecture for our worldwide operations. Time: 6 minutes.
> (Dilbert, copyright 2003 United Feature Syndicate, Inc. All rights reserved. Used with permission.)

While this is a cartoon, it is not beyond reality to expect this type of thinking, which appears ridiculous but often occurs. When was the last time you called your local telephone service provider and thanked them for bringing you dial tone? When was the last time you called your local power company to thank them for keeping your lights on? When was the last time your department was credited for consistently delivering more value for less money, regardless of how the rate of consumption increases?

It is highly likely that your own customers, no matter how closely you work with them, have become habituated to the services provided and have no understanding of the complexity involved in their delivery. Assumptions give rise to incorrect or undesired conclusions.

The marketing effort is not a function merely of communication but of quality, consistency, and high interaction with key players. As an element of communication, a game plan for all interaction must be carefully crafted to ensure continued matching of expectation and business need.

▶ Chapter Overview

In this chapter we explore how IT issues form the backdrop of key topics that a good marketing plan will address. There is a considerable amount of synergy to be derived from key business relationships, and all types of out-of-synch conditions (with the business needs) can be mitigated by a sound marketing *and* communication strategy.

There are a multitude of options the CIO can take. Doing nothing is a certain path to failure, so it's important to understand the effects of not marketing IT. We also attempt to derive a clear definition of what marketing entails (or does not) as it relates directly to IT. Through the application of good marketing practices and the local application of some general examples, the intent is to help establish reasonable results with a minimum of discipline and effort.

Another perceived issue, formerly believed to have considerable effect on the marketing plan but of decreasing value today, is this: Does the IT team serve a constituency that is largely technical or nontechnical? The relevance of the technological sophistication of the customer base is diminishing due to the ubiquity of technology in business life. With this ubiquity comes a breed of Monday-morning quarterbacks who, while conversant in commonplace technology, are woefully lacking in the complexities and challenges of current corporate information technology. This presents a special marketing challenge.

▶ The Importance of IT (to Everyone)

Information technology, while arguably one of the most important infrastructure elements in a corporate operating backbone, is also one of the most underpublicized, undermarketed, and misunderstood components of any corporation. There are two primary contributors to this lack of understanding. The first is a complete misinterpretation of the maxim "The customer is always right." The second is that marketing,

in the form necessary to connect with the customer, is just plain difficult and is viewed as an inconsequential luxury by most IT organizations, which are already under constant pressure to perform with
declining funding and often contradictory business directives.

For purposes of this chapter, we need to define IT marketing:

> IT marketing is the art of appropriately setting expectations between
> customer and service provider such that both entities enjoy a mutually
> beneficial economic relationship.

This definition may appear to contain the grand presumption that IT
professionals all understand their respective roles within the organization. But many marketing problems, by their very nature, stem from
the history of those agents of change, the IT professionals themselves.
In today's state of the art, most IT professionals have come through the
ranks of IT and not through the business. This exacerbates the situation by putting all the emphasis on being a reactive rather than business-driven organization.

The marketing action is, by definition, an overt and proactive step
toward establishing appropriate levels of service delivery and expectation within all layers of the organization. Generally, the customers of
IT organizations perceive them as high-cost, low-quality service providers. This is largely due to IT groups' unsuccessful attempts or complete inability to articulate service value. But IT groups demonstrating
cost competitiveness and service differentiation can construct IT value
chain models to diagnose their deficiencies, improve their images, identify new cost reduction opportunities, link to vendors' value chains,
and build key differentiators.

▶ The Plan

To begin, there are a multitude of great Web-based and text resources
for developing a marketing plan. Because the IT product is targeted
primarily at an internal audience, many of the steps are abbreviated.
The key steps are outlined here.

PEST and SWOT (Conceptual Overview)

There are two key activities that focus the development of the external plan: the PEST analysis and the SWOT analysis. These two concepts are widely used, and there is a plethora of information about them available on the Internet and in texts to help the team make the appropriate assessments, so a quick overview should suffice.

PEST stands for *political*, *economic*, *social*, and *technology* factors. These are all elements that may have an effect on your future business or on that of your company, division, or operating unit. In this analysis, the objective is to make a list of all factors that may be either beneficial or detrimental to overall success in either the business or the marketing campaign. All of the PEST factors tie into and may have an effect on the strengths, weaknesses, opportunities, and threats you identify for your product and market.

SWOT stands for *strengths*, *weaknesses*, *opportunities*, and *threats*, and is critical to any well-crafted marketing plan. By completing the review of your business and your market, you should be in good shape and armed with the information needed to identify SWOTs and PESTs.

Strengths and weaknesses are determined by internal elements, while opportunities and threats are dictated by external forces. Sometimes it is more helpful to identify opportunities and threats (OTs) first in order to more quickly bring to light the product strengths or weaknesses of highest priority.

Plan Outline

Executive Summary: An internal management summary of IT's marketing plan.

The Challenge: A brief description of your services and business objectives to be marketed along with associated goals, such as high-level budgetary constraints, in-process work, and strategic goals.

Situation Analysis: A brief analysis of the organization, the company's context around the organization, and the challenges (financial, product, or other matters) to which IT can bring specific benefit.

Customer Analysis: A somewhat more rigorous analysis of the number of organizations you support, the number of different functions they perform and value drivers they might have for the IT organization, how their decision processes work, and how they operate.

Competitor Analysis: For IT, the competitive analysis is more of an introspective assessment of where core and non-core competencies lay. In this analysis, it is important for the CIO to carefully choose battles. "Outsource non-core competencies" is the background mantra here. Understanding of SWOT and PEST will make this analysis flow more easily and prepare the CIO for the real tests of strength. Outsourcing is not always a competitor, but it can be if it's not initiated conscientiously and with the coordination of internal IT.

Collaborators: In any campaign, it is always important to know who the allies are. These include vendors, internal customers, advocates, technology evangelists, and any other business unit members who have a keen understanding of the IT challenge. They are the business "operatives."

Market Segmentation: At this point, there is enough information to determine how to segment the internal marketplace and "choose those battles wisely." The principle of Occam's Razor is an excellent guide when choosing the low-hanging fruit for any marketing plan. The most useful statement of this principle for technologists is:

When there are two competing theories, which make exactly the same predictions, the one that is simpler is the better option.

So, choose your first audience wisely (on the basis of the best mutually beneficial economic relationships) with a clear understanding of the problems they face (in terms they understand) and what is of the greatest benefit. Identify the messages that most resonate with them, and how the IT organization can best support their objectives. Identify their sensitivities to cost, time, and other challenges.

Alternative Marketing Strategies: List and discuss the alternatives that were considered before arriving at the recommended strategy. Alternatives might include discontinuing a service, repositioning an existing one, or identifying the key benefits the IT organization brings to the company table.

Selected Marketing Strategy: Explain why the final strategy was selected. Finally, identify the marketing mix decision about the four Ps of product, price, place (distribution), and promotion.

Measure the Results and Project the Outcomes: This section of the marketing plan identifies the selected strategy's immediate effects as well as the expected long-term results and any special actions required to achieve them. This section may include forecasts of expense, potential revenues, ROI, and possibly a break-even analysis.

Conclusions: A succinct summary of all of the above.

▶ Assessing the Value Chain

Assessing an IT department's current value chain from the following scenarios (see Figure 14–1) and applying the recommended strategy can help form a successful marketing plan:

We can dispel the misinterpretations of the maxim "The customer is always right" if we suspend our belief that marketing is a luxury. In fact, where a sound marketing plan is laid out, the customer can always be supported properly and therefore be "right." This plan becomes a cornerstone in supporting an appropriately scaled IT and business response plan.

Marketing must be a core competency of the organization and must be addressed to successfully help the customer be always right and therefore satisfied. IT analyst organizations have spent person-years crafting the right catch phrases to accurately describe the issues, results, and remedies for IT problems. IT organizations themselves spend almost no time at all in crafting the right message for their respective target audiences.

Dimensions of IT Value to the Corporation	A possible strategy...
High Cost Low Quality	Establish the IT value chain, detect deficiencies, reduce cost, and create service differentiation.
High Cost High Quality	Improve efficiency (through automation or staff reallocation) while maintaining the same service quality.
Low Cost Low Quality	Identify high-value services, skills, competencies and activities. Focus marketing and value-add consulting while watching cost behavior
Low Cost High Quality	Although this is the desired state, it is seldom the actual state. Balance is maintained between value, cost, and differentiation.

Figure 14–1 Assessing the value chain.

► Operational Excellence: How Will They Know You Are Excellent?

Neither the customer nor IT department members are presumed to be psychic. Many goods and services, no matter how beneficial or innovative, have remained in obscurity due to a lack of presence in the consumer consciousness. Many inferior products (VHS video format) eclipse their superior competitor (BETA) due to excellent marketing campaigns. No matter how technologically sophisticated and superior the services provided, the disastrous results of considering marketing a luxury cannot be overstated.

Undermarketing IT usually results in many or all of the following:

- Low morale in the IT organization.
- Silos of excellence.
- Armchair quarterbacking from the customer community in general.
- Fear, uncertainty, and doubt (FUD); customer dissatisfaction.
- Lack of customer ownership and sponsorship of their own products.
- The blame game.

All department members must be enlisted as part of the marketing force for the remaining techniques to be effective. There are amazing stories about how one incorrectly applied message can undo all of the goodwill generated through a carefully planned campaign. The reinforcement of these key messages through an appropriate rewards and recognition program sets the stage for the remaining techniques.

Because of the serious nature of these changes, to IT's company profile, executive sponsorship is compulsory. For those organizations choosing to use an IT advisory board, the members of the board should be apprised, involved, and encouraged to become advocates in establishing and supporting the appropriate feedback required by their respective organizations. For organizations that do not have those types of business ties, the key managers' performance plans need to include that advocacy role for which they must also be compensated through incentives tied to its fulfillment.

In every sound marketing campaign, the needs of the consumer are identified through market analysis. The internal campaign can more easily harvest information about the needs of the market through systematic analysis of the business requirements. In the process, additional information can be discovered about the various disconnects between customer perception and those of IT.

Once the business requirements have been fully analyzed, key performance indicators (KPIs) should be cooperatively identified by the business and IT groups. These KPIs should then be iteratively refined to form the foundation of routine communication. This implies that *requirements* (not simply "wants") must be carefully culled from discussions with business unit representatives (either business analysts or key business contacts) who act in an analyst capacity. These requirements become the basis of service level agreements (SLAs). From that point, the KPIs become the foundation for harvesting metrics relevant to the business, including:

- Routine and substantial reporting of successes in terms that are understood by the widest possible constituency.
- Appropriate benchmarking inside and outside of the IT organization.
- Establishment of clear and well-focused objectives.
- Correction of the vocabulary at large within the IT organization (group-think).

▶ Walking the Talk

Making It Your Policy

One of the greatest contributors to the poor marketing of IT is a culture of "anti-service" within the organization. An example of group-think gone bad is found in the casual use of the word *policy* throughout most IT service organizations. Individual contributors frequently use the word policy in saying "It's not our policy to do that" as a defense against ad hoc requests for services.

Unfortunately, unpublicized policies used in this manner can generate the opposite effect. Without understanding the reasons for policy, the capriciously applied term can result in undoing the spirit of a carefully crafted marketing plan. Customers assume that the IT organization is a hopeless bureaucracy and look for ways to work *around* the IT organization. While policy is an extremely important part of the IT discipline, volatile, numerous, complex, and ad hoc policies can completely undermine the intent of an effective IT organization. Effective policies (as discussed in other chapters in this book) must serve as marketing tools and vehicles, and as such must meet the following marketing criteria:

- They must serve a specific business need, goal or objective.
- They must be well written and specific, yet generic enough to promote infrequent modification. (If frequent change is necessary, this may be a "standard," not a policy.)
- They must be concise so they can be easily memorized.
- While it is important that policies contain the rules and the consequences of breaking those rules, they must also be fully enforceable and universally applicable. Policies that fail this test, these latter tests are "guidelines" and should never be used as policies.
- They must *never* be statements of current best practice or anything else that is truly a guideline.
- Effective policies (whether internal or external) must be well-publicized, internally and externally.

Success Stories in Effective Communication

Effectively communicating success can be an important operations morale booster both inside the IT organization and for the customer communities. Early wins and internal "reference customers" can be highly effective models in the pursuit of other, less cooperative constituencies.

External benchmarking information (for example, what other services are provided by comparable IT organizations with comparable user communities) is helpful but can be misleading. Statistics regarding spending rates in particular are a poor marketing tool, since these benchmarks are often the results of custom-crafted accounting practices, and surveys regarding spending should always be considered suspect unless their foundational data can be correlated. Benchmarks regarding staffing and support expressed in ratio form are seldom beneficial for external marketing, because they detract from the objective of having negotiated KPIs drive the results stated in the marketing campaign.

In short, while statistics can be highly useful, they can also be misleading and create an uncomfortable position to defend in an institutionalized manner. It is everyone's experience that goods and services can be "sold" using clever marketing practices, but our recommendation is to garner and retain customer and executive sponsorship by using credible claims and estimates.

To best achieve the goals of the marketing activity, it is imperative that we understand the two basic rules governing circumstances under which the customers always right:

- Rule 1: The customer is always right if, and only if, the claim to being "right" is limited to business requirements. The customer's position is always defensible.
- Rule 2: Regarding the ways in which the ultimate solution is delivered, the customer is seldom "right." The technological response to a customer's requirement lies solely with the IT solution provider except...
- Caveat to Rule 2: ...when the solution supports a specific technical requirement better understood by the customer.

  Where this caveat applies, the IT organization must pay particular attention to detail to ensure that it is not missing a future service opportunity or one in which it may add value.

Customer ecCentricity?

Jim Hackett, CEO of Steelcase, recently validated the rules just discussed as he observed the ingenuity of the popular marketing and design think-tank IDEO:

> The popular notions of the last decade were for companies to become customer-centered. Theories abounded that if you paid attention to what your customer wanted, you couldn't go wrong. But the truth is that customers often ask you to do wrong things, not because they're difficult to deal with but because they just don't know better. The distinction is moving from customer-focused to user-centered, and the ability to understand the users of their products is a cultural shift that corporations have to make.

At no time do we assert that the customer is wrong or that a particular solution is wrong. It is important to note, however, that the "right-sizing" of the solution is the responsibility of IT. This is not a bad thing, but it has much to do with the strategic approach to the marketing plan.

IT is in the business of providing *business solutions* to *business requirements*. In a world becoming increasingly dependent on and conversant in technology-related matters, it is important for the IT organization to include a "perimeter defense" message in its plan. This message will assure that the correct accountability, responsibility, and authority remain with the proper players. Solutions dictated by non-IT professionals seldom meet the goals of leveragability, scalability, serviceability, and scalability (to name just a few of the "-ilities").

It is frequently the case that the customer has seen what he deems an appropriate technology solution to his requirements. If so, you have a major marketing opportunity to harness the customer's existing buy-in to properly analyze the proposed solution, and assess (in partnership with the customer) whether it is actually appropriate. This will generally give the IT service organization a clearer understanding of the executive and departmental hot buttons and present an opportunity to focus on the more serious consequences of the final decision.

In the case of a solution that is not commercially available, the marketing process involves not only providing an appropriate solution now but one that is architecturally consistent and reliable. This gives IT a bit of a marketing challenge: How does it provide a product that is packaged properly with respect to the business customer while maintaining a flexible infrastructure within the application? Fortunately, this subject is addressed in Chapter 8, "Architecture," but we need to keep this tension in the forefront of our marketing plan.

Highlighting the Basics

In the case of baseline services such as virus protection, email, dial tone, backups, recovery management, and so on, it is critical to note the built-in value of highlighting the successes buried within these tasks, which IT may consider to be mundane. Customers expect these types of tasks and services to happen but are generally unaware of their inherent complexity. The marketing opportunity lies in the advertisement of these services and their timely accomplishment to build credibility. For example, it is considered good marketing form to highlight risk mitigation activities, such as fast response to a virus threat, in the course of building this enduring credibility.

▶ Marketing Advocate: The Credible Individual

In our definition of IT marketing, we emphasized the setting of appropriate expectations but neglected to mention that it is the attractive force of those expectations that forms a bond between the customer and the product being marketed. Credibility is essential to the success or failure of the overall campaign. Put another way, the goal is to be so successful at delivering on customer requirements that the customer keeps returning freely for those services. As discussed, there are many steps involved in proficiently building credibility, and much of this is dependent on proper preparation prior to marketing the IT organization.

People

Before a marketing plan can be executed, the right players need to be assigned to the team. It is important to establish the appropriate level of accountability, responsibility, and authority in the overall management of the business relationship.

A marketing process for IT begins (generally) with the business relationship manager (BRM). This person's role is to act as the principal business interface with internal customers, with (responsibility for managing the customer relationship. Moreover, this person acts as a primary point of contact for all new work as well as existing support that is not meeting requirements.

Process

The BRM conducts strategic and tactical planning, business analysis, and high-level requirements determination. This IT agent must be the person to call in the IT organization when the customer is unsure how to proceed and the voice of the customer throughout all IT groups. A senior BRM can also act as a planning and forecasting agent by conveying customer needs to the rest of the IT organization while presenting new technology opportunities to customers, and can help customers understand how to use technology toward their strategic and tactical goals.

The BRM's role can be quite complex, because he or she has complete responsibility for managing the IT/customer relationship in every regard. The BRM must take complete ownership of the supporting IT operations product as well as all SLA arrangements and criteria definition; field all customer interaction points; and be a contributor to operational reporting mechanisms. With insights into the needs of his or her particular constituency, this person establishes all of the baseline and ongoing information necessary to properly construct the marketing plan.

Technology

Because the brokering of communication between the customer and IT is an extremely time-consuming activity, the BRM must be conversant in both "business speak" (possess considerable business-domain expertise) and "technology speak" (be able to help abstract high-level business requirements into solution requirements). For this reason, it is recommended that the BRM have no direct reports, handle communication across multiple customer constituencies, and report into the IT organization.

The Right Person for the Job

It is rather rare to find a person in command of all of these disciplines, and the necessary skill mix is typically developed internally. The best practice for compensation of anyone in this role is to tie customer satisfaction (on an individual level, not with general IT performance) to some form of at-risk compensation. The reason for separating individual performance from IT performance is to disassociate the BRM role from conflicting business priorities, which may prevent execution of desirable customer projects.

It is also possible to be a little more creative with the mechanism of separation, as is appropriate for each situation. The key recommendation is to find a means of tying individual performance, as measured by some form of customer satisfaction (CSAT), to at-risk pay.

▶ Borrowing From Established Best Practices

Once IT's marketing advocate is identified, the lifecycle shown in Figure 14–2 (borrowed from sound CRM best practices) should be applied. In short, the plan is to engage, transact, fulfill, service, and report.

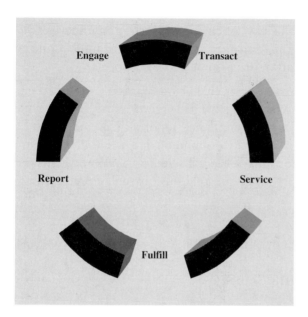

Figure 14–2   Lifecycle.

Engage the customer through multiple interaction channels: face-to-face meetings, email, brown-bag lunches, or feedback sessions (CSAT surveys).

Transact business with the customer and find a means of demonstrating value in each interaction. While this might seem obvious, each meeting should have a specific purpose and identified outcomes. One value that IT brings to the table is a keen sense of process, and the customer must be reminded that there is progress to be made from each interaction. The BRM is the evangelist for the customer within IT and to the customer on behalf of IT.

Fulfillment is the stage at which the customer realizes the benefits of the IT involvement in helping to meet business requirements. The realization may be through the production of working modules, status reports, milestone meetings, progress reports, or other means. The precise form of the fulfillment is directly dependent on the customer and the project, but the net effect is to complete iterative feedback cycles in which the customer realizes the value of IT's involvement.

Servicing the customer is a frequently overlooked step in the lifecycle of CRM. This is especially true if the prior three steps are highly successful in the customer's eyes. An investment in the adage "If it works, don't fix it" is the start of entropy, which inhibits proactive solicitation of status from the customer ("How are we doing?") and will backfire in the next iteration of customer interaction.

Reporting is the most important mechanism in the campaign for customer loyalty. Marketing the IT organization does *not* mean that IT should publish only compliance reports. The good, the bad, and the ugly need to be routinely communicated while developing trust in the customer relationship. If there is a belief that reporting is merely a vehicle for spin doctoring, the relationship will never evolve into a true partnership.

▶ Marketing Consistency

Metrics are the all important cornerstone on which the reporting phases rest. Many ideas are presented in other chapters of this book; refer to Chapter 15, "The Metrics of IT," for details on the development of measures relevant to the customer as well as IT. Topics of common interest are

- Internal versus external performance (benchmarking).
- Efficiency.
- Effectiveness.
- Capability.
- Financial report/budgets.
- SLAs.

Carefully consider the mechanism by which you communicate feedback to the customer. Not only is the function of the communication vehicle important, but also its form can make or break the communication. It is a commonly held belief that IT cannot speak the language of its customers; customers wonder what language IT actually speaks. This is perpetuated in everyday activities such as mass mailings providing status on outages (*if* these appear at all).

The two messages shown in Figure 14–3 are intended to inform the customer base of an intermittent outage. Messages like these, though routine, must consistently reflect thoughtful and deliberate structure so customers can extract only the relevant information necessary to perform their part.

```
To: Everyone_in_my_company
From: IT Helpdesk
Subject: Internet Outage
It has come to our attention that many user are geting intermittent
404 errors when opening their browsers to http://www.some-obscure-
site.com.  You are getting these messages because one of the blades
on our Cisco switch had a bent pin and were getting intermittent
and erroneous supervisor signals and backplane failures.  Even
though our redundant supervisor board was able to take that bad
blade out of service some of your sessions were terminated in the
firewall due to session failure.  We have resolved the problem and
you might need to restart your session to reconnect.
```

```
To: Everyone_in_my_company
From: IT Helpdesk
Subject: Today's Internet Browsing Problems
It has come to our attention that many users are having difficulty
connecting to various internet sites since <hh:mm am/pm> today.
These intermittent errors were caused due to a hardware failure in
our internet connection.  That problem was resolved at <hh:mm> by
our network technicians.  If, after restarting your browser, you
are still unable to connect, please contact the IT Helpdesk at
extension <xxxx>.
Further questions regarding this topic may be directed to our
network analyst <name> at extension <xxxx>.
```

Figure 14–3   Sample messages.

The first example is not only questionable in terms of technical accuracy, but provides nearly zero useful information to the customer.

There are numerous problems with this first message: irrelevant verbiage containing no context for the customer, superfluous information, misspellings, grammatical errors, and copious IT jargon. Although this level of reporting may be relevant in some form of post-mortem with other technologists, it will be swiftly ignored and deleted by the very audience to which it is addressed. It invites the criticism that IT misuses its own resources.

The second example is much clearer and contains only the information relevant to the customer community. The closing line is a marketing tactic that is becoming more frequently used; it helps bring some transparency to the otherwise opaque help desk.

This is also consistent with the marketing "messages" requested by the user community. The criticism received by this company's IT department is that they are a "black hole"; providing the option of asking for details and assigning a named technician is an open-kimono message, which may or may not apply to other organizations.

Conventional IT wisdom tends to hold that technicians must remain anonymous so they may "get their work done," but it also is a dangerous practice, which reinforces an impersonal view of the department. The key attributes of the second message, in addition to grammatical and technical accuracy, are its brevity and relevance to the broadest community. The message answers only the basic reporter's questions: Who? What? When? Where? Why? and How? Though these may appear to be contrived samples, they are frighteningly close to real-life examples we have received.

Each and every customer communication is another marketing opportunity. If the value proposition to the customer community is being in tune with the customer community, all communications must reflect that message regardless of the mode or channel. Simple and routine actions such as using email to communicate a failure of email or the network can do more to undermine a well-crafted marketing plan than any other routine activity.

▶ More Marketing Vehicles

Another marketing vehicle, which requires no significant invention, is a model provided by publicly held companies and forward thinking private companies—the annual report. This report contains metrics, has an established frequency, is a well-understood vehicle with consistent contents, and targets an interested constituency. Figure 14–4 compares a corporate annual report with an IT annual or quarterly report.

COMPANY "X" ANNUAL REPORT OUTLINE

1. Annual report

    a. Letter(s) from the Chief Executive Officer and Chairman of the Board

    b. Excerpts from the annual shareholders' meeting minutes and consequent action items

    c. Restatement and Refinement of Corporate Vision

    d. Quarterly reports

    e. Press releases

    f. Interim announcements and updates

    g. What is going on "behind the scenes"? (reduce the corporate opacity – put a face on the corporation)

2. Expectations management

    a. Information designed to set the expectations of industry analysts and investors

    b. Information designed to tell employees know what to "shoot for" in the coming year

---

Information Technology Annual / Quarterly Report

1. *The IT/IS Annual Report*

    a. Introduction/Letter from senior management CEO and CIO

    b. Client success stories

    c. Status of major projects

    d. Where do the projects stand vs. plan?

    e. How do actual budgets compare to projections?

    f. Interim announcements and updates

    g. What is going on "behind the scenes"? (reduce the corporate opacity – put a face on the corporation)

2. Expectations management

    a. Information designed to set the expectations of business stakeholders and individual contributors

    b. Information designed to tell employees know what to "shoot for" in the coming year

    c. List of major future initiatives and benefactors of those initiatives.

Figure 14–4 Corporate annual and IT annual/quarterly report comparisons.

The corporate intranet is an invaluable vehicle for information delivery, but it is not uncommon for IT to be the shoemaker's children (who don't wear shoes) when it comes to the appropriate monitoring and management of its own content. Companies using Web-based technology for information dissemination must maintain the content properly, or the delivery vehicle becomes useless. It is a common worst practice to simply publish an intranet and forget about site traffic analysis. Knowing the traffic patterns of customers through the Web site is a fundamental indicator to understanding the effectiveness of the delivery vehicle.

Finally, the "human touch" cannot be underestimated and is a strategic element in garnering customer connections. Various forms of reaching out to the customer community can provide tangible value in simple activities such as brown-bag lunches, data center tours, and open house functions.

▶ Conclusion

While it may seem like common sense, only a handful of the best IT operations develop and execute a marketing plan. Taking the time necessary to lay a firm foundation will go far in establishing a high-function, long-term partnership.

The Metrics of IT:
Management by Measurement

by Shel Waggener and Steve Zoppi

Underscored by the common adage "If you can't measure it, you can't manage it," the importance of the three Ms (metrics, monitoring, and measuring) is greater today than ever. Management by gut feeling may still be as prominent as management by exception or management by objective, but the dynamics and complexities of today's fast-paced global environment present a special set of circumstances—circumstances that do not always lend themselves to traditional method.

The days of managing by gut feeling are not completely gone, but today this approach must be supplemented by other methods and real, quantifiable measurements. No CIO will last long if he or she can't quantify what is happening. With greater emphasis on accountability and performance, the three Ms can't be ignored.

In this chapter Shel Waggener and Steve Zoppi outline the history of IT metrics and establish a pattern for the appropriate application of metrics as they might be seen from various constituencies and business partners. They explore:

- *A disciplined and managed approach to metrics.*

- *How to identify appropriate metrics.*
- *The importance of focusing metrics on business value.*
- *Development tools and techniques for creating actionable metrics.*
- *The art of metrics management to improve the business.*

After more than 20 years in this industry, I find myself in the (more or less) enjoyable position of watching history repeat itself. I also find myself reflecting on the wisdom of George Santayana: "Those who cannot remember the past are condemned to repeat it."[1] We all use the expression "hindsight is 20/20," but I am confounded as to why we have made so little progress as an industry in learning from crossdiscipline successes and failures.

I've been CIO in both hardware and software companies. I've seen phenomenal strides and innovation. I marvel at the ingenuity of the human mind in creating complex and intricate products and conceiving of innovation. But the one feature of the technology industry that never ceases to perplex me is how the success-based disciplines of *monitor, measure,* and *manage,* so pervasive in hardware-oriented environments, continue to be scarce as hen's teeth in the sister industry of software.

The evolution of hardware standards has been dutifully tended by industry bodies around the globe, with rigorous requirements for interfacing, fabrication, maintenance, and diagnostics. No such standards have evolved in software—at least, no standards with the intent of seamless integration into a greater whole. Software standards, though gradually (read: glacially) improving, have been largely established and imposed to limit competition—and to make the life of a CIO about as simple as establishing the origins of the universe.

I've worked with hundreds of CIOs and senior managers of technology disciplines throughout my career, and the most expert and successful of those managers have abandoned the hope that unified metrics, monitoring, and measurement will ever come to software, so they divide their focus as follows: Twenty percent effort on hardware monitoring

---

1. *The Columbia Dictionary of Quotations* is licensed from Columbia University Press. Copyright © 1993, 1995, 1997, 1998 by Columbia University Press. All rights reserved.

will bring 80 percent of the benefit, while the other 80 percent of their monitoring and measuring efforts is focused on software and people.

Those of us who have followed technology from the early days of paper tape and front-panel data entry have grown weary of hearing from those of us who have followed technology from the early days of paper tape and front-panel data entry. The old war stories of core-memory failures, faulty wire-boards, and soaked punch cards are, for all of today's intents and purposes, irrelevant. The intrinsic complexities of application and service delivery in today's highly heterogeneous, geographically diverse, multitier environments make monitoring and management significantly more difficult.

Despite the change in our war stories' contents, we have learned from our mistakes. The adage "If you can't measure it, you can't manage it," regarded by some as a cliché, has greater significance today than it ever did. The days of managing by "gut" are not *completely* gone, but the complexities inherent to today's global business scenarios present circumstances that demand measurement because the answers to our most nagging questions are often counterintuitive to our previous experience.

As was the case with our discussions on marketing IT in the previous chapter, this chapter is a sourcebook of ideas from which you must draw your own plans. Measurement and metrics are cornerstones in producing the raw material for any worthwhile IT marketing plan. Therefore, the same rule applies: There are no silver bullets. This chapter outlines the history of metrics in IT and establishes a pattern for the appropriate application of metrics as they might be seen by various constituencies and business partners.

▶ CFO—Credible Financial Obfuscation

The role of the CIO is frequently determined by a number of external factors. Executive reporting structures often dictate management styles and strategies for a CIO. For example, during the 1980s and much of the 1990s, with the majority of IT organizations reporting to the CFO, there was a decided shift toward management by number. While emphasizing IT as a bottom-line expense, this also encouraged a metrics-driven decision process. This approach was tailored to communications with CFOs—success or failure based on numbers. Although communication with the CFO was possibly enhanced, management by numbers also fostered the perception of IT as a bottom-line expense, with little focus on the values IT brings to a business.

Successful CIOs quickly adapted to this challenge by developing the nearly automatic response of inundating the CFO with numbers and metrics to justify anything we needed. Soon, every request for budget was accompanied by one of the now ubiquitous three-letter acronym justifications—ROI (return on investment), SLO (service-level objective), SLA (service-level agreement), TCO (total cost of ownership), TQM (total quality management)—as well the all-important external certification and external sources (ISO9000, TK/IT, Gartner Group, Forrester Group, META Group, Giga Information Group) or any other credible source that would validate or certify the intended position or approach.

▶ CEO—Cross-Examining Opportunity

About the time this "Data War" reached détente, IT spending began its meteoric rise, doubling and in some cases tripling with the urgency of Y2K remediation and the boom in Internet-related costs. With new-found spending power and responsibilities crossing lines of business, many CIOs found themselves promoted—this time reporting directly to CEO.

Suddenly, a whole new set of success criteria appeared. Now, instead of SLA and MTR (mean time to recovery) information touting IT's effectiveness and operational excellence, CIOs were required to provide data about every aspect of the business. Showing *business* success or failure was now dependent on the information IT provided regarding subjects as varied as the new supply-chain management cycle times, CRM customer tracking sell-through data, and unique Web site page views per month.

Most CIOs were barely catching up to the extreme requirements and fast pace when the economy slowed down dramatically and the rules governing metrics changed again. IT was once again relegated to being a bottom-line expense, with cost per employee and IT as a percentage of revenue surfacing as the "most important" metrics. And, by the way, none of the new metric requirements had been relaxed; their relative priorities have simply been rearranged.

Back to Basics—Breaking the Cycle

Through these cycles, one constant has been an ever-increasing torrent of data: massive quantities of data and information to accumulate, store, sort, analyze, report against, and act upon. The noise-to-signal ratio of data-to-information will continue to be unwieldy until the CIO adopts a new strategy for metric management.

So what's a CIO to do? What should be measured by an IT organization, and what should be reported against? How can a CIO avoid drowning in too much data and creating a bureaucracy that does little more than compile numbers? Some have opted to abandon massive metrics entirely, yet the best-managed and most successful companies have been shown to share a few common attributes. One of the most applicable for this discussion is the establishment of a disciplined approach to managing business through *appropriate* measurement. For the CIO, a keen understanding of how to develop tools and techniques that convert these data into business-critical information, including actionable metrics, is tantamount to success.

In this chapter we discuss the art of metrics management that, once mastered, will help zero in on improvement in those areas that are the true indicators of business success while combing out the noise of extraneous data. In each section, there are specific examples of winning strategies and sample metrics as well as some examples of not so successful metrics and common traps to avoid.

Management by Measurement—Keep It Simple

It's the end of the year and time for the annual review. Has it been a good year? How company leaders answer that question varies wildly from company to company and position to position. For the CIO, it is critical to have a clear idea of what success means and, moreover, what it means to each peer executive—specifically to the CEO. Many CIOs have fallen prey to successfully delivering projects and operational gains throughout the year only to find their ideas of success and criticality to the lines of business don't match those of the CEO.

In years past, the classic five-year strategic plan was belabored for months and implemented over years. Executives had the luxury of performing revisions and course corrections throughout the process. This was a world in which business opportunities materialized slowly, and data analysis could take place retroactively each quarter or year to determine what changes to make—and this system worked very well. Today's business climate, however, is led by companies characterized by the ability to acquire data and analyze information in real time with changes in the business. Course corrections are no longer an annual event but, for most well-operated companies, have become a weekly, daily, even hourly (near real-time) adaptation to changing market conditions. It is the era of the "sense and respond" organization.

To accomplish this extreme level of near real-time management, the information pipeline and cycle times need to be substantially shortened. The adage "If you can't measure it, you can't manage it" continues to provide the starting point. In concept, measuring work is a simple task. In application, the expanded evaluation of all technology, business metrics, and pulse points within a business, division, or indeed the entire business, is considerably complex, and the notion of near real-time reporting may not be feasible or practical. Compiled data will be the primary information source guiding the concerted decisions of the CIO and the CEO, and will likely determine the success or failure of your business. While the business sections of bookstores are stocked full of titles purporting to provide *the* magic formula for measuring the health of a business, few are tailored to the health of the IT organization and fewer still can provide the formula that accurately describes the health of *your* corporation!

In reality, a strong leadership team runs the business correctly by *differentiating* it from others and won't approximate a carbon copy of competitors. So in order to run a world-class IT shop (one whose specific solutions truly enable the business's success), CIOs must focus on measuring and managing only those things that achieve this goal. It is a tall order, but one that can be accomplished through appropriately applied IT metrics and management—a methodology providing not just a simple list of the "perfect IT metrics," but rather an approach that can be used to develop a winning metrics management strategy, *customized* to your specific business.

▶ Quality Over Quantity—Always

Successful IT professionals, when faced with challenges throughout their careers, have achieved that success by taking a very measured approach to problem solving. Those problem-solving skills, as applied by line management or some director-level team members, were founded on a more directed and general three-step process for problem resolution.

- Step one: When presented with a series of difficult challenges, evaluate the size and scope of the problem.

- Step two: Develop an action plan designed to solve the specific problem or, optimally, the root cause of the issue at hand.

- Step three: Evaluate the success or effectiveness of the actionable solution.

These steps are very adequate and manageable for solving problems faced by first- or second- and even third-level management as long as the final evaluations of effectiveness (step three) are completed. This approach also has favor because it tends to correctly identify the source of the problem—likely by establishing correct measurement or series of measurements to pinpoint the root cause.

The greatest challenge for any business unit owner (CIO included) is in identifying precisely what measurement will correctly highlight the root causes of a proposed issue or problem. Business owners, even those owners of operating elements within IT, have great diversity of issues, which makes establishing a common system of measurement seem rather futile.

Equally difficult questions to be pondered include the following:

- Should application development groups be measured by lines of code implemented? Applications deployed?

- Should systems administrators be measured by the number of servers administered?
- Should helpdesks or support centers be measured by the number of calls or cases closed?

While each metric is necessary to those organizations, do these numbers give keen insight into whether or not they are being run effectively? Do these numbers provide some insight into the operational performance of that particular team? Moreover, they are unlikely to answer the key (and often rhetorical) question: How do these measurements help drive my businesses success?

All data sought must bring focus to the key issues. Now for the difficult task of finding that data.

▶ The Wheel Already Exists

For many organizations, a substantial amount of previously absent data is made available once ISO certification, Baldridge quality, or other TQM systems are implemented. These certifications, processes, and business process reengineering requirements can sometimes be beyond the fiscal capabilities of many companies. The principles underlying the foundations of these specific certifications, however, are well worth adopting as a foundation for successful metrics and management. While the work involved is substantial, the ability to dramatically improve quality can be achieved by understanding—through appropriate measurement—where operational or methodological problems may exist and establishing a vehicle for correcting those problems.

The beneficial byproduct of these efforts is the creation of test points that the business will use to measure performance against significant criteria and identify key business opportunities. Quality and ISO programs can then become the cornerstone of a business owner's *objective* measurements for operational efficiencies. The most important result of these varied initiatives is that the lines of business (LOBs) develop measures that are specifically designed for *their* success.

Once in place, these documented processes and measures can lead to dramatic improvements in quality and productivity throughout the business. Requirements for applications from the business have a new-found focus, with requests for technical solutions including all supporting data and specifics. Unfortunately, this new ability to measure every aspect of business operations brings with it a new peril: a myopic focus on minute operation detail. Now, rather than having a few isolated areas clarified by hard data, a "manage everything by the numbers" cult can sweep the business. Suddenly, every presentation is awash in bar graphs, charts, and raw data galore.

Every process can now be measured, and you will be faced with more data than is easily deciphered. As trends begin to show, your business partners will request even more data to analyze, looking for opportunities for cost savings or quality improvements.

▶ Money Metrics—You Are What You Eat

So how does one avoid being in the CEO's office at the end of year, only to suffer the fate of many tactically successful but strategically misaligned CIOs? The key is in understanding how to use operational data as a *tool* rather than an end result. Moreover, using the right data, and in sparing amounts, to derive the desired business indicator is the ultimate goal. Too much of a numerical diet can burden the organization, because the metric must be able to change with the business. If a metric is highly dependent on a complex series of other data points (long-term business initiatives like large system development, CRM, ERP, and so on), and the data path is broken by significant changes in business (the abandonment of any portion of these initiatives), the metric is no longer valid.

Additionally, if a company embarks on a long-term project that is capitalized, the budgetary equation for operation *must* change accordingly. Extraordinary expenses in the form of capital projects tend to wreak the greatest havoc on year-over-year planning efforts, because the expense rate may be minimized but capitalized projects now fall into the nondiscretionary bucket (along with licenses, maintenance, and so on). We will illustrate this a bit more later on.

Good metrics should be used to guide the development of strategic objectives, narrow investment opportunities to minimize wasted capital, and continually evaluate status to ensure that progress is being made. During cost reduction periods, the typical CFO uses the poorly qualified but always handy "percentage of revenue" as the key financial performance metric. Inevitably, CxO colleagues have heard from peers (or worse, read in an article in an in-flight magazine) that IT should be spending only X percentage of revenue, where X is generally a very low number. While that percentage has the benefit of being simple enough to easily measure, as mentioned previously, it is a completely inappropriate metric for necessary IT spending and usually results in the goal not being achieved. This particular measure also has the undesirable side effect of making it nearly impossible to tie the IT individual contributor's operational objectives to a meaningful performance number.

In using this metric at face value, there are only two possible results: You failed to meet the objective, or you met or exceeded it. Unfortunately, helping your team make the right decisions to achieve that target is much more complex than the binary outcome. If your team is struggling to meet all the operational objectives laid out by ISO and TQM initiatives, how can you help them relate to a generic percentage of revenue number?

Start by customizing the number to your particular business's operational and strategic needs. Instead of just creating a budget for the IT staff to live with, express the spending in terms of need and impact on the business. For example, identify what percentage of the budget is necessary for operational and fixed expenditures:

- Operational and fixed spending: X percent of budget
- Strategic investment/projects: 100 percent – X percent of budget

For operational groups, tie several key operational metrics not to performance but to dollar impact. Instead of listing "number of helpdesk cases," measure in terms of revenue. For example,

- Total budget = $10M or 5 percent of revenue
- Operational budget = $8M or 4 percent of revenue
- Helpdesk = $600,000 or .3 percent of revenue
  40,000 cases annually
  Percent of revenue per 10,000 cases = .075

A target can then be set for the end-user support organization of reducing the cost per 10,000 cases from .075 percent of revenue to .070 or

.065 percent of revenue. While the percentages may be small, the numbers are simple to calculate and can be tied directly to operational measurements for each group throughout your organization. Rather than a high-level generic measure, you now have individual measurements that are meaningful to each operational manager.

For your strategic projects, you can break down spending by investment in each product area and by each project. Instead of telling your services team that the CRM project budget is $900,000, you can show it this way:

- Total budget = $10M or 5 percent of revenue
- Total strategic investment = $2M or 1 percent of revenue
- CRM Project = $950,000 or .475 percent of revenue

At this point, you have something far more productive to talk over with the CEO. Instead of discussing the generic industry-standard target of spending as a percentage of revenue, you can not only demonstrate your ability to achieve expense targets but show where you missed, met, or exceeded them.

▶ Automate IT

Simply stated, manually compiled metrics generate more work than solutions. With mountains of data to sort into customized metrics, the task can quickly become overwhelming. And the metrics requirements are not just for the IT shop itself; it is not uncommon for IT in smaller companies to also serve as the single source of data reporting for groups throughout the company. The tendency, historically, has been to assign the preparation of metrics reports to administration or other support staff, but with change requests and constant adjustments to business priorities, the workload will very certainly require additional people.

Today's levels of technological sophistication and industrial maturity provide ample facilities to automate the collection of nearly any performance metric imaginable. Depending on the specific business indicator, there may be opportunities to empower the lines of business to harvest and interpret their own metrics. These are generally enabled through the prudent use of the data warehouse or other vehicles for information delivery and analysis.

One of the most commonly overlooked tools in the IT arsenal is the "digital dashboard," a highly versatile and effective means of communicating performance to all portions of the business. Previously, the dashboard concept mandated the assembly of an application development team. Today, with the ubiquity of the Internet and robust Web application tools (for end users and software engineers alike), there is no longer a need to form such a SWAT team, as there is a plethora of commercially available portal-class software products providing sufficient functionality to satisfy this purpose.

▶ The Balanced Scorecard

Humans tend to optimize their behavior in the direction of the favorable performance metric being sought. Due to this behavioral trait, any solitary metric is generally insufficient and can potentially minimize or even violate the overall spirit of the metric. Therefore, it is imperative that overall performance of any organization be well calibrated by measuring the *same data* from *different vantage points*. A useful practice in this checks-and-balances approach to metrics results is a concept called the Balanced Scorecard.

This approach to strategic management and measurement was developed in the early 1990s by Drs. Robert Kaplan (Harvard Business School) and David Norton (Balanced Scorecard Collaborative). Recognizing some of the weaknesses and vagueness of previous management approaches, the Balanced Scorecard approach provides a clear prescription for what companies should measure in order to "balance" the financial perspective.

Figure 15–1 shows an example model of how the Balanced Scorecard approach can be used to measure financial as well as other measurable nonfinancial attributes. This approach will reflect company's performance measured in line with customer, business process efficiency, employees, research, and growth perspectives.

Once the high-level strategic and key operational metrics are identified, the next challenge is presenting the information. While the objective of having consistent measures throughout your organization is important,

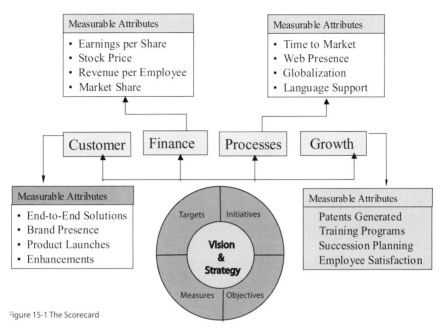

Figure 15-1 The Scorecard

Figure 15–1   The scorecard.

presenting that information to different groups of people requires customizing the message using the same data. One of the most popular and successful techniques for making the metrics part of the core drivers in your company is via the Balanced Scorecard.

Like any management system developed to date, the Balanced Scorecard, inappropriately applied, can yield undesired effects. Nevertheless, it offers one of the simplest and most effective approaches to keeping measurements central to daily operations and long-term planning. A Balanced Scorecard provides a way to constantly monitor the ability of a company's core businesses processes to deliver against the strategic intent. Simply put, it helps to answer the question, Is my company (and your department) delivering in the areas we need to meet our key objectives? Developing a Balanced Scorecard can help focus on companywide strategic objectives at the executive level, which can then be used as the basis for top-down objective setting.

The best first step in applying this model is to set the vision by evaluating core strategic objectives and putting them in categories. The CIO is in a unique position to have visibility across all areas of the business and should take an active role in providing guidance to groups on operational or process failures as they relate to cross-organizational efficiencies. These are likely to reflect the areas from which they are identified: better ways to support customers in the services organization, improved financial performance in Treasury, time-to-market opportunities in product development; improved retention in HR, and so on.

While each department's needs are critically important to that department, spreading IT or company resources across every group equally to address each challenge is a certain path to failure. The executive team must make decisions as to the *relative priority* of *each strategic objective*. To be most effective, these must be companywide, and a stacked ranking should be completed for all areas. Once completed, these rankings will determine the relative weight and resourcing by all groups for each goal. The outcome is a tool to translate and present IT's organizational and individual metrics to the rest of the organization.

Applying this notion to extend the previous example, requiring the CIO to meet a 5 percent of revenue target, we see a change in how the final metric is presented. This constraint maps to a corporate objective of increasing gross margins by *XX* percent or reducing the cost of G&A by *YY* percent. Now, instead of measuring the team's performance based on a percentage of revenue, targets can be established in terms of expense on gross margins:

- Total budget = $10M or 5 percent of revenue
- Operational budget = $8M or 4 percent of revenue
- Helpdesk = $600,000 or .3 percent of revenue
- 40,000 cases annually

This translates to .002 percent gross margin improvement for every 4,000 helpdesk cases eliminated.

The Balanced Scorecard must be a living document, firmly supported throughout the management team and practiced by leadership throughout the company. It becomes the primary tool for ensuring constant course correction, resource adjustment, priority adjustment, and resource allocation rather than just a quarterly report to be reflected on long after the ability to make a change is past.

To make a system like this work, monthly, weekly, or even daily reports that directly tie to a Balanced Scorecard objective are required.

Table 15–1

the CEO	… it can be expressed as Gross Margin improvement.
the operations team	… it is relevant to focus on the reduction in case volume helping to achieve financial goals.
the project management team	… emphasize the project's ability to increase gross margin by eliminating help desk cases as a tangible way to tie the each effort back to the corporation's ultimate goal

▶ Service Level Agreements

The short description of an SLA is a report of operational metrics. Once the organization has established a first-pass Balanced Scorecard, it is important (and much easier) to tie operational metrics for the IT organization and partner vendors to the company's scorecard.

However, making that translation meaningful to the IT staff isn't easy. The IT Balanced Scorecard example above is financially driven, and ultimately, much of IT's business can be analyzed in a similar way. The hard sell to the IT staff members is in expanding their view of the purpose and spirit of the SLA. As mentioned previously, it is human nature to optimize to the metrics. Operationally oriented people tend to forget the greater purpose, the spirit of the SLA as opposed to its letter. It is critical to tie operational metrics to the traditional SLAs and SLOs so that both are meaningful

Following are "10 Truths" about good SLAs, whether they are internally or externally focused.

1. SLAs are a highly useful communication vehicle.
2. SLAs outline services provided, performance levels, and legal ramifications. According to the ASP Industry Consortium's "Buyers Guide to Service Level Agreements," Information that

should be contained in an SLA includes the purpose of the SLA, description of service, duration of service, installation timetable, payment terms, termination conditions, and legal issues such as warranties, indemnities, and limitation of liability.

3. Business goals are always detailed in the SLA.

4. Performance levels drive pricing.

5. SLAs are always customized to the particular purpose.

6. Metrics are always outlined for service performance.

7. The supplier of the services is not the *only* (and should not be the only) party responsible for monitoring compliance.

8. The consumer and the supplier of a service are *jointly* responsible for the terms of the SLA.

9. An SLA is *not* a guarantee of service. However, nothing should be agreed upon unless it is determined to be a commercially reasonable and viable objective.

10. Remediation, revision, and renegotiation are *always* options.

▶ Some Final (and Initial) Thoughts

As stated early in this chapter, there is a long history of techniques employed in the identification of performance gaps, successes, and failures in IT. This chapter has been limited only by the number of pages in which we could distill some of the more prominent approaches to date, but the treatment here is insufficient in light of the rapid pace of technological, social, and global economic change.

Just as it is always paramount to establish the true value and requirements for the outcome before starting any business initiative, so is the case here:

- Survey the myriad aspects of your organization.
- Derive the greatest benefits of metrics and measurement by analyzing only those elements that
  - Are not being well-managed.
  - Are in the critical path of the organization, process, or company.

- – May require optimization due to frequent change.
- Automate whatever will be routinely measured.

Although it may sound trite, in all of our years combined, we have learned to never fear a negative result or discovery. Such a discovery represents the opportunity you were seeking in instituting this discipline by which you will make change for the better.

16

Ladder of Business Intelligence: A Systematic Approach to Success for Information Technology

by James E. Cates

James Cates tells us:

I had just completed an engagement creating a worldwide IT strategy for a small, fast-growing Silicon Valley technology company within two weeks. When this two-week delivery was first requested, I thought it was an impossible task. I met with the client and listened to the requirements anyway. I considered myself to be an aggressive IT project consultant, but I was about to discover a new definition of aggressive.

The company was growing over 100 percent year to year but had very little IT infrastructure in place to support this growth. This inadequate infrastructure included telephone PBXs, data networks, and enterprise transactional systems. The growth and business strategy of the company required it to implement six major enterprise software packages within six months. This included business process definition, package software implementation, and end-user training. As the consultant presenting this plan to the executive team, I stated my concerns over whether such an inexperienced company could complete this enormously complex task within the desired timeline.

The executive team members shared my concerns. They knew that the company did not have a person with the necessary experience to implement this major project. Hence, they convinced me to join them as CIO to lead the company to a successful implementation of Phase 1 of the worldwide IT strategy. I had to lead a team from the inside to implement what my consultant team and I had recommended from the outside.

Incidentally, I tried to talk the executive team out of this aggressive schedule after I joined the company, but I failed in this attempt. Ironically, this whole episode reminds me of an IT consultant advertisement on TV that states, "Consultants don't actually implement anything—they just tell their clients what to implement." This enterprise implementation became one of the key challenges of my career.

In this chapter, James Cates explains the concepts of the Ladder of Business Intelligence (LOBI) model—the IT framework used to rapidly implement infrastructure.

▶ Business Intelligence

Business intelligence—the capacity to effectively enable business decisions through information access—has become a business imperative. Every day, business executives must make key corporate decisions based on information about their enterprise; the effectiveness of these decisions is directly related to the information system's ability to deliver the right information to the right people at the right time.

It is the role of information systems organizations in every institution to enable executive decision making and increase employee productivity by building and supporting an infrastructure that constantly improves the "cycle time to information" for each business role. However, the apparently unique situational issues of each business often deter IT professionals from effectively employing basic systems principles in their actual working environments—what may seem appropriate, even compelling, in an academic treatise is difficult to translate into real-world language and images that contemporary executives with only 30 minutes available for a presentation of new ideas will understand.

The Ladder of Business Intelligence (LOBI) framework is a model that maps fundamental notions of IT to the everyday enterprise and is applicable to companies at every level of the maturity spectrum. The LOBI succinctly captures the stages IT professionals must not only recognize but also surmount if their company is to remain competitive.

To fully understand the application of this model, a brief definition of each stage in the "ladder" is useful. See Figure 16–1.

Ladder of Business Intelligence
Enabled Intuition
Understanding
Knowledge
Information
Data
Fact

Figure 16–1   LOBI in stages.

The remaining sections of this chapter discuss the definitions of the six levels, the value of using the LOBI, and how to implement the LOBI framework.

▶ The Ladder of Business Intelligence

The LOBI is a framework used by CIOs to define the ways in which they can create value for themselves, their organizations, and their supported business units. The objective of the LOBI model is to easily explain the added value and ROI of IT to nontechnical executives and hence to align the business and IT at both the executive level and at the business role level.

A key concept of the LOBI model is that a business operates at different levels of business intelligence (BI)—from *facts* to *enabled intuition*. The purpose of the LOBI model is to reduce cycle time to information (CTI) or cycle time to knowledge (CTK) by business role. Reducing the

CTI for a given business role potentially allows the person fulfilling that role to reduce the cycle time to action (CTA), providing the role with a more timely business impact.

After all, the ultimate objective of automation is to allow a person operating in a business role to make high-impact business decisions in the required timeframe. One of the primary responsibilities of the CIO is to move the business along from a lower level to a higher level of BI; the success of the CIO's performance can be measured by the percentage of business users who reach the stage of enabled intuition. Table16–1 maps the LOBI levels to representative business intelligence results.

Table 16–1   LOBI levels

LOBI levels	Created by
Facts	Spreadsheet or disparate data input
Data	ERP or other transactional applications
Information	FAQs, ticker price, output of BI tools
Knowledge	"What if" scenarios or information with experience; created by business rules
Understanding	Alternative business models; "what if" scenarios
Enabled Intuition	The "Aha!" stage: deep insight

▶ Defining the Stages of the LOBI

Facts are the fundamental entities that an organization deals with. These business truths can exist in a variety of forms, not all of them electronic. Facts are the real-world quantitative representation of useful business entities. It is usually not easy to retrieve facts in the required timeframe because the facts and data are disparate and nonintegrated. Here is a sample fact:

Revenue from client C in month M is: $$

Data is integrated, ordered facts. In today's corporations, most data that refers to fundamental business operations exists electronically. Here is the data corresponding to the sample fact:

Invoice numbers NN through MM, stored as records in application AA, represent all the revenue from client C in month M.

Information is ordered data. Information is data further transformed and delivered within the context of additional business role intelligence. Business role intelligence makes data useful because it places the data in a particular business context. The resulting information can then be used to make better-informed business decisions. The information model is represented in Figure 16–2.

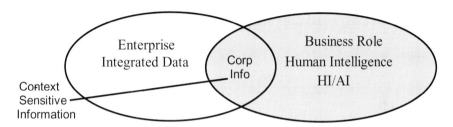

Figure 16–2 Information model.

When the data above is delivered within the context of growth, overall company revenue, or both, it represents information that a business can act upon. Here is the information corresponding to the sample data:

Revenue of $$ from client C was more than the revenue for the previous month by $$+.

Knowledge is ordered information within the context of experience in similar situations. Knowledge enables the reusability of experiential information. This allows an experienced person to use "what if" and "if-then-else" scenarios to solve real-world business problems. An example of a frequently used knowledge base is the FAQs stored in call management systems. Here is an abstract example of knowledge:

If condition C, then action A.

The knowledge model is represented in Figure 16–3.

Knowledge is also the last frontier at which machine intelligence can be directly applied (given the current state of computational technology).

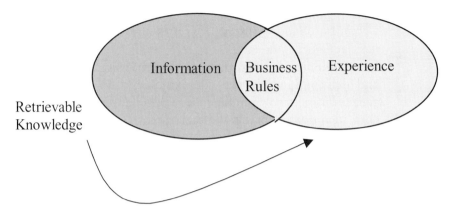

Figure 16–3 Knowledge model.

Utilization of knowledge is the capability to relate available information to a situation at hand and use it to decide the correct course of action, even when you have no experience in solving the particular type of problem in question. Experience with similar situations and scenarios helps to narrow down the decision alternatives.

To continue with the previous examples, if a person in marketing correlates the revenue growth to a promotional campaign run for a set of clients three months previously and is able to extend that correlation across time, geography, and client boundaries, it gives the business a tool to leverage growth.

Understanding is organized knowledge. Although this is a subjective concept, understanding represents a complete comprehension, or grasp, of a set of knowledge. To a large degree, understanding can be described as a personal "internalization" of knowledge achieved through close contact and long experience. Knowledge obviously differs between individuals, both within a business role and across roles within an organization. Collaboration models are aimed at making understanding uniform across groups that work together on executing the same business processes. If a business can reach uniform understanding about its key challenges among the key stakeholders, the quality of its decisions is greatly improved.

Enabled intuition is the stage that is reached when different dimensions of a situation are understood over the course of repeated encounters, and human intelligence synthesizes a completely holistic approach to addressing a whole class of similar situations. Enabled intuition can also be described as knowing or sensing without rational process—that is, immediate cognition. As Zen-like as this sounds, enabled intuition is a very powerful state from which to operate and well worth the journey required to get there.

Insights—the "aha!" moments—normally occur not through planning but in brains that are experienced, prepared, and able to observe and correlate what's happening around them. Such individuals see unusual relationships and draw new conclusions. My observation is that useful business intuition cannot occur without deep understanding of the business problem domain. That said, one of the key differentiators at the enabled intuition level is the ability to operate within an unknown context—unlike the lower levels of the model, which all operate in a known context.

As a business moves from one level to the next through the knowledge level, there is an increase in structure, domain-specificity, and integration. Beyond the knowledge level, business intelligence becomes more unstructured, less specific, and more engaged with collaborative types of communication.

The levels of the LOBI and the process of moving from one level to the next are shown in Figure 16–4.

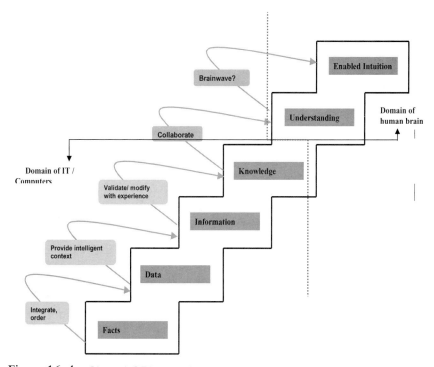

Figure 16–4   Chart LOBI model.

Value in Moving Up the LOBI

One by-product of technology innovations is undeniable: Businesses have acquired the capacity to gather more facts about more entities of relevance to them, faster and across wider geographic areas, than ever before. As this continues, the number of facts that a corporation must analyze to identify those relevant to a particular decision increases exponentially.

The fundamental value of moving up the LOBI is this: The higher a business is on the LOBI, the faster it can transform relevant facts into meaningful business decisions by reducing CTI or CTK. The corporate value of information, or CVI, is composed of data correlation ability (DCA) plus the experience of individuals plus the ability to communicate. Level 3 of the LOBI, information, is the first that empowers a business role. It is therefore to your advantage to get to Level 3 as soon as possible.

Organizations spend enormous resources in gathering facts, but many have no strategies for transforming these facts into information. The value of moving up the LOBI lies in converting these facts into knowledge and beyond.

- Level 1: The *fact* level is simply the foundation—businesses acquire this by virtue of being in business.
- Level 2: Once at the *data* level, the business gains from efficiency and flexibility in referring to facts about its customers, employees, and partners. Data enables other applications and provides economies of scale for support costs across systems.
- Level 3: At the *information* level, the business becomes capable of taking effective action to counter challenges or identify new opportunities. As business roles link information needs to key performance indicators (KPIs), these roles become more effective as the information is utilized.
- Level 4: The *knowledge* level represents leverage that the business has regarding its clients, markets, and partners. Clearly, this is the stage at which the business gains the most value from information by reusing methods, concepts, and *experience across operating units*.
- Level 5: *Understanding* directly improves the firm's effectiveness in the marketplace over the long run. Companies that have

reached this level tend to outlast their competition because they are beginning to gain an insight into the customer's mind and to see opportunities before their rivals see them.

- Level 6: *Enabled intuition* is the level at which out-of-the-box solutions are generated.

Given two organizations that are in the same business and at the same stage of evolution of the LOBI, the one run by people who have greater DCA skills, experience, and communication capabilities outperforms the other. This implies that the superior performing organization has the most effective processes, because *only effective processes* transform data into information and information into knowledge. These transformations will enable the reduction of CTA.

Implicit in these statements is the assumption that as businesses move up the LOBI, they give due care to maintaining and improving all the quality attributes of the data—consistency, integrity, and cleanliness.

Another way of looking at the value of a given LOBI is to consider what a business at each level can accomplish that it could not at the previous level.

- At Level 1, the business cannot make consistent, repeatable decisions because it can't retrieve the data in a timely manner by business role.

- At Level 2, the business can retrieve the data, but the data-to-information transformation process is labor-intensive; hence decisions are less likely to be timely or effective.

- At Level 3, decisions are timely but the business cannot scale, since the decisions are made by the few people who have the needed experience. If they leave the company, decision effectiveness drops.

- At Level 4, these few experienced people have created "atomic knowledge units" and made the decision-making process independent of themselves (this could be as simple as FAQs or as complex as AI systems).

- Level 5 and Level 6 are qualitative refinements of Level 4, currently still achieved by "brain ware."

Clearly, all the major relational database management system vendors are moving their products from Level 2 to Level 3 by incorporating more and more business intelligence into their products.

The LOBI Business Odyssey

How does a business progress up the LOBI? This journey is accomplished simply by repeatedly and systematically executing the *ordered LOBI triple*: business role identification, business process definition, and technology selection.

Simple as it sounds, the ordering of the triple is *critical*; no information system should be bought or built until:

- The business roles that will be made more productive have been identified.

- The process or processes that will gather the data and transform it into information have been defined.

- The technology that is appropriate for encoding the defined processes and displaying the information by business has been selected.

- Business roles include not only those internal to the organization, such as the CEO, CFO, and buyer, but also those that are external, such as channel partner or customer. (The recent, well-publicized inventory debacle in the telecommunications industry is largely attributable to big manufacturers completely ignoring the channel partner business role.)

As used in this definition, the term business role is very restrictive. The CIO should not deal with any generic information system; any and all information must be defined and validated by a business role. (Business Role Information Analysis, or BRIA, is a methodology I have created that requires businesses to follow the ordered triple. BRIA is described in more detail later on.)

Cost and time (CT) are required for execution of the ordered triple at each LOBI level. Depending on the level the company has reached, each triple might require more or less of each of these crucial resources.

The CT of moving from one LOBI level to the next includes:

- educating people about the identified business roles.
- defining and implementing the defined processes.
- setting up the selected technology Infrastructure.

For instance, implementing an ERP solution moves an organization to the data level (Level 2). An ERP includes six major business roles: customer support, finance, logistics, human resources, manufacturing, and sales. Parameter-based functions can be created that estimate the cost of implementing an ERP for a business with yearly revenues of $50 million to $250 million, for example.

The measure of success in reaching a given LOBI level is the coverage of business roles within a business function.

My experience has taught me that it usually takes 10 to 15 percent of the expense of reaching Level 2 to reach Level 3, and another 10 to 15 percent of the Level 2 expense to reach Level 4. I have no experience in the cost of reaching Level 5 at the time of this writing.

To the CIO, evolving a business beyond LOBI Level 1 is a project, and as with any project, the following *always* hold true:

Project success is a function of RS^2 and VEC^3

RS^2 is {Resources, Scope, Schedule}

VEC^3 is {$V \times E \times C_1 \times C_2\,C_3$}, where

V = Vested Interest (that is, aligning the vested interests of key stakeholders)

E = Ego (that is, understanding the values and culture of stakeholders)

C^1 = Communication and alignment with executive management

C^2 = Communication and alignment with your peers

C^3 = Communication and alignment with all doers (implementers)

In most situations, the resources and schedule are limited by organizational factors beyond the CIO's total control; thus the successes really is critically dependent on how well the scope is managed and expectations set. Since scope in turn is a negotiated entity, the key principle deciding the outcome is getting clarity and agreement on this.

The better aligned the vested interests of all the business roles are, the better the chances of project success. Aligning the Vs starts with a realistic assessment of what you (as a business, department, or individual)

know and don't know about the audiences specified in the VEC^3 equation. Before the project starts, you must determine what the vested interests of all key stakeholders are and how they can best be aligned.

▶ Using The LOBI Model

Meaning of the LOBI Rating

The LOBI rating assumes that the higher a business is on the ladder, the more effectively and efficiently the business is operating.

Figure 16–5 shows that at each level, there is a new value for the LOBI triple. Hence, you are enabling a different set of business roles at each level. Note that not all business roles participate at all LOBI levels, but most need to get to Level 3.

You are also creating new processes as you move to each level. Remember, *the lack of corporate process management skills is the single biggest impediment to corporations trying to move up the LOBI.*

Finally, the diagram suggests various technology selections for each level. Since Level 2 is the base for moving to all other levels, it must be attained quickly, with the greatest architectural flexibility. This implies that common enterprise data models must be defined. It also makes the use of storage area networks almost mandatory in order to manage your data in a reliable, flexible, serviceable, and affordable manner.

In Figure 16–5, yellow print indicates a named process and white print a technology selection. (**Figure will print black & white.**)

Figure 16–6 shows the business benefits of each level.

Using the BRIA Methodology

Business Role Information Analysis, or BRIA, is the methodology used to define which business questions are to be answered and their business value. BRIA is used in the earliest stages of the IT project lifecycle and is a necessary part of the requirements-gathering phases. BRIA provides a mechanism by which business users can define their information needs in language and terms they understand and relate to, without getting into a discussion of technical details of the system.

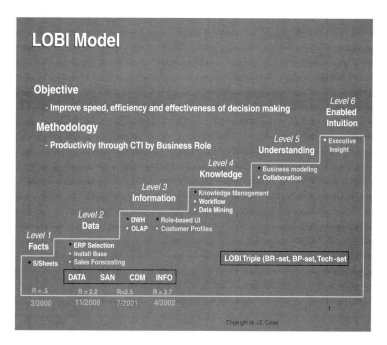

Figure 16–5   LOBI model.

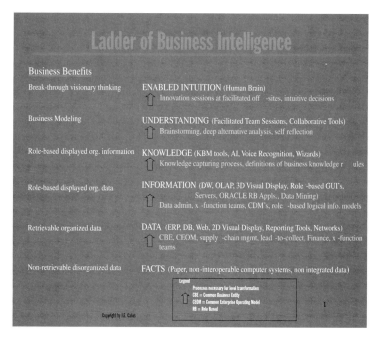

Figure 16–6   LOBI business benefits.

A BRIA document consists of four parts:

- Business role
- Business questions to be answered—information needs of business role
- Business value of the needed information
- Data sources

A comprehensive BRIA document for a business role or roles helps IT drive the appropriate solution set to meet the information needs of the business users. Table 16–2 provides a sample BRIA:

Table 16–2   Sample of BRIA

Business Role	Forecasting Manager
Business Questions	What are the revenue forecasts by customer, product, sales region, time, channel?
	What is the accuracy of forecasts against actual orders?
	How do actual orders compare to the current forecast?
Business Value	Setting revenue targets and expectations
	Measurement of forecast accuracy

This BRIA highlights at least two major points:

- Forecast data must be reported and sourced from a forecasting system if one exists, or a forecasting system must be implemented to hold and report the forecast data (LOBI Level 2).
- A mechanism for consolidation of actuals and forecasts must be in place as must the capability to analyze data across various business dimensions—that is, a data warehouse solution (LOBI L3).

The BRIA methodology helps identify and prioritize the technology investments required to maximize the business value of the investment. Figure 16–7 shows how BRIA fits into the IT lifecycle model.

In BRIA, the user community that requisitions the project relates the project need to a business issue it is attempting to solve. It does this by identifying the key business questions the information will answer and

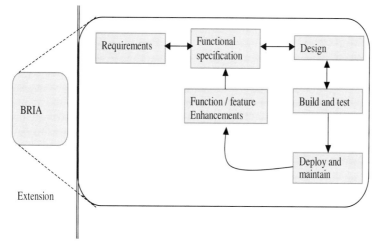

Figure 16–7   Conventional IT project lifecycle.

the business value that answering these questions will have to the business role.

The main reason for BRIA's introduction is its brevity. Why is it brief? Because the executives who deal with the BRIA stage of the lifecycle are busy individuals who have a clear idea of their needs and express them succinctly.

BRIA starts with each business unit's business role population listing a maximum of 10 questions per role, answers to which will help them perform better in those roles. The questions must be prioritized.

Table 16–3 shows one method of implementing BRIA.

On closer examination, it is clear these questions indicate that they can often be derived directly from the major business objectives (MBOs) of these roles. A sampling of MBOs for selected roles in a large organization might include:

- Strategic objective: Improve market share by X percent.
- R&D: Generate initiatives given sustained level of investments.
- Sales: Grow by 100 percent in the next two years.
- Operations: Improve efficiency; include offshore as an option.

The CIO's task is then to build the systems that provide the answers to these questions for his or her business partners, prioritizing among the roles (clients) and deciding which systems to build and in what order.

Table 16–3 Business role of BRIA

Role	Key Questions, 10 or less.	Information	Data source	Existing, or to be developed
CFO	Do I need external funding for the next quarter?	• Info on end of quarter (current) balance • Projected next quarter sources and costs • Projected next quarter uses and returns	• Projected cash flow • Cash flow projections; • Utilization of lines of credit and costs • Projects portfolio • Department budgets	
VP Sales	Do I need to add more sales people	• Market share • Sales person's efficiency • Sales team capacity • Product's adequacy in meeting market needs	• Own and competitor sales • Metrics on Industry and own sales team performance • Causal analysis of order lost situations	
R & D		•	•	
Ops		•	•	
Support		•	•	

Productivity and LOBI Rating

The primary goal of the LOBI and BRIA is to reduce the CTI for each business role. Productivity and efficiency gains are baked into the assumptions of the model; in other words, systems will be implemented to meet the requirements outlined in the BRIA document with well-understood cycle time requirements. If an existing report, for example, takes six hours of manual work to create, implementing a system using the LOBI and BRIA should reduce the cycle time to levels defined by the business roles.

The LOBI rating is used to determine the progress of the various business functions along the LOBI. A LOBI rating template has five parts:

- Business function
- Business roles
- Number of employees in these business roles
- Current LOBI rating
- Desired LOBI rating

A measure of the current and desired LOBI rating helps us define the priorities and a system roadmap to take the organization from the current state to the desired state, business role by business role. The entire set of information users is split into logical business areas—operations, finance, service, human resources, engineering, sales, marketing, customers, suppliers, and so on. Within each business function or area, the various business roles are identified. The BRIA template is used to determine the information requirements for each business role. BRIA helps us define the desired LOBI rating.

The LOBI implies a certain class of systems at each level of the ladder, as follows:

At Level 1, data is scattered across multiple systems or individual desktops.

Level 2 defines an integrated data store environment like an ERP or CRM. Transactional enterprise applications fall into this level.

Level 3 defines the class of applications that transform data into information to aid metrics, analytics, dashboards, KPIs, and so on. Data warehouse, OLAP, and data mining applications fall in this category.

Level 4 defines the knowledge base/expert system class of applications. Knowledge capture techniques are leveraged at this level.

The information needs of a particular business role define the desired LOBI level. For example, shipping clerks or order-entry personnel will stay at Level 2 because all their information needs are met by an ERP system. An analyst or an executive, however, must climb to Level 3 or Level 4 because of the consolidated nature of the reports and metrics he or she will need. Table 16–4 shows a sample LOBI rating template.

Table 16–4   Sample LOBI rating template

Business Function	Business Role	Number of Employees	Current Rating	Desired Rating

All the individual LOBI rating scores up to the business function are aggregated to give an overall rating for the business function. Across the enterprise, this helps us identify the areas in which we should be investing to bring the various business functions closer to the desired LOBI rating.

The BRIA methodology is implemented by an IT business systems analyst working with the business unit. An employee can perform more than one role. A sample *enterprise* BRIA analysis is shown in Figure 16–8.

Enterprise Business Roles Analysis

Functional Areas	BSA Business System Analyst	# Business Roles	# Employees performing role	# Employees Using data warehouse
Finance		21	137	27
Operations		38	97	90
Services		13	31	30
HR		6	1610	26
Sales		5	240	156
Marketing		7	44	
Product Marketing		3	12	5
Engineering		20	362	6
Total		113	2533	340

Figure 16–8   Enterprise business roles.

An Example Using the LOBI Model

Using Figure 16–5, the LOBI model, as a reference, let's apply the above principles.

- Assumptions
  - Small, fast-growing company with no IT infrastructure
  - Limited IT budget
  - No IT strategy in place
  - Small IT staff
- Corporate challenges: Need to estimate cost and schedule for implementing an adequate IT infrastructure within six months; IT systems must be able to support business requirements as indicated in Figure 16–9

Approach Using LOBI Framework

The business is currently at LOBI Level 1, which means it is using spreadsheets and the "hero culture" model to make the company operate. Obviously, this model does not scale. We can estimate the cost of advancement by using past successful estimates based on a given revenue run rate and a desired architecture driven by business needs.

Figure 16–9 is a vision chart that may represent the business needs of any fast-growing company. It is important that all executives are aligned with this vision.

To move from Level 1 to Level 2, driven by this vision, we need to execute the LOBI triple:

1. Identify the business roles we want to make more productive— for example finance, human resources, and services.
2. Define the business processes needed to generate the information to answer the BRIA questions.
3. Select the technology needed to implement the processes defined in step 2.

Since this company is at Level 1, it needs a broad horizontal set of functional software. Therefore, we should pick an ERP system, because this type of system supports the largest number of business roles simultaneously in an integrated manner. This is also the time to carefully architect our storage, data network, database, and data access environ-

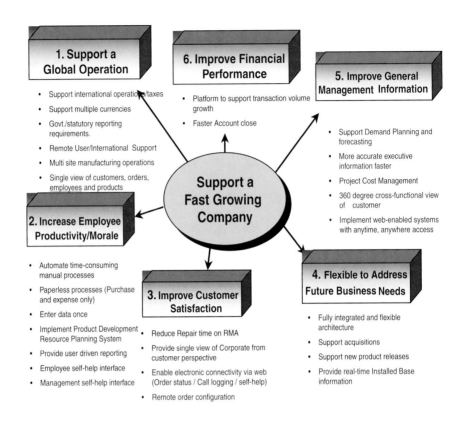

Figure 16–9 Sample business requirements vision.

architect our storage, data network, database, and data access environment. This will be our last opportunity to do this in a flexible and extendable manner at the lowest cost.

In our example, we are solving the manufacturing and product delivery business role sets, which include 38 specific roles (see Figure 16–8). We choose an ERP, a storage area network (Brocade), a network vendor, and a Web services vendor. We must also estimate our cost of implementation. This is done based on experience and is beyond the scope of this chapter.

The idea in the LOBI framework is to purchase only the technology needed to support the specific business roles that will be made more productive. This almost guarantees that you will not create shelfware. Of course, this requires business discipline (see Figure 16–10). We have chosen the manufacturing role sets for this example, but for a corporatewide support strategy, all the other business roles would need to be similarly analyzed. My experience tells me that the average midsize company has over 100 business roles.

Once Level 2 has been reached, you must begin planning for attainment of Level 3, because this is the first level that gives your employees real decision-making power. To reach this level effectively, you need to understand how the employee wants to view the information and the process for transforming the data into information. The technology needed to move to Level 3 includes a data warehouse, a data extraction tool, an OLAP tool, and Web display tools. Of course, you must have adequate network capacity and appropriate security protocols in place.

It is beyond the scope of this chapter to move beyond LOBI Level 3. Not to worry, however—it will take most mid-cap companies three to four years to effectively reach L3.

Manufacturing/Product Delivery Example

Top Business Priorities for Manufacturing

1. **Forecasting & Demand Management:**
   - Plan Capacity, Improve Lead -time, Forecast by Cust. category
   - Reduce operating cost & Inventory costs
   - Improve Inventory Management, Product Lead Time, Order Accuracy,   Product Availibility
   - Support Customer Sales
2. **Invoice Management**
   - Improve Customer Service through: Accurate Shipments, Invoices

Activities	Corp Forecast	Order & Demand Mgmt Outsourced Manufacturing	Corp send Invoice
Business Processes to support for various manufacturing roles	•Field forecast Entry •Forecast Analysis •Revenue Projection •Automated forecast rollup by Customer/Product	**Demand + Inventory Management** • Forecast Analyst tools • Multi-supplier planning • Various Inventory Planning Methods • Hard Reservations/Allocations • Integrated PO system **Online Order Management System** • Online Web OE/detail order history • CTO + ATP Capability	• Automatic Invoicing once • CM has shipped • Capture Built Information
System Strategies	• Use package solution for forecast collection and management •Web based sales forecast collection	• Package Solutions for Order/Demand Mgmt • Retain Built distinct from Installed -Base • Web-based Order Mgmt System for both internal and external users •Customize an Order Configuration Tool • Evaluate Collaboration Software for BOM for Management and Quality Management • Build Data Marts for Order Forecast Analysis	• Transfer advance ship notice file to update ERP system on invoice and customer order information
Recommendations (Packages/Tools) (examples)	Tier 1 Demand Mgmt (I2, Manugistics)	Demand Management : Oracle, Peoplesoft plus integration to ERP Order Configuration Tool: Selecta Web services: IBM, BEA, Microsoft	ERP: (Oracle, Peoplesoft, SAP) Storage: Brocade SAN + Storage Vendor

Figure 16–10

Note: Acronyms used in Figure 16-10 include
ATP = Available to Promise
CTO = Configure to Order
PO = Purchase Order
ERP = Enterprise Resource Planning
BOM = Bill of Materials
CM = Contract Manufacturer)

▶ Summary

I have found that the LOBI framework is very useful in allowing business unit executives to understand ROI expectations at a conceptual level, thereby reducing the time a CIO requires to create business unit alignment. It also allows the IT organization to be very focused on implementing systems that improve the productivity of very specific business roles, which in aggregate improve the efficiency of the entire corporation. If the BRIA methodology is also used, the model helps business units to know exactly what information each business role needs to be more productive.

The most important concept to remember in moving up the LOBI is designing efficient processes. If a company has inefficient processes and doesn't automate them, it will have a slow, cheap path to bankruptcy; if the company automates the inefficient processes, it will have a fast, expensive path to bankruptcy. But it will be bankrupt in either case.

Finally, while I have tried to explain the details behind the LOBI model, in practice I use only Figure 16–5 for most executive discussions.

The proof point for the LOBI framework? I used the LOBI to lead the selling, funding, and successful concurrent implementation of six enterprise applications within a six-month period.

Communities of Practice: Continuing the Learning

by John Moran and Lee Weimer,
Community of Practice Facilitators

So, you've read through all the chapters of this book and assimilated lots of good information. What's next? How do you continue the learning process? Where do you go to get even more information? How do you keep current with changes and best practices in the industry?

John Moran and Lee Weimer describe a powerful approach to these challenges: Become an active member of a Community of Practice (CoP).

Imagine meeting regularly with a small group of other CIOs who are facing issues and problems similar to yours. Some of the CIOs are ahead of you in certain project implementations, while others are taking a totally different approach to problem resolution.

These are regular, informal meetings at which you select the subjects that are on your hot list, and the presenters are qualified to bring in new information on your chosen subject. The different experiences, backgrounds, thought processes, and new information produced during the face-to-face meetings can dramatically increase your professional knowledge and growth. This is the general concept of a Community of Practice.

▶ Overview of the CoP

Communities of Practice (CoP) can be defined as:

> A group of people who are brought together by a desire to learn more about a common class of problems, opportunities, and their possible solutions.

Community members accelerate business results and add value by collaborating. Everyone learns from one another and from outside resources.

Figure 17–1 Communities of practice.

Members find themselves drawn to one another by a force that is both *professional* and *social*. Both of these aspects are key to the success of a CoP. The idea of "professional practice" is critical, because the group's members concentrate on the learning that emerges through "real work" within their organizations. Learning is also social, since the CoP is based on familiarity and reciprocal trust. Thus, CoPs assist both in finding and sharing best practices and in building social capital across organizations.

How can a CoP impact business results? Knowledge management practitioners have recently been investigating the importance of less structured, or *tacit,* knowledge as well as the role played by social networks in innovation and knowledge creation. CoPs are seen by many as providing an environment in which this tacit knowledge can be developed, nurtured, and sustained. For example, the CIOs who authored this book are members of a CoP, and they are sharing their best practices (tacit knowledge) with you.

CoPs can exist within a single organization or within a single discipline and can span several organizations. Because CoPs generate extraordinary learning, they are among the most important structures for organizations in which thinking matters. CoPs contribute directly to an organization's intellectual and social capital. A single idea generated from interaction within a CoP might result in a whole new product line, or in saving millions of dollars through shorter implementation of a major IT project, or in better hiring practices. For example, this CIO CoP has begun the process of defining best practices for contract terms for purchasing software that will directly benefit both buyers and sellers.

We've looked at CoPs as individual learning laboratories and seen how CoPs can contribute to the intellectual, financial, and social capital within a business. So, what does one look like, and how does it operate? As examples, we describe two different IT-focused CoPs that we currently facilitate.

▶ The Silicon Valley CIO Community of Practice (CIO CoP)

This CIO CoP was organized late in 1997 as a fee-facilitated community of CIOs. Its first formal meeting was held in February 1998. CoPs are typically small groups of people that learn together. This CoP is unusual because the members were CIOs from several different companies who wanted to set their own goals and choose the topics that interested them. The participants set their own ground rules and decided who could participate and when they would meet. The topics they wanted to cover would encompass all of a CIO's roles and responsibilities, including:

- **People:** Coaching and developing the capacity of the IT staff and creating a vivid picture of an ambitious future for the IT organization. Building partnerships with executive management and internal or external customers provides the IT organization with recognition as a proactive contributor to business development.

- **Technology:** Selecting and utilizing appropriate technologies to keep the organization connected to its stakeholders and to directly benefit the overall business enterprise.

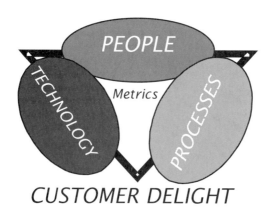

CUSTOMER DELIGHT

Figure 17–2

- **Processes:** Building effective and efficient processes that deliver information to the business enterprise and facilitate its use for strategic and tactical advantage.

- **Metrics:** Setting the criteria and measuring progress to tell us how we'll know we've been successful.

Over the last few years, the CIO CoP has grown and changed significantly. We now have CIOs from over 20 companies participating; the meetings are one-half day each month and are hosted by a member company. Almost all of our meetings include at least two "expert presenters" who interactively lead the community members in topic discussions. Following this session is another important part of each meeting: a dinner that supports both professional and social interaction. We provide a summary of each meeting with the accompanying presentation material, forming a reference library for the CoP members. Table 17–1 lists a few of the topics we have covered in the past.

Table 17–1   CoP topics

Technology Directions for Securing Systems Which Require Multiple Access Methods	Components of Strategy Development for Business to Business e-Commerce	Methods for working with collaborative & remote teams
How do you tie together back-end systems (such as ERP CRM) and e-commerce sites?	Talent Wars in the Executive Suite	Wireless Technology: Status and Costs/Risks
Outsourcing	Business Continuity/Disaster Recovery	Value Chain: Getting Visibility

In addition to our regular meetings, the members have collaborated in writing this book, developed some best practices in software licensing contracts, and initiated the IT Applications/Operations CoP for their direct reports.

The Silicon Valley Applications/Operations CoP (A/O CoP) started in mid-2001 and is structured much like the CIO CoP. The members include up to two director-level IT people from each company. They meet for a half day plus dinner every other month. The members of this CoP are slowly building the level of trust and familiarity required to begin innovative knowledge sharing. One example of this was a meeting set up by one of the members to learn more from Cisco Systems about the role of IT in mergers and acquisitions. Although this wasn't an official CoP event, the organizer felt secure enough in the CoP members that all were invited to participate in the meeting.

CoPs provide value-added benefits. Our experiences with the Silicon Valley CoPs and discussions with members and presenters have provided insight into the value that the different groups have received from their participation in our CoPs. The following is a summary of those benefits:

Benefits for Members

Open, interactive discussion. The Silicon Valley CIO CoP and the A/O CoP settings are business casual, and membership is limited (usually under 25) to facilitate ease of interaction and help build close relationships. The meetings are based on a dialogue model, with discussion of a single IT-common topic and an emphasis on interactive questioning and listening as opposed to debate. Since the objective of the CoP is to facilitate growth and learning, there is less need to be right than there is to be open. This does not mean all of the members always agree with one another or with the presenters. There is plenty of convincing attempted among various members, among members and presenters, and among the presenters themselves. But, however spirited the exchanges may get, they are always good-natured.

Trusted network. Close relationships are critically important to the ongoing success of a CoP for both members and facilitators. People are more likely to trust the experiences of those they have come to know over time and with whom they have also shared experiences.

The dinner portion of our meetings provides participants with the opportunity to become storytellers, assume roles other than CIO or director, and eventually become friends.

Learning opportunities. By sharing best practices and the experiences of others, members are exposed to a range of new and known products, solutions, and services. They may obtain professional opportunities for themselves or their companies, recognition from their peers, or leads for their next new hire (though active recruitment is not encouraged). The members invariably expand their professional circles, grow, learn, and have fun.

Ongoing communication and reference. Outside of monthly meetings, all communication between members, facilitators, and presenters occurs through email, telephone, or an online forum provided by a sponsoring organization. Responsive communications, quality of speakers and facilitation, and attention to detail all contribute to a complete CoP service.

Benefits for Presenters

Target audience. Representatives of companies that have something to offer an IT organization are provided with a rare experience: an opportunity to sit down with members of their top target audience in an informal setting. They must demonstrate their knowledge of the CIOs' problem areas and how their companies and products might help to solve those problems. This is no "hard sell" environment, but an opportunity to demonstrate competence. Through the product or problem knowledge displayed, a vendor can create a relationship with members that the *members* will want to follow-up.

Learning and business intelligence. Presenters often have an opportunity to learn about competitors' products and services, business areas they are unfamiliar with, and opportunities for their own CIOs or directors.

Benefits for Facilitators

Learning and close relationships. Facilitators can guide the learning through the presenters they invite, the questions raised during meetings, and the topics they suggest for members' consideration. Facilitators have an opportunity to grow and learn with the members *and* to make friends and have fun.

Meaningful occupation. Facilitators have the opportunity to provide a needed and appreciated service for a fee.

▶ Finding a CoP

We've presented a picture of the business and personal benefits you can obtain through participation in a Community of Practice. Your next step is to investigate the possibilities of belonging to a CIO CoP in your area. If you can't locate one, consider building a CoP by profession or common interest. This can be done in almost any geographic area.

As facilitators, we have started building a web of CoPs in various areas. We expect to link the individual affiliate CoPs through the Internet in ways that will permit a broad sharing of information across geographic regions. Please join us.

Index

About the Authors

email comments to the authors at
cio-wisdom@collabri.com

Judy Armstrong Judy Armstrong brings more than 20 years' expertise to her role at Benchmark. Prior to joining Benchmark, Armstrong was CIO and vice president of corporate services for C-Cube Microsystems. As CIO for Benchmark, Armstrong has worldwide responsibility for the design and implementation of information systems, applications, infrastructure, facilities, and human resource management, and acts as a strategic advisor to the Benchmark Portfolio Network. Armstrong's expertise includes leading IT through both growth and contracting business cycles by evaluating, selecting, and implementing internal technologies and applications and developing strategic plans.

Ralph D. Boethling II Ralph Boethling brings 30 years of management experience—including more than 22 years in IT organizations—to his role at Change Technology Solutions, where he heads content development and professional services. Prior to joining Change, Boethling held executive-level IT positions in large, complex corporations such as Twentieth Century Fox Film Corporation as well as start-up/early-stage companies such as Financial Pacific Insurance Company and Total Pharmaceutical Care. Boethling's earlier IT career includes eight years in Price Waterhouse's Management Consulting Services practice, where he led several enterprise-level projects for Fortune 500 companies such as the Walt Disney Company and Mattel Toys.

James E. Cates James Cates, CIO for Brocade, draws on more than 30 years of IT leadership, engineering, and applications management experience. He was most recently COO and CTO of Information Technology Solutions (IT Solutions), a privately held IT services consulting firm. He served as vice president, CIO, and CQO at Synopsys, a leader in design automation products for the semiconductor, communications, and electronics markets. Cates was responsible for the successful implementation of a worldwide ERP system. Before joining Synopsys, he was worldwide director of applications services at Silicon Graphics, responsible for defining the company's worldwide IS strategy. Cates began his career at IBM, where he was director of information strategy, architecture, and technology for the IBM U.S. Marketing and Services line of business. Cates serves on the Ohio State University CIS Advisory Board and the board of directors of IT Solutions. He is also a member of the Association of Computing Machinery. Cates received a master's degree in computer and information science from the Ohio State University School of Engineering.

Louis-Robert (Bob) Denis Bob Denis is well seasoned in executive- and senior-level management in the areas of IT, research and development, customer service, operations, and sales support. Prior to joining Trimble Navigation, Denis was a principal at Innovative Management Associates, a consulting firm specializing in enterprise infrastructure design and implementation. As CIO and vice president for Trimble, he has global accountability for the design and implementation of the information technology and telecommunications infrastructure. At Trimble, Denis reports to the CEO and is a member of the company's executive operating council. His expertise includes a demonstrated ability to build and lead teams capable of implementing necessary enabling technologies and projects while remaining aligned with the overall corporate business strategies and budget guidelines.

John L. Dick Currently a cofounder of The StrataFusion Group, which specializes in CIO/CTO executive-level temporary replacement and technology engineering, implementation, and consulting, John Dick is a well-known Silicon Valley technology veteran with over 25 years' experience in the fields of technology management and strategic technology and technology product direction. John's expertise spans networks, enterprise applications, Internet technology and business models, knowledge management, and complex computing environments.

Mark E. Egan Mark Egan is Symantec's CIO and vice president of IT. He manages Symantec's internal telecommunications and computing systems and is responsible for the implementation of all worldwide information systems. Egan led the rapid transformation of Symantec's internal information systems over the past three years, as the company assumed the leadership role in the Information Security market. Egan brings more than 25 years' experience in information systems in a variety of industries. He served as CIO and Venture Partner for one of the world's largest venture capital firms, Walden International Investment Group, and focused on software and Internet companies. In addition, he held several senior-level positions with companies including Sun Microsystems, Price Waterhouse, Atlantic Richfield, Martin Marietta Data Systems, and Wells Fargo Bank. Egan holds a master's degree in finance and international business from the University of San Diego and a bachelor's degree in computer and quantitative sciences from the University of Clarion. He is a member of AMA's (American Management Association) Information Systems and Technology Council and serves on the technical advisory boards for e4e Inc. and Golden Gate University.

Joe Feliu Joe Feliu is vice president of NeoDimensions, a leading technology services provider. For over 20 years, Feliu has held executive-level IT positions at Visto Corporation (a wireless applications and services provider), AllAdvantage.com, Applied Materials, and the United States Postal Service. He was an adjunct professor at UCLA and the University of San Francisco. Feliu is a frequent speaker, panel member, and chairperson at leading conferences and appears regularly in management journals and in media interviews.

Brenda J. Fox Brenda Fox has over 19 years of IT experience with management of global large-scale enterprise systems and technology, ASP hosting, professional services, national support, and R&D functions in high-tech manufacturing, distribution, small business, and government sectors. She has held executive positions as CIO for ReadRite, vice president of application services for AristaSoft, vice president of professional service for CompuCom, director of IT for Safeguard Business Systems, and director of IT for Prime Minister Trudeau's office.

Thanks to business writer John Vurpillat for his time, support, editing contributions and his tremendous insights into the literary process. Thanks to Nancy Gorsich for her friendship and in depth understanding of human communication processes and breakdowns.

Michael Hawkins Serving companies in the IT, financial, government, and oil and gas sectors, Michael Hawkins has over 20 years' experience in a variety of international business and technical environments covering high-availability systems, security, disaster recovery, and IT production operations. He has been responsible for information systems security, strategic planning, network operations, business continuity, and disaster recovery in a large IT enterprises connecting a variety of Web, client/server, and mainframe systems across international networks. In addition to teaching graduate courses in risk management, information security, and business continuity planning, he co-authored four books on implementing and managing business-critical information systems and technologies: *Managing the New Enterprise* (1996), *Networking the New Enterprise* (1997), *Data Warehousing: Architecture and Implementation* (1998), and *High Availability: Design, Techniques and Processes* (2000). He earned an M.S. degree (First Honors) in computer science, an M.A. degree in economics, and a B.S. degree in electrical engineering and computer science. He is also a Certified Information Systems Security Professional (CISSP) and Cisco Certified Network Associate (CCNA).

Dean Lane Dean Lane brings more than 20 years of in-depth experience to his role at Symantec. Prior to joining Symantec, Lane was CIO at Allied-Signal, Morton Thiokol, Plantronics, and Masters Institute of Technology. Additionally, he served as a consultant for Ernst & Young, AT&T Global Information Systems, and Gartner Group. Lane has been a company officer and line manager with P&L responsibility, managed strategic direction and infrastructure, day-to-day operational workflows, budgets ranging from $7 million to $70 million, direct reports of up to 12 managers, and 550 associates. Dean currently serves on the advisory board of BridgeStream and the University of California at San Francisco, and is a member of Executive World, the Project Management Institute, and APICS.

George Lin George Lin, Documentum's vice president and CIO, began his career at Documentum in 1993 as manager of IT. Today he leads the company's worldwide IT organization, which serves approximately 1,000 Documentum employees around the globe and helps to support the company's Global 2000 customers. Having held several strategic roles at Documentum, Lin adds an exceptional balance of management experience and technical expertise. Lin helped to build the company from a small start-up to the market leader in enterprise content management. During his 10 years at Documentum, Lin has served in a number of key roles, including driving strategic direction and revenue opportunities, managing vendor relationships, and overseeing the company's global facilities and IT infrastructure. Lin was also responsible for closely aligning Documentum's use of technology with the company's business goals and processes. For his exceptional IT leadership, Lin was selected as a Computerworld Premier 100 IT Leader for 2003. He is currently co-authoring two books on the intersection of business management and technology.

Howie Lyke Howie Lyke is well known in the IT industry, bringing a unique blend of tactical and strategic experience in IT infrastructure management and implementation. He has more than 18 years of comprehensive IT consulting, management, and business leadership experience. In the areas of distributed data center development and deployment he has overseen the architecture and implementation of distributed client/server data center environments and provided and managed enterprise-size IT advisory services and enhancements for brand-name companies around the world. Lyke cofounded Change Technology Solutions with Harris Kern, of Harris Kern's Enterprise Computing Institute *(http://www.harriskern.com)*, bringing to the company nearly two decades of comprehensive IT publishing and consulting experience in the areas of data center/infrastructure development and deployment. Lyke is also a noted speaker, co-author of the best-selling book *Networking the New Enterprise* (1997), and sole author of *IT Automation, The Quest for "Lights Out"* (2000), part of the Harris Kern Enterprise Computing Institute series.

Daniel Maco Daniel Maco has been involved with the IS industry for over nine years. While he began working with the SAES Getters Group in 1989 as a mechanical design engineer, he was ultimately promoted to the position of CIO. In this role, Maco was responsible for the creation, implementation, and management of a global IS organization with operations across three continents. During a time of rapid company expansion, these responsibilities ranged from organizational design and execution to strategic planning. Maco's breadth of experience comes from direct involvement in projects such as global ERP implementation, merger and acquisition integration, global intranet design, security architecture design and deployment, and global standardization. Based in both San Francisco, California, and in the corporate offices of Milan, Italy, Maco was directly responsible for IS resources throughout Asia, Europe, and the United States.

Guy de Meester Guy de Meester's international experience includes more than 20 years of management in various high-tech global companies. He has played a major role in restructuring the European Technical Support activities under Gerber Garment Technology. In that role de Meester managed the corporate PC environment for the company, which led to his move to the IT world. He joined Adaptec in 1995 to set up and manage the IT infrastructure and applications in the European offices. De Meester moved to the United States in 1997 to manage and centralize the company's remote IT organizations, including leading the integration of the IT systems from various acquisitions such as Data Processing Technology. In January 2000 de Meester joined a spin-off of Adaptec, Roxio, as director of global information systems, to build a world-class IS department. De Meester holds a degree in electronic engineering and a postgraduate degree in business administration from his native country Belgium.

John Moran Blending more than 25 years experience in industry as an executive, product developer, and project manager and in academia as a course developer and instructor, Moran has achieved recognition as a bridge between the academic communities and industry. Moran's courses at the Notre Dame de Namur University, UC Berkeley Extension, and San Jose State Professional Development program reflect the real-life business situations derived from his work in developing Communities of Practice with Silicon Valley companies. His academic experience contributes to his ability to create unique, collaborative environments that facilitate learning, sustainable growth, and increased productivity for his industry clients. His expertise has been developed through the organization and management of marketing and sales support functions for Mips Computer Systems and Optical Storage International; as a team leader developing computer systems products and international markets for Sperry Univac, Control Data, and Unisys; as a student and teacher in systems thinking; and as a principal consultant with Global Gateways. Moran is also the founder of the Software Industry Coalition, a nonprofit corporation dedicated to improving the effectiveness of relationships, workforce, processes, and products of the software industry.

 **Mayra Muniz** Mayra Muniz has been affiliated for several years with Prentice Hall's acclaimed series, Harris Kern's Enterprise Computing Institute as executive assistant to Harris Kern, the founder. Her contributions as an editor, publicist, graphics designer, events manager, and marketing specialist have played a major role in the success of the series. Mayra has also contributed as a co-author in the book titled *IT Production Services*, published by Prentice Hall.

 **Al Pappas** Al Pappas joined Hotwire as the CIO in July 2001 and brings extensive experience in the IT and software engineering disciplines with both mature and startup companies. Prior to Hotwire, Pappas served as CIO for Portal Software, where he built and led their IT organization. Pappas also served as CIO for VeriFone (acquired by Hewlett-Packard) and Adobe Systems. Pappas held a variety of software and systems development positions as a senior engineering manager and executive at Apple Computer, Schlumberger, and several high-technology businesses. In his early career, Pappas developed and deployed the world's largest message switching system for United Airlines. He has a bachelor's degree in mathematics from Brooklyn College of the University of New York and a master's in technical business management from UCLA.

 **Bharat C. Poria** Bharat Poria has over 20 years of technical operations and IT management experience, having served in various management capacities for companies such as Philips Semiconductors and Aspect Communications. He started his career as a systems developer in the days of mainframe computers and has an extensive background in developing and building global technology organizations and implementing global infrastructures as well as CRM, ERP, supply chain, and e-commerce business solutions. Poria has led information offices and architecture and technology groups in building world-class infrastructures by creating the strategic vision and IT roadmaps, introducing and implementing global enterprise architectures, and negotiating major global enterprise contracts for products and services. Placing razor-sharp focus on creating efficient business processes and implementing operational excellence, he brings information to work environments at the appropriate times. Poria has also worked with industry giants such as Morgan Stanley, Bank of America, Chase Access Services, Dole Fresh Vegetables, Tasman Pulp & Paper, and British Railroads. He is a past CIO of Wavesplitter Technologies, an optical components research company, and is currently serving Yahoo, Inc.

 **Stuart Robbins** Stuart Robbins is the founder and executive director of the CIO Collective *(www.cio-collective.com)*, a nonprofit professional association of senior IT executives dedicated to providing strategic guidance to emerging institutions and initiatives. Along with associates of the CIO Collective, he has facilitated advisory panels on technology and business issues for Sigma Partners, Outlook Ventures, InterWest Ventures, the World Bank, and for executives from the International Monetary Fund and the International Development Fund, Bessemer Trust, Morgan Stanley Dean Witter, Jamcracker, Netscaler, BridgeStream, and CRIA Technologies. Robbins currently serves on the CIO/CTO advisory boards for Netscaler, a leading provider of traffic management and SSL technology, and *CIO Insight*, an IT publication of Ziff Davis Media, and is a panelist and advisory board member for Morgan Stanley Dean Witter. Robbins also was the founding CEO of KMERA Corporation, a consulting firm specializing in knowledge continuity solutions for the enterprise. Before founding KMERA, Robbins was the CIO for Jamcracker, a provider of integrated desktop applications for the enterprise. He facilitated Jamcracker's CIO advisory board and has spoken on the changing role of the CIO at conferences sponsored by *The Economist*, the Society for Information Management, Microsoft FUSION, and the International Communications Association and Morgan Stanley's CIO Outlook, 2001 and 2002. Previously, Robbins was the Y2K program officer and interim CIO for Documentum and was a senior director of IT at Synopsys.

Holly Simmons Holly Simmons's background includes more than 10 years of project, product, and resource management in software, service, and Internet application development. Most recently, Simmons was the acting director of development and the acting director of program management for Equinix's IT department, where she supported the CIO role in assessing and reorganizing the department as well as defining and implementing strategic and tactical objectives. Before joining Equinix, Simmons was the director of engineering product management for RealCentric, an application service provider in the commercial real estate market. In this role, she drove functional and technical teams in the design, development, and implementation of a custom Web Java application and data warehouse. In addition, Simmons managed several e-commerce and integration projects as a principal consultant for FutureNext, a mid-tier IT consulting company. Prior to FutureNext, Simmons managed products from inception to end of life and combined her technical and managerial skills to develop leading-edge products and services for large customer bases at Metricom, (Ricochet) and Apple Computer. Simmons holds a B.S. in engineering from Purdue University.

Maureen Whalen Vavra Maureen Vavra has a strong background in strategic planning and Web and systems development. She has held vice-president and CTO roles at Hitachi Data Systems, Delta Dental Plan of California, and Pacific Bell (now SBC) in the past 20 years. She has authored three- to five-year technology plans for high-volume transaction systems in telecommunications and claims processing. As part of her current position at Hitachi Data Systems, she reports to the CIO and has worldwide responsibility for the direction and development of the Web and reporting functions. Her team has implemented major infrastructure development for content management and security and participated in a creative redesign of the Web space. Maureen's global reporting staff is currently enhancing a drill-down Corporate Dashboard and warehouse with a rapid prototyping approach. Major initiatives Vavra led earlier in her career include Pacific Bell's strategic billing system, data resource management, and several data warehousing and Web infrastructure projects.

Shelton Waggener Like many of today's CIO's Shelton Waggener's path to senior IT management wasn't a direct one. After founding his own computer consulting practice in the early 80's, Waggener spent several years abroad throughout Latin America and Asia before returning to Silicon Valley. Most recently CIO at Lucent Technologies' InterNetworking Systems Division, Shel previously served as Director of Information Technology for Octel Messaging and Director of Enterprise Support Services at Sybase, Inc. and is currently Director of Central Computing for the University of California, Berkeley. He has served as president of the IT Support Services Council, is a member of the Bay Area CIO Community of Practice and sits on the technical advisory boards of several leading edge technology solutions companies. A graduate of the University of California, Santa Cruz with double majors in American Studies and Latin American Studies, he is active in many industry groups that focus on solving business problems through technology. Shel and his wife, Julia, reside in the Oakland hills with their two children.

Lee Weimer Lee Weimer has spent most of her career serving the organization development needs of business through their not-for-profit business associations in the United States and in developing and transitioning countries. Beginning as a manager in a chamber of commerce in San Antonio, Texas, she spent 10 years in regional management for the U.S. Chamber of Commerce and the last six years as a consultant to these same organizations. She works with Global Gateways to develop and maintain the Communities of Practice that brought the authors of this book together.

Steven Zoppi Steven Zoppi is principal advisor and cofounder of Collabri Group LLC, a research and advisory services firm. In addition to his research work, Zoppi is vice president of operations for Hotwire.Com, a leading online discount travel vendor. Prior to founding Collabri, Zoppi was vice president and CIO at Electronics for Imaging (EFI), a world leader in software and hardware digital imaging solutions for network printing. Zoppi brings over 20 years of technology leadership experience as an executive-level technology practitioner at both private and public sector organizations and as a recognized industry analyst. Prior to EFI, Zoppi served as vice president at META Group, a leading IT market research and consulting company, where he advised Global 2000, government, and emerging-growth companies on technology, business, and marketing initiatives. Zoppi was awarded the prestigious distinction of META Group Research Fellow in 1999. Prior to META Group, he was director of technology strategies for Adobe Systems and directed the data center operations at Oracle Corporation. Zoppi has held additional senior programming management positions at IBM, NASA/Ames Research Center, Esprit de Corp, and Software AG of North America.

inform**IT**

YOUR GUIDE TO IT REFERENCE

Articles

Keep your edge with thousands of free articles, in-depth features, interviews, and IT reference recommendations – all written by experts you know and trust.

Online Books

Answers in an instant from **InformIT Online Book's** 600+ fully searchable on line books. Sign up now and get your first 14 days **free**.

POWERED BY

Safari

Catalog

Review online sample chapters, author biographies and customer rankings and choose exactly the right book from a selection of over 5,000 titles.

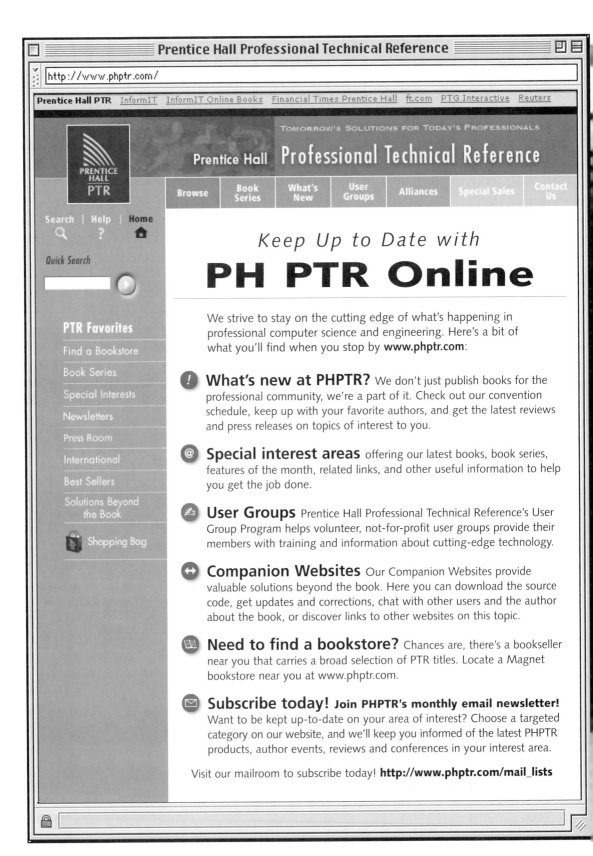

http://www.phptr.com/

Prentice Hall PTR   InformIT   InformIT Online Books   Financial Times Prentice Hall   ft.com   PTG Interactive   Reuters

TOMORROW'S SOLUTIONS FOR TODAY'S PROFESSIONALS

Prentice Hall **Professional Technical Reference**

| Browse | Book Series | What's New | User Groups | Alliances | Special Sales | Contact Us |

Search | Help | Home

Quick Search

PTR Favorites

Find a Bookstore

Book Series

Special Interests

Newsletters

Press Room

International

Best Sellers

Solutions Beyond the Book

Shopping Bag

Keep Up to Date with
PH PTR Online

We strive to stay on the cutting edge of what's happening in professional computer science and engineering. Here's a bit of what you'll find when you stop by **www.phptr.com**:

What's new at PHPTR? We don't just publish books for the professional community, we're a part of it. Check out our convention schedule, keep up with your favorite authors, and get the latest reviews and press releases on topics of interest to you.

Special interest areas offering our latest books, book series, features of the month, related links, and other useful information to help you get the job done.

User Groups Prentice Hall Professional Technical Reference's User Group Program helps volunteer, not-for-profit user groups provide their members with training and information about cutting-edge technology.

Companion Websites Our Companion Websites provide valuable solutions beyond the book. Here you can download the source code, get updates and corrections, chat with other users and the author about the book, or discover links to other websites on this topic.

Need to find a bookstore? Chances are, there's a bookseller near you that carries a broad selection of PTR titles. Locate a Magnet bookstore near you at www.phptr.com.

Subscribe today! Join PHPTR's monthly email newsletter! Want to be kept up-to-date on your area of interest? Choose a targeted category on our website, and we'll keep you informed of the latest PHPTR products, author events, reviews and conferences in your interest area.

Visit our mailroom to subscribe today! **http://www.phptr.com/mail_lists**